THE

ELEMENTS OF CHRISTIAN SCIENCE.

A TREATISE UPON

MORAL PHILOSOPHY AND PRACTICE.

BY WILLIAM ADAMS, D. D.,

PRESBYTER OF THE PROTESTANT EPISCOPAL CHURCH, IN THE DIOCESE OF WISCONSIN.

THIRD EDITION, REVISED.

"All things are double one against another, and God hath made nothing imperfect."—JESUS, SON OF SIRACH.

"Man's perfection is not *by himself*, nor by any thing *in* or *of himself*, but by that which is *to him external*."

PHILADELPHIA:
H. HOOKER & CO., CORNER OF CHESTNUT AND EIGHTH STS.
1857.

Entered according to Act of Congress, in the year 1850, by

WILLIAM ADAMS,

In the Office of the Clerk of the District Court of the United States, in and for the Eastern District of Pennsylvania.

PREFACE.

NATURALISTS tell us that the oak has a northern circle, beyond which it does not grow. It has also a limit that is set for it towards the south Thus it has a region, marked out by definite limits, upon the surface of the earth, within which it grows, and out of which it cannot live. In the language of natural science, this is called its Habitat. Within that habitat it lives, varied in vigor and appearance according to circumstances. The same tree, in sheltered valleys, shoots up a taller and more slender stem than the oak that braves the storm upon the mountain-side. The timber also of that oak, that has grown slowly in the clefts of the rock, has a roughness and a knotty strength that is never found in that which has started up rapidly from rich and cultivated soils. All these differences, and a thousand more, may be produced, and exist in oaks that have come from acorns of the same parent-tree.

To explain this, we know that all of these trees had, each of them, a constitution, a germ of vegetable life peculiar to the oak, suited to take up supplies from external things, and to grow thereby, *because it is a life.*

To use the example again,—wherever the tree grows, in the North or the South, in the valley or upon the mountains, from the clefted rock or in the fertile plains,—there, amidst all variety of circumstance, the constitution is the same,—if the tree is anywhere capable of living, it is as an oak that it lives, and not as any other tree. *Position modifies, but never wholly destroys or wholly changes the nature.*

The vigor of the tree, individually considered, its state and condition, are determined by these two elements, Nature and Position,—and infinite varieties are produced in individuals, but the one element never wholly overcomes the other,—Position never entirely changes Nature,—Nature never wholly conquers Position. We have been so careful in laying out precisely, and illustrating this example, that our readers may clearly see, that wherever there exists organized life, then, if we would examine the state of the individual existence, these two elements must always be taken into account,—first, Nature, and secondly Position.

So it is with all organized life. The Horse, in the dry deserts of Arabia, in the damp climate and succulent pastures of Holland and Flanders, upon the high Pampas of South America, and again, upon our South-western Prairies,—in all these cases, the animals are very different. And in them, all the variety can be shown to have arisen from Position. The Nature can be proved to be the same in all, and the circumstances even be shown, in each particular case, that have modified it into such very different forms.

And upon this principle, all our researches into the nature of the animals are founded. We examine the Nature first,—that is, the organization in its various faculties and organs, its elements, powers, and constituent principles. Then we examine its Position,—the relation, that is, of all these to the circumstances of the country in which it dwells,—as to climate, and soil, and natural features, such as mountains and rivers, and their productions, animal, mineral and vegetable. And often, when in the Nature we have seen organs and faculties, the uses of which we could not at once discern, the consideration of Position shall at once flash light upon these problems, and again the facts of Nature evince the causes of Position. Nay, stranger still than this,—it has often happened in the case of animals that have been for ages tamed to the use of man, that the circumstances, which in the original habitat surrounded them, have explained facts of their natural action that seemed unaccountable to them who had seen them only as tame. The law of Nature and Position is an universal one, and is the foundation of all true philosophy in reference to organized animal life.

To extend the same principle upward to the Life of Man, to apply it to his Moral Being, is the object of this book. It is, as the reader may see, the principle of the motto, that I have chosen from Ecclesiasticus and placed upon my title-page, that says, "All things are double, one against another, and there is nothing imperfect." In other words, that there is no finite being that in itself has its perfection; but only in being compared with a second can it be perfectly understood,—only in being united with another, can it perfectly fulfill its appointed ends,—only in obtaining from some other, that which it has not in itself, can it be perfect. This principle of Twofoldness, any thinking man shall, upon calm and deep reflection, see to run through the world of created life. He shall see it, in reference to man, to be true in the words of my second motto, that "Man's perfection is not *by himself*, nor by anything *in* or *of himself*, but by that which is *to him external*." The Law of Duality, or to use a better word, before employed, of Twofoldness, extends to man as considered in every relation, as in the Home, in the Nation, in the Church,—as in his relation to External Nature, to his brother men, and to his Almighty Creator and Father.

The application of this principle to the moral nature of man, will be found to be the leading idea of this treatise, that from which all its other principles flow,—that in whose light, all the phenomena of our Moral Being are viewed, and by which they are explained.

We take it for granted herein, that man has a Moral Nature and constitution, as well as an animal and intellectual being; and that to man as a moral being there are external facts and institutions that correspond to this moral nature. This treatise seeks to discover, define, and specify distinctly, the various faculties of the moral constitution of man, and so to classify them that they may assume a definite, scientific, and practical form. And to do this, it considers them in the two-fold point of view, as in themselves first, and secondly, their relation to those other external fixed facts, which bear upon Moral Life, as the external circumstances of physical nature do upon the powers of vegetable or animal existence. This, as I have said, is my leading principle, and in reference to this it is, that I define Ethics to be "the Science of Man's Nature and Position."

And I can appeal to the Self-knowledge of every thoughtful man for the proof of the position I assume, that man is a being that has a Moral Constitution, composed of clear and definite elements,—and that this Moral Nature answers to, and is to be explained by moral influences and facts external to us. That this is the case with man considered as a race and as an individual, and that his moral growth depends upon these two conditions.

And he that shall go with me through this treatise, I hope will find that moral science is not without a deep interest. For surely, each man in this world who knows that he is endowed with a Moral Nature, and is placed amidst circumstances, all of which may have a moral effect, must think the question to be deeply interesting, "How shall I so cultivate this my Nature, and so employ this my Position, as to arrive at the fullest maturity and completeness of my moral being, that I am capable of?"

This is the question the author attempts to answer in this book, as a matter both of science, and also of practical action and guidance.

CONTENTS.

BOOK I.

HUMAN NATURE.

BOOK II.

THE CONSCIENCE.

BOOK III.

THE SPIRITUAL REASON.

2

BOOK IV.

THE HEART OR AFFECTIONS.

BOOK V.

THE HOME AND ITS AFFECTIONS.

BOOK VI.

THE HUMAN WILL.

CHRISTIAN SCIENCE.

BOOK I.

HUMAN NATURE.

CHAPTER I.

Is man's nature 'good or evil'?—There is a nature perfectly indifferent as to good or evil.—It is that of the brutes, not of man.—Man's nature is not partly good and partly evil.—It is not essentially evil.—This proved by the monstrous conclusions which would follow.—It is then essentially a nature *good in itself*, not *evil in itself*—but *fallen.*

As I have defined Ethics to be the Science of Man's Nature and Position, it is manifest that the whole subject, scientifically treated, must embrace, at least in effect, all questions that concern his nature and its relation to external things. But as this is a thing plainly impossible, for what scientific system details all its applications, consequences and deductions? And as the purpose of Science is to render such tediousness unnecessary, by giving principles and propositions that will imply all consequences, it seems to me that such should be the course with a true science of Ethics. And therefore I shall try to establish, in regular order, such conclusions as shall be the most natural, and the most fruitful in consequences; so that if possible, I may be able, principle after principle, and conclusion after conclusion, to give a system at once practical and scientific.

This being my intention, the question which naturally comes first in a science of man's nature and position is this—

" *What is Man's Nature? Every man having the idea of good*

and evil—what is it with regard to good, and with regard to evil? Is IT GOOD, OR IS IT EVIL?"

I am aware the question will sound preposterous and absurd to many; but still it is a deeply important question. There are three modes in which man may have a moral quality, in which what he does may be described as good or evil,—his thoughts, his words, his actions. Let the reader mark this. The question is not, are man's thoughts good or evil? are his words good or evil? are his actions good or evil? That is not the question; that can be plainly answered. His thoughts, words and actions are not his nature. They come from it, certainly, but they are no more his nature than buds, flowers and fruits are the tree from which they come. To decide, then, about thoughts, words and actions, this is quite a different thing from deciding upon the quality of *his nature.*

I have said that this question is an important one; I say that it is more, it is the central and primary one of Natural Ethics; one without which there can be no science of Ethics, no knowledge of it. It is not a high theoretic question which we may live in the world without discussing, and be better not discussing than entering upon it, as is the question of the "Origin of Evil," the question "Whence did evil come into the world, since God is all good and Almighty?" But it is a wholly practical one,—the question, "Is this nature, this which I have, this which is *my* nature as a man, good or evil?"

Now, manifestly all the possible answers that may be given to this question are contained in a few words. I may say that "it is good"—I may say that "it is evil"—I may say that "it is partly good and partly evil"—or I may say that it is "perfectly indifferent to either." These four embrace all the possible answers that can be given to the question, and the calm consideration of them all, and the decision of it aright, is absolutely necessary to any progress at all in true Ethical Science. He that will study any science must first master the first principles, and without the complete and accurate knowledge of them he can make no progress; it is to him an utter impossibility. This question is the first principle in the science of which we treat. Decide it aright, and there is only one right answer of the four, and you shall be able to advance further onward. Take to yourself either of the three that are wrong, and the very foundation of religion and morality shall be astray with you; and only by God's grace against your convictions, only by the teachings of God's Providence leading you against yourself, against your ideas and fancied knowledge, shall you go aright.

Now, the fourth of these says that man's nature is indifferent, having no moral quality at all. Are there such natures in existence? There are. Those beings that we call "animals or brutes" —these are of that kind.

We see in animals the most undoubted proofs that they reason; of this all natural history of modern times is full, that they argue and reason from premises to conclusions, just as man does. All kinds of that property called reasoning, we see in animals just the same as in man, the same *in kind*, not the same *in degree;* the reasoning power is very manifestly exercised by the brutes. True it is, that we see it in them vastly inferior to another power, that of "instinct," which works towards ends of which it is perfectly unconscious. Still the reasoning power is not the distinguishing character of man, that which separates him from the animals, nor is "instinct" the peculiar possession of the Brute creation. For the beasts have reason, and man has instinct; each of them, however, in an inferior or less degree. The definition, then, that man is a reasoning animal, or an animal whose quality is to reason, is false; and that an animal is an organized machine, or a being having only instinct, is false also.

Now, what is the character that really differences the two natures, that of man and the beasts? It is not either reasoning power, nor is it instinct; still less is it any of the differences given by Locke or his followers. It is this very thing of *moral indifference*, that the nature of beasts and their actions are really neither *good* nor *evil.* That the sense and feeling of pleasure and pain is to them all, and that of *moral good* and *moral evil,* a good or an evil quality in actions they have no feeling.

I do not say that man has a *moral sense*, as some of our modern philosophers talk; as if there were a peculiar faculty in him superadded to appetites, passions, affections and reasoning powers, which has the peculiar charge of moral objects, as reasoning power has of reasoning, &c.; so that the reasoning power reasons, the moral power feels, &c., *morally.* This is not what I say, but that man *has a moral nature;* so that no thought, word or action but has a *moral quality*, is either good or evil, and will so be judged, both by himself, by his fellow men and by his God.

With regard to animals, it may be seen at once that their actions have *no moral quality;* that there is in them nothing of good or of evil, and that it is only by a metaphor we call them good or evil, *as applied to our own uses.* That is a good dog that watches best, that sets the best, or that kills rats the best, or that churns the farmer's milk the best, or that draws the beggar's cart the best. Change hands and there is no goodness in them.

And even temper in animals, to which with more of plausibility we may apply the terms "good" and evil," even in this case it is only with reference to ourselves and our ideas that we apply the term. The generosity of the lion, the ferocity of the wolf, the untameable fierceness of the wild ass, the cruelty of the tiger, the cunning of the fox, all these are but metaphors taken from our own nature. These things instead of being moral, having a good or evil quality, being deserving of praise or blame, are nought else than tempers arising from the conformation of the animal, and absolutely necessary for its physical preservation. A lion is no more really 'noble,' because, with his immense muscular power and capacity of destruction, he stands out boldly in the centre of the African desert, than a fox is mean and to be despised, because he with a feeble and small frame sneaks through the bushes. In the one temper as well as the other there is nothing moral, nothing immoral, nothing good, nothing evil, only a nature which is neither good nor evil, but *indifferent perfectly.*

The only apparent exception to this is the dog. The response which he makes to our feelings, his apparent sympathy with us, his faithfulness, all these make us lavish upon him epithets that express primarily moral qualities. This, however, is easily explained by the known fact, that there are some inferior animals that seem to have been created in reference to the wants of superior ones; with instincts in their natures binding and tying them to the others, and causing them to rejoice in their society. And thus the attachment of the dog to the man is no more capable of a moral interpretation than the attachment of the pilot-fish to the shark. And the same may be said of the horse and the elephant in relation to man.

But this may be seen, still more plainly seen in the fact that we attribute *no crime* to brute animals, none of their actions come within the moral law of God and of society. The eagle murders not when he slays his prey; nor does the wolf commit a crime when we say that he steals; nor does the scorpion commit suicide or the rattlesnake when they destroy themselves with their own weapons turned against their own life.

And, indeed, with an old master of subtlety, we need have no doubt that their good and their evil are not "Moral Good" and "Moral Evil;" but the Good of "Pleasure and Pain" so arranged, as by its operation upon their animal frame, to subserve ends of which they are wholly unconscious. "I have no doubt," says Jerome Cardan, "that if the ox could speak he would call the grazier good, because he feeds oxen, and the butcher bad because he kills them, and yet there is no difference."

Now, I wish my readers to have it fully and clearly established in their minds, that there is, and exists a class of organized living beings, which has a nature *purely indifferent, neither moral or immoral,* to which *bodily pleasure* and *pain* is the sole guidance from the external world.

Having laid this idea clearly before them, I shall ask them, appealing only to their own experience of their own nature, while it is manifest that the nature of the beast is an animal nature, of itself neither moral nor immoral, is it not equally manifest that man's nature is moral; that while "pleasure and pain" are guides to him as an animal, still as a man he has higher guides in justice and honesty, and law and conscience?

Thus have we established a broad distinction between man and animals. Thus have we excluded one of the answers upon human nature, the one which supposes it to be indifferent, having no moral quality whatsoever.

And before we go further, we shall stamp this opinion regarding our nature as one that always goes hand in hand with Atheism and the worst immorality.

If our nature be indifferent, as that of the brutes is; and, as theirs have no moral quality, then are we like in the ends we have to fulfil to them, we are incapable of immorality. If our nature be animal or indifferent, then, as in consequence of this in them no act is criminal or sinful, or indeed can be so, in us, it must be the same. Then our sole business shall be to gratify our propensities, all of them; our sole excitement to action, physical pleasure; our sole check physical pain. Wheresoever this doctrine with regard to the nature of man prevails, there it is the doctrine of Atheism and debauchery, and of grasping and selfish sensuality.

The next answer to the question, "is the nature of man good or evil," that can be given, is manifestly that it is part good and part evil. The soul good and the body evil; or, the soul evil and the body good. Two strange varieties of opinion these are, but as strange as they are they have had many advocates.

The last, that the soul of man is evil, his body good, implies the Transmigration of Souls; the dogma, that of Spirits that fell there were two classes, they who could rise again and were enwrapped in bodies of clay and passed from one to the other, until being purified they resumed their former state. The first, which answers that the Soul is Good, the Body Evil, implies that there are two Gods. Each omniscient, omnipotent and eternal. The one the God of Good, and the other the God of Evil. These answers, a little thought will show us imply these consequences.

The tenets themselves were once of great importance, now of none. Man's nature is evidently a unity, although composed of soul and body; it must be good therefore or it must be evil; it cannot be both together, the soul good and the body evil, or the soul evil and the body good. We may easily dismiss this the third answer as unsuitable.

And now we have only two left to us. The one asserts that "man's nature is evil," the other "that it is good;" one or other must be true. It is manifest then that the argument may go on by a two-fold division. The establishing of the one refutes the other; the refutation of the one is the establishment of the other. The reader we hope will bear this in mind, for the subjects to be considered in this treatise are so many and so important, that when we can clearly decide upon a doctrine, we shall not always say all we could have said in its defence or in its refutation. We shall be content to say what we count enough.

Now, the nature of man is not indifferent. It is not partly good and partly evil; it must then be essentially evil or essentially good.

Say that it is essentially evil—*the nature of man*—not merely his words, or his actions, or his thoughts evil, but *his nature;* suppose that this is so, and what is the result and consequence?

Why, this, that when he acts in accordance with his nature, thenhe acts evilly. Let him feel emotions of pity arising in his breast, and feel that it is in accordance with his nature to aid the distressed, then, *as his nature is evil*, it should be evil so to do.

He feels that to be just, upright and honorable, is according to his nature, but according to the doctrine that *nature is essentially* evil, justice and uprightness and honesty shall be evil. And the opposite qualities, since opposite of evil is good, shall be good! Then shall all the affections which *are natural* be evil, the love of husband to wife, and the love of wife to husband, *which is natural*, be a thing base and vile and in every way to be shunned; the love of parents to children to be evil. And all the *natural* feelings, the *natural* tendencies, the *natural* affections, all shall be bad, all evil.

And then if man desires to live aright, since his nature is of itself wholly evil, his business shall be to oppose nature. All things *against nature* shall be good, all according to nature shall be bad. To be malevolent shall be good, to be full of pity, evil; to be kind-hearted shall be evil, to be harsh in life and conduct, good; to be merciful shall be wrong; to be cruel shall be right; to be a peaceable citizen of a State, and an obedient child, shall be evil; and to be a lawless and desperate outlaw or a parricide, shall be good. The chaste husband or wife, living according to the dictates of nature in marriage, shall be evil in that very thing; the licentious adulterer shall be good. Monstrous consequences these, and outraging the natural feeling of all; and yet consequences that unavoidably follow from the monstrous paradox that *human nature is essentially evil.*

Let us look at this dogma a little more plainly still. If this be so, then man requires no temptation, in fact cannot be tempted, for his nature being wholly evil, all his hopes, desires, fears, are of themselves evil essentially. He cannot be polluted, for of himself his nature is evil. All crimes are equal, for the nature from which all proceed is equally bad, being in itself essentially evil. All his sins then are equal in the eye of God, each equally deserving condemnation in the eye of infinite justice. And the innocent babe, if his nature be essentially evil, is a subject for limitless wrath equally with the hoary murderer and debauchee of eighty years. And all this in direct opposition to the Holy Scriptures.

Nay, more than this. If man's nature be all evil, as then all his evil temptations, thoughts, feeling and actions must come from himself, then there can be no tempter to evil outside of him,—no devil; but a *principle of evil in him.* And that principle of evil *is in*, and *is*, the nature of man! In other words, man is Satan, and there is no Satan but man!

Now, asking of my readers to look this notion straight in the face, to have in their minds the clear idea of it, is asking of them also to bear in mind that "thoughts," "words," and "actions," are not "human nature." I would ask them steadily to look at this doctrine, "that human nature is essentially evil," and ask themselves, do not these consequences follow from it really and unavoidably?

This is a system of Morality, indeed! which makes it natural to do evil, unnatural to do good; which puts law and conscience and justice all as evil! And all the things that are naturally good, asserts that they are naturally evil. A strange system of Morality indeed, which begins by denying the possibility of any morals, any goodness, and asserting that all actions are bad, and all equally bad!

This is a hideous Moral System, one that nevertheless has existed from very ancient times. They are the tenets of a very ancient sect upon whom the prophet Isaiah pronounces a woe: "Woe be to them that call evil good, and good evil, that put light for darkness and darkness for light;" to them the apostle Paul alludes, when he speaks of those who in the latter days should "forbid to marry, and *command to abstain* from meats, which God hath created to be received with thanksgiving of them that believe and know the truth, for *every creature of God is good*, and nothing to be refused, if it be received with thanksgiving."

Of such philosophising has there been an abundance, and unto it man's nature is essentially evil, and unto it from this central fact all nature and all creatures also become evil, and therefore it is that it forbids marriage, and orders to abstain from meats; whereas the apostle lays it down as plainly that *all creatures are good*, and "that marriage is honorable in all."

But in addition to the display of the natural consequences of this doctrine, that human nature is essentially evil, we may appeal to the consciousness of each individual, to the knowledge he has of himself. Does not each man feel that when he acts evilly or sins, that he acts against the laws of his own nature? That to act rightly and virtuously is in accordance with the law of his nature, and not against it? Does he not each time that he acts evilly, feel ashamed, condemned by his own nature? Does he not feel that to cheat, to lie, to murder, so far from being natural, are directly against his nature? Surely, all the experience that man has of himself, all this tells him that his nature is not essentially evil.

And I confess that I have been most heartily ashamed of men who from the pulpit preach this horrid notion, never having thought of its consequences or of its nature; and then, to establish it, have told untruths as great. Tell the man who has bent in agony over the sick bed of a dying wife, who for months, without hope of reward, has watched, and wept, and sympathized,—tell him this is no good act, but purely evil and sinful! And then, in order to *prove* such a monstrous paradox, tell him *that it was done from selfish motives*, and nature will rise and give you the lie; and the man will feel and speak as strongly of *you* as did Paul of the men that preached this doctrine of old, as "speaking lies in hypocrisy, having the conscience seared as with a hot iron."

Tell him that morality is not only of no good, but downright sinful; and Nature's law shall tell him directly the contrary, and the Bible will say to him, "When the Gentiles, which have not the law, *do by nature* the things contained in the law, then are they a law unto themselves."

Take the hoary desperado, the pirate and cut-throat, and drunkard and debauchee, from the Indian seas, and place him side by side on the same level with a young innocent girl, from an unpolluted home, and nature's consciousness of truth shall declare your notions false.

It follows, then, that the nature of man cannot be in itself essentially evil.

And by the exclusion of the three of the only four possible answers, it must be that we affirm the one remaining, "that Human Nature is of itself and in itself essentially good."

We exclude the three, and this affirms the one. The proof, therefore, of it at the present is exclusive and negative, rather than positive. We therefore insist upon it as a right, of logical necessity due to us, that objections against the conclusion be reserved until we come to the positive proof. In the mean time, we would discuss another part of the subject as preparatory to this positive proof.

Note to Chapter I.

Upon this doctrine, that "Human Nature is essentially evil," it may seem to some persons strange that we should spend so much time in displaying its evil consequences and developing them. Yet let such persons know that all these consequences have not only been deduced as logical conclusions, but they *have been preached* and *acted out* by perhaps the vilest and most evil of all the ancient sects, the Manichæans. These men took it that man's nature is *essentially evil*, and carried out their doctrine to the extremest degree, as history will show.

For this reason we have brought the dogma, in all its consequences, clearly and distinctly before the minds of our readers. We would have them see its untruth distinctly and decidedly. For that man's nature is not *essentially evil*, but a *nature which although fallen is in its nature good:* this is the first principle of all morality.

I would also add, that this is the unanimous decision of the early Christian Church.

CHAPTER II.

What is the nature of Good and Evil?—The highest good, and the means of discovering it.

In our last chapter we used a phrase "Human Nature," for the constitution of man, as consisting of body, soul and spirit. By this word we meant the whole nature of man considered generally, without reference to the peculiarities of individuals or of nations; "the man," generally. We asked, then, whether it were "evil or good," as considering this as the first question, the fundamental one of all Ethics. And we decided it in a negative and exclusive way, that Human Nature must be in itself good, and not evil.

And now we would have our readers remark, that we have used the terms "good and evil" often. We employed them because we knew that human nature was good, and that therefore each one, without explaining, would readily understand that which we meant.

But now it is time to examine more closely into the meaning of these terms.

The first remark we shall make is this, that when we establish what is "good," *we establish also the highest end of man*, that after which he should the most aim, and at the same time we establish *the supreme rule of his conduct.*

For instance, if the supreme good of man be in Utility, then as the supreme law of life he should aim only at Utility; he should make this the measure of all his actions, and casting aside all other considerations, he should not ask, is this right, or just, or my duty? but, is this *useful?* And so with regard to all other criterions or tests whatsoever, that have been established of Good and Evil. The establishment of a Highest Good and Evil is the establishment of a highest law for man's actions, and of the highest reach of virtue and perfection to which his nature may climb.

The question, then, of "good and evil," and their nature and criterion, is a very important one; the question of the "Highest Good" still more important. They are not theoretical, merely, but practical; and that in a very great degree, because they imply a law of action first, and secondly, a knowledge and governance of our own nature according to it.

For clearly, we can see in each individual that he has something which he counts the Highest Good, to which he will sacrifice all inferior; clearly we can see that this feeling is a law unto his nature, acted upon at all times by himself, and always referred to in his actions. I have known Epicures, to whom, by an observation of life and conduct, the Highest Good was the pleasures of the palate. I have known Epicureans to whom general ease and self-gratification was the Highest Good. I have known fathers and mothers to whom the advancement of their children was the Highest Good; men to whom the possession of property was the Highest Good; to whom power was the highest; to whom domestic happiness, or the love of their neighbours, or the sense and performance of their duty, or the doing of justice or of mercy; I have known, in my short life, instances of all these; instances in which I could most plainly discover that these objects were severally considered by men as the main object of their lives, the objects which, to obtain, they would count the highest good of their existence. And I have taken notice that the feeling of the object being the highest, became a *rule of action*, a law and measure by which all action was regulated. Surely, then, the question, What is Good? What is the Highest Good? is not unimportant, since each one in life more or less debates upon it, and decides it for himself.

With regard to the term "Highest Good," if the reader will look at the arrangement of objects of pursuit that I have made, he will see that taken from the beginning, they manifestly mount up from *lower* to *higher*. The pleasures of the mere appetites, such as eating and drinking, are the lowest of all; then the pleasures of the passions are higher still, of the understanding higher, of the affections higher, and of the moral feeling higher still.

And thus is one object pursued as a good, higher and loftier than another; thus, by the fact that man is finite, must there be some that shall be the highest and the loftiest good not merely of the individual man, but of universal Human Nature. And the pursuit after this must be the supreme law of morality and of nature; and he that shall pursue this, shall fulfil entirely the end of his being. The idea, then, of the Supreme Good is a practical one entirely.

Now, in order to understand what this Supreme Good is, the first thing we are to understand is, what do we mean by this term "good"—the term "good," I say, as used by moral beings? "That which is useful to us in the physical world, 'some say,' causes pleasure, and that which is destructive gives pain. So things that are pleasant you call 'good,' and painful, 'bad.' And so from the sweetness of sugar, we by metaphor apply the idea to sweetness of temper; from the harshness of an acid taste, to harshness of conduct; from the destructive nature of poisonous plants, to the destructive nature of vice; and so we mount up to the idea of Moral Good and Evil, even the highest."

And then all these ideas of justice, honesty, equity, truth, holiness; all these are no realities in themselves, but metaphors, coming from mere earthly objects of the sense, and brought thence by our own reason!

What is good, then? A higher class answers, it is "that which is useful; has in it the maximum of Utility." Another makes good to be that which is "in the most accordance with our nature." And this has in it considerable loftiness, as also has that theory that supposes goodness to be that which is in accordance with the "eternal fitness of things," and that too that imagines good to be "that which is according to the idea of moral beauty," and a hundred theories besides, of which the man who has patience may examine as many as he likes.

The last notion is this : that five ideas, Benevolence, Justice, Truth, Honesty, Order, make up the "central idea of morality," or are its elements.* These, undoubtedly, are very good, all of them ; though as for their being the central elements of the supreme law of action, the Summum Bonum, or Highest Good, I myself being a Christian, should rather prefer the ancient elements of "faith, hope, and charity," which, as there are such facts as a God, a Gospel, a Salvation and a Spirit, I conceive are far more peculiarly central elements of a Christian morality.

Now, what is the fact ? This it is, that no compounding, adding together, or intensifying of these ideas, or of any ideas whatsoever, will give us as a result the idea of Moral Goodness. The idea of Moral Goodness is an idea just as simple as any one of these ideas, and manifestly the highest moral idea of them all.

We could easily show this by the old logical method of the consideration of what is technically called the comprehension and extension of the ideas. However, it may be easily seen by another means. In fact we may add a multitude of other qualities, having just as fair a title as these have, for instance, Holiness, Conscientiousness, Temperance, Self-denial, &c., besides the three I before mentioned, of "faith, hope, and love." Because you call these morally good, and it is true that they are so, it does not follow that they are the elements of moral good. So, to live according to the eternal fitness of things, or according to "the idea of moral beauty," these are morally good, but it does not follow that the idea of moral goodness is compounded of these.

In truth, the idea of Moral Good is the highest of all moral ideas, neither made up nor compounded of any, having none above it, itself measuring all other moral ideas, and being measured of none. Of it no definition can be given, therefore ; nothing but illustration, by declaring the persons, or events, or qualities in which it is, or by showing how we attain it, but *no definition.* We may say of a wagon, it is a four-wheeled vehicle, giving thereby a description of its components ; but of this we can give no such definition. When one asks us, "What is the highest moral good ?" we answer, "Moral Good." When he asks, "What is moral

* Professor Whewell. Elements of Morality.

good?" we say, we do not analyze it—we cannot; but we point you to your own feelings, and experience of your own nature, and we say that then you feel a perception of a quality that exists in all moral beings, a quality of moral good, or *the absence of it, which is evil;* which you feel to have a very real and actual existence in responsible beings, and to which you apply the term moral good.

We, therefore, enter not into the vain speculation of trying to analyze the nature of Moral Good, or attempting to define it. We say that man is a being whose nature is good, and not evil; he has the idea of moral good as naturally as he that sees has the idea of sight; that that idea is the same in one human being as it is in another. And that if we show the means whereby the idea and feeling is brought forth in man, and then increased in him, how it is cultivated, and how it is brought to perfection, then we shall have done somewhat of the work we set out to do, the work of a Christian Ethical Philosophy.

In the mean time, how are we to measure the abundance of this quality in others or ourselves? or how are we to learn what we desire to know of it? In the first place, it is manifest that since our nature is *good,* and since it is one that is *under a law,* and its goodness is measured by that law, that that law, more or less, reveals to us moral goodness. It is manifest that the Home, the Family, the Church, that these all bring the idea to perfection, being all teaching institutions that have ever existed, and that for the purpose of bringing forth the feeling in man, of increasing it, and bringing it to perfection.

Live, then, according to your nature; according to what your nature has a feeling, you ought to be. Live according to the duties and teachings of the *Family;* for this, too, is a school of good: and to the teachings of the *Nation,* for this is the same. And above all, remember that there is a Revelation, a Holy Spirit, a Church. The instructions of these agree with, confirm, complete, and as it were, round the whole. But to analyze it, and say these are its elements, or to define it, this you cannot do.

And why is this? Because, simply, that Moral Good is no notion derived from anything that we see or feel, framed forth by metaphor and figure from objects presented to us by the senses. The feeling and sense of it is not gotten in any way from them. The absolute complete Moral Good exists not as a *quality,* but as a *reality—is* God.* The idea of moral good, that idea is the feeling in our hearts of that which is in us or others like in quality to the *absolute moral good*, and the knowledge of the qualities of that likeness. This comes to us in no other way than from God Himself.

When we wish to know what is the Highest Good, then, if we mean absolutely, the only answer is, "GOD." If we refer to man and his conduct, "that which is likest God." It is not Nature, it is not Utility, it is not Moral Beauty, nor Conscience, nor any one of these moral feelings and moral duties that is to be made the rule of action, and is the Supreme Good—it is God.

Men will say, "that is no practical rule; to try to be benevolent is a practical rule, or to try to be useful, or to live according to nature, all these are practical rules; but to make God at once the Supreme Good and the Highest Rule is not practicable!"

I do not much like answering objections when the further development of the subject will put aside the objection, and render it unnecessary to make it as well as to answer it. But this I will say; do you take for your practical rule the Heathen Ethics of Paley, that make "enlightened self-interest" the Supreme Law of Action, or the equally Pagan morality, that makes Benevolence the Supreme Law, or this that makes Justice, Veracity, or anything else the Supreme Law of Action? Take it, act upon it consistently, and be endowed with all the gifts of nature and knowledge, and I shall take a poor uneducated Christian, who never thought of Ethics, but has taken the Bible in the Church, and by them has cultivated his natural feeling of conscience, and other parts of his moral being, and to ten thousand times more moral perfection than you shall he have arrived.

For all these are from God directly, and by conveying to us

* "I Am."—He doth not say, *I am* their light, their guide, their strength, or tower, but only I Am. He sets as it were his hand to a blank, that his people may write under it what they please that is good for them. As if he should say, Are they weak? *I am* strength? Are they poor? *I am* riches. Are they in trouble? *I am* comfort. Are they sick? *I am* health. Are they dying? *I am* life. Have they nothing? *I am* all things. *I am* wisdom and power. *I am* justice and mercy. *I am* grace and goodness. *I am* glory, beauty, holiness, eminency, super-eminency, perfection, all-sufficiency, eternity! Jehovah, *I am*. Whatsoever is amiable in itself, or desirable unto them, that *I am*. Whatsoever is pure and holy—whatsoever is great or pleasant—whatsoever is good or needful to make men happy, that *I am*.—Bishop Beveridge.

Himself, or a knowledge of that action that is likest Him, they are our established guides. Whereas, you have taken an idea! a notion! for your guide.

This is true, if we believe that God made Nature, and that He made it good, and that man, although fallen, is not a beast, so as to do the evil that he does naturally, or a devil, so as to do nought but evil, and that consciously. It is true, if the Bible be a revelation from God, and not "a collection of Hebrew Poetry of the sublimest kind."* It is true, if the Church be a divinely constituted body, to lead men in the way of Religion. If all this be true, then have we the means of ascertaining God, and that which is Godlike, clearly, plainly and distinctly. If it be not true, then you may take anything else you please, and rear up any system you please, make anything the "Highest Good" and the "Highest Object of Pursuit," and your system shall be a system of Heathen Ethics, but certainly not of Christian Morality. And your fame may spread, and your influence may extend, and your eloquence and learning be extolled to the ends of the earth; and the old woman in the chimney corner, going by her nature, her natural sense of right and wrong, as called out by God's revelation, interpreted by His Church, and applied by His Spirit, she shall have higher truth, and more of Ethics than you. For to a Christian the Supreme Good is GOD, the Supreme Law of Action is the revelation of God; "the Pillar and ground of it is the Church," that which applies it the Spirit, and that which receives it the Nature of Man. Any morality that knows not this is Heathen.

Having made this statement as to "Good," the Supreme or Highest Good, and the Highest Law of Action, we go on to obviate several objections that might be made to it, from our ignorance or incapability. This shall be the object of the next chapter.

* German Rationalistic Criticism.

CHAPTER III.

God the Supreme Good, and the only Standard of Good. It must have been so to Christ and to Adam.—The case of Adam.—Adam's Moral Perfection —first, by his nature—secondly, by the gift of the Presence of God, as a Supreme Rule actually. Our fallen nature differs, first, in the withdrawal of that gift; secondly, in disturbance and insubordination of faculties. Still, as a matter of each man's experience, and also of History, God is the Law and Standard of Moral Good to the Natural Man.

Having gone so far as to define that "God is the Supreme and Absolute Good, and the sole measure of Good," the question at once comes up, "But is not God afar from nature and from us, ruling us *by law, and Himself absent*, so that we cannot make of him the measure of Good, or discern its likeness to him?"

To this we answered in the last chapter, "Thy nature is of God and good, made in his image, and although fallen, still not brutal or fiendish, but in his image, although that image be impaired. Still, then, thy nature has a feeling for good, and applies the image as a measure of it. The Bible, and that is the Word of God—the Church of God, and that is his organization—and lastly, the Spirit of God, all these thou hast, or canst have, and all these are nearer to thee, bring the being, and will, and feeling, and nature of God, closer to man than any other fact can come; so close, that none in truth ever disbelieved the being and attributes of God; they that say so are only self-deceivers or vain boasters, trying to deceive others, not Atheists."

But perhaps, in addition to this, our answer to objections, we had better enter a little more closely into the centre of this matter, and view it in another light. We have seen that there is an Animal Nature, one perfectly indifferent. Again, we see that a nature perfectly evil is possible. And neither of these natures is that which man has.

Now it is manifest, that a perfect Human Nature would be that which did good consciously and perpetually, and never did or had even the experience of an act of evil. This consciousness of doing good constantly, and of not knowing by self-experience what evil is but by its effects upon others, this is manifestly the character given of our Saviour, as shown in the whole of the New Testament. It is as manifestly the character given of Adam, our first father, in Paradise.

And as manifestly it is the *ideal image of perfection*, after which each man is led by his nature to aspire. It is manifest, that in this aspiration we desire not an animal nature which is not good or evil, but indifferent; nor a mere innocent nature, whose quality is doing good unconsciously, but one that does good consciously, and that consciously abstains from evil. It is also manifest that this desire of our moral nature is no desire purely imaginary, no image of perfection that never was realized, but one that of itself has had two actual and real exemplars in our LORD JESUS CHRIST, and in Adam in Paradise, the father of the human race.

To examine, therefore, these exemplars of perfection in reference to that which is the Highest Good of man is to bring the definition we have given of Good, and of the Highest Good, to the actual test of historical experience, and both to confirm it, and also to hold out the very highest model, not as imaginary, but as realized. And we beg the reader to pay a close attention to this part of our discussion, inasmuch as the examination of these models not only will illustrate the nature of Moral Good, but also the nature of man, both as fallen and as in Paradise.

Now, with regard to our LORD—HE *was a man;* this is fully and plainly manifest. Human Nature cannot, therefore, be morally indifferent in the same condition as the beasts are, or fiendish essentially, else God could not have taken it; but it must have been Good in its nature.

Again. He was Morally Perfect from birth to death. He did no sin in thought, word or deed: for thought is action, word is action, deed is action. Now seeing that manifestly, therefore, we must call him *perfect*, what is the idea of Moral Good presented to us by Him as *the perfect man?*

Manifestly it may be put *in not sinning*, that positively our blessed Lord, as a man, in everything did that which is according to the will of GOD, and negatively he abstained from doing that against his will.

This is the plain fact, both from his own words and the account we have of his life; for of all other men, whatsoever height of character they have attained, it is an historical fact, there are none who have not been faulted for sin, either positively or negatively, and that He alone was uncensured both by his friends and cotemporaries, and by all since then. That, therefore, by which he was perfect morally, must be the Highest Good, and that which he counted Good must have been Good, and his method of attaining to it the method. And no definition of Moral Good, or of the Highest Good, or of man's supreme rule in life, by whatsoever philosopher it be brought forward, is true but this, that "God is the Supreme Good, and the Supreme Law of man His Will, and the Supreme Happiness and Perfection of man a resemblance unto him."

It is manifest, that to our Lord, the exemplar and model of Perfect Humanity, the Supreme Good was God the Father. His perfection was in his being "the express image of God." And the highest and completest object of his existence to do the will of God. And we can see that he fulfilled the notion of a perfect Humanity, a Human Nature of itself Good, and consciously doing no evil, but all good.

But we see that he was aided towards this; the Human Nature was, as it were, upheld and enabled to effect this, and to be raised to its highest possible perfection, by the union of the Divine Nature with it.

But it will be said, "to Him this was the Highest Good, because being God the Word, the will of the FATHER was immediately known to him, but *to us* that can be no true standard."

To this we may at once say, "He is the express image of His person, the manifestation of His glory;" and "*he that hath seen him, hath seen the Father also.*"

But we go on to another consideration, which will be found to tell upon this part of the subject in a very important way; that is, to consider the moral condition of the other perfect man, Adam; and this we shall find to give us great light upon the matter.

Now, when we look at the situation of Adam, we find enough tc lead us to consider that as our nature is good, even although it is injured by the Fall, so was the nature of Adam good, without that injury.

Next we find that Adam, as Christ, continuously thought, and spoke, and did no evil, and that not as a mere innocent, or as a *righteous animal*, barely without consciousness, but consciously and knowingly. This is expressed by the declaration that God made Adam in the image of God, in the image that is of GOD the

WORD, as St. Athanasius interprets it, which implies that his nature, as a moral nature, was complete and perfect.

And secondly, he possessed the endowment of a direct supernatural communication with the ALMIGHTY, whereby man's nature, "the image of God," should reflect God's attributes. So should man's Will directly be under the influence of the FATHER; man's Higher Reason, of the WORD; man's Conscience, of the SPIRIT.

So that thereby his being in the image, this consisted of these two parts: first, the Moral Nature, and secondly, the supernatural endowment corresponding to that nature. This the Supernatural Gift, consisting plainly of the Presence of God with Adam, not as God was present with our SAVIOUR, perpetually united with his Humanity, but as capable of being withdrawn. Which gift the Catholic Church has accounted to be the HOLY SPIRIT dwelling in a nature, 1st, unfallen, 2d, perfectly free, and 3d, untainted from the beginning with any speck of actual sin.*

This is the account of the First Man and his condition, which seems to have been drawn from the Scriptures by the Universal Reason of the Church. And we can see that it agrees most exactly with the various passages of the Scriptures that concern Adam, or speak of man in general, whether they be historical or doctrinal.

Now, this manifestly implies, with regard to Adam, the same we have shown to be the case with respect to CHRIST, our most Blessed Lord ever to be adored, that His Supreme Absolute Good was God; the measure and standard unto him of all moral good whatsoever. That of his own nature and actions, their good was a similarity in them to God, and that God's will was his law. And that Adam was not then *good of himself*, and *of his own reason*, with no connection with God except that of natural mind, understanding of its natural ability, that which is good, and then of that natural ability doing it. But Adam was good in a twofold way; first, *of his nature*, so made and constituted; and secondly, *of the Supernatural Gift;* the Spirit, thus bringing close to him that GOD WHO in HIMSELF IS THE ABSOLUTE GOOD.

This is the moral doctrine with regard to the position of our first father, which the thought of the Church has wrought out;

* Upon the State of Adam before the Fall, and especially upon the "Supernatural Gift," Bp. Bull's fifth discourse may be read.

and this we shall see, and this only will satisfy the descriptions given us of man's nature in Paradise, that is, of man perfect, and the demands of our Human Nature, that is, of man imperfect; and of the nature of GOD and of CHRIST.

There are, I would also remark, from these conclusions, with regard to Christ our Lord, and with regard to Adam, many inferences that concern our present life and future state of perfect being, which are of the most interesting, and to this age that has forgotten the Church, the fountain of all wisdom, of the most novel and startling kind, upon which I would gladly enlarge, but that my limits prevent it. It is, I hope, sufficient to suggest "that as He is, so shall we be also," to enable others to draw these inferences, and thus leaving this to Christian meditation, we may pass onward to our task.

It will, however, be said, "while we acknowledge with regard to Christ and with regard to Adam, what is here laid down, to us it cannot be so. We are not as our Lord, who was God the Word Incarnate, and to whom, therefore, 'God,' the 'Will of God,' the 'Nature of God' were laws."

We are not, it will again be said, as Adam, who was in the "Image of God," and with whom the Supernatural Gift of God's HOLY SPIRIT, the third person of the Trinity, ever dwelt, and being of himself "Very God," revealed to Adam, the "Nature," the "Will," "the Law" of God, and thus made all these his standard of Moral Goodness and his Supreme Law of Action. "But we are alone," say they, "and therefore we must find out for ourselves some other standard."

I might have given a sufficient answer to this, first, by saying that it is a heathen objection, one that supposes not that "in Him we live, and move, and have our being," but that he has departed and left other powers to rule the world, that in themselves have no moral and spiritual energies, but blind force. Secondly, I pointed out that our nature being itself good, although fallen, the "Bible in the Church," the Affections as brought forth in the Family, and the Natural Sense of Justice and Equity, as brought forth in the Nation, all these are revelations of God, all these are such that of Him we have more evidence and clearer knowledge than we have of any one of the objects of the senses.

These answers were enough for objections; but as my object is not to refute or answer, but to teach, perhaps it may be advantageous to go farther into the subject.

And this I will do, not merely as a proof of what I have now asserted, but as a most important advance in the science of Christian Ethics.

The reader will remember that the objections say, "True: God is the Highest Good; to be like Him is the Supreme Happiness; it was so to Christ and so to Adam. It cannot be so to us, because we are not as was Christ, we are not as was Adam."

We are not as our Lord; this is manifest. Whether that dissimilarity is of such a nature as to cause that Moral Good shall not be to us the same as to him, or that the Supreme Rule of Action to our Lord shall not be the Supreme Rule to us, are matters which, however easily settled, I shall not here meddle with. The objection that says, "We are not as Adam, and therefore the rule and law of Adam cannot apply to us,"—this I shall first take up.

The objection says, "We are not as Adam." What, then, was Adam? That which we have above described.

And what are we? The answer is, we are "fallen;" this is the answer of all Christians. "We are fallen."

But how far fallen—*to what degree?* The answer with reference to degree is, "*so far fallen* as yet to be *men*," not so far *as to cease to be men;* but so far as, *being still men*, we could fall; fallen, but not *so fallen* as to be *Devils, all evil in nature*, or *to be beasts, altogether indifferent to good.* Man's nature is a fallen nature; "*as far gone as it can be*"*from Original Righteousness, but not farther; a nature *still Human*, not a *fiendish nature*, or a *bestial one.* In the first chapter I have shown this; I have shown that we must count that man's nature yet is good.

Wherein, then, is the difference, if man's nature before the Fall was good, after the Fall is also good? Is it not, then, *not fallen?* We answer that it is fallen, although good, and we proceed to explain how it is fallen.

In theological language, the state of man now differs from that in Paradise, in Sin, Original and Actual. We have not to discuss the nature of Original or Actual Sin, for this is out of our way at present, only to show how the two states differ as regards the

* The 9th Article of the Church, "Very far gone;" better translated as above, the Latin being "quam longissime."

condition and moral nature of man. We remarked upon the state of man before the Fall; we showed that his Highest Good was God, his Highest Law the Will of God; that this was so by his nature, by his being in "the image of God." And then we showed that the Supernatural Gift of the Holy Spirit abode with him, revealing "God," the Father, Son, and Holy Ghost, as a law, so that man, "the image of God," as in a mirror, reflected the perfection of God in his Will, in his Affections, and in his Actions. In his own nature being good, he became, because of that Supernatural Gift, in finite and bounded existence, an image of the Infinite and Supreme.

To this we shall add two observations to confirm this view. The first is, that "God *is a law unto himself*, and has a law *under which*, so to speak, *he is;* the Law of his own infinite perfections and infinite goodness." He does not make that evil which is good, or that good which was evil by an exertion of Almighty Power; but that *is good* that *is according to his nature*, and that is evil which is against his nature.

And therefore it is, that he alone is *the good*, all others are good as a quality in them exists, which is kindred to Him. And, so it follows, that of all things that are good, you may use the words, "God is."* Men may have them *as qualities*, but God *is them*—thus "God is Love," "God is Justice," "God is Holiness." Men have them, as I said, as *qualities*, but God *as substantial realities*, and *parts of his very being.*

Now, the relation of finite beings towards the Infinite God, being such as I have observed, such too being the nature of God, it follows that the Revelation, by the Spirit of God to Adam, must have been to him the supreme law of action in a moral point of view, an indwelling, we may say, of the Spirit of God in his heart with a law infallible of action, thought, and word. And that *not as to us*, but *immediate*, *intuitive*, *direct*, requiring nought of thought, labor, or experience, but at once and immediate to his mind.

And this immediate discernment, or rather *presence* of God, as the Supreme Good, the Supreme Rule of Good, brought about by the Supernatural Gift of the Spirit, is that of which mention is made in the Scriptures of the New Testament, as "seeing God."

* The reader will please look back to the quotation from Bp. Beveridge, in the note on page 27, as to the phrase, "I am" belonging to God.

And in this manifestly the highest perfection of a finite being that is good must consist; this gift being withdrawn he will not be perfect, although his nature still may be good.

Now I can appeal to every one, whether the yearnings of the heart do not answer back to this picture; whether we do not yearn after an higher good; whether we do not feel that an internal good dwelling in us, but not of us, and at once revealing to us the Highest Good, and being it, whether this is not that which we feel at once most suitable and most desirable to our nature?

Man feels himself to be no fiend, he feels himself to be no beast, he feels his nature to be *essentially, that is, in its own being, good;* but that there is a correlative wanting to it, because of which it is imperfect. This he knows from the first moment of existence to the last. And as this, his Supernatural Gift and aid, has been withdrawn from him, thereby his Nature, although still it is good, is "very far gone from Original Righteousness."

Now with regard to man's own nature, in its being, is there any change in it? And if there be, what in kind and what in degree?

If my reader will turn back a few pages, he will see that there I recount various objects of pursuit which men make ruling objects of their life. He will see that these range from the very low to the very high, so that very distinctly men shall say, "to make this a governing desire and leading object of life, is base and mean," the pleasures of sense, for instance, and "this" intellectual pleasure for instance, "is higher," and this moral object, the "sense of duty," for instance, higher still. Which observation leads at once to the conclusion, that of our whole nature, no part, to speak in a general way, being anything but good in itself—there are *some parts subordinate* and *some superior.* Hence is it that the perfection of our nature does and must *consist* in this *subordination* or *due proportion and harmony* of the whole nature.

We will illustrate it a little more. There are manifestly governing powers in man. The Will, the Conscience, the Affections, the Reason—these are good *always*, at all times, *as governing powers*, guiding man on his course. We say not any one of these separately, but all of them together, as the proper governing powers of man.

Then come passions, desires, feelings, appetites, instincts.

These are manifestly good also, but *only in their place,* and *in their time*, and *not at all times*, or *in all places;* and not at all as *ruling* or *guiding*, but as *being ruled* and *guided.*

Now herein is man's nature of itself, in consequence of the Fall, weakened, that the lower faculties, the passions, desires, feelings, appetites, instincts, these tend to assume the place of the higher, and themselves *to rule* when they ought *to be ruled.*

And secondly, the ruling faculties are weakened so as to permit this insubordination. The Will is weakened, or loses its power in various ways; the Conscience as a faculty, is in various ways injured; the Affections perverted to unsuitable objects, or wholly alloyed by the passions, and the Reason obscured.

For this, too, we appeal to no dry discussion, but to man's nature and to the experience of every man that has ever thought. Who is the man that is naturally the best in your circle of acquaintance? Why, it is that man that unites, in the greatest perfection, these four governing powers,—first, the Will,—he that having a straight, definite, decided course before him, pursues it with decision and energy from day to day; second, the Conscience,—who in that course makes it his main object to go according to his sense of right and wrong; third, the Affections,—he who, as regards his brethren, observes the great Christian rule of "loving his neighbour as himself;" and fourth, the Reason,—who tempers all this into a harmonious and consistent course by a *considerate mind.* This man manifestly is the man, that of our neighbours we judge and see to be the best, *having perhaps the inferior qualities as strong as others have*, but *ruling them by these powers, which ought to rule.*

And again, when we look about for those whom we count the worst, we see that they are the men whose conduct is not ruled by these ruling qualities, but by some of the lower and baser ones.

And in ourselves, do we not in our inmost soul, whenever we feel that we have acted wrongly, whenever we have a consciousness of evil or of sin, do we not always know and feel, "Oh! that my Will were perfect; Oh! that my Conscience were a sure and certain guide, my Affections rightly directed, and my Reason as clear and active as it might be; *if this were so, then would I be perfect!*" Manifestly this is the feeling of all men; an universal persuasion this, of all men and all ages, that declares the one source of man's imperfections of nature, to be *in the insubordination of his faculties.*

Man's nature then may be good, nay, each faculty of it may be good, and yet the nature in itself be a fallen one, as an insubordinate, a disturbed one.

The consequences then of the fall, are these: First, that the Supernatural Gift is withdrawn, which revealed God to thy nature immediately; and Secondly, because of this, thy nature, which would have answered, and did answer, by *its* law unto God the Supreme Law, is *insubordinate.* These are, according to the Ethical doctrine of the Christian Church of antiquity, the precise injuries inflicted upon man by the fall. These and none else.

Now if we shall look at our present nature as fallen, having clearly and distinctly in mind these truths, we shall see what is the real and true measure of good to the present man. We shall see that it is neither more nor less than that it was to Adam in Paradise, the being and qualities of God, and the being in ourselves like to him.

And in order that this should be so, when we consider the previous elements of the problem, there must be two things. In the first place, there must be a feeling of this in our nature, existing and capable of looking even blindly and by instinct towards Him. In the second place, there must be outward agencies at work upon us, that will call into action that natural feeling, just as the sun and rain, the influences of the seasons, call forth the germ in the plant. That man's nature is good, that of itself it is not indifferent or fiendish, but made "in the image," this affords the first requisite. The nature of man, of itself, feels its own disorder, and it desires to be ordered and ruled by a superior Will, and looks after and towards it blindly, as the new-born child for the mother's breast will open and close its mouth, and desire what it does not know, but knows yet that something is wanting.

I could go over the Heathen writers antecedent to Christ, both Greek and Roman, and also the more ancient philosophy of the Hindoos, Chinese and original Persians, now opened to us by the industry of the modern oriental scholars of England, Germany and France, as well as the Northern Mythology, and show by them, that apart from all revelation, and before it, the attempts in Moral Science of unassisted nature rush towards God as the "Supreme Good," and supreme standard of good, and will be contented with no standard lower.

But I seek not to make a parade of learning, and I merely assert the fact that it is so, and leave it to each thinking individual to measure his own experience of his own nature, and he will find it to be so.

I assert, also, that from these writings evidence just as strong can be given that the evil of nature was felt to be that which I have said, the evil of "insubordination"; and the perfection of Human Nature, the perfection of the Eternal Presence, or as they phrase it, "the direct contact" of a Supreme Rule and the power of obeying it.

In fact, in the Ethical writers of the heathen, we can see perpetually the struggle towards these conclusions, and they come the nearer, the higher and loftier their Ethics are. But bringing this in merely as confirmatory, I go on the further inquiries connected with the subject.

Now, having come so far as to give a matter-of-fact example, proving that although man is fallen, still is God to him the Supreme Good, and the standard of good, we shall make one observation, and then go to the subject of the next chapter. If this be so, is it not manifest that to the *natural man* there must be *naturally some revelation of God?* And that not merely to the man, generically considered, but to each individual man, is it not necessary that there be a mode which communicates to him the feeling of God, now that his Direct Presence is departed; and this by nature, apart totally and entirely from Christianity? So that even to those who have not heard of the name of Christ, still do they make God the measure of moral good, and no other fancied or thought-out standard; or that, in other words, the Spiritual has an access to man by his position, and by his very constitution and being.

This manifestly *is so*, or else all the other truths are useless and invalid. This subject, therefore, *how it is* that even to man, as he is at present, God is the "Supreme Standard of all Morality," is that to which I shall devote the ensuing chapter.

CHAPTER IV.

God has external means whereby he conveys His Knowledge unto Man.—1. External Nature. 2dly. Society.—The operation of External nature upon man's moral being explained.—The operation of Society is two fold—first, of Law; second, of traditional knowledge or Opinion, whereof Society is a channel.

OUR first question is, how is it that to man, even as a fallen being, God is still the Supreme Standard of Moral Good, and that his nature having lost its self-governing power, and the direct contact of God with it being withdrawn, man still measures all good by God?

The answer is, that man's nature being good, the instinct of this, his constitution, must lead him naturally, although blindly, towards God. And secondly, there must be corresponding to that instinctive feeling, external influences that draw forth the instinct of nature into consciousness, as the Sun upon the earth draws up the germ of the plant underneath until it rises into the light.

Now, in reference to our own nature or internal being, we call all other objects *external*—all those influences that bear upon us from without are external. And things external are divided into two parts, Nature and Society. And the question may be easily solved by asking, are there moral ideas connected with Nature and with Society? For then, since Nature exists before the individual man is born, and he is introduced into the world as into a school, then if there be ideas of God connected naturally with the objects of the external world, we are able to see how the germ in him may be awakened, and the dormant life excited to action.

And in like manner, as Society existed before him, and he is born into it; so if Society have the idea of God, it can suggest it to him, and thus awaken his nature and be a school of teaching to it.

From the earliest times we find an association of ideas that connects Nature with God, and makes each object of the material world a letter in the "great alphabet that speaks of Him." Nor is it a vain fancy that of the old Arabs, who, seeing upon the film of the locust's wing the semblance of the letters of their own language, read them into the words, "Desolation of God;" and connecting the stars by lines, and thereby tracing letters in the heavens, thence strove to discover an alphabet of the heavenly wisdom.* For in truth, had we but the eye, were but our senses sharpened to penetrate into the infinite subtlety of the teachings of this that we call Nature, so that we could discern them and be conscious of them, as we are influenced by them unconsciously, we should see that Nature is nought else than a means of bringing the Knowledge of God close to us; of awakening in us the sleeping germs of Spiritual Knowledge. And we should find that not a leaf upon a tree struck our sight even unnoticed amid the myriads of other leaves, not a sand upon the shore among millions has made its unregarded impression upon our sight, but that has tended to convey to us moral knowledge of God, the Supreme Good.

And as the drops of rain being countless that have fallen upon a given field, have nevertheless each single drop a definite and estimable amount in the sum of the harvest, only that it would take the calculus of Infinite Knowledge to estimate it; so the manifold impressions from day to day, from hour to hour, of Natural Objects, these all, although we are unconscious of it, yet tend to form in us the idea of God. Perhaps I should not say to form, but to call out the germs that exist in our own being, as made in the Image, to call them out and bid them expand.

Perhaps the idea here attempted to be expressed as a fact of Ethical science, the idea, that is, of an Ethical teaching of nature, that is universal and pours its influence unremittingly from the smallest as well as the grandest objects, might be as well set before the reader in half a dozen of verses, which I remember to have seen somewhere, in which the author has expressed the same thought very nearly.

"Oh! that mine ears were open, Lord,
Oh! that mine eyes could see,
Then flower, and star, and little bird,
Would bloom, and shine, and sing of Thee.

Then on the world's broad face,
Now so opaque and dim,
The alphabet of heaven I'd trace,
And every line should tell of Him.

* For this alphabet, see the works of the learned Gataker.

Then, sounding clear from ocean's gloom,
Like a far-heard organ peal,
Then booming up from the central womb
Of things I know not, yet can feel

The sounds that now mysterious sweep
Across my saddening soul,
As thunder clouds that o'er the deep
Their gloomy shadows roll,

These sounds that now, confused and dim,
Vague sorrow bring from far,
Clear should they speak—my heart should speak
To the heart of every star.

All living creatures then should speak
With wisdom manifold,
And wide creation that deep silence break,
She held since Adam's fall of old."

These verses, although I must say that the verse is of a very unpolished description, seem nevertheless to express the same feeling and persuasion.

But the same thing is clearly and distinctly asserted in the 19th Psalm. "The heavens declare the glory of God, and the firmament showeth his handy work. One day telleth another, and one night certifieth another; there is neither speech nor language, but their voices are heard among them, their sound is gone out into all lands and their words unto the ends of the world."

In fact, from all languages, and from all nations, we might bring full proofs of this fact, "that all men feel and know that the outward world in all its influences upon man is a teaching of God, an interpretation, as it were, of Him, to our limited intellects; a hiding away, and dimming of His glory, that so it may be softened and adapted to our sight." But still, from the smallest as well as the greatest objects that strike the sense, there flows a teaching, beginning with our life and ending only with our death, which we can never shut out.

And that this perpetually presents unto us, or rather cherishes in us, in a due measure as we can bear it, the idea of God, his Power, Mercy and Wisdom. And that although men may, because they are not conscious of it, dream that it is not so, still that there is such a thing in the science of Ethics as teaching, which *being real is yet unconscious*. And that it is so with this.

Upon which matter of moral teaching being *real*, although we are *unconscious of it*, I shall, perhaps, at a future time of this essay have some words to say. In the mean time, I say, that manifestly Nature, the face of outward, inanimate Nature, is a teacher to us of God, and from the greatest and from the smallest objects, at all times, moral teaching is flowing incessantly and perpetually upon each man. And although but seldom we may know of it, and but in extraordinary cases and under extraordinary circumstances are we struck with it, still, at all times, and in all places, is such an influence acting upon us.

And for the truth of this, I have to appeal to the general sense and persuasion, and the universal reason of mankind.

But leaving External Nature alone, we shall come now to the other sphere into which man is born, that of Society, and proceed to examine what influence it has upon man in revealing to him God, or bringing forth the idea or image of God that is in him by nature.

And here we find a very distinct and manifest influence. An influence that tells upon man in Society as an instructor, in and of the nature of Good. The influence of Law. A second influence, also, the influence of Knowledge, handed down from generation to generation. Upon these two we shall remark.

And first, upon the influence of Law in general. We have stated it as our belief that the organizations of Society are unchangeable; that the Family, the Nation and the Church are always to remain as they always have been, and that man is never without them, has never been without them.

Now, in virtue of this fact of the perpetual duration of these forms of organization, there is a ruling spirit in each of them; in the Family, the Law of Love; in the Nation, the Law of Justice; in the Church, the Law of Holiness; a threefold division of the one Spirit, that influence the manifestation of which we call "Law." Now, what is this?

We take a description of it from a book* of our own, satisfied that the reader will not object to this if it give an answer to the question.

* "Mercy to Babes, a Plea for the Christian Baptism of Infants."

This is an influence from which in the state none can be free. Through all the institutions of society it speaks, for these are its embodiments. The Magistrate, the Husband, the Parent, are mouth-pieces of this Eternal Spirit. To all men it speaks, to all classes and individuals; it reaches even to the babe on its mother's knee. To the good, it is the secret plastic force of Society, which works upon them almost unconsciously, framing and forming them ever with a gentle and omnipresent influence; unfelt, yet not the less real. To the bad, it is a force external and severely felt, sternly thundering out its penalties, its sanctions and its punishments, placing against them a barrier they cannot leap, and calling to its aid, even when men the most reject it, powers in man's own breast and being, and in the feelings of his fellows, and even in the elements themselves, which do and will execute its decrees.

Men have felt this, and felt that there is something divine in Law, and the loftiest and holiest have concluded that this that we call law is neither more nor less than the influence and operation of the Will, and Power and Justice of "the Almighty and All-governing God."

Thus having spoken of Law, we ask our readers to avoid one very common error, when they think of it; the error of imagining corporeal things to be the only realities. A good many do so—they think bread and meat, &c., things that we can see, and touch, and taste, and feel the only realities; whereas there are other things, just as solid and substantial realities, honesty, and justice, and love, and truth, these are just as much realities as if you could handle them, or see them, or feel them. Now, this that we call Law is of this class, a strong and true reality, and yet not to be handled or touched.

It is, too, that means by which mediately the Will of God is conveyed to us as in a channel, which to the primitive man was directly and immediately given from the Almighty; it is the veil in which, now that through man's weakness his eyes are feeble, so that he cannot look upon the full blaze of Glory, God shrouds his effulgence and tempers it to our sight; it is the spirit which from all Nature he pours upon man (as the imponderable fluids of natural philosophy are poured from material things) to teach him of God.

And well and truly does it teach him, for it, "the Law," is the revealer of God to the natural man.

For God, being the supreme fountain and standard of Good,

Law, that is, obedience to and compliance with law, is to the natural man the highest rule of all action, that by which as far as natural action goes, he shall attain to the highest truth of life.

But that not one Law, but ALL LAW in one agreeing and uniting. First, the "Law of man's own nature," the law of the *ruling powers* of "Conscience," "the Will," "the Affections," "the Reason." These are the faculties that make him capable of obedience to the voice of God. And then the Actual and External "Law," which teaching and educating this inward faculty, employs three schools for man; three courts, if I may so say, of law. The one which teaches and enforces the law of obedience and the law of the affections, that is the Family. The second, the law of "right" concerning "life and property," which of course implies justice and equity, that is the State. The third, whose teaching is the law of Holiness, the Church.

Putting these conclusions together, I say, if any one asks me how a natural man, (apart from the influences of Grace,) shall try to reach the good of his nature in the highest degree, and what is the rule that he should make his object to apply in act, thought, and word; I say it is nought but this, "the Law and the whole Law."

The natural man finds the law of his nature to be virtue*—that his conscience should, each moment of his life, be attended to and deferred to, so that he should obey this, for by this faculty it is that the feeling of Law is manifested to us the first. His nature and whole being will assert to him that he ought so to do. Let him then, at any risk, and at any sacrifice, set himself to obey his Conscience, and to go according to its suggestions, and he will find the light, that perhaps at first was a faint twinkle upon the remotest horizon, become brighter, clearer, steadier, larger,—he will find obedience easier, and finally it will become habitual.

And then, having gone upon this for a time with all his might, next will awaken in him the sense and feeling of the Affections as part of the guiding and governing powers of man's life, and he will feel that gentleness, wisdom, patience, love, considerateness, mercy, kindness—that these, somehow or other, give him a rule over

* "Virtue is the law of our nature."—BP. BUTLER.

himself and over others, which he could not at first comprehend, or, indeed, at all perceive.*

And then, if he act consistently upon this that he has attained, he shall come to feel the value of *the will*, of decision and energy in a course of straight forward travel, in a way set out and appointed for him by himself.

And the Reason, too, shall come in, although the last, and declare and show itself to him; and to obey these four, which all are the law of our nature, is to cultivate the principles of obedience to *all law* wherever we find it.

These four, and in this order, Conscience first, then the Affections, and then the Will, and then the Reason; each as a rule of conduct is manifested to man when he has actually, and in action, made the other preceding it, a steady rule of his life.

And as schools and legislative institutions to aid us in this self-discipline, there are the institutions I have mentioned. This is the moral perfection of the natural man; and for him, as far as his nature and his position is concerned, if he wishes to attain this perfection, the institutions are just as needful as is the moral nature.

Now, he that shall look at this influence of Society upon man that we call "Law," must see that it is directly and immediately a good one, and that the only thing that possibly can make it evil, is that it is partial occasionally, that interest is made to override the law of Conscience, the law of the State to smother that of the Family, or of the Reason to destroy that of the Conscience;

*"Gentleness, virtue, wisdom, and endurance,
These are the seals of that most firm assurance,
Which bars the pit over destruction's strength.
And if, with infirm hand, Eternity,
Mother of many acts and hours, should free
The serpent that would clasp her with its length,
These are the spells by which to reassume
An empire o'er the disentangled doom.
To suffer woes which hope thinks infinite,
To forgive wrongs darker than death or night,
To love and bear, to hope till hope creates
From its own wreck, the thing it contemplates,
This, like thy glory, Titan, is to be
Good, great, and joyous, beautiful and free,
This is alone, Life, Joy, Empire and Liberty."

these things excepted, the Law is a teacher wholly good, and is the great means of advance to the mere natural man.

The resolution to uphold it in all difficulties, to defer to it, and to act accordingly, this is the *one and only means* of *natural morality* to individuals or to States*—the only standard and the only source of it.

I may be permitted here, in opposition to the many sophisters and theorists who have erected standards of Ethics from Hobbes, who thought man to be a ravenous beast of prey at eternal war with his fellows, and therefore concluded that his leading character was fierce and warlike selfishness, down to Bentham, who took "utility" for the "supreme rule of conduct,"—I may be permitted in opposition to these men, to urge this view, that Law and Duty, these are the grand standard of morals for the Natural Man, and the grand means of self-development, in a moral way, if he would cultivate his own moral nature, just as I have shown that by means of these, God is ever to man the Supreme Standard of Good.

And this view is also corroborated by the word of Christ to a mere natural man, who asked him, "Good master, what shall I do that I may have eternal life?"—and his answer was, "Why callest thou me good—there is none Good but one, that is God; if thou wilt enter into life, *keep the commandments*."

How completely does this agree with the doctrine above specified, "none Good but one,"—the supreme fount and source—and the supreme law and standard—the treasure of Good in every way, is God the Father of Heaven and Earth. And the way in which that is reached is not by knowledge, nor by wisdom, nor by deep penetration, but by Law; "if thou wilt enter into life, keep the commandments." The great way is to obey the law, by which he manifests himself, the law of God in whatever way it is shown, wherever it is found.

This is the commandment of Christ to the young man; and this,

* Of Law, there can be no less acknowledged than that her seat is the bosom of God,—her voice the harmony of the world: all things in heaven do her homage—the very least as feeling her care, and the greatest as not exempted from her power: both angels and men, and creatures of what condition soever, though each in different sort and manner, yet all with uniform consent, admire her as the mother of their peace and joy.—HOOKER, ECCLES. POLITY.

to the man who is of Nature apart from God's Grace, is the only power, the exclusive means of moral advancement.

And while I have many things to say as a conclusion to this subject upon the relation of the Law to the Gospel, which I cannot take up now, but shall speak of at another time, inasmuch as there is a certain proportion to be observed, which to break through would enlarge this treatise immeasurably,—while I must therefore observe this proportion, I still would ask of my readers to remark the weight of the Principle I have been urging, and exemplifying as the principle of progress in morality to the Natural Man.

For you that are unbaptized in Christ's Name and his Faith, "no arrangement of external circumstances, planned and devised by yourselves or others, can give you the beginning and impetus of moral progress; no knowledge or learning, no philosophy of mind, or subtle examination of the Nature of Man, search it out; no acting upon "Fundamental Principles," or Ethical Theories, such as that of "Utility," that of Benevolence, that of "Sympathy," that of "Enlightened Selfishness," that of "Nature," or any other theory or fundamental notion; nor aught else than this, that of acting up to Law and Duty wherever it is found. Wherever from Country, from Parents, from Society, from Conscience, from Reason, from Revelation, the Commandments come, —there, "if thou wilt enter into life, keep the commandments."

Dwell not in mere sensibilities, or in the luxury of feeling; dream not of some future access of influences, that shall whirl you on to moral perfection by a tornado of overpowering emotion, but *at once*, and *now*, yield to and obey the eternal spirit that is by you, and "keep the commandments." For your own natural constitution is framed according unto Law, external Nature corresponds, and Society guides and directs the influences of Law upon you. And all these are but the appliances and means whereby God, the Standard of Good, is brought nigh to you.

Central art thou, child of man! among all these moral influences; and if thou wouldst be profited of them all, this is the first and the only step—the only beginning of moral improvement to man upon the earth.

And the first and only way to enter upon this path is by the Conscience; then, as I have said, the Affections, as a Moral Law, begin to exert themselves; then the Reason, and then the Will.

How this is connected with the Gospel, as I have before said, I shall leave to another part of this treatise; only at present I shall quote two passages of St. Paul, which may indicate to Christians the future course of consideration, and at the same time afford food for thought, even to the mere Natural Man.

"The Law is *Holy*, (and spiritual,) and the Commandment *Holy, Just and Good.*" And again: the "Law was our schoolmaster, to lead us to Christ."

With those two passages I shall close the consideration of that one of the two external influences of Society, which I before spoke of, as manifesting unto man God the Supreme Good.

Again. Another means whereby God works upon man, is what we call Tradition, "the power that is in Society, by which, if any knowledge of God be committed to it, it shall pass down from one generation to another, and be retained as water in a channel, and influence men, even when they do not think of it, even when they are wholly unconscious of its workings."

That such knowledge shall flow in the channel of "the life of a community as waters in the channel of a river, that it shall imbue the child, the unlearned, the ignorant, with feelings, knowledge and persuasions; this we know from history."

We know, for instance, that among all nations the tradition of a deluge remains; that even now, so many years from the event, still the narration of this handed down from father to son, in various shapes, is permanent, and abides enduringly, although it have been changed into the form of legend and fable.

And the Prometheus of the Greek story, who stole fire from heaven, and thereby restored the human race; he, nailed by angry Jupiter upon the mountains of Caucasus, between heaven and earth, is a true reflex of the old revelation unto Adam. And among the Eastern nations, the character of Gaudama, born of a virgin, to be the Saviour of man, was formed upon the old traditions of Paradise, concerning a future Redeemer. And so Brahma, Vishnu, and Seeva, the Hindu trinity, bear witness to the original revelation of Jehovah.

For, as I have before said, there is this peculiar constitution in Society, this peculiar force, that nought of revelation or of religion that is entrusted to it escapes it, but all flows onward, from one generation to another, in the channel of tradition. We have indications too manifest to be evaded, that arts may have perished and sciences have been forgotten, loftier and more splendid than are now known to man; that nations may have forgotten the history of their own renown, and lost the records of their own civilization; but it seems as if there were in Society a power by which *that which is moral* and *that which is religious* shall, under manifold shapes and obscurations, be retained and enforced.

For, though the life of each individual man is but short, and our generations are only thirty years in length, still the generation is not as a wave, wherein all the particles of which it is composed break at once, and simultaneously are lost; it is rather as the flow of a river, in which continuity is preserved from first to last, or as the rope in which the deficiency of one fibre is supplied by others. So it is with the life of Society; for all purposes of knowledge, death actually makes no difference, the stream continues to flow, although old particles are evaporated, and new ones enter within it; the school abides the same, although the pupils, their education perfected, are called away, for other pupils are entered therein.

I would dwell upon this a little more. Because of the faults of the speculations of our latter time, I would urge it upon my readers more thoroughly.

It has seemed to be forgotten that man is in a school, in a state of trial; and therefore man has got into the notion that he can MAKE the "Law," that which, in the previous part, we have shown to be truly and really the voice of God. So men have thought that they could make this that they call "Public Opinion," and that we have called Tradition. They call it so, because they think that it comes from the men of the present day; but we give it the other name, because we clearly see that it is an inheritance *handed down* (*tradita*) from the Past.

For as in an agricultural country, there is a certain amount of improvements,* as we call them, houses, and barns, and fences, cleared and cultivated land, which no man can take away, but all must leave behind them; which descends from one generation to another, and the importance of which persons having been born to and with it seldom realize until they go to a new country; so is there in Society a certain amount of teaching upon various subjects, and of knowledge that descends from generation to genera-

* Among Political Economists, this is called "Fixed Capital." The reasons for the names are manifest.

tion, that we call Tradition, and this knowledge men for the most part learn without appreciating or knowing its value, just as men inherit Fixed Capital without knowing what relation it has to labor and property.

We would dwell, as we have said, a little more upon this point. We would show how this provision is adapted to our nature. Is it not a fact that the mind awakens but a short time comparatively after birth, say a year or two years, so that then the child is capable of receiving impressions, opinions, ideas?

Certainly this is the case. It receives these, then, while the judgment is immature, the knowledge imperfect, the mind itself feeble; nay, this reasoning being continues more or less unripe for a period of twenty years, and this very period is the time in which most of its ideas are received. Nine-tenths of all the ideas we hold and act upon, during our life, then are impressed upon us.

This idea, I confess, was first fixed upon my mind by a conversation upon the Evidences of Christianity, in which a clergyman of some ability being asked, "Do you not believe Christianity upon its Evidences?" answered, "No: I believe it because my mother taught me." And, really, any one who will take the pains, may find, as I did, that it is the fact that nine-tenths of his opinions upon any one subject arise from this teaching.

He will find, too, that it is suited to his nature; that it is not for nothing that he is so long immature and unripe, but that it is a most gracious and beneficent arrangement of Providence, by which this World is a School to him, and that knowledge is conveyed to him that is suitable to his nature. Nay, more than this, he shall find that only that kind that is suitable to him, shall be received and taken up by it, all else rejected.

And this Tradition is a cord made up, as it were, of three strands; it is a stream from three sources, from the Nation, the Family, and the Church.

In each of these we shall see that it originates and continues to operate. Let a father and mother be honest, and their honesty shall, they know not how, communicate itself to their children. Let justice, or veracity, or high feeling, or natural delicacy, or any other moral idea, be a leading one of the parents, and the children, by this natural provision we have spoken of, shall take it up. And it shall continue in the family, and its traces be seen after seven generations; for the child, with undoubting mind and unresisting faith, shall receive it from the parents, and so shall it become an element in the channel of Family life, and flow therein, we had almost said, forever.

Let the pastor in his church have the high and lofty feelings that he should be endued with, and he shall find that by means of this, they shall communicate themselves from one to another; his flock shall receive them with unresisting faith, and years after he has laid in the grave his Good shall still be working.

Let the Statesman or the Magistrate think upon it, and he shall see the qualities of a Chatham, a Washington, or an Elizabeth enter into the channel of the life of a nation, and henceforth be, until the end of time, a formative power over the character of millions.

For the reverse of what the poet has said is true, "The Good that men do"—this it is that lives after them—"but the evil is buried with their bones."

Two things more, in connection with this subject, I would observe. First, that of this teaching there are three authoritative teachers: the Parent, the Magistrate, the Pastor; and in reference to them none *can fill their places*, or *do that* which it is *their* business to do. For with the Child towards the Parent, in reference to *this teaching*, *belief is easier than unbelief;* the child believes until the assertion of his parent be disproved, instead of disbelieving until it be proved.

And so it is with the Citizen in reference to the Magistrate as regards fealty, and the member of a church as regards his Pastor. These are things that in many cases are called *prejudices* by astonished Radicals and Destructionists, and yet are part of *the morality of our position*, and explain many matters in history and society that men wonder at as unaccountable.

A second thing I would remark: the peculiar mode of this teaching. It seems to have *an inclination almost unconquerable for a "viva voce" or Oral instruction.* The parent to the child shall teach more by a little simple talk, than by the best manual, written or printed. Conversation seems peculiarly the mode of this traditional teaching. With regard to the pastor, also, I have noticed that to speak with his people face to face has a predominant influence.

We have stated that these two influences are teachers, means, and instruments of a peculiar teaching. We are aware that men may dispute it, may even consider it an absurdity, and attribute to the aggregate of individuals that which we attribute to Society as a true and real *organization.*

We, however, submit two considerations that may help men to reach out to our apprehension of the matter.

And previously we will place before them our conception of the position of man. He is under one class of influences from which no being born into the world can be free, those of external nature —under the same class of influences to which the animals are subject, and they produce in him moral ideas, while in the animals we have no reason to imagine that they do so. This is one School.

There is another; that of Society, with its twofold influences, which we have just explained, of Law and Tradition, its authorized teachers of Parents, Magistrates and Priests, its indestructible organization or threefold school, to which these belong. Now the decisive question as to the true and real existence of these is not, "can men do without them?" for men's speculations are far different from facts, and as a fact men *have never been* without them; but this it is—"the moral results that are produced by these means, are they producible otherwise?"

Take a child in childhood, let him be completely isolated from Parents, from the Church, from Society, and will moral ideas arise spontaneously in his mind? Will those feelings, opinions and beliefs, which we see kept, as it were, in solution in the stream of life, imbuing each individual, and thus passed down from one to another generation, will these arise in his mind *spontaneously?*

And as the answer, we have authentic records of perhaps a dozen of children, who were lost before their mind could be so influenced by the Family, the Nation, and the Church, and *no moral ideas* were developed in them, *no intellectual ones—they were perfectly without them.*

From which we draw not the opinion that moral and intellectual ideas are completely artificial—but two conclusions, first, that the *innate principles* of man's being are as those of a bulb or root; that there is a certain outward condition of things requisite to call them forth, which, if it do not exist, they shall not and cannot be called forth. And secondly, that this outward condition is that state we call Society, with it's threefold schools and its triple magistrates, and that *these are absolutely necessary as means of moral culture to the moral nature of man.*

Thus, then, is man placed, and these are his advantages; he has a nature that is not as a beast's nature is, indifferent to good and evil; it is not the nature of a devil, wholly evil in itself, but it is in its *nature and essence* good—but *fallen.*

And in order that it may be led to Good, it is placed in Society subject to *masters* and *teachers* ordained of God, and a member of institutions that by Him are organized, and have their action upon the very roots of man's being. And these teachers teach and instruct in that which is Good; these institutions uphold it also.

And then the Law, in all its phases, enforces it. The Tradition brings to man, consciously or unconsciously, moral elements of Knowledge from the remotest shores of time, the most distant realms of space; and lastly, External Nature repeats and re-echoes all these teachings, from the smallest herb upon the mountain top; from the remotest star; from the stormy sea; from the calm streamlet in the sunshine; from the burning fires of the volcano, and the snowy peaks of the sky-piercing Himmaleh: spring and summer, autumn and winter, all natural objects and all natural scenes, *when once the sense has been awakened,* feed it with a perpetual influence.

Go, ye that think that man is a beast, to pick up his food as he may, to eat and drink, to live according to his own will, and then to die; ye that imagine that this world is a large pen for man the beast to live in, a self-acting patent pen, that supplies enough of food and drink—lull yourselves with this notion, act upon it, but still you shall find that it is not so; still you will find that all things witness unto God; and through them all he witnesses of *Himself,* his *Will,* and his *Law* unto man.

CHAPTER V.

Society brings to all men the knowledge of Good, and the Rule of it.—Man's nature yearns toward it, being good; but it finds itself unable—it is driven then, inwardly for aids—finds within, Conscience, Reason, the Heart, the Will, powers that aid us.—From these arise four philosophies, Socratic, Platonic, Epicurean, Stoic.—These powers the sources of moral progress.—Yet moral perfection by nature unattainable.—Original Sin.—Answer to the question, "How man does evil although his nature is good?"—Difference between Mental or Physical and Moral inability.—Original Sin is primarily in the incapacity of the moral or Governing Powers.

We have in the previous chapters examined points the most important, and drawn conclusions which we believe are, to a system of Christian Science, fundamental. The reader will please remember them, they are these—first, that the nature of man is good; secondly, that all outward circumstances, which wait upon man in this world, are ministers to him of moral teaching.

The first assertion was, that "man's nature is good of itself by nature." This we asserted, with certain limitations.

But at once the question comes up, "Does not man do evil?" and then, "How is this consistent with the fact that his nature is good?"

This is a question of deep importance we will say, and one which, upon this, our theme of Christian Science, has a most vital bearing.

In answer to it, we say then, that man is not as a beast, he is not as a devil, he is a man still, although he does evil; we call him not *totally depraved*, but *fallen;* we call not his state a state of *total depravity*, but of *original sin.* Let our reader remark this and ponder it well; the doctrine we teach in reference to man's state, by nature, declares him "*fallen*,"—that is to say, as far gone as, *still being a man*, he can go from "*original righteousness*,"—but not so far gone as to be a beast, or a fiend; it therefore applies not to him, the term "*totally depraved*," but the word "*fallen*."

Now the very word "fallen," this itself will aid us to comprehend this difficult question,—it implies the having lapsed from a higher condition; it implies inability to come up to a standard; it implies imperfection in natural qualities. A nation degenerated into barbarism would be a "fallen" nation; a hero overthrown, a "fallen" hero; a man of character, who had lost that character, a "fallen" man; but still they cease not to be a nation, a hero, a man. So this word "fallen," implies that Adam originally was created perfect, capable of reaching to and satisfying a certain standard, and in fact reaching to and satisfying it; that to that standard now, no man individually, nor yet the race collectively, can, or do reach—that standard being the *Law of God* and his *Will.*

Now if we look at the third chapter,* we find the subject discussed at some length; we find there that Adam's perfection consisted first in the completeness of his own nature; secondly, in the Presence of God with Adam as a natural rule of life and complete law of action; we shall find, too, that the nature of the fall consists in the withdrawal of that Gift *first* after Adam had sinned, and then in the Insubordination of our natural faculties thereon ensuing. And three means of examining, by example, the nature of man unfallen, we find in Holy Writ, Adam first, secondly Christ our Lord, and thirdly Man after the resurrection.

But our readers may say, if man be thus imperfect, incapable of his nature of reaching a certain standard, surely it is enough for him if he live up to his imperfection, seeing that he is imperfect.

Certainly *if man were alone* in this world—if his own nature were the only indication that he had of a supreme moral law, then that were enough. But let the objector look to our last chapter, there he shall see that, even supposing the man to be afar from the Church and afar from Christianity, still he is not left to himself, to his own nature, or to his own standard; but a higher standard is revealed to him by Society, telling him of *Law*, and through it of the loftiness of duty and the nearness of God; by Tradition or Opinion, which, through the voice of his fellows, brings him religious knowledge and religious conviction from the remotest ages and climes; and lastly, by Nature, which re-echoes and confirms all these.

Let no man then bring forward his imperfection as an excuse, for it is none; if only he will, *in his imperfection*, follow after that which is perfect, he *will be led unto Christ.*

Yes! such is the merciful benevolence of the Omniscient and

* Chapter 3, page 29.

Omnipotent, that, if from one born amidst the barbarism of Africa, amid the Fetish-worship and hideous cannibalism and horrible licentiousness of Central Africa, the desire should arise sincerely to follow the Law of God as it is revealed by Society even there; and the Tradition of religion, faint as it is there ; and the teachings of Nature internal and external; then circumstances shall form themselves to bless the design, and obstacles yield, and ways open through deserts that seemed trackless, and over mountains without passes, and the man shall, by ways he knew not, be led unto Christ and Christianity.*

This is the true answer to them who assert that they have had no opportunity. For the God of the whole earth is not unjust; but in Man's own nature, in the ordinances and arrangements of the outward world and all its circumstances, has he so arrayed the course of things, that "he that will come, may come," and that he who perishes, does so of his own accord, willingly and freely; and not upon the living God Omnipotent, but also All-Merciful and All-Just, but upon himself is the blame to rest.

And he, as I have said, that shall look upon the exposition of the Moral teaching of the External World in the preceding chapters, shall see that it is so.

Now, when we assert this fact of a "fall" from an original type; when we assert that it is in two ways exemplified, in inability to come up to the standard, and, at the same time, in an urgent desire and feeling towards that very standard, manifestly we do a great deal towards settling the moral position of the man and the race.

For first must there be in man, individually and as a race, an inability or a deficiency that is without example in all other animals,—an inability to fulfil functions which we feel we ought to fulfil, and, at the same time, *an external moral stimulus* urging us to strive and struggle in that direction.

That such is the fact, as we know by all experience with regard to man. Because he is not evil essentially, or "*totally depraved*," his natural feeling is towards good. He *seeks nothing but as good.*† The Law as manifested in the outward world and the

* See the Sixth Book, Chapter Second, on the import and meaning of what we call "Circumstance."

† Omne quod petit, petit ut bonum.—Scholastic Maxim.

Tradition show him a perfect good that *is to be done*. And his nature yearns towards it, and he feels that he *ought to do it*, and that originally there is in him the power to do it. And yet, every struggle he makes, he is thrown back unable and incompetent. Is he not then a wonder and a terror to himself?

But it is manifested in more ways than this. The man cannot cease the moral struggle, for, as I have said, the Law is around him, and the Tradition urges him on, and External Nature works with and confirms these two. And this, his vain strife, then forces him to seek back into himself and his inward being, to see whether in that Internal Nature there are moral elements by which he may be able to penetrate and conquer those others of his lower nature that give the opportunity to evil.

He at once sees that there are such; the Conscience he beholds, or feeling of right and wrong. Could he only live according to this exactly, he were absolutely and entirely right, and his nature urges him to struggle toward it. The Will, the power of Self-guidance and Self-determination, could he only guide himself by this; could he only, by a stern effort, shape out his course, and with firmly set and unrelenting Will pursue it, and hew through all obstacles, all difficulties; if there be no moral power in this, at least half the the moral weakness, half the misery of life is lost, and the stern thought of an unyielding and self-determined course holds out to him, if not happiness, at least strength and consistency. Or the man sees the value of Reason, of ruling himself in all cases according to the dictates of Reason, of that which is eternally and immortally right, according to the nature and being of the whole world. Or else he makes of the Affections his standard, seeing plainly that if he could follow nature as far as her teachings speak through man's Heart, then he would be happy.

Now let my readers look at man as he is by nature, and they will see how naturally these philosophies arise, and what they are. In the first class, they will see the Socratic philosophers, those who apprehended the power of Conscience as a guide, a true philosophy, yet inadequate. In the second, the Stoics, with their stern subjection of self, their attempted annihilation of the passions, their ruling of the whole nature by the force of an iron will —a true philosophy, and a grand and noble one, yet as the other, inadequate. Again, in the third class, they find the Platonists of old with their Universal Reason and obedience to it, and this obedience, good and meritorious, still inadequate. And last of all, the moral philosophy that makes the Affections all in all, a theory most liable to be corrupted, but still in men who have advocated and practiced upon it, with a pure mind, the loveliest of all.

Now with reference to these four faculties, is it not plainly manifest that they are to man the avenues and elements of moral progress that exist in his nature,—these and none else, for who can seek a beginning of moral progress, or an element of moral improvement in the "appetites," the "passions," the "desires," while he finds none in Conscience, Will, Reason, the Affections? And yet by them as little can he climb to moral perfection, or to that height his nature requires, as by the baser parts of his being.

And therefore it is, that, in one sense, a philosophy of life is impossible; therefore it is that Christianity has so abhorred this blind Philosophizing; for the very enigma of our nature is this, that while nature indicates these as moral elements, they, *by themselves*, only serve to blind and delude. A moral philosophy founded upon the moral elements of our nature only, or upon them *apart from revelation*, is a delusion.

For the moral yearning is attended with moral inability, and the feeling towards moral perfection is partly a natural reminiscence of a past state in the history of our race, partly the yearning after a post-resurrection state of existence. This desire, and longing, and feeling is the germ *in us* that requires fertilizing elements, that are *not in us nor of us*, to bring it to perfection. And only this doctrine of Revelation, which I have just expounded,* can explain the enigma, or prevent us launching forth into hopes, desires and speculations in search of moral happiness and moral perfection, that end only in delusion and disappointment.

Now, to the Christian, baptized in Christ, I say this, as a result of this examination: "Beware of philosophizing; *act* according to Conscience, to Will, to Reason, to the Affections, but beware philosophizing, forming theories apart from religion, and notions; for the moment you do so, you run many risks of wandering to and fro for years, of dreaming and deluding yourselves and others. For this advice, you can see abundant reason in the position and nature of man, as above specified. The vision and feeling of a

* The doctrine and fact of Original Sin.

perfection of moral nature constantly flashes up before us; the conviction that the elements of moral progress exist in man, is instinctively in us. These are in us for purposes and uses connected with the Gospel, as we shall see;* let us not turn them into delusion, and make of them wandering fires to lead us astray, when they are intended for our good and our guidance."

But in another way, still, must we take a caution upon this point in the leading our nature gives us towards the idea or notion of a "perfect society." Man has a feeling by nature *towards* such a thing; he has the assured feeling that such a thing there was once, that such a thing there can be again, and from the earliest times has the vision been before him; it is before him by nature, and this fact of Original Sin is that which utterly destroys the possibility of it.

For I will ask, as a matter of fact, can sin, poverty, disease, distress, weakness, and irregularity of the moral and mental powers be eradicated from this world, or from the man in this world? Then if it be so, man can individually reach by his own power "Moral Perfection," or there can be a "Perfect Society." *If not, it cannot be.*

To the Christian, that is to him baptized into Christ's Spirit and Faith, I say look at the doctrine of the Fall, and you will see that what I have said is true, and go on with me that we may examine the facts and truths of man's position in the world, and you will see the moral uses of these things.

To him who is unbaptized in the Faith and Spirit of our Redeemer, and has no belief in the doctrine of Original Sin, I say TRY, and you will find that no philosophizing will give you *power to do* that which you *feel and know you ought to do;* no schemes or plans will cast away from Society sin, and poverty, and disease, and death. And furthermore no strife of yours, nay, of unanimous nations, no mass of heaven-high capital or extent of domain, will organize Society otherwise than it has been organized.

These are truths, which denying the doctrines of the Church, you may think false, *while I know* them to be true. Go on, then, my friend; strike your head hard—harder still—very hard—in course of time you may come to learn that rocks do not yield, and that hardness of head will not break them in pieces—a piece of

* This subject is afterwards examined.

knowledge that is very valuable, indeed, though perhaps hardly worth the trouble of acquiring it by experience.

Now, I would dwell earnestly upon this. I would request of all students of moral philosophy to ponder well this fact and its bearings, that the Law, taking the word in its most extended sense, the Opinion or Teaching of Society and External Nature, all hold up before us the goal and object of a moral perfection to be struggled after. And our nature responds to the call. Nay, it indicates to us the elements in our being that serve to this end; and these things all perpetually urge us onward—and yet *of ourselves* we cannot reach the limit! We cannot grasp the object! We cannot attain to that which we desire to attain!

I point out this fact as one of the most important there is in the whole nature of man, and one which at once destroys the whole of many moral philosophies, and renders them, upon the ground of nature, impossible and useless. One, too, which explains the feeling that many have found to arise in themselves, the feeling, "what avail these exact rules, these high speculations, these admirable precepts, when we cannot apply them so as to bring out the results the author desires, and we so much appreciate?" This limitation, then, we would desire our readers all to understand, and all to act upon, for a most vital part it is of a true moral philosophy.

Men may ask, wherefore should it be so? And from their inability to comprehend why it is so, they may, perhaps, incline to deny it to be a fact. We shall tell them why it is so. It is so, that the individual having tried all things, and had recourse to all other means, may finally be led unto Christ! that all philosophies, all plans of moral progress having been acted upon, and found inadequate by all men, they all may be led to the Church of God, and therein find, in the Gospel of His Son, ample and full satisfaction.

We shall, therefore, treat of Moral Science under this limitation in reference to Original Sin, as seated in the race naturally, and in the individual; and for the course of moral action to be pursued by man under it, for man's perfection and man's moral power, we shall refer to the latter part of this treatise.

Here, then, we are able to answer the question, "How is it that man does evil, although in his nature he is good?" How is it? Simply it is this; that the very fault and deficiency of his nature is in the *natural inability to do* that which is in accordance with the Will and Law of God; in other words, that which is Good. His nature is good, and aspires towards it; the Law that speaks to him is good. Tradition teaches him of Good; all things call forth the desire and the will, but the *ability is wanting by nature.*

Now, look at this! Ye who would make of man a fiend essentially evil, say that we have the desire, the wish, the feeling towards good; say that all things lead us towards it naturally, and that there is in man, we will say not the Physical inability or the Mental, but the Moral, what is the case with him? This, that *he does evil.*

And let us remember that voluntary thoughts are *action*, that speech is *action*, that deeds are *action*, and we can see that the nature of man may be good, at the same time that his deeds are evil. For *to act*, and yet that our action should *not* be in accordance with the law of God, which is the "rule and measure of Good"; this is that our act should be evil. In other words, a nature may be in itself essentially good, and yet if it have lost the ability to obey God's Law, its actions are evil. So does man sin, although his nature be good. Nay, more, he *sins always*, in every thought, word and action, wherein he has not Grace.

We would add another remark, to uphold and confirm that which we say; and this is, that we have used the word "*inability*," because we have no other word to express our idea. Now, the very deficiency of the word "inability" is this, that it seems to imply an excuse; that it seems to acquit, to cast off a responsibility, and thereby to make man guiltless, for men will say, "If he is by nature *unable*, why is he condemned?"

The proper answer to this is, "Physical inability excuses, so does Mental, but Moral, never"; before the courts of God, or those of man, moral inability voids not guilt. Say that a duty is bound upon a man, that of defending his country from an invader, that of laboring for the support of his family, that of serving in any office the law enjoins upon him; if the man be bed-ridden, or sick, or deficient in physical ability, then is he not responsible, he is excused. Also, if he is mentally unable, let us say insane, or idiotic in mind, then is he excused, as is both natural and just. But moral inability, *so far as it does not make him physically or mentally unable*, shall still leave him liable, even in the eyes of man. You may prove before a jury, that the man was feeble in Will, but except it be so great as to have touched his Mental or Physical powers, it shall be no excuse. You may manifest to them that naturally he "had very little Conscientious feelings, or that his Affections were of a nature very imperfect"; but the moral inability shall be no excuse, except it have amounted to physical or mental inability. This is a principle in all law, *that natural moral inability, belonging to the race or to the individual, is no excuse, voids no responsibility.* And however men may seek to evade this conclusion by verbal paradox, still, in fact, it will stand, thereby showing that Moral Inability is something altogether different from Mental or Physical Inability, and that the difference is, that it does *not void responsibility* or *annul guilt.*

Now in reference to this subject of "Moral Inability," or that consequence of our natural state of Original Sin, by reason of which we cannot of ourselves obey the Law of God, I may be permitted to quote from a book, written by myself, a passage, which I hope will give some degree of explanation.* "What then is baptism in their case, (that of infants,) considered as a rite for the remission of sins? This may be seen from the nature of sin. What then is sin? This, neither more nor less, 'the transgression of the Law;' this is actual sin. And how does this come? how comes it, that since 'the law is holy, and just, and true,' since 'virtue,' or conduct, in obedience to the law of God, 'is the law of man's nature,'† that men transgress the law, for that law is evidently in accordance with man's best interests?

"Certainly it is not by the bondage of an iron fate predestinating us to be sinful; as certainly it is not the force of external circumstances driving us onward and impelling us to sin, for every man knows, by the fact that he is a man, that *man is the lord of circumstances.*"

"How then does it come? By this, that there is a moral inability to keep God's Law *perfectly*, an inability born with us, and which we clearly see not to have belonged to man's nature originally, but to have been the *result of a deterioration*, which is called the Fall?"

"This inability is in the infant; it developes itself in him just so soon as reason and responsibility begin to develope themselves. And the great end of remission, of forgiveness, of reconciliation, is

* "Mercy to Babes," page 135. † Bishop Butler.

the putting an end to this inability, *not in itself*, but in actual transgression, and in its own guiltiness. The fact of the inability, and of its origin, every one can see from his own nature."

"The nature of Original Sin, the cause of this inability, we do not clearly know in this world, even our deepest imaginings cannot penetrate it. The very consideration of it is involved in the deepest mystery. It would seem that there is a hideousness and horror about it, more fearful than we can imagine, when we think that for its remission and pardon, the Eternal Word must take flesh, and be born, suffer, die, and be buried, that it should be remitted."

"It would seem, too, that if we could only comprehend it, that sin is ultimately an *actual and real death*, of which the death of this world is only the shadow. It would seem also to be of the nature of an infection, reaching from generation to generation, and from father to son, extending as a disease, loathsome of itself in the eyes of God and Man. It would seem also as if it tainted the nature of all men as unquestionably the infected nature of diseased animals, although undeveloped, still is in their offspring. It would appear also that there is some impenetrable and mysterious connection, as it were, between the souls of all men,—between our souls and the souls of all our progenitors, and consequently with the souls of them in whom the deterioration took place."

"And lastly, it is plainly manifest from the Scripture, that in this world . . . . we are all born subject to this evil taint. We were by nature, 'children of wrath.'* 'As by one man sin entered into the world, and death by sin, and so death passed upon all, for that all have sinned.'† So from all these considerations, would it seem that this natural inability requires remission. The sinfulness that is in us by birth must be pardoned. This is called Original Sin."

"I need not say that the explanation of it is difficult from the first,—in that we, as men born in sin, cannot understand what sin is clearly in this life, or how it looks in the eye of a most Holy God. Only this I will say, that any other opinion than this of Original Sin, will and must force us into difficulties and contradictions, overthrowing the whole plan of salvation."

So far I have quoted, that I may the more clearly explain this

* Eph. ii. 3.

† Rom. v. 12.

point. Now, I ask candidly, having, as we must have, by the explanation before given, a feeling of Good and a standard of Good, do we not know from our own consciousness that our fault and the fault of our nature is the inability to reach it? Can we not also refer that inability to the very part and portion of our nature wherein it rests, the Governing or Moral faculties of the Conscience, the Will, the Reason, the Affections.

Certainly, therein we feel the inability to exist. For every man knows that in each act, the will, the conscience, the reason, the affections *should* come in perfectly as the guides and rules of all physical and mental action, so that no act should be done save under their control and by their guidance, just as the helm and compass should influence each movement of the vessel. Every one knows also, that in men's actions naturally these *even now come in*, more or less, in an enfeebled and weak way; and feels that if they could influence him as they ought to influence him, and as they are intended by God to do, then would his life be good, under the governance of the Law of God and man. Every man therefore recognizes this weakness and inability in our present moral position, as an element of the being of an imperfect and fallen nature. Every man also recognizes and clearly understands the seat of this inability to be where* I have placed it.

This remark being made, I shall go on to examine the moral powers of man *as they actually exist.* That is the Governing powers of Conscience, Will, Reason, the Affections, in their present state of weakness and feebleness, doing their work imperfectly; and as I go along drawing forth precepts concerning the strengthening of them, and supplying them with their utmost possible ability.

* I have, as it may be seen, placed *the effect* of Original Sin *primarily* in the weakness of the Governing or Spiritual Powers in the race and the individual. And thereby the Supernatural Gift of the Presence and the Immediate Grace being withdrawn, these powers, which, by means of that rule, had the office and the ability to govern the man, have lost, in a degree which we can hardly estimate, that power. Thereby the other powers that ought to be subordinate, are disordered and out of place. The injury then of Original Sin is *primarily* and *causally* upon men's Spiritual powers,—but *in effect* upon the whole nature, and all the powers of body, soul and spirit. This distinction, a very important one, I hope my readers will apprehend.

CHAPTER VI.

There are in human nature, Governing Powers and Powers Subordinate.—No powers in human nature essentially evil.—Anger analyzed as a proof of this assertion.—Evil action comes from the weakness of the Governing Powers, not the strength of Passions.—Laws of the Governing Powers.—1st, Governing Powers should govern—Subordinate Powers only subordinately act.—Dangers from breach of this first law.—2d, They should act always, others only intermittingly.—3d, They govern according to a Law.—This is the Law of God, which is also the Law of the harmony of man's nature.—The relation of moral to mental power.

We have treated, in the previous Chapter, of the inability or weakness of the Governing or moral powers in man, and that we believe, in a manner so plain and clear, that no one who has thought upon his own being gravely and searchingly, can mistake the truth we have brought into view, and the moral principles capable of being educed from it. We have shown that man has in his nature, Governing or moral powers, the peculiar quality of which is, that their office is to rule the rest of his nature according to the Law of God.

Now the very idea of Governing powers supposes powers Subordinate, whose natural state is subjection—the being ruled and the being guided; so that thereby we shall have two classes established at once, the one of powers *governing*, whose function is to *govern*,—the other, of powers *Subordinate*, whose functions is to be *governed*. This is the first natural division of the powers of man's nature.

Now upon the mere statement of the distinction, there will arise two most important questions and objections, which must be disposed of before any further progress can be made. It may be said, first, "Admitting the division,—instead of powers governing and powers subordinate, should it not be *powers good* and *powers evil?* Are there not in our nature, powers and faculties and principles, that of their nature and by themselves are naturally *evil*, which the Governing powers, the Conscience, Will, Reason, and Affections do check and repress? So that the Governing powers are good in their nature,—the subordinate powers evil in their nature."

This manifestly is a most important consideration, one that is to be gone into fully, and fully resolved upon, before we can make any progress. And so much in its favor we may say, that in all cases of evil action, almost always we can see that it arises from these Subordinate faculties, desires, feelings, &c. Although, of course, this may arise in one of two ways: if they are evil in their nature essentially, the function of the other is to suppress, annihilate, destroy them. If they are in themselves good, and their function is to be subordinate, of course, then, not being subordinate, will be to be in that case, and that only—evil. And therefore upon this last supposition, that evil *in action* may arise from them, does not prove them evil in nature.

Now, this is our resolution. Man has faculties that are good in themselves—he has none that are evil in themselves—he has faculties that are benevolent naturally, none that are malevolent or malignant naturally.

For this resolution we shall appeal to the consciousness of each and every man. All men know wherein they do evil. Each man, therefore, is aware by what desire, or feeling, or emotion of his nature he is betrayed to the evil that he does. Now, let him take that same desire, and by examining it carefully, he shall find that there are cases wherein the exercise of that desire of his nature is not only *not evil*, but is more than that, is *good*. Nay, furthermore, he shall find the feeling *in all cases* is good, *provided only* that it be under the guidance of Reason, and Conscience, and Will, and the Affections, guided by them according to the measure* they prescribe.

We shall take an instance. One of the most violent passions, and of those that give rise to the greatest amount of evil, is Anger—is not that evil in itself, and its nature—naturally evil? Certainly not. Its evil is, that it is not ruled. When it is under the Governing Powers, then it is good, and always good. And so the direction of the Scripture with reference to it is, "Be ye angry and sin not"—a permission, nay, almost an injunction to be angry, provided it be so ruled as not to be against the Law of God. Again, "Let not the sun go down upon your wrath"—it is not to be permanent so as to take the place of the Affections, which are to be permanent, or to become a guiding quality instead of a Sub

* Their measure and rule of course is the Law of God.

ordinate and momentary one. So far the reason of any and every thoughtful individual can see that the distinctions of the Scripture with reference to Anger agree with the principle laid down, that no subordinate faculty is in itself evil, but that its evil is in its being *not ruled* by those powers whose function is to rule, for the direction of the Apostle in reference to anger amounts to this: "Let the Will, the Reason, the Conscience, the Affections govern your natural emotion of anger, according to the Law of God, and then its actions shall be good and not evil—otherwise evil."

But further than this we can go, and evince the same thing in a positive manner by an analysis of Anger itself, in its results and its action. We can show that so far from being an aggressive emotion, that it is strictly defensive. That it has prominent in it two feelings, both of them good. The first, the sense of injustice done to ourselves; the second, the desire of putting an end to it. And whether in momentary Anger or in Resentment, this can be shown to be the case with it always.

Nay, more, further research will manifest to us that to have been born with the natural faculty of Anger predominant, this is so far from being a disadvantage, that it is a positive and decided advantage, if it be only governed and ruled, giving energy, strength, power, and endurance, which can hardly come from anything else.

By this analysis of that one of the Subordinate emotions which most usually produces evil, I believe I have led the student in Ethics upon the way to see that my assertion is correct,—That the Subordinate faculties are not evil in themselves, but actually good, and that their evil is in not being in subjection to the governing faculties. I would refer to the admirable dissertations of Bishop Butler, published under the name of Sermons, for examples at full length of this kind of Ethical Analysis, and would particularize it as one of the books most necessary to be read.

And furthermore, I would to the student point this out as a most important means of improving himself in Ethical Knowledge, that he as an exercise should take Emotions, or Desires, or Feelings, examine and analyze them in their action, and determine wherein and under what conditions their action shall be good, and develope the rules prescribed for it by the Governing Faculties. I know not any habit of mind which more than this lays open our own nature to us and the system of God's dealings. I know not any that more tends to make us charitable and considerate towards the feelings of our friends and companions, and courageous in reference to the events of life.

For the ordinary tone of that which many call Moral Philosophy, looks upon faults of character and temper as *absolute* and *evil* in themselves. And, therefore, instead of seeking down to the good that lies beneath, and trying to guide it and call it forth, and being, therefore, considerate, it is censorious, and gives the individual who has the fault as much credit for natural and ineradicable evil, as it does the rattlesnake or the viper for venom, injuring thereby both society and the man.

Secondly. Persons born with any of these "subordinate" qualities unusually strong, in the earlier part of their life are deluded into the feeling that these, *being evil in themselves*, as they think, are to be utterly rooted out; and they therefore set themselves energetically to this vain task, and often with the most intense agony. Which, when in middle age, they find impossible to be done, they become rebels in a measure, or outlaws to any belief in Moral Government, and give themselves up to live by chance, as may be most pleasant to them.

For these reasons, and to avoid these very plain evils of the time, I do conceive that the Ethical exercise I have spoken of will be very advantageous.

I might go on with a more extended analysis, and by means of it manifest, in the plainest way, the assertion I have made, that none of the Subordinate Faculties are in their nature evil, nor evil in their action when they are under the guidance of the Governing Faculties; but I believe that with the reference I have given to Bishop Butler, and the inducement I have held out to Ethical Analysis, what I have said upon the subject is enough.

Having thus shown that none of the "subordinate" qualities are in themselves evil, and that in their action they are good when guided by the "governing" faculties, the second of these questions comes up. Admitting that there are "governing" powers and "subordinate" powers, you have assented that evil comes from a weakness in the "governing" powers in the race and in the individual. Now "the same consequences will come from an extraordinary strength in the 'subordinate' powers naturally existing."

In answer to this, I say that the relation is that of subordination; and that by the very nature of the Human Being, it cannot be changed from that relation to one of strife and contest between two antagonist powers. The "governing" powers *are to govern;* this is their function, and they always *will govern,* how weak soever they be, if only they go according to their Law. And the "subordinate" powers will always be subordinate to them, how strong soever they may be, for the one is "governing," the other "subordinate." It is the weakness, then, of the one, and not the strength of the other, that originates evil. And the strength of the "governing" powers is according to their law.*

From this it may be plainly seen that there is no man, how weak soever his Governing powers are, and how strong his Subordinate ones, that cannot, *if he will,* rule and check the last, a truth which the experience of each man will confirm.

It remains, therefore, in order to the finishing of this chapter, to examine the differences that exist between the "governing" faculties and those that are "subordinate." And the first and most manifest difference is this, that the "governing" faculties are *always* to govern in him whose life is moral, and according to the truth of his nature. Reason, the Conscience, the Affections, the guiding influence of a self-determined Will, these are to be seen and felt in each and all his actions and words. These are always to come in, and the "subordinate" faculties not always, but only according to the measure prescribed by these.

In this fact will be seen the solution of some difficult cases, even of some that may have carried men away with a false glare. For if we take one of the higher "subordinate" faculties, that of Benevolence, for instance, or that of Maternal Affection, and ask, "May so exalted a faculty as this rule and become a 'governing' faculty?" and the answer is, "No"; from the simple fact that it is "subordinate."

Nay, not even the natural feeling of Theopathy, or love Godward, not even this is to be a ruling faculty; but it is to be enlightened and proportionated in its action by Reason, to be measured as to its ends by Conscience, to be adapted to the good of society, softened and humanized by the Affections, and guided in a fixed and determined line of direction by a fore-thoughted and fore-planning Will.

* This is discussed in the latter part of this chapter.

And he that gives himself up to any Subordinate faculty, even of the highest and purest, and permits this to engross his mind so as to dethrone the "governing" powers from their seat, and puts it in their stead, this man is wholly wrong. This man prepares for himself insanity, if it be made to preponderate over the Will or Reason; destruction of natural honesty and piety, if his desire preponderate over his Conscience; and fierce fanaticism that despises all relations to society, if it overpower the Affections.

For as we have said, the "governing" faculties ought to govern always. And when they do not govern, when the man knowingly and willingly exalts anything else in their stead, then he prepares the way of his own accord for moral disease; we use not the words merely for moral transgression, but for such a state of his *moral constitution* as must lead to moral transgression ultimately, or else be saved from it only by insanity or mental incapacity.

Another inference we would draw from this, which is more important still than the last. It is seen that the business of the governing faculties is to govern always. Of course their weakness is in their non-governance, first, which we have spoken of in the last paragraph; and secondly, *in their intermission.*

For hereby they become as the "subordinate" faculties, which are of their own nature, only intermittent, acting at intervals. Upon this I would remark, first, that the greatest amount of unhappiness that is caused to any individual, is caused by the intermission of the "governing" powers, by the person one time ruling, checking, constraining the "subordinate" faculties by them, and again permitting these faculties to take their place and rule. Upon this all weakness and inconsistency of course depends. And he that shall look at the two supposable although never entirely possible cases of a man, on the one side ruled by the superior faculties entirely, and one on the other in whom one or more of the "subordinate" faculties, even in a faulty shape, have taken their place entirely, such as ambition or avarice, he shall see that these both admit of something of happiness, which the other is not capable of. And he shall see that inconsistency of thought and word, of resolution and action, of moral knowledge and conduct, and worse than all, the feeling of self-contempt thence ensuing, this state, a state in which the "governing" faculties now rule, and now do not, is one of the most miserable in the world.

The second moral inference which we had intended to make is

this, that the "governing" powers by their nature being intended to be always acting, and therefore, as we have shown in this chapter being capable of subduing passions, affections, desires, emotions of any degree of strength whatsoever, and proportionating them to their law; it follows that their strength is in their *continuity of action*, their weakness in their intermission. When they act *always*, that is, when their influence is exerted at every moment of life as *a principle of supremacy*, by the individual man, then will they be able to rule any one of the "subordinate" faculties at any time.

But when the man lives as an animal, indifferent to their action, until it is necessary, in opposition to some of the "subordinate" faculties; then these powers, merely called up for the occasion, shall be invariably vanquished. For "governing" faculties that do not govern *always*, have no strength at any particular crisis. The man who, *in all things and at all times*, rules himself by the ruling powers of his nature, that man shall be able in the one thing wherein he has the most danger to subdue that danger. But he who uses Reason, and Will, and the Affections, and the Conscience *only* against that *one* emotion or passion, and *only* at the time that it rebels, that man shall invariably be overcome. Let the men that are able to rule themselves examine, and the men who are not able, and both classes shall find this account to be true. Hence shall they deduce one of the best practical rules, or rather principles of life and action.

Another thing we shall note in reference to these two classes. The "governing" faculties, in order to be perfect in their action, must, in addition to the two qualifications that we have laid down, have also another—that of *governing according to a law*, and not according to themselves. The Will that places in itself the reason of its guidance; the Reason that puts in reason, or its reasoning the cause of acting; the Conscience that makes of itself the ultimate rule, or the Affections that decide wholly by themselves,—these are, or become evil.

And he that has examined the greatest evils inflicted by man upon his fellows, he will find them to have taken place from those who had the power of governing themselves, and that perpetually, but did so, *not by a law*, but *by themselves*,—a case perhaps permitted only for particular purposes by the Almighty. And he that will look at the misery such men are capable of inflicting, perhaps may see good reasons why so many are permitted to be naturally deficient in their powers.

We shall finish this Chapter by making two observations. The first is, that our division of the faculties into "governing" and "subordinate," is a natural one, supported by nature itself. She tells us that unity of action is, in some measure, the perfection of man's nature,—that all feelings, powers, faculties, desires, should work on together in moral harmony,—that there should be no jarring, no discordance; but, as the Platonists say, there should be in all perfect natures, "unity in multiplicity."

Now, that very "oneness in multiplicity," man, as a limited being, existing under the conditions of Space and Time, manifestly would have, but for the weakness of the "governing powers," which I have spoken of, and it would consist in the constant subordination of all the other powers to them, or rather through them, to the Law of God, who is the Supreme Good and the Supreme Law.

And if man had that "oneness," he would be entirely good according to his nature, as a limited being, without any change in the nature of his present faculties, more than that of complete and entire subordination—that change bringing them in their action, and in themselves to the most complete perfection of which they are capable.

The question comes up here most appropriately of the influence of the moral powers and their cultivation upon the intellectual, or, as they are commonly called, the mental faculties. Now putting aside altogether the fact that Reason is one of the "governing" powers, inasmuch as it will be found, upon referring to the book that treats of it, to be quite a different thing from *reasoning*,—Putting this aside, I think that the view we have given of "governing" and "subordinate" faculties, will give us, upon this point, principles of the highest importance.

It is by that view plain that in all right action of our nature, there is first the subordinate faculty or faculties working towards their ends. And secondly, that along with that force, there always exists another, that is the power of all the "governing" faculties, as ruling and guiding. In all mental operations, then, there will be normally a two-fold action—that of the mental faculty, and that of the moral faculty; and in all cases of perfect and appropriate action, these both will come in.

It follows from this, that there ought to be two ways of increasing the intellectual powers; the first by developing the mental power itself; the second, by developing and bringing to perfection the moral powers, so as to act strongly upon the mental power, which we desire to cultivate; and that this last ought to effect the object as fully as the first.

For the relation of these two *in action* will resemble that of a piece of machinery, in which there is the immediate *tool* that effects the given work, which is united by a certain attachment to a *driving power*; or it will resemble the axe fitted to hew, the saw to cut, the augur to bore, guided and driven by the arm of the workman. The state then of the instrument in itself, as to adaptedness to its purpose, in metal, weight, sharpness, and so forth, is one requisite to action; that of the power that drives it, whether in machinery or muscular strength, is a second.

And much about the same relation do I conceive the intellectual powers bear dynamically to the moral faculty. I have no objection, then, to acknowledge that the mere mental power of many a man have been as great as Shakspeare's originally; but for effect and dynamic action, something more is necessary than power merely mental.

This is enough to indicate and illustrate the connection. We shall, however, announce mose precisely the conclusion we have come to upon this matter first, and then our reasons for it. It is this :—" If you wish to develope to the uttermost your own intellectual powers, or those of youth, whether your own children or those committed to your care: the first and greatest means is the establishment, to the completest degree that the instance will admit of, of the supremacy of the moral power."

We shall not claim to demonstrate this; we shall only give reasons that may show its probability.

In the first place, more persons are kept from a development of their mental powers by impediments to, than by actual deficiency in those powers: and secondly, almost all these are impediments to the "governing" powers. Look at the reasons why children or men cannot develope their mental powers,—" He could not fix his mind to study;" " He could take no interest in studies;" " I believe he could study well enough but I never could persuade him to do so;" or, " He knew he could study, and that he ought to do, but he never did it." What are these excuses which we hear so often? All of them deficiencies of the governing powers, not impairing, but at the very first wholly preventing the exercise of the Mental powers. The first a deficiency of the Will, the second of the Affections, the third of the Reason, the fourth of the Conscience. *Actual stupidity in nine cases out of ten is caused, not by deficiency in the Mental faculties, but by inertness of the moral powers;* and he that examines history and sees how the fierce passions which inflame and set the Will, ambition and hatred and avarice, have enabled the mental powers to act, may see this to be true. He, too, that sees how much the Affections will both give a spring and impetus to mental labor shall see the same.

But most fully it may be observed in teaching. In fact this is the great secret of educational ability, the skill and knowledge of character, to see that "in the moral faculties are the beginnings of mental ability," and the power to discern in the pupil that part of the moral nature that is easiest to cultivate, and then the cultivation of it so as to apply the moral force mentally.

This explains the value of a *teacher* and of *teaching* in contradistinction to mere reading.

But we can, I think, confirm this conclusion by another reason, and that is, that if we look at actions in a moral or religious point of view, we shall find that all immoral actions do more or less impede mental activity. With regard to grosser crimes and sins, it is sufficiently manifest that they decay the mental powers, nay, sometimes utterly erase them. With regard to others, I think that the experience of most men will show, that not only great sins, but even moral faults, errors, deficiencies do more or less impede the mental powers, and, of course, to take them away will be to give *greater* freedom to the mental powers, and greater development.

And he that shall consider the three laws of these governing faculties, as I have laid them out, and then reflect upon the power of Motive upon mental action, the power of Habit and the power of Order, he shall not be slow in concluding that those faculties whose peculiar office it is to guide and govern; secondly, to act continuously; and thirdly, to act according to a fixed law; must, from the very nature of the thing, have an exceeding great effect upon intellectual ability.

But to conclude this subject. I would request the reader to suspend his judgment until he has seen the chapters that treat of these powers separately, and then I hope he shall see so much to confirm his view that he will accede to the opinion I have here enounced.

In the meantime, from a very extended experience, both in teaching and in observation upon society, I will say that there is more mental ability and mental power running to waste in this country than in any other, and that ten thousand times more mental development in general might there be than there is; and the reason of it is this, that as teachers and parents in general we do not see the relation there is between the "governing" and the "mental" powers, and we often omit altogether the cultivation of the first, and apply ourselves entirely to the development of the second: and for that reason mental ability remains torpid, and powers that otherwise would be in vigorous action do not even germinate.

The remedy for this is in a careful culture bestowed especially upon the moral power; a steady and equable discipline that shall exercise and develope to the utmost the Conscience, the Higher Reason, the Affections, and the Will. This alone can remedy the evil of which we speak.

BOOK II.

THE CONSCIENCE.

CHAPTER I.

Of Conscience.—Mistakes with regard to it.—What it is not.—It is the sense of responsibility.—Socrates and Pythagoras.—The action of Conscience is, 1st, Prohibiting, 2d, Recording, 3d, Prophetic.—The Prohibiting office of Conscience considered.—The Recording Conscience.—The books that shall be opened.—The true solution of the facts of Conscience is the doctrine of the Holy Spirit.—Conscience *in us is* not the Holy Spirit, but the ear that listens to His voice.—It is at once *infallible* and *fallible*.

THIS first chapter we have entitled "of Conscience," because, according to a former enumeration, we consider that he who would enter upon the path of moral improvement must begin with this the first, and therefore we place "Conscience" the first.

Now we confess candidly, we think that this matter of Conscience has been confused and disturbed beyond all measure. For there are some that confound it with "Consciousness," and thereby make it merely the knowledge that we have internally, by our reasoning power, as to whether we have acted right or wrong. Again, there are others that make it the sense of right or wrong absolutely, by which we perceive those qualities, whereas there are other faculties by which we feel right and wrong—the Reason and the Affections—by both which we have a perception and measure of right and wrong, as well as by the Conscience. And there are others that call it exclusively the "Moral Sense," as if there were other "immoral senses," whereas all the spiritual faculties are moral, or as if, by it alone, we were guided into morality. And others there are who consider that there is no such thing as a natural faculty, whereby we apprehend a Moral Quality in any action;

and, therefore, when we talk of Conscience, conceive that it is but a short method of saying that such a thing is "useful," or "agreeable," or "reasonable," or "consonant to our nature," or to any other standard that is set up. Now with reference to these opinions, we shall meddle with but few of them. Some are decided by principles previously settled; some others are mere paradoxes which we need not argue against; and for others, it is not worth arguing for or against.

We shall therefore state our conclusion. Conscience is not the moral sense *exclusively*, or that which has exclusively a natural perception of Good. For Reason perceives as a sense that which is good in reference to our individual Self. The Affections perceive that which is good in reference to Society, but *Conscience that which is good in reference to a future responsibility unto God.* In other words, the Law of God is manifested to us through Reason and through the Affections as through Conscience. By all these faculties we perceive that which is morally Good, or as some choose to style it, "the moral quality in actions." Strictly, therefore, do we confine the definition of Conscience to the "perception of the good or evil in action with reference to a future responsibility."

Now, let any man look to these three faculties, and he shall see that they embrace a perception of Good, or of accordance with God's will in all things that can possibly come in contact with man—the Reason in reference to his nature internally, and the agreement of all its powers with the external system; the Affections of Good and Evil in reference to the Home, the Family and the Church, and the Conscience of "Good and Evil in relation to a future responsibility," or what may still more plainly declare it, "the relation of Good and Evil in Time and Space to Good and Evil in Eternity."

The Conscience, therefore, in man, we consider to be the faculty by which he perceives the moral effect of actions in Time in reference to their results upon himself in Eternity. It is that sense which over and above the idea of Right and Wrong, has with it the idea of duty, the sense that it is right, and proper, and suitable to act this way, and not that; and the sense that if we do this way, then are we to be *declared just;* if we do that way, then are we to be *declared unrighteous.* That it is the sense of Duty and of Responsibility. An idea manifestly altogether different in itself from that of a perfect accordance with Reason. For although that which is perfectly in accordance with Reason, shall also be perfectly our duty, yet still in fact the ideas are different.

It needs no other proof than that in all men and in all nations the feeling "I ought" exists cotemporaneous with the feeling of choice in actions. The child feels it just as soon as the man. And oftentimes this feeling "I ought" shall come in, in an action—we shall reject it, yet subsequent experience shall show it to have been right, Reason shall prove it, and Law. It must be, therefore, a separate original faculty. Nay, furthermore, it is the earliest in action of all moral faculties, and that which is the gate of entrance unto all moral action.

Now, in this stage of our examination, it may be as well to confirm our assertions, by the opinions of two men antecedent to Christ and Christianity, Socrates and Pythagoras, of whom the first was clearly that man among the Heathen, who, by the force of nature, came nearest to Christianity, and the other was, perhaps, the man of greatest Genius among the Ancients.

Socrates, as the foundation of his own moral progress, asserted that it depended upon his Demon, or Spiritual Guardian. He asserted that this spiritual being never *commanded*, but always *forbade*, so that if he were going to do anything, and he felt no prohibition, then he might do it, and its consequences would be good. If not, he felt a peculiar check coming from his Demon, which he could not more particularly describe, and if he did not comply with it and refrain, evil invariably followed. And anecdotes without number are told by his disciples with reference to circumstances so ensuing.

Again, with regard to Pythagoras. Although in regard to him we are in more difficulty than in respect of Socrates, in that his lessons were given to a secret society under ambiguous and enigmatic forms, still we can see that his moral philosophy was one founded upon the Conscience and the Reason, as naturally moral and governing powers. His Y was a famous instance of this. The Greek letter upsilon, similar in form to the English Y, was considered by him to be a "deep mystery."

The reader will see that in the figure of the letter there is one path dividing into two, one to the right and the other to the left. The "mysterious" meaning of it, then, is that *at each moment* of a man's life he is at the angle of the fork, *two paths before him*, one of duty, leading to happiness, the other of that which is wrong, and leads to misery. That this position is a perpetual and constant position for each man from birth to death, and that the commencement of Good is for him ever to turn into the one path instead of the other. A parable this is, which clearly depends upon a Moral Philosophy, having for its basis Conscience and Reason.

Now, let us consider these two doctrines. In that of Pythagoras is shadowed forth the twofold nature of action, as right or wrong—the possibility of choice—the fact that we go right *by an effort under instruction*—that going right, we go upon a path whose terminus, while we know it to be happiness, we do not discern. Surely in this emblem of the great Heathen lover of wisdom,* there is an instruction even for us who are Christians.

In that of Socrates we can see that his idea was of a Guiding Power, antecedent to reason, or knowledge, or experience, yet whose decrees were always confirmed by them afterwards; of a power that was prophetic and foresaw evil, yet never told the nature of that result it foresaw, but only forbade or prohibited. And lastly, we find that Socrates invariably attributed this to *a personal influence*, existing *without himself*. If the reader will look further on in this treatise, he shall find that stripped of things alien to them, these notions of these philosophers were neither more nor less than the discoveries of the natural mind in reference to the faculties of Conscience and the Reason.

We will not pretend, as other philosophers have done, to cast ourselves back into the situation of Socrates or Pythagoras, and to enter on the solution of the questions to them insolvable, which the facts presented, upon merely the means that they possessed. For this is "a Christian" Science. And we believe that to the difficulties of Nature there is no other solution than the facts of Grace; to the problem of Natural Religion, nought else suffices save the Gospel. There is no Moral Philosophy true and perfect but one that leads to and ends in Christianity.

We say, then, that these facts of human nature, so experienced and represented by the heathens, Socrates and Pythagoras, have no solution save in the doctrines of Revelation. 1st. That there

* The sages before him had been called "wise men"; Pythagoras took instead the name of "Philosophos," *lover of wisdom.*

is to be a Future Judgment of all men, and all actions of all men. 2d. That no man is condemned without the fullest and most constant opportunity and capacity of having done according to God's Will, or without the sense at each moment of life, as to which is the right way of acting, and whether he was doing so or not. And lastly, That this sense is conveyed to him by a Personal Being having a power and authority, and knowledge above reason—that is, the Holy Spirit, the Paraclete.

He that chooses to examine the facts as represented by these Heathens, shall see that of the questions arising from the facts—these truths are the only solution. Nay, even he who is unbaptized in the name of Christ, and that shall take his own experience of his own Conscience, shall find no solution save this, and that this is one perfectly adequate.

We have already defined sufficiently what we believe Conscience to be; we have guarded it from being mistaken for Reason or for the Affections. It therefore remains to examine it in and according to its action. Now when we examine Conscience in reference to its action, we find that its actions are in succession, clearly to be divided into three classes,—the first, Prohibitory; the second, Recording; the third, Prophetic,—that the simple* action of Conscience is so to be considered, and in no other way.

Now if our reader look at those three distinctions, he will find them represented by three steps, answering to a Sylogism.

The first is Prohibitory.

"This act thou shouldest not do."

The second, Recording.

"This act I have done."

The third is Prophetic.

"Therefore for this act I am responsible."

He who examines Conscience in all its relations, will find that this embraces the sum of its action. The Prohibitory has reference to the Present; the Recording to the Past; the Prophetic to the Future.

Upon these three phases of Conscience we shall proceed to discourse, warning our reader at the very first, to think that these are not always separate and distinct in time; but that we so divide them

* By "simple," I mean considered in itself abstractly—not complicated, as it is generally in connection with the other moral powers.

for the purpose of more fully considering them, and because, in an act of Conscience, the three elements always exist in effect.

Another remark also we would make, that the action of Conscience is in many cases complicated with the action of Reason; that which, in and because of our own nature, assigns a reason for action, and also with that of the Affections; but he that wishes to analyze Conscience, shall find that its action is distinct from that of both these; and that whatsoever we call, in mere ordinary unscientific discourse, by that name, if it come not under these heads, is to be attributed to the Reason or the Affections.

The sense of "justice," for instance, is an Affection of Society, and to act under it, is to act under the influence of the Affections. The feeling which we have, that action upon that sense suits and coincides with our own nature, and is ultimately that which is most appropriate to it,—this is Reason. But that emotion which, at the very first, when we are upon the point of doing an unjust action, says, "this is *not* to be done," thou *shalt not* do it;" and then upon our doing it, says, "this has been done, and the end of the action is not yet;" and then henceforth anxiously looks forth and says, "the end of this action is what I know not, but a something that is to be feared, although unknown,"—this is Conscience.

It is manifest, then, that the Affections *enjoin* having *assigned a reason* in Society and its laws. Reason does as the Affections. only that it gives for its cause the *advantage of the man;* not barely his immediate advantage, but his ultimate, complete, and entire advantage. But Conscience prohibits and *gives no reason.*

Now we have said that the first office of Conscience, considered exactly and scientifically, is Prohibitory. We say exactly, for that which is called ordinarily "Conscientious conduct," is conduct predicated upon the three moral faculties of "Conscience," "Reason," the "Affections," and acted out with the power of a determined "Will." But we have said, that the first action of Conscience, abstractly considered, is *negative* and *prohibiting;* that its formula is not "*thou shalt,*" but "*thou shalt not.*" We know that this may be objected to as not being sufficient; but he that considereth, that voluntary action embraces thought, word, and deed,—that within voluntary action, all morality and immorality lies,—that voluntary action is not divided into two parts, the one good as a separate, independent quality, say as the quality of red is, and the other evil, a separate existing quality, as green is in colors, but the one which is good, an actual and really existing quality; and the other evil, which is *not an actual and really existing quality*, but is the *negative of good:* he may easily see how it is that Conscience is negative,—that its object is to *shut man out from the evil*, by prohibiting it, and thereby to *shut him into the good.*

And in illustration of this, we will say, that in children the first clearly marked moral action that we see in them, is from *negation.* In fact, the very situation and position of childhood renders it so. For if there were no morality to be taught to children save that which had a Reason sufficient and adequate assigned for it, morality could not exist until the reasoning power had been fully developed; whereas the fact is this, that with voluntary action there awakes this sense of Right, and it is negative and prohibitory, not reasoning. And when we look to children, we find a very great capacity and tendency for the Negative, and none, or very little, for that which founds obligation upon reasoning. Let a mother say to a child, "John *do not* do that, for it is wrong,"—a something merely negative, for it is a prohibiting command, founded upon a pure negative, and the child shall obey, his internal sense, the first and initial moral sense, agreeing with the external prohibition; but reason, argue with, try to persuade, convince and so forth, and the immediate effect is confusion and doubt. Hence we may see how exactly the Internal Nature of the child agrees with the Scripture doctrine of the Authority of Parents, as well as with the account here given of the nature of the Conscience.

And he that shall listen to the experience of savage nations, and of those without Christ, shall find the experience of all men universally to testify to the existence of an "Inward Check," a something that prohibits and forbids some actions, and is close beside the will and desire to do these actions, and says "No" to that desire. But furthermore, we shall find this observation confirmed by another remark. Let a man go according to his Conscience, and he shall go easily, without feeling any bond upon him, any guidance, or any direction. Let him go against it, and instantly he shall find obstacles and prohibitions, not for a moment only, but momently and perpetually; showing, that in the right course, voluntarily taken, he can walk freely, without compulsion or sense of compulsion, but that the moment he goes wrong then has he a sense that *negatives* that wrong each moment of his action.

It will be seen thereby, that the faculty we are considering is a *moral instinct* awaking in man the moment voluntary action awakes; a part and portion of his nature, just as the sense of sight is a portion of his nature. And he that shall consider how the physical instinct of a bee actually works upon a principle that supposes the knowledge of a mathematic investigation of the very deepest kind in him who implanted the instinct, and actually and practically takes the principle for granted unconsciously, he shall have no very great difficulty in believing the existence of this moral instinct* of right and wrong existing in man.

The second action of Conscience we shall note, is its Recording power; and when we speak of it in this view, we shall say simply the Recording Conscience. Now with regard to this, the assertion is, that it naturally, in some way we cannot explain, *records* and *keeps recorded* each action of the man's life.

This is a fact of Metaphysical science fully established by all the evidence which is required in Physical science for any law of nature. Of the truth of it enough examples are to be found.†

* In a volume of the London Quarterly Review, which, being in the country, and far from libraries, I have not access to, the following story is told of Lesage, the mathematician of Geneva. A natural philosopher of the same city came to him and asked him, "what should be the vertical angle of the side of a pyramid with a hexagonal base, so that it should contain the maximum of solid contents with the minimum of surface."

Lesage took the problem, worked hard at it for a long time, and then told his friend the answer—so many degrees, so many minutes, and twenty-one seconds. His friend told him that he was wrong, it was twenty seconds, not twenty-one. Lesage took his papers back, went over his calculations again, at a great cost of time and labor, and found that it was so. He was very curious to know how his friend, who was not much of a mathematician, had solved it. He had taken a mathematical instrument for the measurement of angles, and had measured the angle at the bottom of the cell of the bee, presuming that these were the conditions, and then set the mathematician at work to test his experiment.

And it was so. The bee had unconsciously worked upon a principle and rule that it took the highest intellect and the highest science of that time so long to investigate.

Is the assertion in the text with regard to the moral instinct of the Conscience in aught more extraordinary than this?

† There is a great mystery about the memory. Men have apparently for-

Now, upon this we assert, that in all acts of the Conscience whatsoever, beside the first Prohibitory or Checking action, there is a second, divided into two parts. The first, *for the present*, is to "be conscious" of it, to know and feel at the time that it is the "*I*" that is doing and none else, that the action is "*mine*," and excludes all other personal agents.

This consciousness is manifestly an indispensable and immediate attendant upon all voluntary action, a clear knowledge connecting the individual's "Self" with the action, so as to infer responsibility. And this consciousness, when the action has gone backward into the Past, then becomes a Record, which, from what we have above seen, seems incapable of being erased from the being of the individual. So does it seem that actually and really the Recording Conscience of the individual man is a book in which, day after day, and hour after hour, events, as they pass, are enrolled in all their minutest circumstances; and that, although to me now but a single leaf is open, and I may have forgotten the contents of all the rest, still they may be opened again, and once again the judgment of the Withholding Spirit, and of my own self-knowledge or Consciousness upon them, appear.*

Hence, too, may it appear that at the day of judgment the books that shall be opened may be the Consciousness of our Omniscient Father in Heaven, wherein the actions of all men are perpetually and eternally enrolled; and secondly, the history of the events of our life that has been written in and upon our being by the Re-

gotten entirely circumstances and impressions, and then, under the influence of some great stimulus, the memory of them has risen up again clear and distinct, as the sympathetic writing traced upon paper comes out to view under the excitement of the peculiar chemical action it requires. Men have forgotten the language of their childhood, and spoken it again on their death-bed. Under the influence of delirium, the slightest impressions of past life have come up again to consciousness. The flames of fever have brought again tc view the tracery of records long forgotten.

For these and other facts, for which I have no space in a foot note, I refer to modern investigations into the nature of the mind. The conclusion is, that there is such a thing as "Latent memory." That by it "no impression, no feeling, no thought is ever actually forgotten, but is written down upon our nature; so that there exists in us and in our being a most exact transcript and record of all the events of life, *to be called forth when requisite, according to the wisdom of Almighty God.*" This is Latent Memory.

* "The Spirit beareth witness with our spirit."

cording Conscience, and has gradually rolled back into that which to us seems oblivion and forgetfulness, and yet is not so.

Some call this "Conscience as Witness, Accuser, and Judge;" we have preferred the appellations we have given, both for the sake of precision, and also for other reasons which will be seen as we proceed.

We come now to that last class of operations that we attribute to Conscience; that is, what we shall call the Prophetic Conscience. By this we mean, that there is a third operation of the faculty, in consequence of and along with the feeling of the Check, which is the first part of the action of Conscience; and the knowledge that it is Recorded, the second part of its action. Along with these emotions, there is, coexisting with them, an apprehension for the future, a kind of dim vague feeling, hardly explaining itself, yet manifestly existing, of consequences of infinite weight in recompence to our act.

This, as well as each of the other two, we shall find in every action of the Conscience distinctly considered; and this will and does always exist, and sooner than not be visible and palpable to the man, it will take to itself any shapes whatsoever, even of false religion or superstition.

And when we look at Conscience, unaided by the light of Revelation, this is the most mysterious and unaccountable of all its actions; but when we think that we are creatures *existing in time* and yet *framed for eternity*, then can we see what it is. We can see that it is the stirring of the immortal and the undying within the mortal and perishing; the dark instinct of our nature lifting its unopened eyes towards heaven; the peeping of the young bird over the nest out towards its home. And therein is the function of Conscience completed, that it is that sense which in Time prophesies of Eternity.

And at once, when we consider this Prophetic power in it, and when again we look at the revealed facts connected with Eternity, of Death, Judgment, Heaven and Hell, we can see that these are the objects towards which its instinctive action points,* prophesying to all of Infinite fear and Infinite pain if they will not be ruled and checked by the law of God.

* If there be a power in a loadstone that shall point to the north, is it a wonder that in man there should be an instinct that looks blindly to the judgment throne of God?

We have now gone through the characters of this that we call Conscience, according as they appear to the natural man, or what may be called the natural ethics of the Conscience; and now we come unto that which completes them.

Let the reader consider the first office of the Conscience, and he will see some things in reference to it that strangely correspond to the facts of revelation. We attribute to this faculty a *personal power*, as if it were the influence upon us of an individual who is *not ourselves*. We say "Our Conscience checks us," "We must obey our Conscience," "It is wrong for a man to go against his Conscience." What is this but to say, that this influence is a personal agency, separate and distinct from that of the individual, and operating as such upon him. Again, what is this but to say, that this personal influence has *an authority* over the man in all his powers and faculties, which authority, *without any reason save its expression*, the man is bound to obey, and is therefore that of an entire and complete supremacy, a complete and unqualified veto upon actions of every kind. Moreover, we can see more plainly this notion of a personal being, in the fact of its Recording, in the fact that those things that, with reference to the responsible being, man, are enrolled in the Omniscient Knowledge of God his judge, these things all are known by that Recording Spirit, and at any time may be brought up by it. Herein, since it is the same Spirit that waits upon all, we see Omnipresence and Omniscience manifested.

Again, in reference to the Prophetic office of the Conscience, in the forethought it has of the Future Judgment, in the fact that it ever attaches the idea of endless pain or happiness in a future eternity, to things that are done in Space and Time in this fact we behold again the attribute of Omniscience.

These are things that all men see. We do not say that all men are brought to this conclusion, so plainly as we have brought it out; but this we say, that the facts of the action of Conscience are plain to all, and that these facts are most easily and most naturally classed as we have classed them, when we have separated that which really ought to be separate—the Reason and the Affections from Conscience.

And then, when we come to Natural Religion, we find that if there be an Almighty and Omniscient Being, not only Maker and Creator, but Father also, and Teacher, there ought, upon the very idea of Responsibility, of filial relation, of pupilage, to be a Personal Influence proceeding from God, and dwelling in God—one attached to each individual in the world, and therefore Omnipresent; knowing the hearts of all men and the will of God, past and present and future, and therefore Omniscient; and commanding all men without reasons assigned, yet infallibly true, and therefore Omnipotent. This influence, thus invested with the attributes of the Deity, ought therefore to exist if we follow up the facts of Natural Ethics, with the reasonings of Natural Religion, and build upon them the edifice which the considerations of Responsibility and of Natural Justice require of us to build.

And so stringent and imperative are these, that the most ancient philosophy of the east has ever attributed to the influence that produces these actions, the attributes, and all the attributes of divinity. And they in modern times, who have begun by denying Christianity, have almost invariably been driven by these motives into making our own personal being to be God; and that against the very first fact of the Natural Conscience, which clearly distinguishes between *our personal being*, that which *ought to submit*, and that other person that acts upon ours, which *has the right to command* with an unlimited supremacy.

But we say, that in Revelation alone is to be found the fact that explains all this enigma; in the doctrine of the Holy Ghost. Revelation teaches us that each son of man, from birth to death, is attended by the influences of the Third Person of the Trinity, the Holy Ghost; that He is "God of one Substance with the Father;" that he "Proceedeth from the Father and the Son," and "is Jehovah and the Giver of light and life." And the plain doctrine of the Holy Scriptures in regard to the Spirit is, that His operation with regard to *all men* is to warn them against evil, or that which is not good, and to do this with an influence that carries authority and power with it, and admits of no dispute. That being a personal being, and Omniscient, He knows and records all the actions of the individual man; and at the same time He knows all the will of God and the things of God, as being of "one substance with the Father," and "one with Him."

"The Spirit searcheth all things; yea, the deep things of God," "which no man knoweth but the Spirit of God."

And thus the actions of Conscience, as Checking, Recording, Prophesying, are explained. Thus is man witnessed against without possibility of mistake; thus, at the moment he is warned and the moment passed, his act recorded, so that he cannot deny, and then ultimately before the bar of God, he is convicted; "his spirit bearing witness with the Spirit," as to evil done in a full sight of his responsibility. And thus the Omniscience of the Holy Spirit, the forethought which He who is one with the Father has of the Future Judgment, the authority with which He enforces his injunctions, and the absolute certainty with which He can warn of the future; all these attributes of the Holy Ghost, as the great agent of prophecy, both to the Church universal as also to the individual; explain the influences of the Conscience, and show the reason of its prophetic power.

Thus do the whole of the Facts of Conscience manifest to us the agency of a Personal being who has the knowledge of God, an infinite knowledge that concerns the future as well as the past,—an Authoritative Power, to which, without reason assigned, the man must bow,—a Recording Power, which has reference to eternity solely, and a future judgment,—and a Prophetic power, that connects time with eternity, this life with a future existence, and the actions herein done, with the high throne of God.

We have said that Revelation alone affords a solution for the facts of nature. And we say, in conclusion, that he that shall look at the facts of the natural Conscience in all its influences upon man, he shall see that no other solution completely and entirely accounts for the facts of Conscienee, except this fact of Faith, the doctrine of the being and influences of the Holy Spirit.

And this leads us onward to another question, which is most important in all matters of Conscience. "Is not our Conscience then, the Spirit of God?"

How important this is, may be seen by supposing it to be answered in the affirmative; for if it be, then the sole judge is Conscience; then a man has in himself the *only rule;* then he is the judge of all things; then he needs no learning, no knowledge, no education; but only to go according to his Conscience, and he shall go right, infallibly right. Nay, more than this, he shall need no Bible, no Church, no Religion; for if his Conscience be God, then being Omniscient, it must overrule all external things; and all he has to do is, go by that rule; and, with regard to his fellows, he has only to require that they all should submit to him without questioning. These are conclusions which naturally should follow from the notion that "Conscience *is* the Holy Spirit," and which are its legitimate results. And he that shall look to men, shall find that a great many hold these conclusions. A great many consider Conscience as infallible, and make it the sole and ultimate test, who have never thought of the premises upon which the conclusion depends.

Now this leads us onward unto one of the most important principles of Ethics; we will say a fundamental one. That is, the distinction between *Conscience, the natural faculty in us*, and the *voice of the Holy Ghost without us;* Conscience, the eye existing in our nature and being, whereby we see the light, and that Light which we see; Conscience, the ear wherewith we listen to the voice from heaven, and the Voice from Heaven, the voice of the Holy Spirit that is audible to us through that part of our nature.

We say, then, that so far as Conscience is considered under the one aspect of a *natural faculty*, so far it is liable to the same infirmities as the other natural faculties. For the light may be as the sun, and yet the eye which is blind by nature, or blinded by accident, never see it. The voice may be that of many waters, and yet the deaf ear not hear it. So it is with regard to the Conscience, the *faculty in us* and *in our nature*, wherewith we listen to the voice of the Holy Spirit, is a different thing altogether from the Spirit Himself. And yet in the consideration of Conscience, both the Natural Faculty and the Divine Energy to which it answers, are to be considered.

Now, he that shall look at this last principle carefully and considerately, in the full light of his own experience, will see many conclusions to follow of the most important and the most interesting kind.

In the first place, the eye and power of sight in man proves to him the existence of things visible, at the same time that it is the means of bringing him to the knowledge of them. And no argument will disprove their existence, simply because he has a natural faculty whose business it is to *show* and *manifest* them. So of a Future Eternity, no argument whatsoever can disprove the existence, no absence from sense or sight annul it, because of it the Conscience is our sense, and because, corresponding to the Conscience, there is a *power that manifests the Future Eternity to us as far as concerns the actual duties of the present life.* This is an inference of great practical importance, binding and connecting, as we have said, finite acts with infinite consequences, Time with Eternity, the limited being of man with the Infinite God, and that through the Eternal Spirit.

But the most important conclusion that follows from it is this: "*So far as the dictates of our Conscience are the dictates of the Holy Spirit of God, so far Conscience is infallible.*" This is the rule of the governing power, Conscience, which follows from its own nature as twofold, a natural ear or a natural eye, with a heavenly voice or a heavenly light; and this combined with the other laws of it as a governing power,* shall give us completely and entirely, as a result of Ethical Science, the doctrines and rules of Conscience as applied unto life. This shall be the subject of the next chapter.

CHAPTER II.

The value of Conscience.—Our position in consequence of it.—An examination of it in action, as, 1st, Withholding; 2d, Recording; 3d, Prophesying.—The emotions that are sanctions to it, 1st, Moral Restlessness; 2d, Shame; 3d, Fear.—The mark upon the Nature, 1st, the Stain; 2d, the Guilt.—Conscience is not properly a "judge," nor the pain from it properly "punishment."

FROM our examination of the nature of Conscience in the previous chapter, it is manifest what an exceedingly precious endowment this is to man. A secret adviser, so secret that although inaudible to all others, it shall yet speak to the man himself, clearly, distinctly, perpetually, upon all emergencies wherein it is necessary, and upon all occasions.† One too whose advice is not to be measured by the man's own degree of knowledge or his station, but that gives to the ignorant, the poor and the weak the proper and suitable guidance for the circumstances in which they are. And that with such an accurately proportionate action, that it has, with no small degree of plausibility, been maintained that

* See the three laws of the "Governing Powers"—Book I. Chap. 3.

† Of course here is to be made the exception—except he have neglected it, and therefore it have become "dull" or "insensible," or "seared, or "dead." For this part of the subject, see an ensuing chapter of this book.

Conscience *always a step, and only a step in advance of us,* and this has been by some made one of the laws of the Conscience.

However, be this as it may, it is such an adviser that to the ignorant it says, "Ignorant as you may be of worldly knowledge, you are still a moral being, and can live as such; follow *me*, and you shall *be* so, and shall *do* so—for the position to which I call you is but a step from your present one—within your reach, and to be attained by you, by my help."*

To the poor the adviser is present, too, with a riches that surpasses all earthly wealth—the announcement from the Eternal Throne, by the Eternal Spirit, through its natural adit to the soul, of its infinite value as a Spiritual Existence.

To the ignorant it tells of this sure knowledge that ever rises to the level of our necessities. To the self-distrusting of Omnipotence it speaks All-holiness and All-justice, ready to support him that will go after its guidance. It tells them that no obstacle shall permanently remain in the way, that all passes shall be opened, all barriers burst that oppose *his* upward progress, who follows this guide.

Such are the advantages to us of this gift and faculty, looking at the matter generally as we have looked upon it, in the twofold

* The Christian will see in these words, combined with the account given of Conscience in the preceding chapter, the solution of a great question. "By my help"—that is, "Not of *you*, but of *me;* not of your nature *alone* and *unaided*, but of it *as aided* by me, the personal and omnipotent being who speak, through the Conscience, to all men—the Holy Spirit."

Hence is all moral strength and ability of God, coming *first unto us from him*, and not arising in our nature from nature itself.

Moral strength given, to the unregenerate first, wholly undeserved, nay, often against their own will, in order to habituate them to the thought of good, to teach them by making them to act upon that power for which they have no merit, to lead on in the way of life by support and secret upholding powers: This *probationary moral power* in the unregenerate is a help given even to the evil, according to the will of the Holy Ghost, the Infinite Teacher, for his own wise purposes. The solution, therefore, of the question, "Does the natural man do good"? is this—all the good that even the natural man does, he does of God's Grace, given him according to the will of the Spirit, and *Grace comes first.*

The regenerate man is in a different position, having from the Word the strength and power of *a son*, but still not of himself, but of *his new birth*, and *his new privileges*, and *new position.* But of this last, which is also very interesting, more at another time.

point of view of the *light outside us*, which we see, and the *eye in us*, by which we see that light, and also not as yet considering the deficiencies or weaknesses of *Conscience the faculty*, or the rules for its guidance, matters which we shall in a future part of this work consider.

Having thus seen the advantages to us of Conscience as a gift and faculty, it remains now to examine the position in which we are placed by it—the responsibility that is upon us by that gift.

Now, when we look at the action of Conscience, we see that there are several characters that belong to it, as considered in its relation to our nature, and these we here enumerate by way of summary.

1st, It is commanding.

2nd, That commanding is negative, or prohibitory.

3d, It is ever present with us.

4th, It pronounces upon all our acts.

5th, It witnesses of all.

6th, We naturally apply personality to it.

7th, Making the distinction we have made, as to its twofold nature, Conscience, *the faculty in us*, we may consider as weak, as liable to errors and mistakes, but Conscience, *that which is perceived through the faculty*, we consider to be incapable of error or of mistake, in one word, to be *infallible*.

And, 8th, As the crown of all that we attribute to the Conscience, we may say that it is authoritative—it has authority. We consider that it is *entitled* to *rule*, and that we are *privileged* and *bound* to *obey*. As the Father, within certain limits, is by his very position as Father entitled to command his children; as the Magistrate, within the restrictions established by law, can command; as the Master orders and guides his servants, such is the privilege of the Conscience over the man. It has *authority;* its dictates are binding upon us.

We shall carry out this subject of the authority of Conscience at another point of this treatise; for the present we would apply it in elucidating the position of the individual man. Observing, then, the rule, that if we would understand fully the Moral Powers, we should consider them rather dynamically as powers in action, than statically as powers at rest, we shall see, as regards the man, plainly what the nature of Conscience is, by considering it in action. All actions, then, having in them a moral quality, and

Evil being, as we have above said, not the contrary of Good, but the negation of it, the Conscience in its twofold nature is that which checks the man as he is about to do evil.

It follows from the first principle, *that if the conscience does not check him in any action, that action is right, provided his Conscience be in a natural and healthy state.* This is in accordance with that which the Scripture says, "If our 'heart' condemn us not, then have we peace with God."*

In the second case, the man is about to act when he feels conveyed to him a check, a sort of inward force opposed to and negativing his intended action, yet that in such a way that he *can* always *overcome it if he will;* and has the full consciousness *that he can.* This authoritative *check* he feels; and if the appetite or desire which awoke him to action, carry him on to overcome the check, then has he acted *against his Conscience.*

The act would be evil in itself—but it has immediate consequences even in his nature. There are passions of his being which are at once brought into play as sanctions† of such a transgression, and these are properly three, and only three.

1st, Moral restlessness, or the negation of Peace;

2dly, Shame;

And 3dly, Fear.

We introduce the consideration of these three in this place, because they are emotions, or passions, or feelings, which we consider as being directly and immediately connected with and caused by the Conscience. The first resolution upon them is that they are not faculties, as memory is a faculty; they are not natural feelings or sensibilities, as the sense of honor or the sense of justice is; they are "emotions," peculiar emotions, whose existence and being depend upon Conscience. But not upon the existence of Conscience do they depend, but upon the fact that it has been disobeyed. They are emotions *whose possibility only* exists in the nature of man, the *realization of that possibility* depending upon the violation of the law of the Conscience. And so far is this true, that when we come to consider our apprehension of a perfect

* 1 John iii. 20. This which in our English version is translated "heart," in the Hellenistic Greek means "Conscience," from the Hebrew usage of the word "heart."

† "Sanction" is the Penalty legally attached to the breach of a law.

man in reference to this part of Nature, we find that our idea is that he should have the Conscience *perfect as a guide*, and that he should *perfectly obey* it, and therefore that in all his actions he should possess a perfect sense of *moral approbation*, and a perfect consciousness of right. In other words, to such a person moral restlessness and dissatisfaction would be altogether strange and utterly unknown. Moral calmness and peace would of itself be the natural state and condition of his mental atmosphere.

Again. Shame—the sense of stain and pollution—this would not exist at all in man unfallen, for the simple reason that evil would not have been done, and that the purity of the nature would not have been polluted in or by any action. Thus Shame is the feeling of an actual Stain upon our moral nature. The emotion that attends our knowledge that we are defiled by sin, never could have existed in the man unfallen, in whom the Conscience was unviolated, but in us arises from its violation.

With regard to the Moral Restlessness and Shame, that they could not exist in an unfallen nature may be easily granted. With regard to the Fear, I know that objections may be taken; it may be said that Fear is a natural faculty or passion, having reference not to Conscience, but to Pain. Upon this, I say that if my reader will only examine, he will find that caution against pain, or apprehension of it, is not fear; that the only real and true fear, properly so called, is that which, with violation of Conscience in Time connects consequences in Eternity—that is Moral Fear.

The truth of this view of the nature and origin of these three emotions, Moral Restlessness, Shame and Fear, may be seen in the manifest difference between the unfallen man and the fallen nature of the same person. There is no mark of any of them in Adam unfallen; but he is represented as calmly dwelling in innocence and peace, feeling no sense of Shame, no emotion of Fear, but as a limited being, perfect in his nature, communing with the Unlimited Perfection of the Almighty, and at once upon the turning point of the Fall all these emotions then make their appearance. Adam and his wife hide themselves from the presence of the Lord among the trees of the garden; and in reply to the questioning of the Lord he said, "I heard thy voice in the garden, and I was *afraid*, because *I was naked;* and I *hid myself.*" Restlessness, and Shame, and Fear, at once become constituent

U of M

elements of that nature, which before in perfect calmness and tranquil self-assurance, had walked face to face, unreproached, with the God of perfect purity and almighty power.

This fact that these emotions did not exist in the man unfallen, but that at once they manifest themselves upon the instance of the Fall,—this confirms the account I have given of them, as emotions depending upon the Conscience.

And when we come to examine, in reference to this point, the life and acts of our Lord, we find an utter absence of these emotions,—that Moral restlessness, which is an especial quality of our Human Nature unregenerated by God's Holy Spirit,—in fact, of all men that are not "born anew of water and the Spirit," and "renewed day by day in the spirit of their minds,"—of that restlessness we cannot discover a trace in Christ our blessed Lord. There is no sign of it at any period of his life in Him. His self-consciousness is calm and quiet, and assured. No evidence is there in Him of "moral progress;"* of "newness of ground," or "advance of position," or "expansion of views;" but the same undisturbed moral position, he keeps, adequate completely and entirely to the position, and abiding in it patiently.

And then, with regard to what we call Shame, an emotion that we may plainly say there is none of the Human race b ut Christ that has not felt; as for this, in all Christ's relations, as a man born of a woman, there is not the smallest evidence that He even felt it in any degree.

Moral Fear also, he seems not to have felt, while of mental as well as bodily suffering and pain, he seems to have had the apprehension. But upon this point, I shall not dwell too closely, seeing that it would be to attempt to enter into the gates of a mystery which angels cannot comprehend, the mystery of the Atone-

* These are part of the ordinary talk of so-called reformers. I need not say how they jar upon my mind, whose doctrine is that expounded in this book, "*duty to God* and *man, acted upon from childhood to old age.*" The sole "moral progress," I believe, is Duty better done; the sole "expansion of views," is the consequent clearer view of God and Heaven. No "advance of position," save in this, no "newness of ground," do I consider possible morally; no ground in fact can support us save that old ground of "Nature explained and guided by Grace." If I have erred in bringing these cant-phrases of a wretched and self-deluding, yet earnest philosophy, in proximity to the name of our Lord, I hope I may be pardoned by my readers, for this error.

ment of our Most Blessed Lord, both God and man; because while I can see that he endured Physical and Mental agony; while I can argue that this was Infinite, still from the fact of its Infinity I cannot comprehend but must only believe and adore.

And, moreover, I know that the Church has, in a measure, determined that over and above the agony visible to man, of which man can judge, the infinity of bodily and mental agony, borne by Christ the *man*, because at one and the same time, *he was* God; besides this, the Church has determined in her liturgical prayer, used in the Greek Church, "By all thy sufferings known and *unknown*, have mercy upon us," that over and above the mental and physical agony, there was another infinity of Spiritual Pain borne by him, to the bare knowledge of which, in our present state, we cannot reach. Into the holy gloom, and the divine mysteriousness of Christ's sufferings, we shall not then attempt to penetrate; for, in view of that *infinite suffering which he bore for us*, it is manifest* that he "feared," nay (Hebrews 5 and 7,) "That he was heard *in that he feared.*"

Upon this point, therefore, since it is beyond our apprehension, we shall not press, nor shall we suffer it to be pressed against us, but will leave it with two remarks: First, that His suffering he bore not for himself, but for others, and it was infinite; and secondly, that of either selfish or Moral Fear, we see no speck in his whole life. These two remarks will, I hope, go then rather to confirm than to weaken the view advanced.

I might also refer to those before Christ, who came nearest to the moral teaching of the Gospel, to show that these emotions, have, by them, ever been connected with the Conscience. In fact, the wisest of their poets and of their philosophers, unhesitatingly declare it. I might also refer to the experience of all men in these latter days, to declare that calmness of mind and tranquillity can only come from a Conscience determinately and consistently obeyed; that from such a Conscience only, can come the mind that will abide through life unashamed, and fearless, and that will, if Duty requires it, stand up in its behalf unterrified. This, each man, whose rule is to obey his Conscience always, can say, is the invariable result of that obedience, freedom from Restlessness,—that is, Peace of Mind; freedom from Shame,—

* Matthew xxi 39.

UofM

that is, Self-approval; and freedom from Fear,—that is, Moral Courage.

But the Scriptures fully assert the same, "Brethren, if our Conscience (Heart in the original,) condemn us not, then have we confidence towards God."* "The wicked are like the troubled sea, casting out mire and dirt continually."† Again, "He that believeth in him, shall not be ashamed."‡ "There is no fear in love, but perfect love casteth out fear; for fear hath torment."§ "He that feareth, is not made perfect in love."

The way in which we connect these texts with our subject is, that the Conscience in its action upon the life of man, can only reach perfection under Christ; and that in these, and innumerable other passages that can be quoted, the sum and completion of Christianity in its effects, is in an Holy Peace; first, which is the very opposite of Moral Restlessness,—2ndly, in deliverance from sin and its "Shame,"—and 3dly, in the freedom from "Fear,"—which doctrine, it is manifest, fully confirms our statement as to the nature of these emotions, and their relation to the Conscience.

Having shown, therefore, the nature of the emotions that are the sanctions of the Conscience, we shall now proceed to examine its action.

The individual man in his course of life, we will say, intends to do some act; in the moment of intention, before he has acted, he receives the feeling of an internal check, a moral negative to action, which is suddenly interposed as an obstacle *between the intention and the action*, under the conditions I have before noted, and which I will not here again repeat. To overcome that obstacle, he must use *an effort*, and that a *conscious voluntary effort;* so that he *knows*, that of *his own will*, *freely* and *knowingly*, he *breaks across that obstacle or impediment.* Now if the Conscience be in its due state, and perfect, invariably its negative shall be only upon the evil,—that which it forbids shall be evil. The man, therefore, in breaking through its obstacle, shall have willingly and consciously done evil,—done it *freely* and *knowingly*, and therefore have been guilty.

But to resume, when he has done the action against which the

* 1 John, iii. 21.
† Isaiah, lvii. 20.
‡ Rom. ix. 33.
§ 1 John, iv. 18.

MOU

Withholding Conscience protested, *freely* and *knowingly* and *by an effort* overcoming the barrier placed in his way, then at once it is chronicled by the Recording Conscience, and evermore it is liable to be brought up to him, and presented to his view as connected with a stain; a feeling that to his moral nature, being of itself good, this evil action, done freely and knowingly, is that which to pure white a blotch of filth is, a Stain. And this, therefore, is one effect of evil done—the Stain upon the nature producing the Shame. The Stain is the effect on the nature; the Shame is the mental emotion corresponding to that effect.

The Recording Conscience has the power, as we know, of bringing up that act with its Stain again and again to the individual man; but under what conditions this takes place, it is in vain for us to guess; and, so far are we from being able to decide upon the laws by which it happens, that when we attempt to classify them we are perfectly unable to reach any decision. In some men sickness or danger shall always bring them up; in others, peculiar circumstances of life; in others, mere trifles at long intervals; and in others, the recalling of these things shall be almost hourly: so that, perhaps, looking at the circumstances that concern the bringing up of past misdeeds by the Recording Conscience, the best thing to do, instead of trying to form laws of their re-presentation to the mind, is to say, that they take place according to the purpose and will of the Omnipotent and Omnipresent Spirit, whose organ the Conscience is. So far with regard to the action of the Recording Conscience.

We come now to the last action of the faculty, that of the Prophetic Conscience; and with regard to this, we have already said that Conscience, "by its very nature, attaches consequences in Eternity to actions done in Time." This, in action, is that part of the offices of the Conscience we call the "Prophetic Conscience;" and he that shall look at the two-fold nature of the Conscience, the first part as a faculty of man limited in power and in action to Time and Space, and *yet immortal;* and the second, the action upon that faculty of the Spirit of God, infinite in power and knowledge, he that shall consider that in this faculty there is thus a concurrence of the Infinite with the Finite, and of the Spirit of God with the spirit of man, shall be at no loss to see how it is that naturally the idea of infinite consequences is connected with acts done in Time and Space.

UofM

It is in vain to say that it ought not to be so, and thence to argue that it is not so, just as it would be vain to argue against our seeing a star eighty millions of miles away, because one fact and the other takes place by a *natural sense receiving an external light.* It is a matter of fact, that we have the natural eye; that the eye receives a light which originates millions of miles away, strange and incredible as it may seem. And so the natural faculty of Conscience is a fact; the existence of the Holy Spirit is a fact; his light upon us, connecting Time with Eternity, is a fact: better far make use of these facts for the purpose intended than attempt to argue against their existence; for facts lose not their reality by assertion, nor yet by argumentation. He that shuts his eyes does not annihilate the sun, nor will the arguments of a man that is blind by accident prove to me that there is no light. Upon all these matters, the universal persuasion of all mankind is naturally taken to be true, and *is* true.

Now as with regard to the "Withholding Conscience," it checks, and the Recording Conscience presents again and again the fact of our transgression as a Stain, and the consequence in the man is the emotion of Shame; so with regard to the Prophetic Conscience, this is its office, that it connects acts of transgression against the Conscience, that have taken place in Time, with a responsibility in Eternity. It tells the man "what you have done *here* is not ended, although past, apparently come to an end, but it has its consequences *there.*" Thus the Prophetic Conscience, unto the breach of the dictates of Conscience, attaches the peculiar idea of responsibility for evil; the idea that although our act is done, and no earthly consequences but those that are beneficial may happen, still most certainly *evil* will, *in the future,* ensue.

For I think it a thing not to be denied, but a most certain fact, that men, in some cases, have done evil, from which, *in this world,* they have received not only no harm, but even good; so that no law of their own being or of external nature recompenses to them the evil they have deserved. I think it most certain that some men, acting against their own Consciences systematically and habitually, have yet in this world received no harm from it, but rather a superabundance of that which they estimated as good; and that the penalty of Evil and the reward of Good is not the consequence of a law of nature, but is the immediate infliction of punishment by the Will of a just and intelligent being, who is God.

The Prophetic nature of Conscience, then, consists in this, that by it acts against the Conscience are perpetually brought up and re-presented to the mind, with the intimation that the being who did them is liable to punishment, and *that that punishment is in Eternity;* which two ideas, as combined in the mind, we term by that one phrase, "Guilt;" so that, with regard to an act against the Conscience, the effect of it upon the Conscience, in reference to the *future, is* the sense of its responsibility to a Judgment and Condemnation in Eternity. This liability we call "Guilt," and the corresponding emotion we call "Fear."

Now when we look at the facts of human nature, we find this of Responsibility a fundamental fact of our nature, a fact that for all evil we count ourselves "under the liability and obligation of punishment;" and that this liability exists to a *person;* not to a physical or natural law, but *to a person.*

Secondly, that it implies to the eternal being an eternal punishment adequate to each act it has done in time, however numerous the sum total of the acts may have been.*

And thirdly, that for all men, up to the very date and hour of their death, the Prophetic Conscience places the punishment in the Future.

Hence may it be seen, from the first point, that the instinct of nature is towards the truth of a *personal God,* when declared to us, as universally it is, by the Tradition of Society; so that the feeling of Guilt in us is a proof of a personal Deity. The second fact implies that Eternity is a different state from Time in kind, not merely in degree: and the third, that the place of justice and true recompense is that state, and not our present one. We find all these ideas embodied in the feeling of "Guilt" and the emotion of "Fear;" and the truths to which they answer are those of Responsibility to the One God, of a Judgment that gives to all acts their due, in a state that admits of complete justice, the state of Eternity. These are truths which no argumentation will refute, no denial invalidate, because, as we have shown, they are truths of our own nature, evinced by the facts of our own being, and witnessed unto by Almighty God through his Spirit.

* "That servant which knew his Lord's will, and prepared not himself, neither did according to his will, shall be beaten with many stripes; but he that did not, and did commit things worthy of stripes, shall be beaten with few stripes." Luke xii. 47, 48.

Thus do we see that the Prophetic Conscience brings up to us acts against the Conscience in reference to Eternity, and with that peculiar mark upon them that we call "Guilt," the sense of obligation to a punishment after Time is passed away; and answering to this is the emotion of "Fear."

There are two supplementary questions that may be considered in this chapter. The first is this, Is Conscience a *Judge?*—the second, Does Conscience *punish* us?

The answer to the first, from the account we have given, is that in the sense of pronouncing upon the quality of *action*, as liable to future condemnation, so far *metaphorically* Conscience may be called a judge; but in the true and real sense of *finally* and *authoritatively pronouncing decision judicially*, it is *not a judge.* It declares to us first the quality of action with great certainty; then again it records our transgressions, and *in the future judgment* it shall from that record be a *most certain witness.* And again, of that trial and its result, it gives us a certain *prophecy.* All this it does, but this amounts not *to being a judge* in any strict sense. The Judgment is in Eternity, when, instead of conferring with Him by means and faculties such as this of Conscience is, we shall be brought face to face with the Almighty.

Still, this warning, this recording, this prophesying has in itself a most important value, from the fact that it is by the Spirit of God, who is God of one substance with the Father,* that it takes place. But, as we have above said, *it is, in this world,* warning, recording, prophesying *of judgment,* and *not judging.*

The next question is this: Does Conscience punish? And the answer here again is: "No! Conscience does not punish in any proper sense."

If we say that† "suffering pain, in consequence of any action, is the punishment of that action," then we may say that "Con-

* Nicene Creed.

† The opinion that "personal suffering is always the punishment of personal transgression of the laws of the universe," in other words, of Sin, is, I am sorry to say it, a very wide spread opinion in these days. It is an old error, held by the Pharisees, those men of hard hearts, in our Saviour's day, and by him rebuked severely. "Master, *who did sin,* this man or his parents, *that he was born blind?* And He said, "Neither this man did sin nor his parents, but *that the works of God might be made manifest in him.* Again, they told him of the Galileans, whose blood Pilate had mingled with their sacrifice. And he said, think ye that these Galileans were sinners above all

science punishes." But the principle is *wholly untrue;* for suffering is not so connected with evil, as to be *always* its consequence; so that you can say, that *always* where there is in this world suffering, there has been sin on the part of the sufferer; and in this case, we can see that "Shame" being the sense of Guilt, in no sense is the punishment of the act recorded, but *only* the feeling coming from the Stain; and the Fear corresponding to the Guilt is by no means *the punishment*, but *only the anticipation of the punishment.*

To speak, then, of Conscience inflicting *punishment upon us*, is a thing wholly and entirely wrong; while to speak of the "pain," or the "torments" of an accusing conscience, is perfectly right.

the Galileans, *because they suffered* such things. *I tell you nay*, . . . or those eighteen upon whom the tower in Siloam fell, think you *that they were sinners* above all men that dwelt at Jerusalem? *I tell you nay.*"

This opinion destroys the doctrine of a future judgment. It tells the man who is robust, healthy and prosperous, that he has broken no law, whatever his conscience may tell him to the contrary. It tells the weak, the diseased, and the poor that their evils are punishments, by them justly deserved. To the one class, then, it puts an end to mercy and compassion; in the other, to any belief in God's mercy and his justice. It destroys the idea that this world is a state of trial, and that pain may, in God's wisdom, have many other reasons besides punishment,—be a moral guide, a preventive of greater evil; nay, often a positive and actual good. Lastly, it is at variance with the phenomena of hereditary disease, as well as with the facts of that which ordinary men call accident, and the Christian calls Providence.

I would ask my reader, as an Ethical exercise, to investigate the consequences of this opinion, and he shall find them as I have said, most pernicious to all moral action, and subversive of all right ideas of God, and of the uses to us of the outward world.

And if he be a parent, I would, for the sake of his children, warn him against such books as "Combe's Constitution of Man," whereof this notion is the staple. For the idea, as he will see on further thought, by tracing out its extreme consequence, puts God, "the Personal and Ever-present, Omniscient, and Omnipotent, Governing Being," out of the world, by substituting for Him an "All-sufficing, Physical Law." It is therefore nothing in spirit, but a coarse Physical and Natural Deism.

One thing more I would add as not unimportant. This idea, in another shape, "that sin has always attached it as a natural consequence, a Temporal Penalty of bodily pain,"—a belief as false and as easily refuted,—is a peculiarly Roman Catholic doctrine, and lies at the very root of their doctrine of Purgatory, and of their horrible self-torturing penances. For this, see that most able work, "Palmer's Letters on Romanism."

So do extremes meet. The Romanist and the Deist unite in preaching the same false doctrine, of the natural and unavoidable connection of sin with bodily pain.

And upon examination, we shall find that these two phrases have done an immense deal of harm to religion; for if Conscience be, *in this world, a judge*, in the true and real sense, and truly and really the pain that comes from Conscience be a *punishment inflicted by it*; then, by a natural and unavoidable logic, the truth that the Holy Spirit is the true agent in the Conscience, combined with these false notions, "that conscience is a real judge," inflicting "real punishment," at once leads to the conclusion that the Judgment is already past,—an heresy, stamped by St. Paul as ensuring condemnation, and in these days, because these false phrases, very frequent indeed.

CHAPTER III.

The deficiencies of the Conscience and its laws deduced from its nature.—The deficiencies of Conscience,—the various kinds classified and enumerated.—Its Laws are three: First, of Obedience,—Examination of this law,—Practical inferences from this law.—2d Law of Conscience, Permanence. Its nature and effects.—By means of this second law all passions can be resisted, not otherwise.—Reason of sudden and unexpected moral falls.—Besetting sins, or obstacles to moral progress.—3d Law of Conscience, The law of Subordination; that is, "while it rules us, itself must be ruled." The rule of Conscience is the law of God.—Evils that arise from ignorance of this law.—Morality is eternal and immutable.—Scruples of Conscience. Explanation of their nature, and how to treat them.

It is our object now, after that which we have said in the previous chapters upon the nature of the Conscience, to consider the two parts that remain toward the completion of the subject: the deficiencies of the Conscience first; and secondly, the rules by which we shall be able to remedy those deficiencies, and to bring it to perfectness of action.

Now, upon the subject of its deficiency, we have already in our description of the nature and faculties of Conscience, shown that it consists of two parts, the first of which is the voice of the Holy Spirit of God speaking to us; the second, the natural faculty in us whereby we listen to that voice. Hence does it follow, as a necessary consequence, that all deficiencies are in the natural faculty,—that is, *in the man*. Hence the moral cultivation of the *faculty in us*, is the remedy for deficiencies; for in this only it is that the deficiency can exist. This we can easily see is a necessary and absolute deduction of the Science of Morals.

Again, there is another deduction, as necessary to be made. When we look at the bodily organs and their deficiencies, we see at once two things. In the first place, there is the organization visible and tangible, and as such formed and purposed for a certain function; in the second place, there is the function itself. The *organization* is the means towards effecting that end, and the *function* is the end. Now in judging of bodily organs, the means being visible and tangible, we are judges of the means to the end; as for instance, of the arm, we know all its functions, such as reaching, pushing, holding, and so forth, and have in our mind a full notion of all. And more than that, we have all the machinery for those functions before our eyes, and can judge of the suitableness of it towards the end. We can say, because such and such a bone, muscle, or nerve is deficient, diseased, or inadequate, therefore such and such a function of the organ is unfulfilled. But with regard to faculties, moral or mental, *the function is actually the only thing that we know;* the organization by which that particular faculty works, of that we know nothing.

And, therefore, from this at once we come to a conclusion of very great value, as a means of limiting our researches,—that is, that it is vain to attempt to penetrate into mental or moral organization, for it cannot be known; or in some fancied organization, supplied by own over-daring, to place the cause of deficiencies.

To illustrate this, we shall take the memory; "the memory is the faculty that remembers;" we know not the organization of it as a faculty,—that is, *the means* by which remembrance is brought about. We only know *its function*, "that it remembers." Hence that "memory" shall be good that "remembers well,"—that remembers *firmly*, and *readily*, and *fully*, and *particularly*, and so forth: everything that can come under the word "remember," and the word "well;" that shall be a bad "memory," whose function of remembrance is characterized by all those defects which come under the word badly. It is not *powers* and *organizations* that we know, but *functions*.*

* In Mathematics, the "function" of a quantity is always expressed in "terms of that quantity," 2x, x^2, x^3, d.x, all these are functions of x, the

To apply the principle, then, the deficiencies of the Conscience, are those by which it does not fulfil the functions that belong to the Conscience; and if we have fully and truly described its functions in the previous chapter, the perfect Conscience shall be that which effects these functions perfectly, the imperfect Conscience that which effects them imperfectly. A Conscience, then, that Checks or Withholds adequately when evil approaches, that Records, and, according to its law, re-presents to the man the evil done, and that Prophesies of a future recompense in the same measure, that shall be a good Conscience. A Conscience whose effects are less than this, is not a good Conscience, but an imperfect one.

Having thus stated wherein the deficiencies of Conscience are to be found, it now remains for us to enter upon the consideration of them under these limitations.

The Conscience, then, may be considered as faulty by excess, or as faulty by deficiency in reference to any of its three divisions of function.

That Conscience, for instance, that does not warn against that which is actually evil, is in one degree a *thoughtless* Conscience; in a higher, a *careless* Conscience; higher still, a *hardened* Conscience; yet higher, a *callous* Conscience; and, highest of all, a "*seared*" or "*dead*" Conscience,—all these terms implying deficiency in the sensibility of the faculty to that which is actually evil.

And then, again, an over sensibility, tending to present to us as evil that which is not actually evil, a tendency which any one that considers the analogy to the eye or the ear can at once comprehend, is represented to us as a "weak" Conscience, a "scrupulous" Conscience, or a "sore" Conscience. The true Withholding Conscience being that which is faulty by neither deficiency or excess, and therefore is called the "*sure*" or "*perfect*" Conscience.

Now with regard to the second part of the Conscience, its deficiencies are manifestly in reference to the power of recording or re-presenting, first, faults of deficiency or faults of superabundance,

original quantity x, *is seen* in them all. So in the example in the text of "Good memory," "bad memory," "feeble memory," all the phrases we use bring in and employ the word "memory," they are "functions" of that unknown quantity. The nature and the machinery of the faculty is unknown as far as they are concerned.

wherein that which is evil, when done, is not represented to our minds as evil, that is, the record written is not brought out, and that which is not evil is represented as such. These cases are denoted by the same terms as we have noted in the first.

But more than this, there is a peculiar fault belonging to the second kind by its very nature, when the actions recorded and re-presented have the peculiar note that we call "Stain" attached to them; so that they shall be recorded with this note, and when brought up again to the recollection shall have it associated with them, and shall rouse the feeling of "Shame" in the mind.

This Conscience, in reference to that "Stain," is called a "foul," a "polluted," or a "defiled" Conscience; and the opposite, that in which the record is in a more or less degree without "Stain," a "pure," or "clean," or "undefiled" Conscience.

Again, with reference to the Prophetic Conscience, the same remarks that were made with reference to the second function of the faculty may be made with regard to it as to deficiency or excess. But with reference to its operation, as it presents actions in respect to the future, and in connection with *liability to punishment*, that is, as we have established it, "*Guilt*," in reference to this, the Conscience, in which, when acts done and past are presented to the mind in connexion with this liability, is called "a guilty Conscience;" and that in a degree more or less according to the number and flagrancy of the acts: and a Conscience the opposite is called an "innocent" Conscience.

Thus does it appear that with regard to the function, the worst of all kinds of Conscience is that which is "insensible," or has lost its warning power, commonly called a "seared" or "dead" Conscience; that to which evil is good and good evil, the discriminating power being wholly lost.

With regard to the effect—the Conscience that is "foul" or defiled, and that which is "guilty" or covered with "Guilt," this is the worst of all.

Here comes up a question which once was one very much debated, and still is in some measure interesting: "Can there be naturally such a thing as that one should be born without a Conscience?" This question we believe we have in a degree forestalled, and as it were given our readers the means of deciding it; we therefore merely indicate it, and so pass on.

The best, then, of all shall be that Conscience which in reference to these functions, is *tender*, in reference to the Recording faculty, is *pure*, or free from Stain, to the Prophetic part, is "*innocent*," or free from Guilt.

And between these two extremes there are various degrees, all of which are combinations of these elements, and therefore enumerated "in posse" by the enumeration of them.

And also there is a multitude of practical questions, of the most interesting kind, which it is enough to have indicated, as the examination of them in detail is to our object, which is a "system" of Moral Philosophy, unnecessary. We shall, therefore, in the mode of all proper science, leave the multitude of problems deducible from our main principles, to be as exercises for the student in the application of these principles, and content ourselves with those that are leading and absolutely necessary.

The next subject, therefore, that will most naturally engage our attention is the question, "How and by what means we are to so regulate the Conscience that it shall be for the individual man in the best possible condition that it can be in; that is, what means shall we pursue, if we would derive all the advantages from the power and faculty of Conscience, which God intended that we should derive?" This, manifestly, is a question of the most serious importance, for there is no doubt but that the majority of mankind, so far from subordinating the action of their passions and appetites *to any rule* or *to any governance*, are actually led by these appetites. And some are actually so audacious as to set forth a philosophy that says, "that an appetite, a passion, a desire craves gratification, is a sign that it should be gratified to the fullest extent! and that the outward frame of Society imposes some restraint, indicates that that frame-work is wholly wrong! and must make way for a new one, all whose end and rule shall be, 'that all appetites, all passions, all desires shall be gratified to the utmost of their demands!'" a horrid and brutal Philosophy, that gives liberty to all vice, and destroys the very basis of all Morality.

In view of this fact, I think it is of no small importance to vindicate the Supremacy of the "governing" or "moral" powers, and to point out to the individual man, who is desirous to live according to the law of God, the means whereby he shall be enabled to give to the first of these governing powers, the Conscience, its due perfection, that is, the "supremacy" which it should possess over the rest of our nature.

Now the reader, on looking back to Chapter VI. of Book I., will find there laid down, that there are Governing Faculties whose office, by their very position, is that they are to govern, and that the Conscience is one of them. Again: he will find that of these governing faculties there are laws, in consequence of the obedience to which and by which, from their very nature, they attain and uphold their "supremacy": guided, then, by those rules, they uphold their station; abandoning these, the laws of their being as Governing faculties, they abandon their sway.

Their laws, as governing faculties are, first, that they must govern. Secondly, that they must govern always. Thirdly, that they must govern by a law not by themselves. He, then, that would have a Conscience pure and perfect, must apply these rules unto its action upon his nature, and by these rules, and by these alone, can it attain to the completeness that it is by God intended to possess, and is by its nature capable of having. Let us apply these rules.

The first says, that unto a perfect Conscience it is necessary that it should govern; that is, that no Conscience is a "sure" guide, or can be appealed to as such, or trusted in, save and except that as a *principle of life it be made supreme by the man.*

This may be seen to be so from the very nature of man's constitution in even his bodily faculties. When extreme sensibilities are given against any emotion or sensation that is injurious, if that emotion or sensation be pressed upon the feeling, then the sensibility becomes sometimes almost wholly dead, so as to cease being any guard or protection. So would it seem that the faculty that warns against evil, by its warnings being neglected, loses its power altogether, and resigns its seat to inferior competitors.

This analogy from bodily faculties would be of itself sufficient to illustrate, and to rest our proof upon, backed, as it is, by the experience of the whole world, and of all both heathen and Christian moralists; for who is there who does know how easily one step downward from the straight course of steady and conscientious action, will end in plunging the man in guilt, of which a little before he deemed himself wholly incapable? Who does not know what a fatal fascination evil once familiarized to us has? There would be proof enough in defence of the assertion that we have made, that Conscience as a principle *must govern* if we would have it perfect, as showing that once deprived of its position it loses, as it were, its very nature, and ceases to be that which it was; for then becoming merely a principle among other principles, it loses its nature, and acts only as the subordinate principles do, at intervals, and neither constantly nor reliably.

And when we consider the universal persuasion with regard to it, we find that this which I have called the first law of Conscience, is, under various forms and shapes, the solid conviction and belief of all men as to its action. They represent it as a light which we are to follow—dim and indistinct at first, but which, *if we pursue it steadily*, becomes brighter and yet more bright. Again: they paint man as in darkness, gloom and storm, in the midst of a desert by night, needing guidance; and Conscience as the minutest and remotest speck of light, appearing upon the verge of the horizon, yet to be followed *because it is light*, and *the only light.*

Here, then, in this comparison, which is a familiar one to all nations, is exemplified its increased value as a rule, as depending upon our constancy and perseverance in following its guidance. The brightness is considered to be always growing as long as we press onward, and never to decay while our face is turned towards it and our footsteps are pursuing it.

We have given this example, and shall omit any further enumeration of instances. Suffice it to say, that in all those metaphors which men have employed to designate this faculty, or to denote the mode of its operation, the conviction of the same law is universally to be discerned, a hint which, while it may set the student upon a more extended examination of this particular point, may serve to excuse our further consideration of it. But, however, as an additional support of the doctrine implied in these illustrations, we beg to refer our readers forwards to our notice of the effect of Habit upon the Moral Nature,* so far as "active" and "passive habit" are concerned, by which he shall find the doctrine of the foregoing paragraphs most strongly supported. And we shall now go forward to the support of our first law from other and more weighty considerations.

He that looks to the preceding chapters shall see that the constitution of the Conscience is two-fold; of a faculty in us, and

* Book IV. Chap. 3.

working upon us through that faculty, the Holy Spirit of God Now the doctrine of the Scriptures as to Him is, that his influence upon the spirit of man *is given in proportion*, not capriciously, but *after a certain proportion*, though what the elements of it are we cannot precisely say, it not having been revealed. But this is clearly said, that it is "*grace for grace*,"—Grace as a reward for grace well employed, and as a means of obtaining more Grace.* Here, then, in this fact we find the ultimate reason of this first law, that except we are as a matter of principle governed by Conscience, its action is incomplete, for its completeness is in constant progression, depending for light and clearness upon the continual gift of the Spirit, in reward for the continual reception and use of that gift.

And adding this fact to those others previously noticed,† the conclusion, as a matter both of moral science and inward conviction, shall be established, that if we would have Conscience a sure and trustworthy guide, then, as a fixed principle of action, we must obey it. *It must rule*, and no passion, nor desire, nor appetite within us, and without us no object towards which they may lead us must be sought or pursued, if doing so will contravene our Conscience or lead us into evil in the slightest degree.

This is the first law of the *perfection* and the *governance* of Conscience, and the man that takes it to himself, however blasted in character, and condemned by the unanimous verdict of his fellows he may be; he that shall take, even in the depths of his degradation, this for his guide as a ruling principle, he shall arise out of the deepest pit, he shall be lifted up from his abasement, he shall become a man standing upright in the dignity of manhood.

Let him rely upon it, "*for a man who will do so, how deep soever*

* This, I believe, gives the full sense of the Greek idiom "grace for grace," and this only adequately expresses it.

† The fact, that is, of man's moral inability, as he is by himself apart from the influences of Grace; the fact that the Spirit is Jehovah and infallible; that his Grace *comes first* unto us and awakens us; that the dictates of conscience, assigning no reason for themselves, are yet confirmed by all after experience; that they are authoritative, it is our privilege and duty to obey. All these facts are those referred to in the text. They all, together with this Law of Grace, that is combined with it, declare and prove that the power of the faculty depends upon "supremacy," that made "subordinate," it loses its natural and normal influence.

he may be sunk, there is all hope and no fear." This declaration, here written with pen and ink, is written upon the hearts of all in the records of Providence, nay, upon the Very Throne of God; for the Holy Spirit, co-essential with the Father, whose voice the Conscience is, has made it a first principle, and a primal truth in the self-experience of all: and to all men the course of the outward world, arrayed and set forth as it is by Almighty power and Omniscient wisdom, echoes back and reasserts that internal conviction. There is none to whom the light does not appear, faint as it may be through their own fault, but still to all, while they are alive upon the earth, it appears and invites to follow; and therefore to all men, even to the vilest and worst, there is *hope, all hope,* if they will only follow it.

And to those most elevated in their moral qualifications, to them, by the very same reason, *all fear,* if they abandon this supreme guide and ruling power, and permit themselves to be ruled and governed by anything else than this.

It is a cheap Morality to discourse of virtues and vices, to harangue against this vice and that vice, to give set and commonplace argument against the love of money, against luxury, and against licentiousness: but the plain truth is, that *these* are but the occasions and external causes of falling, as the storm is to the tree that is rotten at the root; for no external fall has there been into open and flagrant guilt, but *first there was an internal fall,* a dethronement of the Moral Power from its seat of guidance: and where this once has taken place, then external circumstances may, by the Grace of God, keep the man from the abyss of vice, but he has left the only moral ground, and whatever good he may do, incidentally, yet by his very position, as one closing his eyes upon the light that is given to guide him, and renouncing its guidance, he is ready for the deepest plunge into the foulest degradation.

Such is the first law of Conscience, the law of "Obedience," the law that *it must govern and we obey*—govern supremely, obey entirely.

And this matter of the governance of Conscience, its entire and absolute governance, this which to men in ordinary may seem so exceedingly difficult, this depends not upon the agony of a sudden effort, putting forth unusual strength upon emergency, but upon that second rule of "Permanence," so that one law, in some measure, derives its strength from the other. He whose Conscience governs *permanently*, by *that very fact attains the habit that it should govern supremely.* The permanent and constant habit, that is, of referring all things to Conscience, and as a matter of fixed and steady principle bowing to its decision and acknowledging its "supremacy," this shall give, even to the weakest in mind, the power of resisting the most exceeding temptations.

Nor does this depend upon the force of Habit as its peculiar cause, though this, too, will confirm the power, so much as upon a vital and real distinction between the nature of that power which the "governing" faculties have, and that which the "passions" have, that the "*power of the 'governing' faculties is in their constancy of action*, and *the power of 'passion' in its concentration to a small interval of time.*" This, we have already remarked, comes from their function as "governing," which implies action constant, not intermitted. And he that shall consider the faculty of Conscience with care, shall find that it is so with it.

To those, then, who may not, at first sight, consider the assertion* of our last chapter as credible, to them we say, let them, instead of looking at vice in the mere outside point of view, in reference to injury done as to money, position, character, and so forth: and thus, when they are hurried away by that evil they are hitherto prone to be conquered by, at that moment calling up the moral powers in arms against it, so that the strife is, *for the moment*, to place the moral powers to war against the temptation; let them observe the nature of the two as different powers, and give the moral powers a "governing" influence, one that *always* and *in everything* reigns; and because of this, in the *one thing* wherein is their danger, it shall rule the wildest assaults of "passion" within and temptation without.

He that does not *cheat* from the motive only that "honesty is the best of policy," who does not lie from the sole motive that such a character would ruin his trade, who commits no adultery from the mere fear of the law and the verdict of a jury; this man may be counted a good moral man in the ordinary outside acceptation of the word, even at the very time when inwardly, in his own heart, he knows that he would do all these things but for the out-

* The assertion, namely, that in any human being, however weak his moral faculty may be by nature, and however violent the force of passions, the moral power is able, by nature, to check and subdue any passion whatsoever.

ward penalty. And his neighbors and himself may wonder why drunkenness is such a temptation to him, or any other of the twenty vices we may mention, and may laugh us to scorn when we say that even that man's moral power is able to conquer it; when the fact of the matter is, that the man is hardly *a moral being at all.* His Conscience never acts efficiently at all, for it is never obeyed systematically.

To such a man, we say, let your Conscience act,—let it act always and *in everything,* and *as a matter of principle;* and soon you will find, that *in this law of action,* it has power to overcome any gust of temptation and hold it under.

At the same time, we must acknowledge that so far as we have hitherto gone, these two rules of Conscience, as to its action, are more ready to uphold and secure its mastery, when it has been obtained, than to obtain it by themselves. Still, the consideration of them is such, as we conceive, to cast much light and hope upon the course of man.

As depending upon this law of "permanence," we will note one other fact, which is sufficiently strange. It often happens that to the individual man there is some little thing that may be *wrong to him,* not wrong *in itself,* but *wrong to him,*—relatively wrong that is. And this little matter,—it may be the very least thing and the most unimportant in the world, in which none of his friends see any wrong, but which is *wrong to him*—this a man shall often do, through the force of habit, with the *feeling full in his own mind that it is wrong.*

And *so doing,* he breaks the second law of Conscience, and *shall make no progress whatsoever.* All the good in greater things that is done, is then felt to be good, but is not to him a means of moral progress. When the Conscience declares against any act, how small soever it may be, and *in full view of its being wrong* that act is done again, *then there is no moral progress,* no bringing to perfection of the power of Conscience. It is as the small impediment that hinders the starting into motion of a body, which, were the body in motion, would be crushed into dust by a thousandth part of the power that it impedes. Small things, then, as well as great, there are to be brought under the law to which I allude.

But to conclude our examination, the immediate effects of this law of "permanence," observed as a principle of life, are very extraordinary to the world, and sometimes even to the persons concerned very astounding. In the first place, the individual who has been as I have described the man a little above, with these acts that properly and truly should have been founded upon Conscience, placed upon the false basis of "enlightened selfishness," or mere "external law," or "the custom of Society," this man, during the time that these things have been so placed, shall have hardly felt the existence of a Conscience, and to him it shall almost be a word without a meaning.* Let him, then, however weak may have been his perception originally, however dim the light, begin to act upon it; and then, under the influence of this law, there shall spring up within him the stream of a new internal life. It shall be as if a wide extent of unwholesome marshes were transformed into the continuous current of a river. The principle then becomes a living principle when it is *continuous*, and only then.

It needs but very little experience of men to see how few of them ever make Conscience supreme. But few as these are, fewer still are they who are always guided, in reference to it, by the second law, that of its "permanence."

The question then of the possible perfection of Conscience, this becomes not a mere theoretic question by any means, but one entirely practical. But it is highly probable that no man *by nature*, apart from Revelation, has ever followed his Conscience so strictly after these two laws, as *to perfect it according to them.*

I do not, then, suppose that of natural power any one has ever got beyond these two rules of the Conscience so as to rise above them towards the third, although I can see in divers even of the heathen an appreciation of them.

But the third law I count to be the most important; this says, that "Conscience is not to be ruled by itself, or to make *itself* a rule, *but to govern by a law—itself is not to be its own law.*"

Now, we see many people who keenly appreciate the first law, that "Conscience is to be supreme"; few, indeed, that know the value of the second; but in the most of even good men a complete

* Men, in such a case, usually delude themselves with the idea that Conscience is not a faculty, the organ and sense of the Divine Voice; but that it is the mere mental conclusion as to what is "right" or "wrong." And that "right" and "wrong," "good" and "evil," are *not* immutable in their nature, but depend on circumstances. These two notions do, as I have said in the text, render Conscience "almost a word without a meaning."

ignorance of the third, and this is in so extraordinary a way, oftentimes, that it makes men torment themselves and others by the most fantastic scruples. They feel the "supremacy" of Conscience as an authoritative governor over the man so strongly, that its rule over them seems to them to exclude *any supremacy over it.* And thus the disease or derangement of the faculty, which as other faculties of the human constitution is liable to disease, and is manifested in irregular action, this disease of the faculty shall be permitted to tyrannize over themselves and others. Therefore, the man under this idea holds himself bound to bow down to the most ridiculous scruples, and to compel others to yield to them. All this from taking Conscience to be *absolutely infallible,* and from not considering its twofold nature.

He, however, that shall look at the nature of "moral good," as having in itself an unity and sameness in all individuals; at the nature and being of man in the world, as under the One Lord, and Father, and Teacher, must conclude that the law of God's goodness, and justice, and mercy, in other words, the Law of God, must be the Law and Rule of Conscience. And taking especial care to avoid the common mistake by which we attribute "Self-Will" unto God, instead of "Will," the Will of God, which is the Eternal Law of his being, the law of unchangeable and infinite goodness, and mercy, and truth, this, in whatsoever way reached, *if it be only reached, is the Law of the Conscience.*

For we shall mistake, if we attribute to God a Will in the sense of self-will, unconnected with these his eternal attributes, as if by the power of Will, that is *self-will,* he made "good" "bad," or "bad" "good," by an omnipotent fiat; which is to attribute *self-will* to God, not Will, is to make him deny himself, and is to destroy the nature of his attributes. Whereas, goodness, mercy, justice, truth, these, as parts of the being of God, are *in their nature His nature,* and the law of its being and unchangeable.

And the qualities in us that herein resemble God, these, as qualities, are eternal and immutable in their nature. Mercy is not one thing in me and another in you, and a third thing in a Hindoo or Negro; but is the same in all men. Evil never can be good, nor good evil—nor can one become the other. *The laws of Morality are immutable and eternal.*

These things, then, being so, it is manifest that theWill of God, the law that is of His being, the law of eternal and immutable goodness, this is the law of Conscience and by this it must be ruled.

This has thus been shown from the nature of that with which the Conscience has to deal; but more plainly still it is manifested from the nature of the Conscience itself being twofold, first, the voice of the Holy Spirit, and secondly, the organ in us that listens to that voice. And the perfection of it will therefore consist in the organ *perfectly* receiving and *perfectly* transmitting to us that voice. Now, the office of the Spirit, by the Scripture, is the manifestation of the Will of God, hence by the very nature of the Conscience its law is the Will of God. And by whatsoever means the Will of God is manifested, by this we shall be able to test and examine the dictates of our Conscience, and see that we are not deceived by that part of it which is a faculty in our own nature, and which as such is liable to irregular and abnormal action.

We can see, then, that each man in measuring the action of his own Conscience over himself, must measure it by the *Will of God* in whatsoever way revealed, whether in the Scriptures or the law of Society, or the law of man.

This, manifestly, is the truth of the case in reference to himself, but in order to give it a practical tenor, so that men may be able to apply it, I would place it in this position: "When you are afflicted with doubts, or scruples, or questions of conscience; then your own secret troubles and torments, in the most of cases, will render you unable *yourself* to apply the *law of God as a rule* to correct the errors of your Conscience; because *had you been able and accustomed so to do,* you would never have fallen into this state."

In this case I would advise you to consult *confidentially* persons whom you see to be qualified for this very thing—those who *can understand what scruples are,* and *sympathize with the real pain that comes from these trifles*—who *are* Conscientious in themselves, and *familiar with the application of the law of God* to particular cases. And lastly, who are in the situation naturally of Judges; as being Parents, so in the family—or Clergy, so in the Church—or Judges, so in the State. He that has a scruple of Conscience that torments him, if he go and reveal his scruple, *under the bond of confidence,* to such a man as I have described, in the most of cases he shall get an opinion and advice that shall correct his Conscience *by the law of God.** And if this do not satisfy him, then let him go to a second or a third person having the same qualifications, and for the most part finding them to agree, he shall be set entirely at rest.

So much importance do I put upon this, that I think that founded as the advice is upon the very nature of Conscience, the suggestion acted upon as it may be acted upon, may save persons from an immense amount of secret pain, suffered in secret, because of the unsympathizing nature of men, and often laying the foundations of a morbid and brooding temper, whose natural issue is insanity.

This is all we have to say in reference to what are called "questions" and "scruples of Conscience." And this because we count a *living adviser, applying the law of God, under a pledge of confidence, and himself possessed of a sympathizing tenderness of disposition*, a thousand fold preferable to any system of rules laid down upon paper, and to be applied by the person himself whose Conscience is distressed.

But one caution we add to the individual: "If this free you, as most likely it will, then delay not to let Conscience *govern you;* and *always*, and by a fixed principle and rule, that is *the law of God.* For as to the drowned, where the means have been employed to recal them from the torpor of death, the first sensation is that of intense pain, arising *not from disease*, but *from the fact*

* To the young, upon these grounds, we say, that the one best adviser in such a case is a pious and judicious Father or Mother. Here is natural sympathy, here natural guidance, here confidence of the purest and most unselfish kind. If evil thoughts, then, enter into your mind, and you are secretly distressed by them; if temptations come to you from acquaintances, or schoolmates, or from servants, to do that which you suspect to be evil, but are not certain of it, being shaken by their persuasions; if you are internally tried by the violence of evil emotions, such as "anger," or "envy," or "malice": in any and all cases of internal distress, do not brood over it alone, but make your Father or your Mother your *confidential adviser.* And in such a case, often in half an hour, you shall get relief from that which might, being kept a secret in your own mind, cause even years of torment.

And let parents sympathize with their children, be tender with them, and be themselves purely and entirely conscientious. And *above all, let their children's confidence be unbroken*, and as silent as if it had never been spoken.

The neglect of this, at the present day, causes a great deal of misery, and permits a great deal of sin. The observance of it would nip much evil in the bud.

that life is again reviving, and the vital principle coming again into action; so with a Conscience which *has not had its due supremacy*, when it is roused to vigorous action from its insensibility; these scruples are at the first most frequent and most painful, and are signs of returning life. But to the man, when the Conscience is ruled by its laws, they vanish; or if they come up, are attended by no pain, for at once he can decide them.

However, to resume. The third rule of Conscience being that instead of being governed by itself, it is to be governed by a law; and that law being the Will of God, this leads us at once to two subjects of the deepest importance; the first the adaptedness of our "nature to religion," which in a different way might be expressed, as "the connectedness of natural and revealed religion;" and the second, the deficiencies of the natural Conscience, and the aid that it demands to supply them. These two subjects, with the help of the principles established in this chapter, we hope to expound in the next.

CHAPTER IV.

The facts of Conscience render Natural Religion possible—and the facts of Revealed Religion perfect Conscience.—In whom the Conscience is perfect.—Conscience cannot pardon.—It leads us towards the Atonement of Christ.

Note upon the Practical nature of Justification in its connection with the Conscience.

THE questions which in our last chapter we proposed, were the first with regard to what is called Natural Religion,—its extent and possibility. The second, with regard to the deficiencies of the Natural Conscience.

Now with regard to the first, he that shall look upon the principles we have established, shall have very little difficulty. If "man's nature be in itself good," and its state be that which is expressed by the words *fallen*, so that it is *not* the state of a beast, a state of brutal indifference, unconscious of Good and ignorant of God; if it be not a devilish state, a state of pure, unmixed hatred and abhorrence, and utter antagonism to light;

but a state in which *all objects sought, are sought as good.* If then, our natural deficiency be that of insubordination and of inability in our nature to obey God's Laws, and if Evil is not a *positive existence* in itself, but truly and really "the absence of Good," and sin is not some mysterious quality having a substantial reality* in nature, but is a trangression of the Law; if, moreover, the Law of God is revealed as a law to man by Society, and by the face of outward Nature, then it is manifest that Religion is a possible thing; nay, that naturally man is suited and adapted to it, and that it has a foundation for itself in his Nature and Position.

But when we come to the consideration of the nature of man, and look closely at the Conscience, then we find more clearly and more plainly the correspondency between man's Nature and Religion. We find, that as the earth, in its qualities, considered as fertile and capable of producing crops, answers to the heat, and the light, and the moisture, and the air, and the frost, and the snow; and all these influences are external to the earth, and yet these, with its qualities of nature, conspire unto fertility; so it is with our Human nature and Revealed Religion. Between the natural facts of a Conscience understood by all who follow it, *and by none else*, and the facts of the Gospel incapable of being known save by Revelation, there is precisely that relation.

The natural Conscience tells us that evil is supremely to be avoided. It even hints to us its own two-fold nature,—it gives us even naturally indistinct notions of its personality and its divinity. It feels the guilt, and evermore it leads us towards the idea that this guilt may be wiped away, though not by itself.† It feels that the shame may be wiped off, so that the man may stand upright. It acknowledges also the responsibility. It connects the deeds done in Time with a result in Eternity,—a judgment before an Eternal and Almighty Judge, and the same one who has been to us here an Eternal Witness. Of these things, the heart of man speaks to him wherever man exists.

Not, I say, clearly as now, under the broad light of Christianity, but in that dim, instinctive way in which the root of the willow shall blindly, yet infallibly, direct its course, as I have seen,

* "For sin is the transgression of the Law." 1 John, iii. Chap. 4 v.

† "The blood of Jesus Christ His Son cleanseth us from all sin." 1 John i. 7.

twenty and thirty feet towards a well; as the plant that has begun to germinate shall, on being removed to utter darkness, send forth an exploring root of many feet in the direction of the light; as the young shoot, planted in a cleft wherein there is only earth enough for itself at its present age, shall, in its after-growth, send out an exploring fibre towards the deeper earth, which shall root itself there, and ultimately become the main root. So it is with the relation of the natural Conscience to religion,—it blindly and ignorantly yearns towards the facts of religion,—it does *not know them*. But it instinctively tends towards them, so that *at once*, upon their revelation, nature accepts them and confesses the facts to correspond to its feelings, and acknowledges that these facts revealed and applied, then are that which brings itself to perfection.

I have now analyzed the Conscience as to its nature, its operations, its laws and sanctions. I have shown how it works, and that in such a way, that I have no doubt that each man who has thought upon his own nature and striven earnestly, however weakly and feebly, yet earnestly, to follow that light, has seen that the representation is a true and correct one of the faculty according to its workings.

And in the heathen world, antecedent to the coming of our Lord, when the only knowledge of facts they had was from the Tradition of a primitive revelation, I can show the same representation of facts as to the Conscience; nay, the same facts. I will not say that they were clearly and distinctly set forth in order, but in a confused way, as a stormy sea reflects the image of heaven,—in a dim or broken way, as a mirror in fragments shows the human face. But still, in such a way, that to us, to whom the facts of Revelation have been unveiled by Christ, it is manifest that the corresponding facts concerning the Conscience have been known to them by nature.*

This may be seen in the works of all the Greek Philosophers antecedent to Christ; chiefly in those of Plato and Aristotle. It may be seen, too, in the philosophy of the remotest Eastern na-

* "For when the Heathen, (Gentiles,) which have not the law, do by nature the things contained in the law, these, not having the law, *are a law unto themselves:* Which show the *work of the law written in their hearts,* their *conscience also bearing witness,* and their thoughts in the meanwhile accusing or else excusing one another." Romans ii. 14 and 15.

tions, their leading doctrine of Pantheism, having for itself no other natural foundation than that of the God-head of the Internal Voice; and the same facts, in the same way, are witnessed by all Heathen nations of modern times, when as yet they have received no knowledge from Europeans, but are fresh from heathenism. Of this I could bring forward the proofs from the authors, but I deal not in the affectation of learning. It suffices me that these can easily be obtained by my readers that are ordinarily learned, and that those of them who are unlearned have sufficient confidence in me that it is so.

This being so, the facts of Conscience that come up to all men by nature as enigmas and deep mysteries, these in Revelation have revealed truths that are their solutions, corresponding unto them most accurately and exactly. Revelation tells us that to avoid sin must be our supreme endeavour—a motive that must ever and entirely reign in us. It tells us, too, that no ignorance is an excuse, no absence from the sources of knowledge, no hiddenness in the remotest depths of barbarism, but that there is a light that shines upon all wheresoever they may be, whose brilliancy and illuminating power is measured, not by rank, or riches, or station, or abilities, or knowledge, but by our actual zeal in following it. It tells us that the τὸ θεῖον (the divinity), which the philosopher* ascribed to it, and the δάιμων (personal deity) of Socrates, and the personality which in universal speech all men give it, these are no chance dreams or vague illusions, but that it is the voice of the Holy Spirit, "God of God, Light of Light, Very God of Very God, of one Substance with the Father;" and hence that he speaks to each man with the same voice, through a similar faculty and organ.

And thus the two discordant facts of Conscience infallible, authoritative, controlling with a voice requiring absolute submission, and Conscience fallible, and weak, and needing to be ruled, which otherwise could not be made to agree, are reconciled.

Hence, too, its insight into Eternity, its dumb speech regarding the Future, its prophecy of judgment, its connexion of Time with Eternity, all these are made clear.

And, finally, its feelings of Shame, and Stain, and Fear, and Guilt, and of Moral Restlessness, all these manifestly have in the

* Aristotle.

revealed facts of our Fall in Adam, our Redemption in Christ, their due and only explanation. *The facts of the Natural Conscience are only to be explained by the facts of the Gospel.*

Having thus shown how revealed religion is related to natural religion, in reference to that governing faculty that we have examined, we shall go on next to an examination of the deficiencies of Conscience which prevent its being a perfect guide naturally. He that shall look to the illustrations we have just given, will see that its natural perfection only is in this, that it leads the man who follows it onward, and gives him a feeling towards the facts that perfect it, *so that if it is to be perfect*, it is so only in connexion with these *facts known* and these *facts applied.*

So that the Heathen, or he who is left to the natural Conscience, feels the faculty to be a useful one, but very mysterious; he, again, who knows the facts of Revelation, can explain a great many things to the other deeply mysterious; but that man only to whom the facts are applied, "who is born of the Spirit," to him the Conscience has obtained its due perfection.

That is to say, the man "who is born of the Spirit," he who being so by God's grace *then governs himself by his Conscience, always* guiding his Conscience by God's law, this I count to be that man in whom alone of all men the Conscience is perfect; for he it is in whom alone the perfection of the three parts of the Conscience exists: and he who shall examine who that man is, or in whom these qualifications meet, shall find they do so only in the "*Justified Christian.*"*

Now, he that examines the faults of the natural Conscience, and compares it with the perfect Conscience, that is, the Conscience of the man unfallen, he shall find that the Conscience of the man unfallen must have been completely free from all error, and a perfect guide. The result of the fall, therefore, is that God the Holy Spirit remaining the same, the natural deficiencies of the Conscience, as a faculty, that it has now, it has from it. The first effect of the Fall upon the nature of man, is the inability of the Conscience adequately to transmit to us the voice of the Spirit.

Of this deficiency, and the means of correcting it by the restoration of its Supremacy, I have already treated; and there is no

* See note at the end of this chapter on the practical nature of justifying faith, page 126

doubt that in a very great degree the sensibility of the Conscience may be restored by these means; indeed, in so great a degree as to make men almost conclude that Conscience may be made by nature a perfect guide.

But when we come to the third law of the Conscience, and see that it must be governed by the rule of God's law, then at once we see that the natural Conscience is no sure guide; for to them who are "born of the Spirit," the Spirit *dwells in them* in consequence of that birth, *informing and internally guiding* their Conscience by an influence which, if it come not within our knowledge by sense, is yet not the less manifest in its effects. And secondly, as an *external law*, the will of God as manifested in the Scriptures, and interpreted and applied by the Church, is the law by which the Conscience is to be ruled.

The "Birth of the Spirit," then, in consequence of which He becomes the *internal law* of the Conscience, and the outward *law of God's revelation*, these are the actual gifts of revealed religion, in consequence of which the Conscience is perfected, and to which no strife of our own moral nature can attain of itself merely. No internal working or struggle of the Conscience of Socrates could cause him to attain unto the gift of Spiritual Regeneration, given in consequence of our Saviour's death, or to a knowledge of the completed canon of the Holy Scripture.

But again, we shall make another remark which will more fully manifest the truth of that which we have asserted. In the primitive man it has been seen that the Conscience was a perfect guide, the natural faculty being perfect, and from the Supernatural Gift the power perfectly to obey it was his. Hence was there no Stain upon it, and no Shame, no Guilt, and thence no Fear. The Recording Conscience detailed no transgression of God's will, and the Prophetic Conscience prophesied no punishment; but the past was without the consciousness of evil, the future without dread of misery.

Now, herein is a difference, and a vital one; there is none of fallen men that has a Conscience that is without Guilt and Stain; this is to each human being an effect of the Fall. Nature tells us at once that there is no natural means of removing this Guilt and Stain. Good is not antagonist to Evil, so that the "plus" of one shall make the "minus" of the other, and that we can keep a debtor and creditor account with Conscience, so much

Good against so much Evil, the surplus of our good balancing accounts against our evil. But Good is the *living according to a law* which we are *bound to live by*, and Evil the transgression of that law. We cannot, therefore, balance the one against the other.

Nor does Conscience reveal to us any way of getting rid of the Stain or the Guilt; in fact, to express it clearly, Conscience has first a Warning power, and then a Recording power, and then a Power Prophetic of punishment, but it has no *pardoning power* naturally.

Thence are we to seek the completion of Conscience in the *Atonement* of our Lord Jesus Christ, *applied to us by the Spirit;* the effect of His death by which our sins are forgiven, in consequence of our Regeneration by his Spirit, the Stain of them wiped out, and the Guilt pardoned, and ourselves set free from the Shame and the Fear. This fully completes, as far as Conscience is concerned, our illustration of the relation that nature bears to grace, and Natural to Revealed Religiôn.

And besides illustrating the first part of this chapter, it fully shows the position of Conscience in man as a secret force in the heart of each which he may resist, overthrow, conquer again and again, so as to feel that he is perfectly *free from compulsion;* and that in his actions, if he do evil, *he must act in a full sense of his responsibility and against light and knowledge.*

So that herein the Freedom of Man, the Justice of God, Ignorance and Unlimited Knowledge, Time and Eternity, Mercy and Judgment, all meet together in this one faculty.

And by this faculty in its action, the dealings of the Almighty Creator with us his creatures are justified, so that whatever man may have to say to his fellows before their bar, before the judgment throne of God, the evidence of the Recording Spirit and of the man himself shall, in each man's case, manifest that "the Judge of the whole earth has not done wrong."

We have thus examined the nature of Conscience, and shown its uses; we have gone into its laws, and the means of perfecting the faculty naturally and spiritually. In the next book we shall proceed to consider the Reason as a governing faculty, the second of the governing powers.

NOTE UPON THE PRACTICAL NATURE OF "JUSTIFICATION BY FAITH," REFERRED TO ON PAGE 123.

We are "justified *by faith*," *working by love*, and *showing itself in true Christian works.*

In the justified man there must be first, "faith—a sincere belief in the Gospel, and an appreciation of the Atonement of Christ as sufficient for the sins of the whole world, and as applied to himself."

2dly, This faith must realize itself in his heart by the Spirit of his Lord, that is, *true love* towards his God and towards his fellow men.

3rdly. This must issue forth *in actual works of love*, in "the fruit of the Spirit, which is love, joy, peace, long-suffering, gentleness, goodness, meekness, temperance, against which there is no law;" in works of mercy to the wretched; and in subjection of his own thoughts, words and actions to the Spirit and Law of Christ.

In the Regenerate Christian it will be seen, if this be so with him during life, that the voice of God, at the last great day of judgment, will *declare him just* through the blood of Christ; and even in this world the voice of the Holy Spirit, through his Conscience, *will witness to his justification.* According to that which the apostle says, "the Spirit beareth witness *with our spirit that we are the sons of God;*" (Rom. viii. 16;) and again, "We have not received the spirit of bondage again to fear, but we have received the Spirit of Adoption whereby we cry Abba, Father." Herein is seen the connexion of the natural faculty with the Spirit, and the relation of both *under the Gospel* to *justification.*

This, I conceive, to be the doctrine of the Church, against both the Roman Catholic doctrine, that we are *made just* by an *infused righteousness*, instead of being *declared just* or "acquitted" by the *Atonement*, and the Solifidian scheme, that says that *love* and *works* are not necessary. But for more ample information, I refer the learned to Bishop Bull's treatise, the "Harmonia Apostolica."

To the unlearned, then, I say, as a practical inference, if, after you are Regenerate, "made a member of Christ, a child of God, an inheritor of the kingdom of heaven," for after this point only in your existence you have the full filial privileges of the Spirit's power—if after this you know that you have true faith, that faith that is vivified by "love" and realized by "works," *then you are justified;* justified, if before that secret tribunal which the Spirit of God has erected in your heart, you can, (*having faith,*) truly say, "I love God according to the measure of his Grace and of my own weakness, with all my heart, and soul, and strength; and I truly strive to realize this in Christian works of mercy and love." The man is "justified" who with faith in his heart, can *truly* say this, before his God.

But if having had faith, and being baptized in the name of Christ, faith becomes dead, and in our hearts *we know* that we do not love God above all things, but our own will or our own pleasure; and that we do not love our neighbors; if we also do no Christian works of love, but all our works are founded on motives of "Self-will," or "Sensuality," or "Selfishness," so that we care not for our neighbor, but rather despise and evil intreat him, when it suits this Evil Concupiscence in us, THEN are we *not justified*—our faith is not a "*living faith,*" it neither is enlivened by love nor realized by works. It may not be so dead as that the root should perish, but the growth is stopped, the leaf is withered, and the fruit is blighted.

How, then, shall the man recover? Not by any excitement, not by any extraordinary means. He knows what is that inward obstacle or outward sin that impedes his course. He knows in his own heart, *although others may not know,* what is the peculiar *besetting sin* to which he yields. He knows what that is *in thought, in word,* or *in deed* that he does, through interest, through thoughtlessness, through pleasure, through habit, through *outward temptation* or *inward feebleness, that is clearly and distinctly against his own convictions of Christian duty,* as manifested to his Conscience by the Spirit. While he does this that is so, the Spirit says to his Conscience, "Thou art *not justified,* thou art *condemned;*" and his own consciousness tells him the same. His Reason and his knowledge of the Law of God assure him of the same. God to be sure may, in his wise purposes, permit him to remain in the world and in the Church even in that state, but still it is not the state of one who is *justified.*

The man, then, in this condition, knowing that he is in the wrong, he should instantly set himself with all his might to abstain from *that particular sin;* to wrestle with prayer, with fasting, with all the means prescribed both by the Gospel and by his own knowledge of himself to overcome it, according to the direction of the apostle: "Wherefore . . . let us lay aside every weight, and the *sin* which *so easily besets* us, and let us run with patience the race that is set before us, looking unto Jesus, the author and finisher of our Faith, . . . lest ye be wearied and faint in your minds. *Ye have not yet resisted unto blood, striving against sin.*"

If in struggling with our besetting sin, it should bring us to our death, or wring drops of blood and agony from the dearest affections of our heart, still are we to persevere. And then, through the prayer of Faith, through God's Grace, through the power of Christ, we *shall overcome*, and be led on conquering our sins, till we reach that state wherein we are Justified, the state wherein the Spirit bears witness with our spirit that we have Living Faith that acts by love, and realizes itself by true Christian works.

In this note I have considered only the case of that man who has been once born again. The state of men outside the Covenant is different.

BOOK III.

THE SPIRITUAL REASON.

CHAPTER I.

First, Reasoning is not Reason; this illustrated.—The composition of human nature is not double, but three-fold.—Man having an Animal Mind and a Spirit, these faculties in him correspond to two worlds, the world of the Seen and that of the Unseen.—Hence two reasoning powers, the "Animal Mind" and Spiritual Reason.—Moral ideas are received from Society *by* the Reason.—All ideas of which it may be said "God is," are of it.—A remark in reference to our future state, and the grounds of our perpetual progress in it.—The question of innate ideas.

OUR readers will have remarked that among the "governing" powers, as we place Conscience the first, so the second is the Reason. To examine the nature and laws of this faculty, therefore, shall be the object of the present book.

The subject we acknowledge to be one of considerable difficulty, and yet we believe to the reader who shall give us his considerate attention, we shall be able to bring forth the laws and offices of this great power so that the principles educed may be something of a guide to him in his course of moral study as well as in actual life practically. The first distinction we would have him observe is this, that "reasoning" and Reason are things wholly and entirely different, so different indeed that very often considerable powers of reasoning shall exist in him who has of Reason very little at all.

A strange paradox, one may say, and yet literally possible,—reasoning is properly a logical exercise, the power by which, "premises" being given or assumed, we draw the conclusion—this is "reasoning." Now if we look at the definition of insanity, we find it is "that *madmen *reason rightly* from wrong premises." The *reasoning power is unimpaired* in them, the *Reason is diseased.* And this is so well known among physicians attending upon such persons, that it is a rule never to "*reason*" with them; and that because their "reasoning" powers are very often even more perfect and vigorous than ordinary, while their Reason is diseased. This shows that there is a real distinction between "reasoning" and Reason.

But, indeed, it is ordinary to mark it, the man who is forever arguing, proving, disputing; in short, he that has a taste for "reasoning," this man seldom we find reasonable, and seldom attribute Reason to him. So far we have gone, and as there are two ways of explaining what we mean, and the first is that of fencing off outwardly from our conception that which does not belong to it, so we beg our readers to mark this first, the distinction that "reasoning" is not Reason.

Having thus noticed the verbal distinction which our readers will find brought out still more strongly afterwards, we go on to examine what Reason is in its own nature.

And here we must be permitted to enter into an examination of a point which is of very great importance to the question in hand, as well to the whole question of Christian ethics, the investigation and decision of which, according to the truth of Christianity and Nature, we count absolutely necessary to a true Ethics—and this is the composition of that which we have called "Human Nature," as to its parts. The individual being that we call a man, of how many parts is his "Human Nature" compounded? "Of two," at once it is answered; and these two are "body and soul."

And they that give this answer undoubtedly will be very much astonished to learn that it is not so; that the two-fold division of Human Nature is not the one given in Holy Writ, but a three-fold division, and that that three-fold partition is not only in express terms made by an Apostle, but also uniformly observed; so that the division of man's nature is not into Body and Soul, but into "Body," "Animal Soul," and "Spirit," a division three-fold, not two-fold. "I pray God your whole spirit, (πνεῦμα, pneuma), and soul, (ψυχή, psuche), and body, (σῶμα, soma), be preserved blameless unto the coming of our Lord Jesus Christ."†

* This refers strictly to maniacs or monomaniacs, not to idiots.

† 1 Thess. v. 23. See upon this passage the commentary of the great Eng-

So that here the constituent parts of our nature are enumerated as three, as furthermore when we go through the Scriptures we find that there are in the original three adjectives derived from these three parts, employed to denote three different classes of men or natures, not two. If there were only two kinds of nature, the one "spiritual," under the influence of God's Spirit, and the other "totally depraved," as it is called, of course there would be only two, the "spiritual" and the "carnal," (pneumatikos and sarkikos). But there are three, (pneumatikos,) spiritual, (psuchikos,) animal, and (sarkikos,) carnal. "Carnal" being those who are under the dominion of the body and its lusts and desires; "spiritual," they who are under the Spirit of God ruling their spirit; and "animal," they who are as animals, are indifferent to all religious feeling, insensible and unawakened, with no spiritual perception and no spiritual feeling.

Having gone so far, we need not say that the doctrine which this treatise adopts, is that in Human Nature there are the *three* parts "Body," "Animal Soul," and "Spirit."* It remains to

lish theologian and saint, Dr. Henry Hammond, in Patrick, Lowth and Whitby. He calls this the *ancient and true* philosophy; shows that all the noblest heathen philosophers held it, and also that those eminent fathers of the Church, Clement, Origen, and Irenæus, were of the same opinion. He declares, too, that the conflict between the Spirit and the flesh cannot be understood without believing in an Animal Mind; and that the governing power in us cannot be comprehended except we suppose a spirit, an inferior animal soul, and a body—a tripartite existence in man. He furthermore shows how, because of following this mind of the flesh, the man is styled ψυχικὸς, the animal man; and the body, before the resurrection, is the "animal body," as after it is the "spiritual" body.

* Perhaps I may add to this another illustration. The Jewish commentators, some of them translate thus: [a]"And the Lord God formed man of the dust of the ground, and breathed into his nostrils *the breath of two lives,* (nephesh chayim,) and man became a living soul;" a translation of which the original is unquestionably susceptible.

This, then, will imply in man two principles of life; the one the psuchè, or animal soul, which he has in common with the beasts, the mere brute life, with the faculties that belong to it, and the other the spiritual life, which belongs to man peculiarly as a spiritual being. Original sin will thus be expressed as a mortal wound of the spiritual life, whereby the animal mind, with its desires, becomes enabled as against an enfeebled master, to become insubordinate. And thus the spiritual life in man is so diseased, that

[a] Gen. ii. 7.

apply these principles to the elucidation of the point in hand, of the Reason as a moral power, or the "Spiritual Reason," as we call it, in opposition to the "Understanding," or, as in this treatise we should choose to call it, the "Animal Mind."

Now taking it for granted that there are these three divisions— of "Body," "Animal mind," and "Spirit,"—man has the three, the beasts have the two. Whatsoever then we find in the beasts of mental power, that is in man also, this may be considered as belonging to them in virtue of the "Animal Mind;" and in man it is not as Spiritual, but as Animal,—but those powers which *man has* and *they have not*, these may be considered as peculiarly *spiritual.* The powers, then, on the one side of this line, we consider to belong to the "Animal Mind," the others to belong to the "Spiritual Reason."

Now we do not ask this matter to go upon speculation, we are content that it should go upon experiment. And we say this upon the best authority that, acccording to the experiments of the best natural philosophers, there is no operation of the mind that may not *in kind* (we do not say *in degree,*) be traced in the Animals, *save only moral ideas.* So far, then, have we gone closer to the real difference of the "Spiritual Reason," and the "Animal Mind;" the one deals with *moral ideas*, the other *is excluded from them.*

This deduction we have before established, but now we would limit it so as to express it more clearly in reference to the "Reason." We have before shown that there is an Animal Mind, and its functions we can determine by a consideration of the sphere from which its impressions are derived.

Now, when we look at the Universe, at once we feel and know that it is of two parts,—the one Corporeal, the other Spiritual,— the one Visible, and the other Invisible,—the one Finite, the other Infinite,—the one of the senses, the other above the senses. In one word, that there is a world material, corporeal, visible, in every way as to itself and its objects, limited in Space and Time: and that we will not say side by side with this world of sense, but

except the man receive healing from the Word, he will die the *second death,* undergo that unquenchable and unrevealable Death Eternal, which is the real death. the substance that, backward into the world of Time, casts that shadow that we call death.

co-existing along with it there is another world of things *unseen, incorporeal, spiritual.*

Of these two Worlds, their being and their co-existence, we offer no proof. The universal belief of all men, in all ages, is for it; the natural instinct of the heart of the youngest child, and the highest and surest persuasion of the broadest-winged intelligence, all unite in believing, all agree in asserting that man is a dweller in two worlds,—the world of the Senses, and that of the Unseen and Infinite.*

Not that God made a world material wholly and acting machine-like, and put man in it, shutting out the Spiritual and keeping it somewhere apart, (an idea or notion, upon which a great deal of modern education is founded,) but that with the Natural World actually and really the Spiritual World co-exists, (we use the phrase only in a figurative sense, in order to express that the impressions, sensations, emotions, and teachings from the one are just as many, just as great, just as close to us as from the other.) This Spiritual world co-exists with the Natural one, and as *man, one being,* lives in the one, so does he live in the other, an idea which is clearly the persuasion of universal human nature, and the doctrine of the Holy Scriptures.

True it is that man dwells in two Worlds, so that, applying to the Infinite appellations that belong to Space, and Time, and Body, and therefore are only figuratively correct, the Spiritual

* The Platonists make two worlds, "The world of the things of Sense," "The world of the things of Spirit." The Hebrews named the universe by two words implying the same thing, "heaven and earth,"—that is to say, the whole compass of the world, things spiritual and things earthly, they expressed by naming the two extremes. And not until Pythagoras, had the ancient Greeks any other name for the whole; he invented the word, "Cosmos," as a name for the universe, which we translate world, but really means "the harmonious whole." As identical with this phrase, "heaven and earth," the Greeks used also the words, "all things visible and invisible." This also is in St. Paul: "By him are all things created that *are in heaven* and *that are in earth, visible and invisible,* whether they be,"* &c. He speaks to the Jews in their phrase, to the philosophic Greeks in theirs, asserting to both that God is the creator of THE ALL.

And in the Nicene Creed we recognize the same distinction, that the created universe is composed of two parts, the "Spiritual world," and "the world of Sense," when we term God the Father, "Maker of *Heaven and earth,* and of *all things visible and invisible.*

Col. i. 16.

World is *here* and co-exists along with the visible world,—we dwell *in contact* with the one as with the other.

And as our unconsciousness in sleep of our relation to the one the material universe does not disprove, much less annul the fact of that relation, or of its existence; so our waking unconsciousness of the other will not disprove our being and existing in it, and our being influenced by it.

We have brought this forward and these views precisely at this time, because thereby the reason may be seen in the fact of man's external circumstances as a being *dwelling in two worlds* that *co-exist together*, for that other Scriptural doctrine of St. Paul as to the three-fold division of the nature into Body, Animal Mind, and Spirit. Dwelling in the World of Sense, manifestly his Body and his Animal Mind, these he has to deal with the objects of sense, its impressions, feelings and ideas; dwelling in a Spiritual World, his Spirit is the power by which he is fitted for this. This, then, we conceive, is that fact which lies at the bottom of the division we have given, and to which we adhere.

Hence then, those natural faculties, common to the animals and to man, and clearly shown so to be by natural science, these we consider to belong to the "Animal Mind," we call them the "Animal Reason," or, if the phrase be preferred, the "Animal Understanding,"—both which we shall thenceforth use technically or scientifically. And we shall now form our distinction that the Animal Mind embraces and deals with all ideas or notions derived purely and entirely from the senses,—all ideas that is, that are merely physical.

We know that Mr. Locke deduces* *all ideas* from the five senses and the reasoning power, internally "compounding," "comparing," "dividing," and so forth,—but how it has happened that the brutes, having the five senses and the reasoning† power, have not got the ideas of "God," and "freedom," and "immortality," and "law," and "worship," and "heaven," and "hell," and "conscience," having, according to Mr. Locke's notion, all the ways and means of getting them that man has, we do not see.

And *we do see* that all these ideas connected with the Infinite,

* See his "Essay on the Human Understanding."

† This has been distinctly proved by late naturalists,—"the same in kind, although not in degree,"—and is a fatal blow to that philosophy.

man receives first *from Society*, and *without examination*, upon a kind of natural faith dependent upon his inner being. Nor is there any man that has ever existed to whom the knowledge of these things has not been *conveyed* in *a language* existing before he came into being, and then received, as before mentioned, upon the faith of an inner nature.

Nothwithstanding, therefore, Mr. Locke, we believe in the existence of an "Animal Mind," which deals with the ideas derived by the senses from the world of sense, compounds, compares, divides, and which man has, in virtue of his being an Animal. And then, in another faculty in him, the "Spiritual Reason," which he has in virtue of his being a Spiritual Being, having a Spirit and existing in a Spiritual world. This divine endowment, then, we consider to be that which has to the Spiritual, Unseen, and Incorporeal, the same relation that the "Animal Mind" has to the world of sense. This the man has in virtue of his being a Spirit, as he has the other in virtue of being also an Animal.*

We thus make a broad distinction; the "Animal Mind" is that which deals with ideas and notions derived from the World of the Senses, ideas that are finite, sensible, material; and all these ideas upon examination shall be found to be in reference to Morality *purely indifferent*. This is the distinction that we here establish. The "Animal Reason," then, or "Understanding," this we by no means place among the ruling or governing powers, but the Spiritual Reason we do.

From the previous examination one question, doubtless, will arise to all our readers: "Seeing that the Divine Reason obtains not its ideas from the external visible world, from whence does it get them?"

The motto of this book, our reader will remember, is, "All things are double, one against another, and God hath made no-

* It may thus be seen that we do not believe with Locke, that all our ideas come *from material objects through the senses*. We believe they come from two sources, first, from the Spiritual world; and *from it*, either *through* the senses *by* the teaching of Society, or else *from it, without the medium of sense*, as is the influence of the Spirit upon our souls. And secondly, another class of ideas, those of the Animal Mind, come exclusively from the sense and material objects. The theory of Locke, therefore, in effect denies the existence of a Spiritual World and its connexion with man.

thing imperfect." If he look to our treatment of Conscience, he will find that we treat of the Conscience as twofold, and in and upon that doubleness rest the explanations we have given of it and their truth. With regard to the Spiritual Reason in man, he has seen the same principle in one way illustrated, and if he look again he may see the same in another.

Man, as an existence, is what we call a "fixed fact;" he in nature is not a fixed and determined fact, and all around the spontaneous and haphazard accumulation of accident, rubbish, and weeds, and waste, which the ceaseless tides of time and the current of circumstances have caused to accumulate around him. Not so—far from it; as Human Nature is the same in constitution through all ages, so is Society; as the *man* is a fixed fact, so *it* is. The picture is not a fact, and the frame a non-existence; the gem a fact, and the setting nothing; the ship a fact, and the river in which it sails nothing. Not so. Society, in its three forms, is the frame, the setting, the channel of Human Nature; no accumulation of waste rubbish, which is floating up and down by chance, but as true, and real, and fixed a fact as it is.

And now are we prepared to answer the question. Let our reader look backward in this volume,* he will find that Society serves a twofold purpose, that of supplying externally the Law and the knowledge of God and his attributes; that it is a channel whereby there is no man, even in the remotest countries, that is without His name.

"Whence, then, does the Spiritual Reason obtain originally its ideas of the Spiritual, the Infinite, the Unseen?" We answer, not from the five senses,† or any operation of the Animal Mind upon the ideas therefrom derived; not from any spontaneous rising up

* Book I. Chapter IV.

† There is a plain distinction to be noted here; an idea may come to me *through* the senses, and yet not *from* them; the one expresses that the senses are the channel merely of an idea which did not originate in them—the other that *they* or *material things* which they perceive, are the origin of it. The idea of "God," of "freedom," of "immortality," these are conveyed to me in a language the *words of which I hear—through* that sense, therefore—but not *from* it, but originating from the Spiritual world. The idea of green, the colour comes to me *through* sight, and *from* the objects of that sense originating in them. Again: the influence of the Spirit upon my spirit is neither *from* nor *through* the senses, yet causes in me, as I know by faith, which is "the sense of things unseen," very important ideas.

of these ideas in man's own mind, as some Philosophers have supposed, but from an original and primitive revelation of himself, the qualities of his being, made by God unto man. The qualities of God as a Spirit, down through the channel of Society are borne in language, that divine gift, and then by man as a Spirit, received and applied in virtue of his "Spiritual" reason.

This is the source and origin of these ideas, and let any man examine, by constructing logically a proposition which consists, as every one knows, of "subject" and "predicate," as, for instance, "man is just;" he shall find that to all ideas of the Spiritual Reason, God shall ever stand as the subject, and the idea as the "attribute," as "God is just," "God is holy," "God is true."

Nay, as before remarked, God shall be the substance in which is all the *essence* of each of these truths, and the idea shall be only a quality in man, but in God a reality.

For instance, "God is just," "God is holy," "God is true"—these assertions are *absolutely* and *without exception** true of God at all times and under all circumstances; but of man not so always. And of God they shall be so true as "that God is justice," is "truth," is "holiness," in a sense applicable to none but God.

These ideas, then, and all that the Spiritual Reason deals with of the "Infinite," the "Unseen," the "Spiritual," these are attributes of God's Nature. And being revealed by him to man, (man's existence as a Spiritual being in a Spiritual world rendering this possible,) are carried downward, through a channel made for this purpose, to each and every man. And thus, as all fires on earth have been lighted from the sun, so do all moral truths and and moral ideas come from God.† And the Spiritual Reason, this

* The test of these ideas is, that you may say of each of them "God is," and that of which you can truly say "God is," comes not from the World of Sense, but from the Spiritual World.

Another test there is of them; they are "necessary:" we know when we hear them that they are so, and must be so. For instance, the proposition "God is Good," this at once is seen to be "absolute," or necessary; it must be so, and is so, we at once confess it. But the proposition "man is good" is not so. The same proposition also in reference to God is "universal." "God is Good," there is no exception to this. To man it is not so. It will be seen, then, that these qualities of "necessity" and "universality" belong only to ideas coming from the Spiritual World.

† Of course by the very nature of the faculty this may be in a twofold way.

is the power in man's Spirit; or in other words, the spiritual faculty that perceives and applies to the whole being of man these moral ideas and moral laws, that spring from the very being and attributes of the Eternal God.

And these moral truths are not as some have dreamed, arbitrary enactments of an Omnipotent Will, making Good to be Good, and Evil to be Evil, because it is omnipotent, and able to make Good Evil, and Evil Good by its decrees; but Good is Good immutably, because God is Good, and Justice is just eternally, because God is just; and so of all the laws and facts of Morality, they are all immutable and eternal, as being facts of His eternal Being.

And here would I note, that in this view that notion of later moralists by which, when they see a moral instinct incapable of being analyzed, forthwith they make from it a "faculty," as some have a faculty or sense of "benevolence," of "justice," of "veracity," and so on, to the amount of as many moral ideas as they can find: all these belong to that one and the same power, the Spiritual Reason. Attributes they all are of God; and what these moralists call "senses of," are not at all senses, in the way at least that seeing is a sense, but rather the feeling of the one sense, the Spiritual Reason that is, of the eternal moral attributes of the Almighty, the realizing of them and the application of them by it.

And herein is the wonderfulness of the Spiritual Reason, that when by the will of God one of his attributes is to it revealed, it embraces that one so much with its whole nature, that of that it seems all formed and wholly composed; so much so that men shall talk of a "sense of veracity," of "justice," of "law," of "benevolence," of "holiness;" the whole truth being that in this one *manifold faculty* of the finite spirit, that peculiar attribute of the Infinite, is, as it were, mirrored.

And herein mainly do we consider that the ever-growing and ever-expanding progress of the blessed is to be found in the opening and revealing unto the Spiritual Reason of new and still newer

First, by the ordinary operation of the Spiritual Reason, whereby the teachings of Society through Law and Tradition, convey to man spiritual knowledge and spiritual ideas.

The second, whereby the power of the Holy Ghost, the influence of the Angelic Ministry and of the Communion of Saints, work upon our Spiritual Sense, and cause to rise up in us thoughts and ideas of Good.

moral attributes of God; and in the consequent awakening in the glorified man of what we should call new spiritual senses, and hence of ever new spiritual enjoyments.

So that attributes as much higher than the highest we can now feel or express of God, as these are higher than those of the Mosaic dispensation, and these again than those of bare natural religion, may be unveiled to us in eternity; and increasing knowledge and increasing love, hand in hand, may unceasingly ascend towards the loftiest throne of the inscrutable God.

This, then, the Spiritual Reason, the sense of the Unseen, the Incorporeal, the Infinite, I count to be in man that power that is peculiarly adapted to apprehend and feel the attributes of the infinite God as applicable to the finite man, as the mirror catches the image of the sun and reduces it to its own size, the proportion being yet retained; that which brings the Unseen to bear upon the Seen, and which, when awakened in us, is the faculty whereby we are bound to the Spiritual World. This, then, is peculiarly "*the moral sense*," seeing it is that that has in itself an unbounded aptitude for all moral ideas, all the aspects of His perfection that God may be pleased to reveal.

Nay, it would seem, therefore, that there is no perfection of His, no loftiness of Glory, no unrevealed splendor, but there is in the Spiritual Reason a feeling towards it, an instinct which, when the ray of new glory strikes upon it, shall open as a bud to the sun, so that "we shall be transformed from glory to glory."

And so in this, the divinest of the governing powers, in this consists the fact told us in the Scriptures, that we are made in the "image of God;" that in us finite beings, limited both in time and space, there is a faculty that reflects his attributes, and with manifold buddings forth and brightenings can be "after his likeness," eternally renewed with new knowledges constantly received, and new senses of them constantly arising in it.

This, that the "image of God in man" consists in his having "the Reason," is, however, not my private opinion or my argumentation, but the continued interpretation of the Universal Church. I invent it not, but only expound it.

At the same time there are certain moral dogmas that shall lead us to the conclusion if we assert them; and if we deny them, or any one of them, we shall deny the above conclusion. These are:

First. "That morality and its laws are eternal and immutable, not *factitious or arbitrary.*"

Secondly. "That the law and ideas of good originate in and are attributes of God, and are not *derived from outward objects of sense, or anything finite or corporeal.*"

Thirdly. "That the nature of man is the same in all ages, and does not *change from age to age.*"

Fourthly. "That there was a* Primitive Revelation of God to man."

Fifthly. "That Society is a fixed and established channel of moral law and moral knowledge."

And to these we may add, sixthly, "That language is not an invention of man, so that the primitive men were dumb, and gradually, from the grunts and screams and howlings of mere animals framed themselves that wonder—a language; but *that in itself it was the gift of God, and of his framing.*"

Now these six opinions are all taken for granted in that our elucidation as true,—drop one, and it falls.

Another observation will aid us very much to discern the importance of the Spiritual Reason in man. We have shown how this, in the peculiar and proper sense in which we have defined it, is that wherein the "image" consists, and so it was held by the Ancient Church universally; so that in reference to God, it is his image *in us;* and truly so since it reflects his attributes and applies the Spiritual, the Unseen, the Infinite to man, who is finite. This, then, is its relation unto God,—His image in man is the Spiritual Reason. Now in reference to the first faculty of man's nature, the Conscience, we have before made a remark that we give to it a personality different from our own, and that, especially, when we attribute unto it the high and supreme authority which Conscience has, we speak of it not as "I," but as another being commanding and ruling, by a legitimate and infallible sway, over that which every man understands when he says "I."

But with reference to the "Spiritual Reason," as an acute author has remarked, the Reason we consider to be our *personality;* the "I," it is *the exponent of our whole nature*, that which in action reveals the man, the *representative in action* of his nature.†

* For an exposition of the circumstances of this, see first Book.

† "But though each man's desires and affections belong specially to himself,

Having thus seen the relation of the Reason to the man, we go on now to examine its offices and operations; and by the description we have given of it we see that to perceive the ideas that we call moral is one of its offices, seeing that by means of it alone we receive them, and not from external nature. The second office is manifestly the retaining and keeping them in the mind as rules and laws and patterns after which to model our action: and the third is the applying them to our action.

Of these we shall at length enter into the examination, but previously to this discussion we would point out to our readers a critical remark of some interest. The attributes of God in the first are perceived, in the second they are retained in the Reason as "rules and models." Now models are in Greek ἰδέαι, (ideai); in us, then, these are ideas, ideai, models, after which to form our conduct. The Platonists transfer these ideas to God, and ask, are not these the "models" in the Eternal Mind after which he made the world? This I conceive to be a fair representation of the Platonic doctrine of "ideas," in their sense, and of its origin.

Again, the famous question of "innate ideas" herein is resolved by the same consideration, a question which, as it is discussed, is like the question as to whether the fire is in the flint or the steel: and which we answer in this way, that the "Reason" is in man the image of God, and *in it*, therefore, all ideas that are not of sense, but of the "Infinite," "Spiritual," and Eternal, are *innate* and *existent as germs*;* *but latent*, *the feeling*, *aptitude or instinct*, *rather than the idea*, so that of itself spontaneously, except the same idea in a definite external form be brought to the mind from without, it could never arise to consciousness. But when the Tradition and the Law, through the channel of Society, touches upon it, then, from the union of the two, the idea is consciously developed. The fire *is in* the flint, *it is not* in the flint; *it is in*

while Reason is a common faculty in all men, we consider our Reason as being *ourselves* rather than our Desires and Affections. We speak of Desire, Love, Anger as mastering *us*, or of *ourselves* as controlling them. If we decide to prefer some remote or abstract good to immediate pleasure, or to conform to a rule which brings us present pain, which decision implies the exercise of Reason, we more particularly consider such acts as our *own* acts. . . . . *We identify ourselves with our Rational part.*" Whewell, Elem. of Morality, vol. I. §§ 58, 59.

* This manifestly can be so only because man is made in the image of God, and only so far as he is so.

the steel, *it is not* in the steel,—but *from* the flint and the steel *together, it is.* This, then, we count the resolution of the problem of innate ideas.

Having thus touched upon these two questions, we shall now proceed to the examination of the powers of the Spiritual Reason, and their laws, in the next chapter.

CHAPTER II.

The Spiritual Reason.—Its Modes.—1st. Moral Perception; 2d. Moral Feeling; 3d. Moral Principle.—These established and illustrated.—*Mental* cultivation is different from moral, and cultivation peculiarly moral is necessary.—Is ever the Divine Spiritual Reason wholly undeveloped?—Answered in the affirmative.—The Reason may be developed consciously and unconsciously.

In our last chapter we have sufficiently established the existence of the faculty, which we have called the 'Spiritual' Reason. We have indicated its object in the attributes of God, manifested unto us as moral truths,—eternal and immutable truths,—brought to bear upon us by the channel of Society. We proceed to examine it a little more fully in reference to its action.

Now we have divided the operation of the Spiritual Reason in a triple way, and if we take all ideas whatsoever that belong to it, all that belong to the Infinite, the Spiritual, the Unseen, or, in other words, all those qualities of which we may say, "God is," for this is the formula that includes all the truths that are the objects of the Reason; if we take these in their action upon the mind, we shall find these modes exhaust that action,—"It is perceived," "It is felt," "It is held as a principle." These, then, we make the faculties of the Reason as regards the eternal truths of God,—"Moral Perception," "Moral Feeling," "Moral Principle," —three faculties or functions of the reason in man, by which he deals with truth.

Now at the very first we shall be met with the assertion, that this is strange that we should, as it were, assign in the mind a particular sense called "Moral Perception," as if one man did not perceive the value of a Moral Truth as well as another. With reference to this, we say that it is so; that take any two men, one man shall hear the assertion, or make it, that "God is good," or that "man ought to be benevolent," or any other of the same kind of assertions in the same way, as a man in a dream speaks or hears. He shall say that they are true, just as he shall say it is true that "twice two are four." Nay, he may be able to talk about it and argue on it ingeniously and eloquently, but this shall be in an outside, unimpressive, unimpressed, and unrealizing way, —a way not realizing his theme *as a truth intimately suited to his nature,—not feeling it as of any importance,*—not applying it *as a living law of life.*

We have known, we say, men purely and entirely selfish, *so far* as God will permit man to be so, that had been taught in our Colleges that most destructive doctrine, that "Enlightened Selfishness is the main and only principle;" and we have seen their perception as to their own interest, tremblingly alive,—watching, with a prophet's eye, the slightest gloom over their horizon,—guarding, with an intense sensibility, against the remotest annoyance,—searching with microscopic vision for the smallest addition to personal comfort; we ask, have not these men an intense "Perception" *of self-interest* and *self-gratification,*—an intense "Feeling" of *self,*—have they not? and a fixed and set "Principle" of *self,* guiding their conduct?

And, then, let us try them with regard to any moral idea. They have, as to it, no Moral "Perception," only a *verbal,* or *logical,* or a merely *mental* one. They are like Gallio, who understood Greek as a learned Roman, and Law as a wise governor, and heard St. Paul and the Jews disputing about the highest truths of religion, and thought them "words and names," having no realities to correspond; or, like the acute heathen philosophers, who thought that St. Paul preached certain new deities, because he preached to them "Jesus and the resurrection," taking undoubtedly, as St. Chrysostom remarks, "Jesus" for one new God, "Resurrection" (Anastasis,) for another.

This is the aspect such men turn to Moral Truth,—an aspect wholly unperceptive, insensible, frozen, dead, because they have merely a *verbal perception,* while towards self, or ambition, or money, their apprehension is endued with the keenest sensibility.

Again, this their object, or passion, or feeling, shall dwell upon their mind anxiously,—their thoughts naturally shall run that way, —their feelings gather themselves around it as a nucleus of emotion,—perpetual meditation shall consecrate it, and all moral subjects shall be unthought of, unfelt, unregarded. This desire shall be a living spring of action perpetually at work; consciously, so that the man knows and feels it himself; and also unconsciously, so that others feel and know it when he does not,—a *principle*, in other words an *energic spring of action*, ever at work, when no moral truth, no moral principle ever abides with them as a motive power.

Now we have given examples as to immediate deadness of the mind as regards moral truth. And we say, that if we consider any moral truth in these three modes,—if we look to one class of men and then to another, the one shall be found to hear a moral truth announced in words, to apprehend the meaning of the words *logically*, *mentally*, *verbally*, yet to have no living and realizing sense of its value,—no feeling of its worth,—in short, no perception of its relation and connection with themselves. While to the other, the words convey a truth which the individual apprehends as precious and valuable as his very existence; and the very knowledge of which will seem, as it were, to cast a glory over all nature, and a new light over heaven and earth,—to disclose a thousand secrets and a thousand mysterious ties that bind us to all men,—to open and awake in our being new founts and sources of joy that before had been hidden.

These are effects that each one perhaps in the world, at one time, has recognized in himself or in others,—a process that is perpetually going on; either the man becoming hard, and cold, and dead morally, or becoming more and more sensitive to good.

The power of Moral Perception is as much a power and faculty as that of Sensation, or that of Memory. Its objects are as definite, its action as manifest. We consider it to be determined, and we shall give rules and laws for its exercise when we have sufficiently determined the other two modes of the Spiritual Reason.

The first, then, of the faculties of the Spiritual Reason we consider Moral Perception to be—and we define it to be the "Spiritual apprehension of the immutable truths of Morality."

The second mode of the Spiritual Reason, Moral Feeling, is very hard, indeed, to define, or bring clearly out in words, so that one should be able to recognize it as a moral faculty. Still let the man who has ever felt a spiritual truth or apprehended it, let him reflect, and he shall see that when once it has been spiritually apprehended, it seems as if in the Inner Nature there were a hidden Treasure-house* wherein it is stored up as a peculiar treasure and a possession. It seems that therein the soul dwells with it, and delights in it, and feels it to be a particular and precious acquisition, and rejoices over it. And when the man walks abroad, he recurs to it again and again, with perpetual and constant reiteration of thought, as to a something that comes to him *from without*, which he can feel and know to have become his own, and yet cannot reveal in its fulness to others.

In fact, each Moral Apprehension of the kind I have above specified becomes to the man an internal spring of action and life, independent altogether of outward things, which is to him, if he only avail himself of it duly and properly, what a new sense, unawakened before, would be as regards this external world.

We may not be able precisely to define this thing; but take one man, and you shall find him speak falsely in such a way as to show that he has no sense or feeling of truth. Take another man, who has once, in the way we have spoken of, *apprehended morally* the value of Truth, and enquire of him and he will tell you, it may be in a very confused and indistinct manner, and yet sufficiently brought forth to declare the truth of this our exposition, "that the *feeling* of *truth dwells*, he knows not how, in his being—that it is a new element, as it were, of his nature, which he constantly recurs to with affection, and loves it, and struggles to retain the perception as keenly as at first he felt it."

And so shall you find to be the case with the mind of man as regards all of these that we have defined as Moral Ideas—after he has spiritually apprehended them there is a faculty of the Reason that *retains them, as it were, internally*—the faculty of Moral Feeling.

The third mode of the Divine Reason, which we proceed to define, is Moral Principle—a thing very easily understood in fact, but very difficult, as all these are, to explain in words. But let us take an illustration. Suppose a man to make up his mind that he

* This is the Synteresis, or "Spiritual Treasury in the soul," of the ancient moralists, that faculty of holy contemplation and meditation, whereupon mainly the ripeness and mellowness of Christian character depends.

will attain wealth, and to make this the supreme end of his conduct, without any other rule. There is, we will say, in a neighbouring bank an immense amount of specie; he could lay a plan and rob that bank, and become immensely wealthy; he does not do so, *because* "the chances are so great that he will be detected, imprisoned, become infamous, and be prevented thereby from attaining the object of his wishes," and *so he does not so;* but he *would do so* if he were *absolutely, entirely certain* that he would escape, that he would thereby attain the wealth he desires, and keep it. *That man does not act from moral principle,* but from *policy.* His merit is as great, his moral deserving as much, as that of the wolf who refuses the bait upon the trap which he has seen take his brother wolf.

Again: you shall see another man, who having apprehended a moral truth, having had it established as a feeling, has it also in his Mind as a *rule of action,* that is not altered by any external consequences that may take place, that holds it as a principle—a "principium," or "beginning" of action, before and antecedent to which there stands no motive but itself; which is of itself a fundamental motive, that is not based upon any other; an ultimate rule that decides all disputed points; a measure which measures all actions, and is itself measured by no consequences.

Such, to the man of moral principle, is "honesty," "justice," "purity," "veracity," or "mercy." Because he has realized them as principles, he loves them for themselves, not merely for the good they may bring him. And if a time come when they bring evil, still he loves them, and acts upon them the more. For the treasure of a moral principle, first apprehended, then realized as an inward principle, and then applied to action as a law of life, is an inward wealth that countervails and outweighs all earthly gain or loss. This many men have felt and acted upon—many men, many women, and many children. This constitutes moral principle; this, and *nothing less than this.*

And we shall find many such persons in this world, men that shall take a principle, because of itself, and suffer no accumulation of profits, no pile of temptations, no assurance of impunity to move them; but in little things, in great things, that shall move onward measuring all things external by their internal Law, or Rule, or Principle, saying, "Thus I do because it is honest; it is just; it is pure; it is true, or it is merciful." Is

there not a difference between the one person and the other—a plain difference, and easily tested?

This the old Christian Moralists called the "Spiritual Law," as the other they called the "Spiritual Treasury," and thus I consider that this mode of the reason is most manifestly and distinctly established.

These, then, are the three modes of the Spiritual Reason: "Moral Perception, Moral Feeling, and Moral Principle."

Having, then, specified these three modes as to their operation, we shall now proceed further on in the consideration of the subject. The faculty itself has been established. The modes of its operation, and the object upon which it is employed, as well as the channels through which that knowledge that is its object awakens it in man, have been shown. Various observations, then, of the highest importance are here to be made.

In the first place, from our examination it is manifest that *mental* cultivation is not cultivation of the Spiritual Reason, but there may exist a very high and complete degree of cultivation merely mental, in conjunction with the most neglected and uncultivated state of the Spiritual Reason. A man may be a most complete Geometer, or Mineralogist, or Botanist, or Chemist, with his powers of observation trained to the utmost acuteness of perception, and his mental power, as far as these sciences are concerned, highly exercised, and yet in the higher qualities of the Spiritual Reason be more of a brute than an inhabitant of Caffraria, or a native of New South Wales or New Zealand; because all these sciences, when reduced to the simplest elements, are founded exclusively upon the ideas of the Visible, the Corporeal, and the Seen, the objects, that is, of the senses; and upon the Understanding or faculty that deals with the ideas derived from the senses, not upon the High Spiritual Reason, does proficiency in them depend.

We say, then, with reference to what are called the "Exact Sciences," and the "Sciences of observation," that a training in them does not *necessarily* awaken the Spiritual Reason in the slightest degree, or exercise in any way its powers. We say not that it is adverse any more than we say that any other exercise of the *mental powers* is adverse, but merely that increasing the *mental powers*, it leaves the *moral power* wholly unexerted and unexercised so far *as itself goes*.

And he that shall send his son to a school wherein his *mental*

UofM

powers are trained in the very fullest way, and expect that by reason of that training his *moral powers* shall be educated, without a *direct training addressed* to *them*, that man has mistaken the very nature of things. To call forth muscular power, you exercise the muscles; to give strength to the lungs, you train them; enfeebled powers of voice are strengthened by exercise and training directly applied to its organs: how absurd, then, the notion that you add to the Moral Powers *by utterly neglecting them*, and attending wholly to those powers that *are exclusively mental!*

Teach the youth the Law of the Conscience, the first great step in morality. Teach him how he must act in obedience to it at all risks; then point out to him its nature, and the progress he shall make heavenward if he will only follow it. Teach him then the law of the Spiritual Reason and its nature; supply him with the food for that faculty whereby man is in the "image of God." Point him out the nature of the Affections, and the holy balm for misery and sorrow that lies in them, the glory and the light from heaven shed upon the meanest hut by them; the awful consequences that arise from their perversion. Then instruct him in the power of the Will, the energy residing in that spring of power. Point out to the youth all this. Say to him, "this is in thee; all these powers and all these possibilities are in thee, by thyself to be called out and exerted." And then show to him how the Heavenly is a supplement of the Earthly; how the pillar let down from heaven unites with that which springs up from the earth; that not a want, not a weakness, not a misery, not a deficiency of our Human Nature but has its fulness, its strength, its joy, its sufficiency in the Divine Nature of God the Word, who became Flesh for us. This, methinks, would be a direct moral training.

In short, I plainly say this, that in order morally to educate, you must not trust to mental education, you must educate morally. You must instruct in two things, which constitute together moral education, and directly develope the Spiritual Reason. The first of these is Christian Ethics, the "Science," as I have defined it, of "Man's Nature and Position:" and the second, that which is the crown and complement of this, "Religion."

And furthermore, the education in these two must not be Mental, but Moral and Religious; not "*discussions*," "*proofs*," "*essays*" upon "prayer," "hope," "good works," but *prayer*, *hope*, *good works done;* for mental discussings are not *religious works done:*

not *discussions*, *proofs*, *essays* upon *conscience*, *reason*, the *will*, and so forth,—but direct and immediate action and training in the individual of these, the "governing" or moral powers. This I count a distinction of the deepest importance, that "the Mental Powers may be occupied *about the Moral Powers, or moral subjects derived from them*, and the moral powers be at the same time utterly unexercised." And teachers should most exceedingly be on their guard lest at the very time they think they are the most educating the *moral* powers, the *mental* powers only may be engaged. A direct exercise of the *mental* powers is necessary to give *mental* strength, so is a direct exercise of the *moral* powers to give *moral* strength.

This discussion I have introduced here because here is the most appropriate place for it; and he that shall look back and consider the nature of the Animal Mind or Understanding, and then shall think upon the Spirit and its faculties, of which, as the first is Conscience, so the most cultivable is the Spiritual Reason, he shall see very plainly and manifestly the cause why it is here introduced.

Another question concerning this faculty and its modes, is very interesting, that is to say, "Can this faculty of the higher reason be wholly undeveloped in any one?" The answer is, "not in any one that is in Society;" for this, in its various organizations, is the channel of "law" and of moral "knowledge" that awakens in each and every one in Society, that is, in every one *that speaks a language*, the Spiritual Reason more or less. Men, in order to be brutes, in whom the image of God is not, must be retained apart from *all* society, *all* language; apart from the Family, the Nation, and the Church, that they may be as the beasts are. And then the Animal shall be dumb, without language, with the cunning of the brute, and without the Spiritual Reason. The idea of Pleasure and Pain it shall have as the brutes; these shall be its whole motives, and from them shall come its various notions. But the ideas that are the objects of the moral power, as Truth, Mercy, Justice, Benevolence, all these of which we may say "God is," of all these it shall have no idea, the sense of them never shall have been awakened: for Society it is that is the channel of these ideas by which they are carried to each individual, and awaken in him the Spiritual Reason, whether he will or not. But in the case we have supposed, it shall be as the eyesight which from birth has

been unexcited by the light, when it should have been excited, and is therefore dead and perished.

This is the only case in which such a thing can be; but for the man who is in Society, the circumstances of his position and the effect of its schools, will even unconsciously develope in him, to a more or less degree, the Spiritual Reason.

From this comes a question most exceedingly interesting, it is this: "Can moral truth be learned unconsciously, *without our knowing that we learn it?* Can the moral faculty be developed in us *without our knowing* that it is so?" A question this is, that is most deeply important. It would seem, from the above example, that it can be so. And when we look at the Principle of Imitation, implanted as it is in man's nature, when we consider how far Sympathy leads—when we see how much the men of a nation, even those that strive the most against it, are formed and moulded into the National Character, we may be inclined to consider that it is perfectly possible that the Spiritual Reason should be capable of development, by means whereof the individual is utterly unconscious that they are means, or even that they have any influence at all upon himself or any other.

And herein do I consider a most important difference to exist between the Conscience and the Spiritual Reason,—that in reference to the Conscience, we must be "conscious" and know our own act in order to profit by it; but with reference to the Reason, *first*, we may act upon it ourselves Consciously; and *secondly*, others without our knowledge may act upon it, and form it in us of their purpose and knowledge, without our being conscious of it.

And so the man who, with fixed mind, has trained himself in the practice of the truths of Eternal Morality, he may go forth into the world knowing the Inner Treasure and the Inner Law he possesses, and feel himself rich in them. And not less rich may he be who, from the example of a Holy Home, from his sympathy with pious relatives, and the practice of religion, has developed his moral powers *unconsciously*, by *moral action*,—learning moral truth by acting upon it, and *being taught so to act*, and yet not knowing it as teaching, or conscious of it as such, until brought in contact with temptations to the contrary evils. This to the young is no small blessing.

But with regard to the modes of training and developing the Spiritual Reason, we purpose to resume the discussion in the next chapter.

CHAPTER III.

There are two states, one of Consciousness another of Unconsciousness.—To exhaust man's Consciousness is not to know all his nature.—Unconscious teaching of moral truth exemplified.—Moral application of this and grounds of it.—The Reason may receive Spiritual teaching from Spiritual beings unconsciously.—Cultivation of the Reason produces, first, Moral Harmony, secondly, Moral Progress.—Moral teaching of Parents.—Viva voce teaching, its power.—The Spiritual Reason awakes before the Mental Power is ripe.—Spiritual truth may become a family inheritance.—Application to Parents and to Children.—Cultivation of the Reason in ourselves.—Perfection of the Reason.

The question of the modes of exercising the Reason, this is to be the object of the present chapter. This we account to be one of the most important in all the range of Christian Science. We have shown that the Reason, in one respect, is certainly awakened unconsciously, which we count enough to enable us to go on and advance farther upon the subject.

Now first, we will remark that in the life of man there are two states, alternating the one with the other, the state of Consciousness and the state of Unconsciousness; the one corresponding generally to the time when the hemisphere which the individual inhabits is presented to the sun, the other to that when its face is withdrawn; waking corresponding with the light, sleeping with the darkness. We are Conscious in the one, Unconscious in the other. These two are separate and distinct states of being, each of them truly and really belonging unto man, each being a portion of the circle of his existence.

The Germans, then, in their examination of nature and mind, start upon a ground entirely wrong when they say, "when we have exhausted that which *is in man's consciousness*, then we see the whole of his mind and the whole of his nature." Herein they blunder,—for because his "Consciousness" contains a great deal, his "Unconsciousness" does not therefore contain *absolutely nothing*. The negation of knowledge about it does not imply non-being in it. On the contrary, it is a state, a very peculiar state, and one which may be seen to be necessary for our physical being; and which, as nature is one, may also be very fairly considered as having, if we only could adequately discern it, in itself a necessity for our mental and moral nature. And so it may possess peculiarities of mental action,—of moral and spiritual impression and emotion, which, if we only could know them, would be of the greatest value in explaining the mysteries of our being. But as we cannot know them by Consciousness, or, indeed, by anything else than by vague speculation on facts that can hardly be systematized, we will not press this thought any further than merely to assert that the philosophy that says, "there is nothing in man's nature that is not in man's Consciousness," and that "to exhaust our consciousness is to give a complete view of mind," is and must be false.

For men have gone to rest with the determination to awake at a certain hour, and their minds, unconscious, and by no action of which they were cognizant, has, in their sleep, measured time, and at the appointed hour has awakened them. Students have retired with their mind set upon a lesson half-learned, and have awakened with it wholly understood. Nay, as in a case specified by Rollin, the anxious mind, without the knowledge of the individual, has awakened his body, and he has gone through the whole process of composing a copy of Latin verses set him as a task, as well as through all the bodily labor of dressing himself, looking for his desk and pens and ink, and writing; and in the morning he has been utterly unconscious of it.

Many other facts might be brought forward to show the fallacy of the German fundamental, that "we are to search in our consciousness for a complete account of our being;" and to show that the state of unconsciousness, instead of being a *state of blank negation*, is a *state of mystery*, in which most certainly the nature of man, physical, mental, and spiritual, is at all times *alive* and capable of receiving impressions, and unquestionably is many times actively and energetically at work when we know it not. A full and complete account, then, of man's mind could be given only by cataloguing and classifying the phenomena that occur, first, in the mind when it is "conscious," and secondly, when it is "unconscious." And as the mind of man is regular, and his nature one, we may not doubt that as we call one set of waking mental actions "Memory," and another "Reasoning," and another "Sensation," so if we could penetrate the "Unconscious" state of our neighbor's mind, we should see belonging to that state peculiar modes of action and impression and feeling needing to be classified by new names and a new Terminology. And therein we should see how it comes to pass that all theories of dreaming, &c., are so imperfect, being solely the applying to one state of mind of those terms and laws applicable not to it, but to the contrary one ; and we should learn, at least, in the absence of all means of penetrating into the "Unconscious" state, to be a little more cautious in theorizing.

But more than this, we assert that there is in this world, even in the waking man, a state in which the individual is taught, and taught in the most efficient and powerful way, moral principle and moral truths unconsciously to himself; and that *acting first*, he then learns, *after he has for a long time acted*, the truth and ground of action.

We look upon the child taken by his parents to the house of God, and there, by the principles of Sympathy, Imitation, and Habit, acting as others do, and feeling as others feel, to be thereby learning principles without knowing it, which years after he may apply consciously, with full knowledge of their value.

We look upon the father, with his rightful authority, the natural respect that he claims, and natural obedience he enforces ; and the mother, with her maternal love and her sympathy and counsel, as both of them thereby guiding their children constantly into action, and habitual action, of which the children cannot fully see the principle and consequences ; and yet by action so enforced upon them, they plant in them that principle in their nature, so that it really exists : and thus children receive moral and religious teaching of which they are perfectly unconscious. We look, too, upon the Nation as teaching in the same way, unconsciously ; the citizen, from earliest childhood, being trained to act in certain ways and habits and modes of thought that are exclusively national, by means of habit, sympathy, national pride, and all those influences which are comprised in what we call the Spirit of the nation. The Family frames and moulds the child ; the Nation frames and moulds the citizen, at a time when he is perfectly unconscious of that teaching; nay, when he is incapable wholly of judging or of exerting his mental powers, we will not say against it, but in any way. The fact is a plain one, and we cannot get rid of it. It is a fact of the moral position of man.

Another fact is equally plain in Morals. Get a man to act, and act habitually, so that his actions shall *imply a principle, although he does not know it*, and that shall prepare him for the acknowledgment of the principle. This is a fact realized by every one, *so that there is indeed a moral teaching that is unconscious, as well as a moral teaching that is conscious.* The justice and grounds of this I shall now proceed to examine, and they rest on these facts.

First. That "moral truths are the eternal facts of God's nature, not factitious or arbitrary notions, but the same for all, and immutable."

Secondly. That "man has a faculty made expressly for the reception of these truths, which corresponds to them as does the bodily appetite to food."

And thirdly. That "there are peculiar institutions organized to teach them, for that express purpose—the Family, the Nation, and the Church, the teachers of which schools teach with *an authority* which they possess by *their very situation*, and are heard with a reverence and obedience which are in their pupils by virtue of *their* position."

This, then, I say, that Parents *in their houses*, in all their actions, are teachers; unconsciously often to themselves, unconsciously, at the same time, to their children. The Family is a school in which, of the father that is holy and good and true, of the mother that is affectionate and loving, there is not an act, not a word, not a perceptible emotion that does not teach; not a command to a child to act in this way or that, *even although that child does not understand the principle of the action*, that is not a teaching of that principle; and that this is so because of the nature of the things taught, because of his nature in relation to them, and because of the nature of the institution.

There is, then, a peculiar work intended to be done by certain and peculiar workmen, and *not by others.** And this is a work that nature gives to one class of workmen, the training in religion and

* There is another religious training of the young in the *definite and distinct doctrines* of the Faith by the *Clergy* in the *Church.* Of course this is

morality of the child by the Father and by the Mother in the Home; and it is capable of being done *until the age of maturity;* and is done by *none else as it is by them.*

Pious Father and pious Mother, look to this! There is an influence, a power, an authority *you* have, *by your position*, over *your children*. *You* can give it or delegate it to none. No amount of talents, or learning, or educational ability, or personal holiness can give to another, who is *not their Parent*, the power that *you* have by your position as parent. Although your lips may stammer and your knowledge be small, still *from you* to *them* (this is the rule by nature) a word shall be as a kindling flame, as an awakening trumpet, as the voice of doom, as the infallible oracles of God. A gesture shall teach, a glance of the eye be remembered for a life-time, an action bidden implant a principle.

For the *parent* in his *home*, *teaching* and *acting* upon God's *laws*, has *authority* which none else has, and which he can transfer to none else. And in the heart of the child there is a *power*, the Spiritual Reason, whose food this teaching is, and which is adapted so to receive it.

And upon this ground, the ground of the Spiritual Reason and its peculiar powers, we warn parents, whoever may be the teacher of their children in other things, themselves to take a share in the religious and moral education of their own children at home; for they by their position, by the nature of Divine Truth, and the faculty that receives it, can do what none else can do, and teach as none else can teach.

And the same we say with regard to the *Magistrate*—his position is a natural position of *authority;* the position of the ordinary citizen towards the Magistrate is by his very situation a position of obedience *to him as the executor of the Law.* The Magistrate's actions, therefore, unconsciously teach; the acts he does have in themselves a significance that is powerful to the heart of men, that awakens in them knowledge and principle. And none can take the *Magistrate's* place, none can do the work he has to do, and make the impression that he has to make but himself. And this not simply because "*we the majority will support him*," but because of his

not excluded by the assertion in the text. A series of similar remarks may be made upon it, as to its teachers, its faculty, and its material of instruction. The student may follow this hint out for himself position, and the nature of that position in a divine organization, the State, which cannot fail.

But we shall follow this out still further. Our reader will remember that the "Animal Understanding" is especially the sense of the Visible, of those perceptions that come from the senses, and of the ideas that are derivable from them, that the Reason is the faculty of the "Unseen," the "Infinite," the "Spiritual," these which are not perceptible by the senses. Let him then think that close by us is the "Spiritual World"; that in it we live, and that in it besides facts that are Spiritual, there are *beings* and *persons* that are so also. Then may he think that the faculty of the Unseen may receive instruction from Him who is Unseen and them who are Unseen, and thus unconsciously the faculty of the Infinite be taught by those who do not exist in Time and Space; the things of Eternity and Immortality be taught to us by beings eternal and immortal, directly acting and influencing us immediately, and yet not felt consciously; the faculty of the Spiritual from Spiritual beings draws Spiritual sustenance.

Sincerely do I believe that moral teaching, yea, that moral teaching which is the very highest and most effective, may be unconscious, when I see that the highest agencies to which we are handed over by our Baptism in the Church of God are invisible; that their instructive influence, working upon us most decidedly and most effectually, is yet wholly imperceptible to the senses, and incapable of being brought to direct Consciousness.

By this train, therefore, of argument and elucidation, I consider that I am sufficiently authorized to divide moral instruction of the Reason into the "Conscious" and the "Unconscious."

Having thus come so far, it would, perhaps, be good to enter into an examination of the modes of teaching; but there are other preliminary questions to be investigated previous to entering upon this. And these are, first, "the effect of a development of the Reason upon man." And secondly, the actual state in which Reason is by means of "Original Sin."

The first of these questions, therefore, we shall first examine, that is, the effect of a development of the Spiritual Reason upon the mind and character of the individual man. Now, we have shown that the Reason is, as it were, the mirror of God in man, so that as the image of the sun is reflected in the mirror and reduced, so in the finite man does the Reason receive the image of

God, and confer upon that which is finite the proportion of the Infinite.

And secondly, that in the Reason awakens by cultivation the sense of God's attributes, which in him are the glorious realities of His being, and to us are the eternal and immutable laws of morality. The two effects, then, I conceive of a cultivation of the Reason to be, first, the establishment in the man of "Moral Harmony"; and second, a constant and perpetual Moral Progress in him, a constant and increasing advance in all things that are like unto God.

And the measure of these is in no standard established by the Society wherein we live, or by our own opinion, nor by the Reason itself; but solely in God and his Eternal Attributes, the standard is whereby we measure our advance.

And though our Nation should establish another, and by an unanimous decree assert it though philosophers should prove and demonstrate it in the most eloquent and convincing way; still the invariable institutions of Society, and the instinctive feeling of man's Reason, shall manifest to him that of the "Moral Harmony" in the man, and of his "Moral Progress," there is no other model,—no standard, no means of advance, other than God and His Law.

With regard to this which I have called "Moral Harmony," when a man calmly and considerately looks at his own moral nature, he shall see that the first stirring of which we call the Spiritual Reason in him by nature, was the sense and feeling of the want of "Moral Harmony" in all his powers of Body, Soul, and Spirit,—the sense and feeling of the want (not merely deficiency, which is one kind of want, or desire, which is another want, but both together,) of an inner proportion of the facts of his whole nature; a feeling of incongruity and disjointedness, in which, recognizing clearly that there are in him the elements of one harmonious unity, he feels that these elements are all in a state of chaos,—a threefold feeling that his nature *has a law*, and *is not yet obedient* to that law, but *ought so to be.*

This feeling of Insubordination, there is no man that has not felt, the aspiration it is after unity of action in our nature, or what we have called "Moral Harmony." The feeling is one that arises in almost all, and as the "sense of Responsibility" is the peculiar and instinctive feeling of the first of the governing powers, the "Conscience," so this is that peculiar to the Spiritual Reason. The one says, "Oh! that I could abstain from that which is evil, and which my conscience tells me to be so, then should I be good,"—the other says, "Oh! that my nature in thought, and word, and deed, in body, soul, and spirit, were ruled by one LAW, its own inner law, then should my nature be as it ought to be."

And then this feeling of the want of Law from internal searching, turns the mind externally, and everywhere to the man the same lesson is repeated. Society speaks to him of Law: all things that meet his eye or his mind, suggest Law, Proportion, Harmony of manifold parts, working in unity of end and object. The most ignorant and uneducated sees it and acts upon it, and the deepest natural philosopher, the further he goes the more he feels the presence in all things of Law. In man's nature only seems to be the want of it, and this is combined in him with the deepest estimation of its uses and its necessity.

Now to him who shall ask wherein the Reason in man is affected by Original Sin, or wherein it manifests itself, let him look at this desire of Moral Harmony, this sense of its want, this desire towards it, and this exceeding conviction of its necessity; and then let him consider, at the same time, the internal conviction that the healing power is not in or of man's own nature,—there he shall find Original Sin in the first of its effects upon the Reason. He shall find that that faculty, which ought clearly and distinctly to reproduce in man, the finite creature of clay and the dust, the moral proportions, if I may use the phrase, of the Infinite and Immortal God, and thereby rule by His Law all elements of man's being;—this divine faculty is reduced to the state of natural inability, which I have before illustrated.*

Again, the consequence of a cultivation of the Divine Reason from the previous examination, our reader shall see to be an awaking, as it were, of his "Moral Apprehension," his "Moral Feeling," and his "Moral Principle," to the truths of God's Being as eternal truths of morality. He looks and sees the very word awaking,—implies previous blindness to those truths,—he can see also that by nature, apart from Society, man's blindness was total,

* With regard to "Insubordination of Natural Powers," and "Moral Inability," as effects of Original Sin, see the First Book.

and that even in man existing in Society, there is more or less blindness or insensibility, even to the most striking and the most convincing truths. The exemplification of this, the reader will find under the articles upon "Moral Apprehension," "Moral Feeling," and "Moral Principle." The effect, then, of "Original Sin" upon our Reason, may be put down as secondly, "Moral Blindness," or the incapacity of the mind in our present fallen state for *apprehending*, *feeling*, and *applying to action* moral truths.

We are now prepared to enter upon the question of the means of cultivation of the Spiritual Reason, the subjects previously discussed having been, as the reader may see, absolutely and entirely necessary to the examination of it. There are manifestly in this, two distinct divisions,—the cultivation of it in ourselves first, and then in others,—these, for the most part, we shall discuss together.

Now, according to the principles above stated, the most efficient and most perfect teaching, is that of the Teaching Institutions, embracing, as we have shown, instruction so completely in its whole circle, that even acts not meant to teach, yet shall teach. So that the Father and the Mother, the Magistrate, the Clergyman, these of the Reason in the Family, the Nation, and the Church, are the best Moral Teachers,—teaching *consciously*, and also teaching *unconsciously*.

The power of their conscious teaching, seeing it is addressed to a *peculiar* faculty, which is adapted to receive *peculiar* truths, *peculiarly* apprehended, manifestly shall depend upon their having themselves *those truths, so apprehended*, and *so addressing them*.

Let the father, for instance, as a matter *of feeling* and *of faith*, with his heart and soul apprehend the fact that "God is," and that truth so apprehended seems, because of *his* feeling and faith, easy to be spiritually apprehended by the child. The same truth addressed, without any apprehension on the father's part, shall make no impression upon the spiritual power of Moral Apprehension, whatever it may upon the mental faculty.

Again, we shall find that of the "Conscious Teaching" of parents the truth must be *peculiar*. There shall be no difference between the teaching of the parent in Arithmetic and the teaching of any one else in the same; but there shall be a vast difference, admitting both to be in earnest, in matters of Religious Faith. Therein the parent, as we have noted, *shall teach by a word what others cannot by the labor of a day.*

And truths of the Gospel shall have a capability of being taught, that falsehoods have not; for instance, that God is most merciful, or that there is an eternal punishment: this the parent shall teach the child easily, but "that God, *for his mere will and pleasure*, pre-doomed, irrevocably, an unborn man, millions of years before his birth, to eternal hell, and *that for his own glory*,"—this notion shall very hardly be taught by parent to child, because it is so far from being a truth of the Eternal and Infinite God, that it is utterly contradictory to all we know of God, and utterly abhorrent to His nature.*

Again, they must be addressed to the *peculiar* power suited for their reception, not to any other. A mere assertion on the part of father or mother of an eternal and immutable truth in which he or she earnestly believes, *in love* to the child, this, as before noted, shall convey that truth to the Spiritual Apprehension of the child: let them set themselves to *prove* it, as Paley does, to *demonstrate* it, and then they address to the *mental* powers that which should be addressed to the spiritual faculties, and the immediate effect is to close the mind against it.

To complete these remarks upon the "Conscious Teaching" of the Parent, I shall adduce one or two other things that, from my own observation, I have noticed; and the first is, that "in instruction of a moral kind from parent to child, there is *an extraordinary power in 'vivâ voce' teaching above all book instruction;*" so much so, indeed, that it would almost seem that the same truths, in the same words, *being taught by reading*, lose the power of being morally felt and apprehended, and *being spoken*, have it —as if divine truth could be conveyed in its fulness only by the living voice of affection and faith. But that the being read, in

* These extreme and harsh notions, preached of old by that peculiar class called Supralapsarians, are not, I believe, held now by almost any of the very respectable denominations that call themselves "Calvinistic." They have modified the system by other elements, and soothed and softened such asperities as this is. In fact I believe the bold and harsh declaration in the text is such that it could only be made hundreds of years ago, in a foreign land, by men frenzied with Papal persecution, and fighting vehemently against Papal man-worship, and Romish ideas of human merit.

some measure, should interpose a non-conductor, so that only the mental statement is received, and not the spiritual influence. I cannot account for the fact, but I can, by a long experience, see that it is so. In the moral teaching of parent to child, there is a force in "vivâ voce" instruction which no printed lesson has.

Again, another remark I shall make is this, that in the child the Spiritual Reason is awake and acting long before the *mental powers*—I will not say are ripe, but before they begin to act with any degree of perceptible effect. The mother who, under these conditions above specified, shall try it with regard to her baptized* child, shall often find it so; shall find that of the things of the Infinite and the Spiritual, there is an apprehension and a power of Knowledge and Obedience long before that mental faculty,† whose instructor is experience, shall have reached to anything like ripeness of its powers.

A third remark is this, that the formation of character depends mainly upon the development in youth of the Spiritual Reason as to its appreciation of Divine Truth, its unconscious development, or, if I may use the expression, *its institutional* development by the Parent in the Family. The Sense of Veracity, for instance, or of Justice, or of Benevolence, or of Honor, or of Purity, when awakened in the Reason, in the family, under the moral tuition of the parent, shall become, as it were, an element of the being of the individual, and a plastic principle whose close adherence to his nature shall frame and mould him to a higher harmony and a nobler type of existence than otherwise the man could have attained. And the moral character so formed shall be calm and tranquil and self-possessed; it shall be living and fresh, and free from the affectation and the tendency to grotesque extremes that now usually pursues those who, by themselves, attain to an insight into any moral truth higher than those around them hold, and then try to realize it and carry it out in their lives and actions.

To the parent then, we may say: "Here is a sphere wherein, by means of God's ordinance, you are placed, in which *your position* makes you a moral teacher, addressing the highest faculty,

* I say "baptized child," inasmuch as a human being who is really in covenant with God, whether Adult or Infant, in reference to "the things unseen that fade not away," and the "powers of the world to come," is in a quite different position from him who is not within the covenant.

† The Understanding, a logical or reasoning power.

and gives your slightest word a weight that your weightiest exhortations and most vehement and energetic efforts cannot have *out of it*, and makes even your unconscious actions means and elements of instruction. *Here*, then, remember is your great influence; *here*, your formative power: *before all things* the duties of this sphere *must be done*, and if neglected, then the consequences are, within the same sphere, evils and keen misery such as many Parents have endured and lamented.

And for the child, let him know that the station of a Father or a mother is of itself to be viewed with the deepest reverence, not merely because of character or mental power or influence, but *because of their position* as Father and Mother. Let the child know, then, that the first of all injuries *to himself* is to rise against that influence, to rebel against it, to scorn and despise parents. And that it comes not merely from the Providence of God, or from his threatenings in Holy Scripture, that the child so doing shall be unhappy in life and unsuccessful, but from the law we have specified whereby the Spiritual Reason of the father is made the ruler, former and teacher of the Reason of the child, the one as central, and the other as revolving around it.

And as if a planet could be supposed endued with rational powers and will, and to desire freedom from the forces that cause it to revolve around the sun; the accomplishment of that wish would be the whirling of it off to the abyss of ruin, and the fulfilment of the desire would be of itself destruction: so it is by the natural law of the case with the Child towards the Parent; the nature of the act makes the nature of the consequences, and the denunciations of the Scripture are prophecies of them.

We have made these observations so much at length, because we believe that the mass of the moral delinquencies in Society, as well as the deterioration which we see very rapidly taking place in many classes, arises from the neglect of this, the Institutional Education and training of the Reason by Parents in their proper sphere. And therefore we have set forth the law and the grounds and consequences of it, perhaps, a little more amply than we otherwise would, in proportion to the other parts of our work, have done.

The same doctrine in reference to the State and to the Church, we shall only say applies in the same way in regard to the peculiar ideas which it is the intent of these schools to awaken and train in man; the ideas, namely, that concern "right to man" and "duty to God." We leave them, therefore, to the student to develope for himself.

Having gone so far in the examination of the Spiritual Reason, it now remains to show the best modes of exercising it, and bringing it to perfection in ourselves, as we have in others. Remembering, then, that the modes of its action are "Moral Apprehension," "Moral Feeling," "Moral Principle," and supposing that hitherto the individual has lived by chance, loitering along the pathway of life, without moral cultivation from himself or moral attention to his own state, "how shall he begin?" Suppose that his Spiritual Reason is so blunted, that as an animal his mind is occupied only with animal pleasures, and that the Highest Good, in his estimation, is so far from being any of the goods of the Spiritual and the Infinite, that it is altogether of Time and Sense; so that "truth" to him is nothing, and "holiness" and "purity" nothing, and "justice" nothing, but "names and words invented by dreamers which wise men use to govern them with, but which no man permits to stand in the way of his own interest when he safely can do it."* Suppose he take "all men to be rascals if they durst,"* "Each man to have his price,"* "all virtue to be, at bottom only selfishness";* in other words, suppose his Spiritual Reason to be utterly uncultivated, (as far as God permits it to be so,) and utterly blind. And yet should the man,—hearing the assertion, or we will say reading it in this very book, that there are Spiritual Truths that are realities—that there is a spiritual sense of them that may be awakened—as a blind man should hear of the sun, and moon, and stars, and of the sense that perceives them,—then honestly desire that in him that sense might be awakened, and those truths by him perceived—*how should he proceed?*

I answer, there being three modes of the operation of the Reason in reference to any moral quality, "Justice," we will say, or "Benevolence," or "Honesty," he is not to begin by an endeavour to sharpen and excite by *mental* means his apprehension of that quality, for this will not bring it about. Reading about it, even in the most sincere and ardent way—this is so far from producing Moral Apprehension that it may blunt it, and even in some

* All these are sayings of worldly-wise men, who no doubt drew them from self-experience.

men it may altogether eradicate moral principle. This, then, will not do.*

Again: he may think that by bringing himself in contact with "circumstances" that shall excite the emotion, and cultivating *feeling* upon the particular virtue or moral quality—that he can so stimulate the growth as thereby to cultivate the Reason in the highest degree. This ends in a stimulability of the feeling, a resting in that feeling, an unreality which every one that is honest and true can see; and may terminate not in moral growth of the affection, but in the mental and literary affectation of extreme sensibility. Such has often been the case with those who have begun sincerely to cultivate the Moral Power by the way of exciting their own feelings or their mental powers.

I have before said that in moral progress the Conscience, and a fixed determination to follow it *must be always* the first step. Supposing, then, this step to have been taken by the individual, I say, *let him try in the way of principle;* that is to say, let him take that moral principle, of whose power he may be utterly ignorant, may neither feel nor apprehend it, *let him take it into life as a rule, a principle of life.* He has hitherto not cheated, because of divers and sundry advantages which *not to cheat* brings him; let him set aside *the "advantages,"* and their result the *non-cheating*, and establish for himself as a *law of life internal*, affected by no external circumstances whatsoever, but measuring them all, *honesty.* And if for a day he *act* upon it, if for a day he use it as a *principle*, if but for a day it be made a "governing principle," so that it rule, secondly, "rule always," and thirdly, "that it rule according to its law," as I have expounded with regard to the principle of the "governing powers:" if this principle to which he was we will say in the morning utterly blind and insensible, be willingly and steadfastly adopted for *one day* as an inner "*rule*," *swaying and bearing supremacy over circumstances:* if he act so for a single day, then, before the day is over, his apprehension of it shall be more or less opened—his feeling of it awakened, his power to act upon it as a rule increased very perceptibly. *The acting upon Principle*, not feeling or arguing, is the way wherein, as regards ourselves, we are to cultivate the Spiritual Reason.

* See upon this subject the Chapter upon Habit, in Book IV.

And when the three powers or modes of the Spiritual Reason are brought, all of them, into action under the condition that it should rule; secondly, should rule always, and thirdly, should rule according to its law; then the result upon the character is the gradual growth of that "Moral Harmony" that we have spoken of; that internal law whereby the mind is governed and ruled, so that it is uniform with itself: and there is no jar, no sense of disagreement, but all the powers work on together equably; the manifold workings of the powers and parts of the whole nature, the body, soul and spirit, all consciously uniting in harmony of action:—this is the completion and perfection of the Reason, and it is brought about by the Reason as a governing power, guiding its own operation or workings according to its laws.

This question, then—what is the Law of the Reason? manifestly shall complete our examination of the subject, and show the perfection of nature as far as this faculty is concerned. This shall be the subject of the next chapter.

CHAPTER IV.

The highest law of Reason is not Nature, nor the law of the Family, or of the Nation, but the Faith of Christ,—and this in a three-fold view.—1st, as *written*; 2ndly, as enforced *by* the Church and *in* the Church; 3dly, as dwelling in the hearts of the Sanctified.—Other practical inferences.—The source of fanaticism is in denying its food to this faculty.—Practical conclusions.—Exhortation to those who are the teachers of this faculty to teach without fear.

We have now examined the subject of the Spiritual Reason with the exception of its "Law" and its results; that is to say, that "Law," by which, according to the third principle of the governing powers laid down in the First Book, it may be brought to the highest practical perfection in the man; and secondly, the effect and consequence upon *man's* nature of that perfect operation of the faculty, which we have indicated as "Moral Harmony and Moral Progress."

To enter, then, into the examination of these two subjects, and fully to consider them, this will complete the discussion of the Reason.

We are now to seek the law of the Spiritual Reason, and as a guide in this, the reader will please bear in mind the principle before maintained, "that no governing Power can be a law to itself." He will also remember, that it is not *a* "law" of the Reason we seek, but "*the supreme Law of the Reason*," that which will embrace and in itself contain all others, the Law emphatically.

For to him that has been separated from all Society,—by the very fact of the harmony that goes through the whole world, and the analogy that all things have to one another, and the spiritual meaning that they bear, this the external harmony of Nature shall become *a* law to his Reason,—shall interpret itself with a manifold significance, and shall be an awakener of the Moral Apprehension, the Moral Feeling, and "the Moral Principle" in him. Thus Nature shall be *a law*, and to him, *if he have none other*, the *highest* law and bounden therefore upon him.

Again, to him that is in the first form of Society, the "Family," where there is no Nation nor Church, to him the law of the "Family," enforcing itself upon his actions, is a law of the Reason, and, as we have shown, will, from the primeval revelation, bring him knowledge, and enforce in him, even unconsciously, action that developes the Reason. This, then, becomes to him a higher Law than that of Nature, with higher knowledge, which does not supersede the other, but makes it, as it were, weightier and broader: so that what was the sole law is now associated with another, and transfers to it so far its supreme authority, becoming itself an auxiliary.

Again, the man is a member of a Nation—and then to his Spiritual Reason there are three laws,—the one of the harmony and analogy of nature, the other of the Family,—and the one that is to him the supreme Law of the Spiritual Reason, the law of the Nation. Not simply its *enacted* or statute law, but its "Universal Law," its "Common Law," everything that dwells in the universal consciousness of the nation, as a general rule of action and government for all men of that Race, and Nation, and Country; and this, then, shall be to the man the Supreme Law of his Reason.

It will be seen that it is taken for granted that the analogy and harmony of nature teaches so far the truths of Eternal Morality, —that the law and knowledge of the Family teaches the same,— and the law of the Nation, even of pagan nations, the same.*

This may be manifestly seen from the fact that whatsoever "Law" prescribes anywhere, it prescribes it *as good,* and it is bad by ignorance, "corruption," "mistake," "misapprehension," or by stepping out of its sphere, but not by *intention,* or *by its nature.* And everywhere it has a corrective in that which it supersedes, for it cannot *contradict,* only *confirm.*

But higher and higher as these laws go from the outward harmony of Nature, up to the law of the Family, and from it to the law of the Nation, a higher law still is to be sought, in a more complete and perfect declaration of God's Nature and Will,—that is to say, in the Revelation of Jesus Christ, the institution of his Church, the Regenerating power of the Spirit of Christ. In His truth and His light, it is to be sought: "I am," he says, "the way, the truth, the life; no one cometh to the Father but by me."†

This, then, is the highest law of the Reason, the supreme one, that which does not destroy the other laws of the reason, but confirms them all and agrees with them all, while itself is supreme in authority over all,—*the Faith of our Lord Jesus Christ.*

We take "the Faith" for the whole Gospel, all that is written in the Holy Scriptures as the *written word;* the same word upheld as *doctrine and law of life* by the Universal Church; and the same as *enforced by the Holy Spirit* in the hearts of the "Communion of Saints,"—the body within the Church of the Sanctified. This "the Faith of Christ," as, first, *written* in the Scriptures; 2ndly, *enforced doctrinally and practically* by the Church Universal; and thirdly, as living in the life and actions of the sanctified; the word and faith of Christ in this three-fold aspect is the highest Law of the Spiritual Reason, that which brings it to perfection,—"this Faith of Christ our Lord."

* I would recommend upon this last point, my readers, to obtain the "Hulsean Lecture for the year 1846, by Richard Chenevix Trench." The subject hinted at in the above paragraph is there gone into fully, and it is shown, "that Christ" was "the desire of all Nations," and that even "Heathendom prophesied of Him unconsciously." This, in fact, is the title of the book. The style is very beautiful, and the sentiment and argument exceedingly interesting.

† John xiv. 6.

And here natural Ethics and spiritual Ethics touch; here is seen the truth of that principle, "That Revelation is the complement of natural Religion and Grace of Nature." For here is seén that the Spiritual Reason, in man, can be only perfected by Him who is in God, "the Divine Word;" or, as it otherwise may be translated the Divine (Logos) Reason.

Nay, when we look at all those truths of natural Ethics, that upon this subject we have brought forth in our last few chapters, we shall see that each and every one of them has in the Gospel a corresponding truth of Revelation, which completes, perfects, and crowns it—so that although Human Nature is by itself a wild tree that bears no fruit; yet upon it, by its being, as made in the Image, a true and perfect fruit-bearing scion, may be grafted by Almighty Grace, that shall bring forth much fruit.

To illustrate this, we take "this Spiritual Reason" to be ourselves personally, that which is truly and properly "I,"* or what represents the being and attributes of the individual; and at the same time, in this, the Reason, the wisest in the Church, nay, even the Heathen,† who have thought most deeply upon it, have placed the "Image," or resemblance of man to God.

Now when we look to the being of God we see that the Son is in the Father, the "Divine Reason," the "Word," the "Manifestation of his Glory," the "express image of his Person:" being, therefore, in the Father, as the "Spiritual Reason" is in us; with the essential difference, that in the Almighty Father, since He is Infinite in power, knowledge, wisdom, and all attributes, the "Word," and "Wisdom," and "Manifestation" of the Father is the Son,—a Personal Being, who is "God *of* God," "Light *of* Light," "very God *of* God."‡ And we, made in the Image of God,

* See a previous quotation from Whewell's Morals.

† Plato for example.

‡ The word "of" in the phrases, "God of God," "Light of Light," "Very God of Very God,"—is often read as if it were the sign of the possessive case, as in the phrases "the son of the king," which is identical with the "king's son," the "nature of God," that is "God's nature." Whereas the word "of" is the emphatic word, answering to "ἐκ" in the Greek original, or "de" in the latin version, being the preposition "of," as in the phrase "he was descended of noble ancestors."

The English preposition "from," perhaps, would be in our present idiom the clearest and most unambiguous translation, thus,—"God from God," "Light from Light," "Very God from Very God,"—expressing the great fact are made in the Image of the Word: and the faculty that shows that Image, the Spiritual Reason, this faculty has for its supreme law, the Faith of Him who is the express Image of His Father's person—not the image, as Reason is in us, of the Infinite in the Finite, but, the image in that He is "God *of* God," Light *of* Light," "Very God *of* Very God."

Such a natural congruity is there between the Relation of the Word to the Father, and the Relation of the Spiritual Reason to the man. And secondly, in the fact that man was made in the "Image of God," that is of the Word, which image, by the Fall, is defaced, but not become the image of the devil, but of Adam, a man fallen, yet still a man. These two natural congruities should surely indicate to us the truth of this that I have asserted, that the perfection of the "Spiritual Reason" in man, is the "Faith of Christ the Word." A natural truth of the higher Ethics is thus completed by a truth of Revelation.

And he that doubts need not seek far; in the most ordinary Ethical books of the Heathen before Christ, he shall find the natural side of this truth stated as a fact, yet losing itself in theory and speculation, and folly, because the Spiritual complement of it had not yet been revealed. And in the Church's doctrine of the Divinity of the Word, and His relation to the Father, he shall find the other part, a truth of Nature and a truth of Grace, the one answering to and completing the other, from both which combined, we draw our inference, that to that natural faculty in man, which we have called the "Spiritual Reason," the supreme law and means of bringing it to the highest perfection, is "the Faith of our Lord Jesus Christ."

We might, as other philosophers and other moralists have done, dwell upon the other Laws of Reason, which have been once to

of the "Eternal Generation of the Word." That from the Infinite and Unoriginate Father came forth eternally a personal being, the Word, who is the "Manifestation of His Glory," the "Express Image of His Person," the second person of the Holy Trinity, who "was incarnate and died for us! The agent (if we may use the phrase) of the whole power of the Father; the sole access and adit unto the Father for all men; the exclusive fountain, the one source of all Spiritual Life to man, is the Word eternally proceeding from the Being of the Father; and yet eternally dwelling in Him. God then OF God, light OF light, very God OF very God, is the Almighty and Eternal SON in his relation to the Almighty and Eternal Father.

individuals or even to races and nations, supreme laws of the Reason; and which are in being still, *but not supreme.* We might, as Wordsworth, gaze upon the face of Nature and from it struggle to call forth the Law for man's being. We might bring up, again, the reasonings of Plato, or of Aristotle, or the lofty Stoic guesses at the truth under laws that were to them true and the highest they had, but were not *the ultimate, the adequate,* and *supreme law.* But *we* are not as Plato, or the Stoics, or Aristotle. For us the Supreme Law of the Spiritual Reason is in the Faith of Christ, finally revealed and manifested.

It is literary trifling and absurdity to go back and imagine that we can place ourselves in the situation of the Heathen Philosophers. The same train of argument which in them, at their date, was deep and solemn enquiry, in us shall be frivolity and affectation. We cannot place ourselves in their position, and it is absurdity to imagine it. Instead therefore of going over their speculations to their results, we take the natural facts they had, and show the completion of them in the faith of Christ. For a Supreme Law we point not to outward Nature, to Platonic or Aristotelian Morals; to the Grecian "sense of Beauty," or the Roman sense and feeling of Justice—not to these but to that upon which all these rested, "*Nature;*" and then to that which all these had not, "*The Faith of Jesus Christ;*" and then, according to the maxim which makes and constitutes our Philosophy, "*Grace is the complement of nature,*"—we say, the Faith of Jesus Christ is that alone which as its Supreme Law perfects the Reason of Man.

Here then have we reached the highest point of Natural Ethics and the lowest of Spiritual Ethics, the point wherein the one unites with the other; and as, in reference to the "Natural Conscience, we showed that to the justified alone was the Conscience perfect, so now do we assert that to them who are "*Sanctified*" only is the "Spiritual Reason" perfected; and this takes place in both its results of "Moral Harmony" and "Moral Progress," by the constant influence of the Grace of our Lord Jesus Christ upon the Spiritual Reason of the Sanctified. The examination then of these two points, although we are led in search of them and towards them, and even within a very little of them, still lies outside the domains of Natural Ethics, and within those of Spiritual Ethics, it is therefore deferred to a future time. We shall therefore recall some other characters of the Reason that illustrate the views we have given.

We would point out that the Reason is the faculty of the "Unseen," of that which is not tangible by the senses or to be brought under their examination—and side by side with this we would place the Apostle's declaration, that "Faith is the substance of things hoped for, the evidence of things unseen;"* his declaration also that "the things that are seen are temporal,"† that is, they flee away and abide not for ever. So that it would seem that the power in us by which when it is awakened we discern the Unseen, this power is the Spiritual Reason, and Faith is its act when under Grace. And, when God has awakened it, then only can it exert itself in Faith, as the Scripture says, "Faith is the gift of God."‡

Hence from Natural Ethics and from Revelation we have three truths.

First, There are things Unseen, which alone are real and fade not away.

Secondly, There is a power in man that may be awakened to see them, or may be left unawakened, so that it does not see, but still it is the sense of them.

Thirdly, There is an influence that awakens and perfects that power. This influence is what the Scriptures call the "Grace of our Lord Jesus Christ;" and the sight by it awakened is called "Faith." Here again Nature rises upward, and the truths of which it speaks in dim enigmas are declared and interpreted by Revelation. The nature and effects of living faith and the enlightening and illuminating influence of Grace upon the mind, these explain and make clear this doctrine of natural Ethics.

Again, that it is the "sense of the Unseen." This, combined with that other fact, that "it may be trained unconsciously"—this bears witness to the Church's doctrine of the "Communion of Saints," and the influence that the angels of God and the Holy Departed have upon us.

For indeed the Spiritual Reason or Sense of the Unseen, is so far the witness and the faculty of a Spiritual World, that as no man who has the eye, the sense of natural vision, can be without a con-

* Heb. xi. 1. † 2 Cor. iv. 18. ‡ Eph. ii. 8.

viction that he sees, so with regard to an Unseen World, men may chase away the doctrine, call it absurdity, reason, argue against it as they will, and yet they cannot by all their labor get rid of it. It will cling by them.

Cultivate, then, in your children the sense of the unseen world of Spiritual things—the feeling of the actual and real influence of the Spirit of God, and of the guardianship of his "holy angels," and of the "Communion of Saints,"—and the sense of the Unseen shall receive its due nutriment in the truths of Revelation, and shall produce a sanctifying result upon the character, in that calm and holy habit of meditation which seems to be the highest grace of the perfect Christian mind.

But chase this belief away; sneer it down; call it superstition, &c., and you shall find that the faculty *will not* be deprived of *some food;* it sought for that "above human reason,"* and could not reach or obtain it, so it shall take refuge in that which is "against reason." Not being fed with the truths of the Unseen, it will turn to the garbage of the "Absurd." He that cannot believe in "one Baptism for the Remission of sins," he shall

* There are "things above reason," and "things against reason." This is a plain and manifest distinction, referring to the limited nature of man during his present state of existence with his present faculties. It asserts that there are truths in his life revealed to him which, while he takes them to be true upon the evidence of the revelation of God, still, owing to the limited nature of his faculties, and their adaptation only for this gross and earthly state of being, he cannot comprehend the grounds and reasons of them. They lie far *above him,* in a purer and clearer atmosphere, in which his mental faculties cannot live. And to rise to them a change must take place in him, from the animal and earthly to the pure celestial body.

These facts, whose reason is *above* our faculties, while we know them to be facts, are called *mysteries.* Such are the mysteries of the Atonement, of the Incarnation, of the Spiritual Body, of the Marriage Union, of our Regeneration and Spiritual Life through Christ, of the nutrition of our souls by His Body and Blood, as our bodies are nourished by the Sacramental symbols of bread and wine—all these are mysteries, facts revealed to us by God, to be received in faith, and yet incapable of being comprehended. *Above reason,* they are not *against it;* for we can, by reason, refute all gainsayers, whatever arguments they may bring forward. We can refute the opponents of these truths, *but we cannot explain the truths themselves.* For the explanation we must wait for a future life and a loftier state of intellectual being. Such is the distinction between "things above reason" and "things against reason," a distinction every student must see to be of deep importance in Moral and Religious Science.

believe in "Baptism for the dead" General Washington by Joseph Smith, the Mormon. He that "cannot believe in a Church of God existing upon the earth with its Divine Powers," he shall come to believe that "an impostor, half crazy, half knavish as Matthias, was the Shiloh."* And they who from youth upwards had set at nought all the truths of the Christian faith, they shall be converted by the frantic ravings of the Millenarian prophet, announcing the doom of the world, and the triumphant entrance of the Messiah into,—not Jerusalem, but New York!

Give the man the truths of the Unseen World, the truths "above reason," revealed in the word of God, upheld and interpreted by the Church, impressed by the Holy Spirit; and "the sense of the Unseen," the "Spiritual Reason" in him shall embrace them naturally, easily, readily. Keep the truths of the Faith of Jesus Christ away, and any absurdity, any superstition, any folly, he is prepared for. The natural faculty that is deprived of due and appropriate food and denied it, this faculty shall, whether in body, soul or spirit, thus become a depraved appetite, feeding upon garbage.

Upon these grounds, I say, the man who trains up his children without the truths of the Faith of Christ our Lord impressed upon their mind, this man (especially if they be unbaptized) by the very nature and reason of the case, trains them up as victims, by himself made ready for any absurd and unreasonable fanaticism. If they are baptized in the Church of Christ, then have they the teachings of the Spirit pledged to them, and of the Communion of Saints, and this in its secret operations upon their souls, may perhaps, through God's mercy, in some degree supply the neglect of the parents, without, in any degree, relieving them from the guilt.

Again: I would point out how much the fact that the Spiritual Reason can be taught and trained by an influence of which it is unconscious, illustrates the operation upon us of God's Spirit, whose teaching is known but by the fruits it brings forth; how much it agrees with the truth of the Scriptures, that "the angels minister to us," and that "our dead friends may not be apart, but near to us." All these, which are matters of Revelation, at the same time are matters of natural belief, which, because man has

* See Stone's "Life of Matthias the Impostor."

a "Sense of the Unseen," he will not give up to any argumentation whatsoever. And the fact and truth which the man can see in his "family," that Moral Teaching may be true and real teaching, although it is not consciously perceptible to the subjects of it, this aids him to see that all these influences, which are asserted in the Holy Scripture, and yet he feels not consciously, may still exist and be good, and have a true and real effect.

And again: we find the faculty ever seeking "Moral Harmony," ever testifying by its desire after it to the natural want of it, yet ever struggling towards it as an object. Here, then, in its sense of incongruity, unsuitableness, inability in the natural state—here is its testimony to the doctrine of Original Sin. Ten thousand orators may prove to their own satisfaction that "men are now born as the first man came out of the hands of his Creator," but the "Spiritual Reason" of each man shall say "No" to their eloquence and their arguments. It shall say, "I wish,—desire,—seek after,—aim at 'Moral Harmony;' and in *Nature by itself* I feel it not." And the inner voice shall confute the eloquent argumentation of the orator and man of genius, and to the plain preacher of the Gospel, that proclaims the doctrine of Original Sin, that "man is fallen," it shall uphold and support the truth he asserts.

Having thus brought this subject to a conclusion, so far as it is in the province of Natural Ethics, I would recapitulate; and from that recapitulation enforce another inference that may be drawn very distinctly.

First. There is a certain, distinct and clear body of definite, eternal moral truths, which are ever the same, and do not vary with circumstances.

Secondly. These have Institutions organized for the purpose of teaching them, which do, under all circumstances, teach consciously or unconsciously.

Thirdly. There is a peculiar faculty in each individual man, adapted to receive these truths.

Therefore to them that have these truths, and know them by earnest and true realization, whether Parent, or Magistrate, or Clergyman—these three principles say,—"That which you know as Divine Truth of the Spiritual Reason, that teach *fearlessly*, *earnestly*, *zealously*: and no matter though a multitude were against you; the Harmony of Nature, the frame of Society, and its institutions, nay, the very unseen world itself, Angel and Archangel, Cherubim and Seraphim, shall lend you aid; and in the very being and frame of the individual man, even of him who opposes you, therein shall that faculty that is the Image of God desire and yearn after the Eternal Truths that come from God; and a word of these from you shall be a seed that shall bear fruit after years are gone.

Let the Parent, then, not fear his own weakness,—or the Magistrate his want of eloquence,—or the Clergyman his want of influence:—if the "*eternal truths*" are *in him held* and *acted upon really* and *honestly*, he has a power that shall and will tell in the strongest way.

But if he only talks, and is "eloquent and impressive," or even learned, in a *mere logical*, or *mental*, or *rhetorical way*, upon things of which he has no "Spiritual Apprehension," or Feeling, or Principle; he may be sure that he cannot communicate to others that which he has not himself. He need not wonder that in uttering to children, or pupils, or citizens, or congregations, the *words* and bare *verbal* enunciation, the outward shell of that Eternal Truth, that they should not make quite so great an impression as the *same words* shall from the mouth of the man who feels, and apprehends, and realizes that truth, as a Law of life more precious than gold or silver, and which he would be hewn asunder before he would transgress.

This subject, then, of the Divine Reason, we here dismiss, leaving it here, because only under the light of Revelation can it be completed; but yet so far as Natural Ethics go, discussed and examined, we trust satisfactorily. The remainder of the subject, the "Moral Harmony" of the Spiritual Reason, and its progress to perfection, properly belong to Religion.

BOOK IV.

THE HEART OR AFFECTIONS.

CHAPTER I.

Heart or Affections.—Its meaning.—Towards Persons.—Appetites and Desires towards Things.—It is towards Persons in Society.—Society in reference to this Power is a School of Love.—Errors that may be avoided by this consideration.—Use of Instinct in Animals.—Moral Principle and Rule of the Affections deducible from this.—What is "Nobleness" of Heart, and what Meanness.

We have entitled this book of the "Heart or Affections," thereby manifestly taking the one phrase and the other to be identical, as to that particular class of emotions that they signify. And we have given the two titles to the book, because each of these words is liable to be used in a somewhat varying sense, so that either might be mistaken for something that we do not mean; but the union of the two in the title, and the use of the one as an equivalent to the other, will, better than any formal definition, convey to our readers that particular idea that we wish to give to them.

By the "Heart," then, "or the Affections," we mean to imply the third of the "governing" powers of man,—those four powers, namely, by which we take him to be a moral being, and which we take him to have, as a living creature having a "Spirit;" and the animals not to have, as not having a "Spirit." While we admit, at the same time, that as being an "Animal," he has the "Animal" Mind and all its qualities; just as being an "extended" and "material" body, he has the qualities that belong to "matter filling space." But as a "man," he has to these last two, *superadded* the "Spirit" or "Rational Soul," of which we have taken "Conscience," "Reason," "the Affections," "the Will," to be the four *faculties*.

For this word "Heart" which we have employed, there are doubtless many significations which may occupy the attention of those that wish to quarrel and argue upon words; but there is no doubt at all that the one predominant meaning, setting aside peculiarities of idiom and metaphor, is that one which we have given. And he, who in ordinary discourse hears the word, save that its meaning is determined to some other of the other senses by the connection, he shall generally understand "the Affections," and these Affections, as not belonging by any means to the brute creation, but as peculiar to man; in one word, he shall conceive it to be peculiarly a *Human faculty*, and only by a very high metaphor, which every one that hears shall understand to be an exaggeration of speech, shall he apply the words to the brute creation. To the Dog, the Horse, or the Elephant, those that come nearest to the human race of all mere animals, the word "Heart" is never applied. This, then, is one distinction which serves to mark off and limit the meaning, that it is a quality that belongs not to brute animals, but to men

And when we look at it as so limited to man, notwithstanding a multitude of meanings derived from various idioms and various circumstances, still in our own Anglo-American, and, indeed, I believe in all the Gothic dialects, we shall find the predominant signification to be that the Heart means the "Affections."

True, there are other meanings. It means memory, or seems to do so, in that strange phrase, "getting by heart," commemorated and illustrated in the epigram:

"John has no heart, they say,—I do deny it:
He has a heart—and gets his speeches by it."

Again, in the dissolute times that followed close upon the English Commonwealth, there was a translation into English of a French Idiom, in which profligate men spoke of "Affairs of the Heart," (affaires du Cœur,) meaning seductions and adulteries; and licentious women spoke of "wanderings of the heart," (egaremens du Cœur,) meaning thereby adulterous love and profligate amours. And there is undoubtedly a whole range of English literature, that of the age of Charles the Second, in which this word is so employed as the vile translation into English of the word cœur, employed in as vile a sense in French. But it is now antiquated, the word has cast off the meaning, and but few would understand it in that sense. This meaning, then, being merely the idiom of a time, and now fallen into almost total disuse, we shall pass by, having noticed it merely for the sake of distinctness.

Again, there is another idiom which is naturalized in our language, that which makes the "Heart" to be an idiomatic expression for courage or strength of mind as noticeable in the phrases, "Take heart," "Faintness of heart," "In good heart." And this we at once distinguish as an idiom, by using it in the phrase in that sense; but even in the same words apart from the phrase in an utterly different meaning. For instance, we say such "man is of a good heart," this is a moral commendation,—but "be of good heart" denotes courage.

Again, there is in a passage of the Bible an idiomatical use of it for the "Conscience," by the verbal translation of which, the verse is made almost unintelligible, "Brethren, if our *heart* condemn us not, then have we peace with God; if our *heart* condemn us, God is greater than our *hearts*, and knoweth all things."* A passage in which the Greek and English are only verbal, not real translation of the Hebrew word, "leb," (heart,) meaning "conscience."

So far with regard to the idiomatic meanings of the word. We shall now proceed to the metaphoric meaning. It means unquestionably, in metaphor, the innermost part of anything; as for instance, "the heart of the earth," "the heart of the country," "the heart of a tree," all which are figurative meanings for the "innermost part." And in this sense it may employed as a metaphor for the "*whole moral nature*" of man as the inner and most mysterious part of his being,—but still this shall be only metaphoric, and not a proper and peculiar sense.

Another metaphoric meaning, derived undoubtedly from the heart, the physical organ, is that which signifies that part wherein the strength lies, as "the farmers are the heart of the country;" and "to give heart," is to give strength.

* John iii. 20.

Putting aside all these peculiarities, we come to this conclusion: the word "Heart," in the idiom and metaphor of the English language, applied to persons in respect to Human Nature, means the "Affections." And this, in our language, is the predominant meaning, and the one generally understood by every one that hears the word, setting aside the peculiar cases under the peculiar circumstances above mentioned, in which each one naturally understands the exception, and takes it to be an exception, although perhaps the principle upon which he does so, is not present to his mind.

Having thus, with regard to this subject, obtained as much knowledge as we can obtain from the verbal examination, we shall now go onward to the examination of *the thing* itself,—that is, the governing power, which we have called by the name of the Heart or Affections. And the first and most evident character of the Affections is this,—they are turned towards *persons*, they dwell upon *persons*, and in *persons* have their end and object. We have "Appetites" for *things* that are immediately required for the support of the body, as for food and sleep; "Desires" for other *things* which we would possess, as money, real estate, power. "Appetites" and "Desires" for *things*, but "*affections*" for *persons*.

It is plain that the "Appetites" belong to the body, and that in a manner so exclusive, as in the animals, almost to shut out the idea of reasoning or mental interference in any way. There seems to be a peculiar conformation in the animal, by which a certain particular kind of food shall, to the sense, give an overpowering pleasure. And he that shall look at the intense occupation and hurrying eagerness with which animals eat their food, he need not doubt that "appetite" in the brute is almost entirely exclusive of reasoning; brute-mechanical, if we may use the word, depending upon the "Sensation" almost wholly, and its power of being moved in a particular way, by a particular object. And that these appetites are required for the direct and immediate support of the body.

Now "desires" are likewise directed towards "things" as well as the "appetites;" and when we look at these last, we find that there is not one of these that does not tend just as directly, though more remotely to "physical good,"—the good of the body, as the "appetites" do, though it be through a more complex series of channels.

We find also of each and every one of the desires, that although they exist in a vastly superior degree in man still in as distinct a way do they exist in animals. Desire of applause is very manifest in the dog, and is in him, I conceive, precisely the same quality that in Achilles and Alexander was the "love of immortal fame." "desire of property" is seen in the monkey, the jack-daw, the ant, the marmot, and seems to be the very "wish for accummulation" that works so strongly in the miser and rapacious man; and so we may go on, and we shall see that there is not a desire, how mightily soever it may have wrought in men the most renowned, that does not exist the *same in kind,* though *not in degree,* in the animals.

These "desires," then, we call Desires of the Animal Mind: and if we are asked, why they are more complete and more perfect in man, being the same in kind; we say, because in him "the understanding" or mind that deals with objects of sense, and the notions derived from it, is more perfect; as in him, it dwells in his nature in union with "the Spirit" or Moral Being of man.

We come next to "the Affections," or Heart, and in their case we see a plain and direct distinction, at once recognized by all men, between them and the Appetites and Desires. These last, as we above said, are towards "things," the appetites directly, with hardly any mental interference in the case of the lower animals; the "desires," with more interference of the reasoning powers, are towards "things," the Affections towards Persons.

Having thus established this very important distinction, we shall proceed to the further examination of the subject. There are Affections—they tend to *persons,* not to *things,* and are thus distinguished from Appetites and Desires. Have not brutes "Affections?" We answer, they have very manifestly desires directed to the qualities of individual men, who are persons, and to those of other animals, who are not *persons,* (at least the phrase "person," we have never heard applied to any animal, and we do not believe it can properly be used of such,—*Spiritual beings only are persons*). But, omitting altogether the conclusions that might arise from this last consideration, we remark that the "Moral Affections" tend not only to "persons," but to "*persons*" in "*Society.*"

This phrase, "Society," we at once see means something else than the *instinctive bond* that unites a communion of ants or bees together. We have already shown that it is a channel of manifold teachings which, by means of the natural principles of Imitation, and Sympathy, and Obedience, train the individual man whether he will or no, in moral knowledge,—that so it is actually a "School," in reference to the faculty of man's nature, called the Reason. Again, with reference to the "Conscience," as has been seen, Society is to each man a "Probationary Institution," one that exercises in manifold ways the first of his moral powers, the sense of Responsibility. And so, in reference to "his Affections," Society is a "Home," a natural place of training, wherein the "Heart" is taught in a congenial atmosphere to expand with "love," and "sympathy," and "respect," and "kindness," and all the feelings that tend to our neighbour's good, and seek it mainly and rejoice in it, and so by blessing him do, in a reflex manner, bless ourselves.

Now Society has, to each *man*, these uses, and he feels it and knows it to be a fact. It is, a "School of Knowledge," an "Institution that trains him in the law of his nature,"—a "Probationary state," that exercises his "Conscience,"—and a "Home," wherein the "Affections" are developed. Then let us take the animals, the ant, or the bee, or the beaver that live in what you may call a sort of society,—have they, by it, more knowledge than the ant, or bee, or beaver of a thousand years ago? are they more disciplined? or, indeed, disciplined at all? Is it to them any "trial state" preparatory to another? or, to them, any training school of the "Affections?"

No certainly,—Society to man is an idea that involves all these things; to animals their union is entirely mechanical, caused solely by "instincts" and "adaptations of nature." *Instinct seems to do for animals that which the Affections do for man;* and to do it in such a way that there shall be no moral, or even mental progress of the individual or the race, no teaching involved or implied.

Having presented these views in this condensed form, upon the nature of Society, as related to the affections, I would ask,—do not these views suppose God *ever present* in this world, in Providence, in Power, in Fatherly Justice, and in Tenderness; as a God that "teaches" all the sons of men in knowledge of His Law and of His Will? The Almighty and Omniscient teacher, as the *God* who from birth unto death, unto each son of man, affords trial after trial, so that no man passes away as guilty before the throne of God, that his own spirit shall not acknowledge that he willingly sinned against all light and all knowledge and all opportunities? Do not these views imply Him, as the Almighty who organized this world as a "home," wherein He, as a father, *being present*, trains His children's hearts to love? Is not this so, by our own Nature in its Moral Being, by Society working upon that nature in its several ways; and by the revelation of God's Nature, as He has manifested Himself in His Holy Scriptures unto man?

I would ask, then, of the Fatalist, how it is that he, in defiance of all this, has dared to destroy this knowledge and this belief? to put this truth aside and to take the circumstances that happen in these wonderful institutions of nature, and freeze them into an icy sea of destiny and doom? to say "there is no end of good in these, no uses appropriate to the nature of God and man—Society is no divine institution for appropriate purposes—no, it is an accumulation of circumstances under one fixed law, that of Fate, and absolute Doom!"

The tenet has been held, and by good and religious men;—I ask, can any man hold it that once casts a thought upon "Society" as a Divine organization, for the express purpose of training the Moral or Spiritual Nature of man, in his Conscience, his Spiritual Reason, his Affections, his Will? Certainly not. No man who has calmly thought upon the Spiritual Nature of Man, and the uses of Society in reference to this nature, can hold such views. It is only by looking to "Power," as the sole attribute of the Almighty; and by forgetting that man has a moral Nature; and that there are means and institutions to train it, which are as permanent as the existence of the Human Race, and are the institutions of an ever present God, that the religious man can possibly hold such views.

Again, another person sees the phenomena of man and of Society as facts only, and thinks not upon the Moral and Spiritual Nature of man, or the Institutions for instructing it, and then knowing and feeling that "destiny," or "fatalistic doom" is no fit explanation, says "God organized this world upon a system of laws, which laws were to act, and by their infiniteness bring under their rule all natural consequences whatsoever:"—and thus with him this world is actually a machine in which physical laws are the wheels, and "cause and effect" the "power and weights;" certain causes bringing about certain effects mechanically. His theory evidently supposes that God acted at the beginning so far as making a system first, and secondly "setting it a going;" but that He has never acted, nor ever interfered since. To him who holds this Mechanical Theory of the Universe, I say, if he had looked at the nature of man, then had he seen influences above all merely "physical law," in the possession, by man, of an actual Spiritual Nature, one of the very qualities of which must be *actions originating in no antecedent physical cause.* He had seen also influences, which arise not in a single "cause-and-effect," physical law binding all things in a chain to the original movement of the system at the beginning of the world, but in three schools for teaching, each existing in the one many-formed and many-purposed institution of Society, and each working out the Will of a present, ruling God.

Think of the four links in the chain of being; of God, first; and secondly, of Society, the organization instituted to teach His Will; and thirdly, of the Spiritual and Moral faculties of man, which by nature belong to him; fourthly, of Man as the individual to whom they belong; and hardly shall you fall into these errors. But without considering the *existence of Society as a moral fact*, and the possession of *Spiritual Faculties* by the man,—look only upon the Power of God, and over the manifold tide of events, the millions upon millions of facts and influences that bear upon the man, and hardly shall you escape manifold errors. The fact that God is a Spirit, and that man has a Spiritual being, these two are united together by the fact that there is a Spiritual Teaching, and Institutions for that purpose organized. Forget the two uniting links and there is a great gulf between man and God, which you shall in vain attempt to bridge over with systems, whether Fatalistic or Epicurean, Stoic or Platonic.

"Society," then, "Human Society," considered as different from mere animal communism, which depends solely upon instinct supplying common uses of bodily support by a kind of natural "division of labour"—Human Society is distinguished from this brute-mechanical Socialism of the beasts, as spreading over all nature in one wide family, or "School of the Affections," wherein God as "Father of the Family," is the present teacher, to them who will learn.

A teacher God is in Society, even by the scourge of affliction and the fire of suffering,—to *them that will learn.* For clay is hardened and wax softened by the same fire; the same punishment which subdues the good, only exasperates the evil:—and so convinced are we of this, that we will say that there is no affliction, no suffering, even no wrong and no evil or injustice, that is, by his fellows inflicted upon a man, that may not *by himself* be made the means of calling forth more clearly in his heart the fire of the affections, and rendering him towards man more lovely and more loving; and no joy of theirs that shall not awake in him a like emotion, and by Sympathy, give him, as it were, a two-fold pleasure, one of his own and one of his neighbour's.

Having thus examined these two points* in reference to the "Heart" or the "Affections," we would bring forth a moral inference deducible from them, and urge it upon our readers.

The "Affections" are directed towards "persons" and not "things," and in them receive their full and perfect exercise and gratification. The "Appetites" and the "Desires"—these are towards things. This is the law of their nature, and so a rule of it.

And from it comes most plainly the principle of Moral Action, that when the affections are directed exclusively towards the Person or Individual, *without respect to the advantages that may come from the Affection,* then are they so far pure and noble. *He that has friendship and love towards any individual, must keep altogether out of thought the benefits he may derive from him in consequence of that love of his.* If once the thought of these benefits be mixed in with his Affection and *calculated upon,* then *desire* takes gradually the place of *affection,* which becomes decayed, and may perish utterly.

So it is with regard to the child in respect to the parent and the parent in respect to the child. Nature tells us that filial love should be directed to the Parent as Parent; and the moment the child begins to think of loving, *because of* benefits or advantages, of measuring its love by these advantages, and weighing so much of the one against so much of the other, so soon does Affection depart, being adulterated with Desire. So with the Father towards the Child: Paternal Affection, if mixed up with thoughts of benefit

* That the affections are towards "persons"—and these "persons in Society."

is alloyed and changed into something else that is not "affection," but is selfishness and "calculation." And so of the Husband "towards the Wife,"—of the betrothed or engaged towards one another. Let Father or Son, or Brother or Sister, or Husband or Wife, or any else whose bounden duty it is to render "Affection," let them permit selfish considerations to enter in, and "the Desires," whether of money, or comfort, or station, or of anything else to intrude, and they shall find out, that craftily as they may disguise it, there is an instinct that pierces through this concealment. And they may find, too, that even in the Social Nature of man, there is such a law as this: "*He that hath, it shall be given unto him, and he shall have more abundance, and from him that hath not shall be taken away even that he hath.*"

I say not this under any high romantic feeling, or in any hasty fervor, but in a common sense way, as a natural inference from a natural rule. And seeing the amount of unhappiness that has been in families for the last seventy or eighty years, seeing also how generally men calling themselves Moral Philosophers, have taught *actual selfishness as a rule*,* I believe that the cause and effect are these two—"Selfishness in matters of the Affections," taught by these philosophers and acted upon by persons that knew not the wrong,—and then misery as a consequence from that action.

Now, all the relations existing between persons wherein "Affection" is due, all these are attended with a multitude of actual and real advantages over and above the Affection, upon which, as the Highest Good† of them all, the relation is founded. Each and all of them, in their natural and proper operation, tend to heighten the "Affection," but if each and all of them were gone, then *the Affection should be retained.* Now, the assertion we make is this: that if any of them separately, or all of them together, assume the influence, or be the leading principle, then the Affection is degraded and debased into a "desire," and the relation is injured in its integrity and pureness.

The husband that truly loves his wife, loves her the more for her various wife-like qualities, for everything that makes him in his house more happy, more comfortable, more respectable. All

* The Moral Philosophy of Paley has been commonly called the "Selfish Philosophy."

† See in Book I. the doctrine of the Highest Good.

these qualities become, as it were, fuel to increase his affections and love. But he that desires to *have all these*, and *for that reason* takes a woman to be a wife, *he may* find himself disappointed. And so for every relation in life wherein affection is due—if men *would have all*, let them *have this the first.*

A parallel case I may state as confirming this conclusion. I have known many men who *because they were religious prospered in worldly affairs;* and I have noticed that just as soon as they began to substitute the consequence as a motive for its cause, to say in their hearts, "I shall remain religious *in order* that I may prosper in worldly affairs," just so soon their religious feeling begins to decay. The one fact and the other depend upon the same principle.

Now, wherein "the Affections" are kept clear from the Desires by the man, with his own will, consciously, there is seen a peculiar character of mind easily recognized by all, and in the common language of all given as a distinguishing name. This word is "Nobleness;" and he is "*noble*" in Heart who to all to whom affection is due gives that affection unalloyed by the "Desires" and "Appetites."

"Nobleness of mind" we shall therefore use henceforth as a word to which a distinct and definite meaning in Ethical Science is attached. And opposite to it directly is what we call Meanness, the character of which is that it makes "*affection* a *pretence* and a *means* for gratifying and indulging the "Desires,"—lawful, indeed, in themselves, if lawfully used, but when taking the place of the Affections and substituted for them, most evil.

That the "Affections" are intended for "Persons" in "Society:" from this the second principle, a multitude of practical inferences of the highest moral value are deducible; but these, most properly, shall come under the particular examination of the several relations to which they are referred, and therein our readers shall find them. In the meantime we go on to another part of this subject.

CHAPTER II.

Sympathy.—Two kinds.—Passive and Active.—Passive Sympathy, the sense of harmony of feeling with others.—Illustrations of it and its uses.—A moral precept founded upon it.—Second kind of Sympathy, the active power of entering voluntarily into the feelings of others.—It is vicarious.—Misery is in this world more than happiness for man unprotected.—But Society in all its forms is defensive against misery.—We sympathize more with sorrow than joy.—Hence its uses manifest.—Sympathy in a great measure voluntary.—Natural and acquired deficiency of this affection.—Hardheartedness.—Its natural punishments.—Sentimentalism a disease of the Sympathy.—Rousseau.—Law of sympathy.—Moral conclusions from this arising.

There is one especial difficulty about Ethics, in that it is a science of which each one has the requisite knowledge *in* his own consciousness; and the presentation of it, then, in an external systematic form, is almost impossible. The business, therefore, of the writer, so far as he can, is to present the truths in such a manner, that each one may recognize them as facts of his own nature, and accede to the rules drawn forth by the author; but for putting it in a mechanically systematic order, it is a thing which the very nature of the science forbids. The true system in it is not of external arrangement, but of internal sequency, so that fact shall lead to fact, and principle be made a foundation-stone to principle: that so the reader shall be led to think upon his own nature and to see by it, that the principles of the science are true. For often it happens that a fact or truth shall be denied by him under the influence of prejudice or of ignorance, which, had he seen it in its Ethical connexion with others of which he would make no doubt, though they have never been brought up consciously to his mind, he would at once have acknowledged to be true. Let not the reader, then, expect this external, mechanically systematic order from us; we are content if we present the various truths of Ethical Science in the peculiar systematic method which we have described above,—that form which we feel most appropriate to a science, all the facts of which are in existence in each one's breast. In accordance with these views, we would, in this chapter, as in its peculiar and appropriate place, present the subject of Sympathy (and perhaps some kindred truths,) to the thought of our readers.

The original meaning of the word Sympathy is "Harmony of the Affections," (sympatheia). It originally implied not merely that state in which of two persons the feelings of the one being affected in a particular way, the feelings of the other, because of sympathy, shall be so affected,—so that "we rejoice with them which do rejoice, and weep with them which weep," although we have not the motive to rejoicing, or to sorrow, that they have, but only our sympathy with them. It was not taken, then, solely as this the passive effect, but also as a particular power that brings about the effect, and is a part of our nature.

And by many beautiful comparisons this idea was supported,—by marvels of the most wondrous kind it was proved or impressed. The Philosophy of ancient Greece and of Middle-age Europe, teems with the wonders of that miraculous principle, Sympathy. It was pointed out that two harps being tuned alike, and one being played, the chords of the other would follow the tune with a faint, sympathetic music. It was believed that precious stones had sympathies with peculiar persons and characters. Nay, even the influence of the stars shed their virtues upon men by Sympathy. And the herbs of the field wrought by "Sympathy." And, stranger still, wounds could be healed at a distance by an ointment whose force depended upon "Sympathy," the ointment being smeared upon the weapon, not upon the wound! In fact, he that shall look at the works of "Baptista Porta," or "Albertus Magnus," shall find there the strangest Natural Philosophy ever dreamed of, and all of it founded upon the one principle, Sympathy.

But perhaps the Platonic notion, that supposes marriage to be the union of two souls that once, in their pre-existent state, were one, and the "sympathy" which urges them again to union, to send them unconsciously seeking it over the world, is the most interesting fable upon the point. Although hardly inferior to it may be counted that which supposes the mother's heart to be endued with such natural affection towards her child, that after it has been lost, if brought again into her presence, through secret sympathy her heart shall yearn towards it. And then again, that Middle-age persuasion, by which two perfect friends shall, at the remotest distance have, under certain conditions, a true and perfect knowledge of one another's state; because of their friendship, the feelings of their hearts moving with a perfect sympathy. All these are interesting fables, showing nevertheless the feeling and persuasion of the existence of a Great Power and Principle in the Being of Man.

We hold that there is actually and really such a power, perhaps not performing works so wonderful as these attributed to it, and yet rightly understood and rightly employed, very wonderful, and truly bringing about extraordinary results. We say, that taking away the marvels, and fabulous dreams, and high poetic fictions, the idea, as it was conceived of old, of a Sympathy or "Harmony of the Affections," by means of which effects ensue, that come from no mental power or conscious effort of the mind, but from an instinctive "harmony," or "discordance" of that power we have called the "Heart" or the Affections," is most perfectly and entirely true.

The idea, we say, as it was of old conceived, such as we have defined it, and as it is now understood by the ordinary and common mass of men.

The idea, then,—that we may clearly define it, so that men may know precisely what they are required to examine,—is this, that "Sympathy is a natural harmony by which, upon matters especially that concern the Affections, one human being shall, under certain conditions, feel, in despite of all concealment of language, the real state of the other." This asserts that there is in some men, under some circumstances, a naturally penetrative power, in a very great degree, that shall see the real state of others in despite all concealment; and that this power being particularly prominent in some minds, is yet an element in all.

It asserts, for instance, that for that man that is really and sincerely compassionate in heart, we will say, or meek in temper, or truly pure minded, or affectionate, this feeling does, as it were, give a tone to his thoughts and emotions, all of them, and become a sort of key-note to his mind. Nay, that such is the power of this that we call "feeling," that it frames and forms anew, and gives an expression to all the features and all the gestures. So that really and truly the predominant feeling comes in as a flavor in all actions, a key-note in all thoughts, a subtle writing upon the face, a lauguage that speaks through every limb. And were man's senses as subtle as they are dull, and obtuse, from the slightest glance, the merest gesture, the fullness of the mind might be seen.

Yet still, though the conscious sense be dull, the mind *unconsciously* will, by the power of sympathy, penetrate into the Heart; and at a glance, the man knows not how, feelings of suspicion will arise in his mind, or of dislike, or of liking, exactly in accordance with the particular tone and temper of his own mind. So that if the Heart be pure and holy, and just, then shall *that heart have a prophetic power*, by which, when the impure, and unholy, and unjust are brought in contact with it, a secret warning shall speak in it, and enjoin caution, and watchfulness, and suspicion, *to be measured afterwards* by facts *carefully observed* and *inferences strictly drawn*, and *proofs;* but still,—*before all these, a warning*, and *one not to be neglected.*

Passive Sympathy then is the instinctive feeling of the harmony or discordance of the Moral Affections of others with our own. Perhaps it may be accounted for by the two principles above mentioned; first, that the predominant affection frames all the features and gestures to a form peculiar to itself, and gives, if we only had the subtilty to perceive it, a peculiarity to all our words, even to the very tone of our voices; and secondly, that the mind often acts so swiftly that we are unconscious of the action, and only perceive the result; as it is when the experienced musician continues to play while he is conversing—that so the mind perceives the predominant moral feeling, or the want of it in the face of the man, unconscious of its own action, and presents the result only as a suspicion. These two principles, both which the reader will upon consideration see to be true, perhaps may explain the nature of "Sympathy,"—perhaps only its operation.

We are inclined to the latter view, that Sympathy is a separate power, and that these will only show the means by which it may operate. And the following are some of the grounds upon which we do so think. In the first place, we see clearly and distinctly that while men are individuals, and therefore each man is one—yet they are not individuals in the same sense in which the grain of sand upon the bank is one. Each man is *one* individually,—but the Human Race is *one* also. And the race is not one, as the bank of sand is one, by mere aggregation or accumulation of individual particles, but rather is an *organized oneness*, as is the tree or any other living body; and hence, because of this, the individual shall not only have tones, tempers, feelings, powers, that terminate in himself, but even *against his own will, even unconsciously those that terminate in others.* Hence is "Sympathy" the feeling preservative of that vital oneness of the race, by which the heart of one man shall vibrate in unison with the heart of another; and even by such things as may appear to be unreasonable, likes or dislikes, jealousies, suspicions, and other movements, of the nature and uses of which the man himself may be unconscious, may the vital coherence and unity of the Human Race be preserved: and then we may, in support of this, point out the fact that all men are of one blood upon the earth, of one heart, and one feeling naturally, and that this oneness of being naturally suggests and warrants such a harmony as we çall Sympathy, as well as the sense and feeling of it.

Hence it is that many, in all ages, even of the wisest and best, have believed in this mysterious power and its warnings; and although we may not be able to establish the rules and laws of its action, still the condition of human nature and of the hearts of men, renders it very probable. We look upon it as at least so far established that a rule of action may be founded upon it, that may not be lightly disregarded.

Man knows the things of his own heart. Each one knows for instance whether in religion he is sincere or an hypocrite; he knows whether he is inwardly licentious and adulterous, or inwardly pure; he knows whether he is inwardly honest or dishonest, and so forth. Now to those *who are truly sincere* within, truly honest, truly pure, I say, "there is sometimes against individuals a feeling of dislike even at the first; and this is often a movement of "Natural Sympathy,"—a warning to the pure in heart of the presence of impurity, to the honest of the presence of dishonesty, to the sincere of hypocrisy;—*not a proof*, but only that which if we follow it up and keep it in our mind *may lead* to proof;—a kind of secret caution which secures the good in heart against the wicked, and defeats evil in its most crafty snares.

This by its nature, as I have said, is not to be taken as a proof or a demonstration, but only *as an indication.* It is to be taken as *for ourselves* not for others, a something that *we should ponder over*, but hardly *give currency to* against the individual.

But to the young, who have been reared in a holy Home, in purity of heart and thought, and in the great blessing of having been members from childhood of the Church of God, under

Parents that have realized and acted up to their duty—to them I say:

"Never neglect the mysterious warning of Sympathy, *if you yourselves know* and *feel* that *you* have *purity of heart* internally, and sincerity of *religious faith;* if this be so, often shall you find this secret warning, to reveal to you that which to others of maturer minds is perfectly unseen,—and *this for your own good.*"

So far with regard to "Sympathy" in one, and that a very important sense. Sympathy is taken in another sense as "the active power that one man has naturally of entering into the feelings of another, and being himself affected as that other is:" of this we shall now treat.

It is a very evident thing, that in all the feelings whatsoever that belong to the Heart, there is a power on the part of all men of entering into those that belong to another, and in it thus making them our own, and that without our having the causes for these feelings that the persons with whom we sympathize have.

For instance, a neighbour shall lose a husband or a child, and the natural emotion shall excite in her grief—and then from the "power of Sympathy," *we* shall have the ability to feel her grief, actually and really, so that *without suffering the sorrow* we shall *feel the emotion* that it causes.

I do not say, always to such a degree as the person upon whom the affliction has come; and yet I dare not say that it has never been so, for I myself have seen grief by Sympathy, in which there was, to all appearance, more deep and vehement emotion and more suffering in those who sympathized than in the person with whom they did sympathize.

But this I do say, that sympathy in this second sense, is a real and distinct power, by which one man is enabled to enter into the emotions of another's heart,—all emotions, I say, that belong to the Affections,—and actually to take a part in them, to bear them, to suffer them, without the having had himself the original exciting cause, or indeed any exciting cause at all, save the Sympathy. A *power of transference*, as it were, belonging to our Nature, by which the man shall be able to convey to his own Affections and lay upon them the weight which the person with whom he sympathizes is bearing, or ought in proportion to his affliction have borne. A power by which the sorrow of one shall be divided and borne in part by another. A faculty by which, as in the external world, we help by the lever in lifting material burthens, and distribute the weight; so are we able to distribute the weight of the burthens and sorrow of the heart.

Active Sympathy therefore we define to be the power of entering into the emotions of a fellow being and bearing them with him *vicariously.*

The reasons that justify us in believing it so to be are,—first, the divine institution of Society as a real and vital organization, which exists coeval with man. Sympathy, then, we consider, as it were, the vital harmony in the body of Society by which one heart is adapted to the other, and the needs and necessities of the one supplied by the other. It arises from that organization which makes humanity to be as it were one great body universally spread over the face of the earth, each member bound to the whole and to each individual by that vital harmony. Thus the oneness of the human race shall not be the oneness of *aggregation* by which the sands make up a bank of sand, it shall rather be the oneness of *vital organization*, by which the particles of the human body are one by vital force and vital harmony. This vital harmony in each particle of the human frame we consider in the body of Society to be represented by Sympathy.

We consider it again to be a separate power, and one primary to the Heart, which may be conjoined with almost all the feelings whatsoever, and which gives them a second range and a further flight that they had not of themselves. For instance, you may be righteously angry for injustice done yourself: again, injustice is done your neighbour; by the "power of Sympathy" your emotion of anger shall again be raised, and you shall be angry *for him.* It is manifest the cause for the emotion, and the emotion itself, may exist *in him;* and the capability of the emotion of anger being excited, may be *in you.* But more than this is wanting, that *you* may feel indignation *for the injury done to him:* the faculty in your nature that supplies this power of entering into his feelings *vicariously*, is "Sympathy." The utmost similarity of nature, temper and habits may exist, but more than this is requisite to connect these parallels, and that is this power. And any one may look at the definition we have given, and by his own experience he shall see and feel that there is such a power; that it is not the agreement that arises from mere similarity of temper, nor the mere harmony of emotion arising from oneness in any emotion, but that it is a separate power that looks to society as an actual organization, not an aggregation, and that it may be united with any one emotion or feeling of the Heart, so as to transfer that emotion to ourselves.

We have placed it as the primary power of the Heart; that by which all *other affections are extended from ourselves to our brethren in the one common human nature.*

And he that shall fully consider it, shall see that the Appetites or Desires can hardly be objects of Sympathy, but strictly and only the "Affections." For instance, "hunger" and "thirst"—the emotion with which we see them is not Sympathy,—towards mere hunger we have no such feeling. But let "hunger" be the cause of "misery" and wretchedness, and at once we find our sympathy flow forth, and "compassion" is the result, the feeling that makes the distress of others and their misery our own. Again: it is not united with mere "Desires," the mental emotions that turn upon things, "love of property," "love of power," "love of fame," all these, which are turned towards things, we find that hardly can we sympathize with. But all those that are turned towards "persons," all, in other words, that are of the Heart or Affections, whose object is "persons" in "Society," to all these Sympathy may be united, and thence make these emotions existing in others our own. Hence we have correctly placed it among the Affections, and as the first of them.

But there is another observation with regard to its nature that we may make, and that is, that the power we have of entering into the "Affections" or Emotions of others varies very much. And the first broad distinction is this, that far more both in amount of emotion and in easiness of being moved do we sympathize with the sad than with the joyful emotions. This is an assertion which each one's experience will manifest to him as true; and the uses and ends of this provision of nature are easily seen. For, putting aside the question of Good and Evil, with regard to which it is that preponderates, and confining ourselves solely to that which regards pain and suffering, there is very little doubt that these last, *which are not always evil,* and are not *in every case* the attendants or the consequences of evil, do as to their amount greatly preponderate.

This opinion we offer as an opinion, as to the actual amount of pain *considered in itself physically,*—believing, at the same time, that a great deal of it, even by man, using his moral nature, can be converted into direct moral satisfaction, and that by God as our Father, it is used as the pain inflicted by a Father. This estimate as to the preponderance of pain, we say not unhappiness or evil, but *pain*—we shall support by the opinion of Bishop Butler.

In his Sermon upon Compassion, he speaks thus:

"Suppose that we are capable of happiness and of misery in degrees equally intense and extreme, yet we are capable for the latter for a much longer time beyond all comparison. We see men in the tortures of pain for hours, days, and except the short suspension of sleep, for months together without intermission; to which no enjoyments of life do, in degree and continuance, bear any sort of proportion. And such is our constitution and that of the world about us, that anything may become the instrument of pain and sorrow to us. Thus almost any one man is capable of doing mischief to any other, although he may not be capable of doing him good; and if he be capable of doing him some good, he is capable of doing him more evil. And it is in numberless cases, *much more in our power to lessen the miseries of others* than to promote their positive happiness, any otherwise than as the former often includes the latter; ease from misery occasioning, for some time, the greatest positive enjoyment."

"This constitution of nature, namely, that it is so much more in our power to occasion, and likewise to lessen misery, than to promote positive happiness, plainly required a particular affection, to hinder us from abusing, and to incline us to make a right use of the former powers, *i. e.*, the powers both to occasion and to lessen misery; over and above what was necessary to induce us to make a right use of the latter power, that of promoting positive happiness."

Hence do we see the opinion of Butler that our nature is far more susceptible of misery than of happiness; that is, *of itself*, apart from all things else, and taking misery merely to be suffering of the nature, not to be "evil."

From which susceptibility of the nature we may well argue that to man, standing apart from all protection, by himself, as an individual, misery clearly predominates. This can be, I think, proved distinctly by removing, first, the Church; secondly, the Nation, and third, the Family; and by so doing you place Man and Nature face to face, and see that to him life, *apart from these sheltering influences*, has more misery a thousand fold than pleasure.

Again: by this we see clearly and distinctly another use of these organizations to be "the sheltering of man from misery," the interposing, as it were, of the shield of a positive institution between him and suffering. He that looks at the state of a well ordered Nation, in which the Law reigns and the national organization is in perfection of action, and considers the security to Life and Property thence ensuing, and then contrasts it with anarchy and its consequences, may truly see that one end which the Nation fulfils, is to fence off from each individual within it sorrows he would have endured but for its existence. He that looks, then, at the Family, shall see that in reference to all its members it is the same. And as a Minister of the Apostolic Church of Christ, I will say that there is no one that has been new-born within her holy fold by "Water and the Spirit," and has fed upon the bread of life from her altars, whether we interrogate him as to his own experience or that of others, but must say that the Church of Christ is protective against many evils, preventive of much misery. Men who are non-professors may not believe it, but they who are and have been within the fold, know that such are its effects. The Family, the Nation, the Church, are institutions defensive against misery of their very nature, and tend to shield us from it.

Now, this being seen—it being seen, too, how "man is made to mourn," we can see why we have Affections directed towards "persons;" why those affections are led by one, the first, that enables us to enter into the feelings of our fellow men, and why "Sympathy" is so much more with sorrow than with joy. Far more can we "weep with those that weep," than "rejoice with them that do rejoice."

Hence the uses of the Affection are very clear and manifest; it causes us directly to ward off misery from our neighbour, by making his sorrow affect us as if it were our own. The Affections are to Persons, and with every one of them it is joined, but chiefly with those that are remedies for the weakness, the woes, the miseries of man. In each of these it affects us with the emotions of others, and makes us aid them as so moved we would aid ourselves.

Another remark we would make that is very important. It is

well known that in the physical world the cause produces the effect infallibly, and by a mechanical operation, by which when the "cause" comes into being, then the "effect" ensues. Now, with regard to instinctive actions in the animals, they are manifestly of the like mechanical nature; that which is done in man by those peculiar agencies that we call the Affections, is done in them by an instinct which seems to be necessary, compulsory, mechanical. But with regard to man, it seems as if over the higher qualities of his Spirit this law of "*cause and effect*" had very little sway—these the higher or spiritual qualities seeming *to be causes to their own action*, or to have the power of originating internally their own operation, just as if a machine should set itself going. So seems it the Conscience can be influenced *from without or from within*, the motive in this last case coming from the Spiritual nature of the man, the Reason be influenced in the same way, and so also the Affections and the Will.

But external physical circumstances are bound in one law, that of "cause and effect." They form the web that

> "Hither and thither,
> To and fro,
> Is woven in the thundering loom of Time."

Within this law, and in this web, are *all things not Spiritual.* With them "cause" produces "effect," and this again is "cause," again generating "effect." And so as from the first link stricken with the hammer, the sound shall vibrate into the last of the chain; so is power propagated through things physical, whether they be organic or animal, but the "Spiritual originates power internally," and can resist that which is externally conveyed to it.

The animal is, in respect to the emotions towards its fellows, mechanical. The irresistible mechanical force of instinct shall cause the male wolf to aid the female, during the period of nursing the young, with the most anxious solicitude. Let her be wounded, and under another animal law he shall aid in tearing her to pieces. The instinct he cannot resist under its law of "cause and effect."

But with regard to Sympathy being a *spiritual* faculty *in man*, it is manifestly in a great measure a *voluntary thing*. Misery is presented to you—then, naturally, the Emotion of Sympathy arises—you *may* indulge in it or you *may* repress it; this you feel;

you *have power over it* more or less—nay, in the course of time, you have a power so complete that you may almost entirely eradicate it. It is a known fact that men are able so completely to abolish in themselves the feeling of Sympathy that it shall attend upon none of their emotions; that their own pain, their own weakness, their own sorrow, they shall feel with a most acute and sensitive affliction; and shall see in their neighbours the extremest instances of the same, and feel no emotion leading them to aid. This, as the common experience of all, men can see to be a thing that occurs not unfrequently, and that it arises from a free and intentional exercise of the Will over the Sympathy, repressing it so constantly and habitually that finally it ceases to act, at least as to its functional actions, even although the faculty have not been entirely destroyed. The natural deficiency of "Sympathy" in an individual is called "Cold-heartedness," or "Apathy," or an "Unsympathizing Disposition" in the nomenclature of Natural Ethics. For the Ethical systems of so-called philosophers need an artificial and invented nomenclature, but the system of Nature has no deficiency in natural epithets, or in natural arrangement of the subtlest kind.

The acquired deficiency of "Sympathy" goes by another name, the appellation of "Hard-heartedness." And there is no doubt that there are such men as we have described a few paragraphs above, who have so cut off the fountains of natural sympathy in their bosom, that they shall walk through life with an unfeeling eye, as cold as the gaze of a marble statue,—a heart never warmed by aught of natural sympathy towards their fellows, but cooly calculating upon the extra gain of money that the hard pressure of poverty upon their fellow-men, or the agony of distress, may wring out from them for themselves. That such a thing is a very common circumstance indeed, is manifest to all.

But nature will hardly be defrauded of her dues, and they who have so schooled their hearts, in this "Education of Selfishness," towards their fellows, they often find that for all their gains, God, and truth, and justice, cannot be escaped. For he that shall look at this purposed closing of the heart and the cutting off of the Sympathies, he shall see that naturally it has consequences that flow from itself and do avenge it.

And first, to shut off from our fellow-men the flow of our sympathies,—to harden the heart voluntarily, and look upon them solely with an eye to gain,—this Self-discipline, if we know anything of the nature of the mind and of its diseases, is neither more nor less than a *preparation and a training for Insanity.* And were a physician to be asked how a sound-minded man could the soonest turn himself into a suicidal maniac, by a course of internal and voluntary mental action, he would give this, to cut off and restrain the Sympathies, so that they should not flow towards his fellows, that so the Heart should be perfectly alone and isolated from all participation and communion of feelings with other human beings.

And when we look at the set and fixed ambition after money of the many, and the keenness with which they are alive to that object alone, and the coldness which they assume to all besides; and then see the accumulated number of cases of insanity growing year after year, we do connect the one with the other. We do say, if you would have a healthy and a sound mind, free from all taint of disease, then let your Sympathies flow forth freely towards the poor, the distressed, the miserable, all that need succour and aid. "Rejoice with them that rejoice, and weep with them that weep,"—and so you secure much rejoicing to yourselves, and avert much misery.

Again: I know not how it is, but it is an observation of nature that I have made myself, and have heard others make, who had good experience and thinking minds, that those, who to their fellow-beings were "cold-hearted" and "unsympathizing," to them it seemed that Providence reached, in some measure, an avenging hand, *through their families*, so that these who had *secretly, in their own hearts*, locked up and closed for selfishness-sake these emotions that should have flowed out in acts of compassion to their fellows,—to them, by the retributive justice of God, it has been allotted to find

> "How sharper than a serpent's tooth it is
> To have a thankless child."

But this is an observation of Providence, which, while I may bring it up as a confirmatory remark, I cannot clearly assert why it should be so.

Upon these considerations, regarding the nature of Sympathy, the only question that now remains to us, is the rules that result regarding it. And these come mainly from its nature as we have expounded it. It is in fact a most true principle, that the functions of a moral faculty, fully and adequately expounded, shall give true rules as to its guidance in reference to the external facts to which it is applicable. Thus Sympathy is in us the "faculty," and the external fact of the world to which it corresponds is "misery." Sympathy, then, bears us onward naturally, to take a share in others grief,—this is the nature of it in us,—and the action and end of it is that thus we may relieve misery.

Now we see many persons of naturally acute feelings of Sympathy, who are deeply and easily moved by facts of sorrow and misery, or even by high-wrought descriptions of it. They sympathize strongly, the feeling is deeply moving, delightful to a generous heart, has in itself something of the noblest and loftiest character. And so is it one that is in a measure pleasurable, an excitement, a stimulus; nay, a luxury,—"the luxury of woe." It ought to be carried out in action,—not carried out, it becomes a mere stimulus, and causes a moral disease of the worst kind, the disease of "Sentimentalism."

Let me not be thought to exaggerate, or to put undue importance upon it; but there is such a disease of the moral powers, and one that is most deeply injurious. Sympathy is given *that we may share in and feel the grief of others*, and *from this be led to alleviate misery*. And it is no harm to be susceptible of its influence; nay, to be acutely and exquisitely susceptible. But *to indulge in the feeling*, and *to cut it away from the end;* this is to harden the heart to a degree which hardly can be understood in its magnitude.

And this is Sentimentalism, "the indulging of the feelings of sympathy as a stimulus and a mental excitement, without in any way aiding the distressed or diminishing the sum of Human Misery."

Now I will say, that upon reading the biography of men of note in the world, some of the least generous, the most selfish, and the most devoid of all true feeling that the world has ever seen, as well as some of the most blood-thirsty and obdurate in heart, villains without pity and without remorse, have been of this kind.

Look at Rousseau,—the base, thieving, lying impostor;—the man whose "Confessions" are a record so shameless of all that can degrade man, that the only thing that can in any way acquit him, is the assertion of his insanity;—the cold blooded wretch, whose legitimate children, immediately after birth, were placed in a basket and fastened to the gates of the Foundling Hospital, with a studied and systematic prevention of all future recognition. And this wretched fellow, overflowed with the finest Sympathies!

But they made his stock in trade of Eloquence and Pathos. And he made his bread by it, such as it was. And to himself he was, while he lived, a cancerous misery, and to a nation after his death, the cause of infinite corruption and infinite sorrow. This is the character of Rousseau, I believe, fairly and moderately drawn; and I think I may say that the whole wretchedness of this most miserable man arose from no one thing, besides this, that, possessed of the finer feelings of Sympathy in the highest and naturally the most exquisitely organized mode, he indulged in the feelings, and the excitement, and stimulus arising from them, at the same time never carrying them out into action. And hence the highest gifts that might have ripened into the noblest character, and might even have corrected all the evils and disadvantages of his youth, actually perverted his nature, and aided in producing a heart thoroughly bad.

We have dwelt upon him so long that we have hardly time to mention any more, although the tenderness of Robespierre's Sympathies are we believe matter of History. And so of many other monsters of the same period. Suffice it to say that examples enough can be found in proof of our position, "that an indulgence in the feelings of Sympathy without carrying them out to the relief of actual distress, produces hardness of heart to such a degree that the most pitiless and cruel, the most licentious and unnatural, and ungrateful conduct shall be joined with the most overflowing and deeply thrilling sentiment." And so shall natures that were intended to be of the noblest be turned into the basest and vilest.

Having thus illustrated our position, we will say, as a practical conclusion,—"When you feel the emotion of Sympathy towards distress—let it *always* issue forth *in actions*, and *in relief of sorrow*. Be even jealous of it having any other issue. Let it not give eloquence to your tongue in describing it, save that this be made a means to aid you in relief. Commit it not to paper eloquently, nay *not at all*, but turn the whole current of emotion unto the actual relief of wretchedness; and drain not one streamlet from the full channel to devote to aught magnifying self; and so upon your own heart and moral character in the fullest degree shall you find the effects of this first and most blessed of all natural affections."

In fact, the highest and most ennobling of all actions of the moral faculty is the exercise of this quality under the laws that result from its own nature, and the laws of the governing powers generally. And if the many who are really and truly anxious to improve their moral nature by the natural means, and who now in vain seek it in books;—if the many Christians in the Church that wish to be ripened in their hearts for Heaven; if they only could feel and know in practical truth, the effect of that "Sympathy" which *in secret, apart from all motives that may be selfish, "feels"* distress and misery, and *at the same time "relieves" and aids*—if they knew this and acted upon it, there would be higher and loftier characters in society, and a deeper and most sanctified Christianity.

As the "Law" then of "sympathy" we say that the "feeling" is good of itself morally when it is joined with the "action,"—bad when it is indulged without the action; and as the rule we say—"never indulge an emotion of Sympathy apart from an attempt to diminish the sum of misery."

If you can relieve distress, do it subject to the law of Conscience and of Reason. If it is by any means out of your own power, utterly impossible—then *at least you can pray to God through our Lord Jesus Christ* for relief to the individual—for prayer is action of the highest and noblest kind; *but never let an emotion of sympathy be excited in your heart that you do not aid misery in some way,*—in this way at the least if none other be possible.

And never let it be turned by you in any way to yourself, your glory, your praise, your benefit, for it is best directed, according to its nature, when wholly and entirely it tends to the relief ot another's wretchedness. Then best for *your own nature* when it is *wholly directed to another.*

Again,—be jealous of opportunities; and *yourself, personally,* come in contact with misery and distress for the sake of relieving them—*delegate as little as you can to others,* for in giving aid by the hand of another you give money—*but you give not that which is more precious than money,* personal sympathy; and you *lose which is worth a great deal more to you,* the moral schooling that the actual and personal exercise of this moral quality in your own Spiritual being shall give to your Heart.

Two questions more complete the examination of this subject. The first, "are we always to permit the feeling of sympathy when it arises?" The second, "are we always to relieve distress when it occurs?"

The first I think we can answer in the affirmative, provided—first, that it be not forbidden by the Law of Conscience or the Law of the Spiritual Reason—that is, the law of God: and secondly, that the feeling be made to issue forth in action.

Again, I think it is manifest that Human misery *is always to be diminished* under the same conditions. For instance, a cheat and an impostor, or the vilest character you can conceive, is starving—and that in consequence of his own villainies, or his own profligate conduct,—if you give him *money* wherewith *he may* relieve his misery, reason and experience tell you that with that money *he will* purchase the means of debauchery; your Conscience and your reason both tell you therefore that *the gift of money is wrong*—but they tell you *not* that *therefore you are to do nothing.* The money was only for the purpose of relief of misery,—and that under the circumstances *it* could not relieve; this only excuses you from aid in that particular way—you are still bound to seek some other means, which *shall effectually bring about the result.*

Misery is, *in all cases,* so far as men are individually concerned, to be alleviated and put an end to. As far as men are not concerned individually, but where the obligation of the Family or the Nation is concerned, it is manifest that it is a different thing. Higher relations here come in; and the authoritative power of inflicting not merely *pain,* but *actual misery* for beneficial purposes, is a power which belongs primarily to God, but to them secondarily, as institutions organized by God, and serving to carry out his Law.

But with regard to personal misery between man and man, I think there is little doubt, that when the emotion of Sympathy carries us towards the relief of it, the failure of the readiest means, or even of *many means* does not at all excuse us from the obligation to relieve it, but only from the using of that particular means.

And secondly,—that it has been the consequence of sin or evil conduct, this by no means is an excuse from action of relief—but between man and man, the *misery of the individual man* is *ever to be relieved, and aid that shall do this* under the above rules and limitations, *never to be refused.*

CHAPTER III.

Habit; Active and Passive.—Passage from Butler quoted, and practically applied.—Affectation.—Sentimentalism.—Unreality, or Romance.—Day-dreaming.—Remedies for these diseases of the Moral Nature.

In our last chapter we treated upon "Sympathy," because we look upon it as the first of the Affections, and as the one which must go with all the rest in reference to our own moral improvement and our neighbour's; a peculiar moral element, that is capable of union with all the others, and therefore to be considered as antecedent to them all. There are some other powers of the same kind, which, if we consider them now as capable of being united with many of the affections, we shall thereby have clear ideas of them; if we leave them to be considered in their complication with other Affections, we shall be liable to great confusion and indistinctness.

And the first of these considerations is this: "Upon the Affections, what is the power and influence of Habit?" There is an "*emotion,*" for instance, of "Compassion;" there is an *act* of "Compassion;" there is a *habit* of "*Compassion.*" What is the moral value and the moral difference of these three modes of the one Affection? Wherein is the Habit more than the Emotion or the Act?

Upon this subject of Habit we shall enter in this chapter, and we clearly tell our readers that the chapter shall be little more than the remarks of Bishop Butler upon the point, with comments of our own, pointing out and illustrating the most important sentiments in the passage which we quote from him.

If this book be used in teaching Ethics, we advise the teacher, having himself practically realized, (which is to a teacher of Ethics the most valuable process of Ethical knowledge,) the influence upon morals of these principles of Butler, to turn the attention of his class upon them, and line by line, and word by word, for we count them more precious than gold, to *illustrate, enforce, explain*, by all the means in his power, until each one feels the principles and their value in relation to his own life; and to think no time wasted that will bring about this result.

And if, on the other hand, our reader be a student of Ethics, whose object is as a man to know his own Heart and Nature, and so to use and apply its powers that he may reach the height that his Nature and Position enable him to attain, we ask of him *to think, and think again*, over this passage.

And warning him to expect no brilliancy of expression, no eloquence, no striking point or antithesis; for as one who was a good writer but no thinker* remarks, "for one who was so wonderful a thinker as Butler there hardly ever was so bad a writer;" I again express the opinion that the passage contains for him who is in pursuit of Ethical truth and Ethical progress, principles more precious than gold.

These principles are applicable to all the moral powers as well as to the "Heart," but upon it the bearings of them are of the deepest importance. Here, therefore, I introduce the passage, at the same time avowing that it tells upon the whole moral life of Man. Having thus premised, we shall now quote the passage.

"There are habits of Perception, and habits of Action. An instance of the former is our constant and even involuntary readiness in correcting the impressions of our sight concerning magnitudes and distances, so as to substitute judgment in the room of sensation, imperceptibly to ourselves. And it seems as if all other associations of ideas not naturally connected, might be called *passive habits*, as properly as our readiness in understanding languages upon sight or hearing of words. And our readiness in speaking and writing them is an instance of the latter, of *active* habits."

"For distinctness, we may consider habits as belonging to the body or the mind, and the latter will be explained by tho former. Under the former are comprehended all bodily activities or motions, whether graceful or unbecoming, *which are owing to use:*

* Sir James Mackintosh;—a very eloquent composer of beautiful essays that have nothing in them, a man in his day much overpraised.

under the latter, general habits of life and conduct, such as obedience and submission to authority as to any particular; those of veracity, justice and charity; those of attention, industry, self-government, revenge. And habits of this latter kind seem produced by repeated acts as well as the former. And in like manner, as habits belonging to the body are produced by external acts, so habits of the mind are produced by the exertions of inward practical purposes; *i. e.*, by carrying them into act, or acting upon them, the principles of obedience, of veracity, justice, and charity."

"Nor can those habits be formed by an external cause of action otherwise than as it proceeds from these principles; because it *is only those inward principles exerted* which are strictly *acts* of obedience, of veracity, of justice, and of charity. So likewise habits of attention, industry, self-government, are in the same manner acquired by exercise; and habits of envy and revenge by indulgence, whether in outward act or *in thought and intention; i. e.*, inward act, *for such intention is an act.* Resolutions also to do well are properly acts; and endeavouring to force upon our own minds a practical sense of virtue, or to beget in others that practical sense of it which a man really has himself, is a virtuous act. All these, therefore, may and will contribute towards forming good habits."

"*But going over the theory of virtue in one's thoughts, talking well, and drawing fine pictures of it, this is so far from necessarily or certainly conducing to form a habit of it in him who thus employs himself, that it may harden the mind in a contrary course, and render it gradually more insensible; i. e., form a habit of insensibility to all moral considerations.* For from our very faculties of habit, passive impressions by being repeated grow weaker. Thoughts, by often passing through the mind, are felt less sensibly; being accustomed to danger begets intrepidity, *i. e.*, lessens fear; to distress, lessens the passion of pity; to instances of other's mortality, lessens the sensible apprehension of our own."

"And from these two observations together, that *practical habits are formed and strengthened by repeated acts*, and that *passive impressions grow weaker* by being repeated upon us, it must follow that active habits may be gradually forming and strengthening, by a course of acting upon such and such *motives and excitements, whilst these motives and excitements themselves, are by proportionable degrees growing less sensible; i. e.*, are continually less and less sensibly felt, even as the active habits strengthen."

"And experience confirms this; for active principles at the very time that they are less lively in perception than they were, are found to be, *somehow, wrought more thoroughly into the temper and character;* and become more effectual in influencing our practice."

"The three things just mentioned may afford instances of it. Perception of danger is a natural excitement of passive fear and active caution, and by being inured to danger, habits of the latter are gradually wrought at the same time that the former gradually lessens. Perception of distress in others is a natural excitement, passively to pity and actively to relieve it; but let a man set himself to attend to, inquire out, and relieve distressed persons, and he cannot but grow less and less sensibly affected with the various miseries of life with which he must become acquainted, when yet at the same time, benevolence, considered not as a passion *but as a practical principle of action*, will strengthen; and whilst he passively compassionates the distressed less, he will acquire a greater aptitude actively to assist and befriend them. So also at the same time that the daily instances of mens dying around us, give us daily a less sensible passive feeling, or apprehension of our own mortality, such instances greatly contribute to the strengthening a practical regard to it in serious men; *i. e.*, to forming an habit of action with a constant view to it."

"And this seems again further to show, that *passive impressions made upon our minds by admonition, experience, example, though they may have a remote efficacy and a very great one* towards forming active habits, yet can have this efficacy *no otherwise than by inducing us to such a course of action;* and that it is, *not being affected* so and so, *but acting* which forms those habits; only it must be always remembered that *real endeavours to enforce good impressions upon ourselves* are a *species of virtuous action.* Nor do we know how far it is possible, in the nature of things, that effects should be wrought in us at once, equivalent to habits; *i. e.*, what is wrought by use and exercise."

"However, the thing insisted upon is, not what may be possible, but what is in fact the appointment of nature; which is, that *active habits are to be formed by exercise.* Their progress may be so gradual as to be imperceptible in its steps; it may be hard to explain the faculty by which we are capable of habits throughout its several parts, and to trace it up to its original, so as to distinguish it from all others in our mind; and it seems as if contrary effects were to be ascribed to it. But the thing in general, that our nature is *formed to yield*, in some such manner as this, to use and exercise, is matter of certain experience."

"*Thus, by accustoming ourselves to any course of action, we get an aptness to go on, a facility, readiness, and often pleasure in it. The inclinations which rendered us averse to it grow weaker; the difficulties in it, not only the imaginary but the real ones, lessen; the reasons for it, offer themselves of course to our thoughts upon all occasions, and the least glimpse of them is sufficient to make us go on in a course of action to which we have been accustomed.*"*

"And practical principles appear *to grow stronger absolutely in themselves by exercise*, as well as *relatively with regard to contrary principles*,† which by being accustomed to submit, do so habitually and of course; and thus, a *new character* in several respects *may be formed*, and many habitudes of life, *not given by nature but which nature directs us to acquire.*"

We have taken the liberty, in reference to the truth of these observations from Butler, for the sake of greater distinctness of impression upon the students of this book, first, to divide the extract into paragraphs, and secondly, to mark with italics the passages which we wish them to reflect upon more attentively; and having made these observations, we shall proceed to consider it in the way of comment and remark.

Now with regard to the affections, our readers will have seen that there are three modes of their action; the first is the *feeling*, or *emotion;* the second, the *action;* and the third, the *habit;* and with regard to these, it is manifestly a thing deserving of consideration, to examine wherein does Virtue as regards the Affections consist.

And first, with regard to the Emotion, when we consider what has been said in the last chapter, we shall see that in respect to any affection of the Heart, the *Emotion considered by itself may exist along with a great degree of viciousness of heart and life, even as regards that very virtue it was intended to promote.*

* I would wish my reader to weigh this well in reference to Conscience.

† And this also is most important in regard to all the moral powers.

For instance, in the vicious sentimentalist, such as Rousseau or Sterne, the *Emotion of Pity* may be exceeding great, and yet the *virtue of Pity* have no existence, and the vice of baseness and hardness of heart be most luxuriant in growth.

Again, in this world, the fact is, that the Heart of the vicious is not entirely hardened, only partially; and then the emotions that would lead the man against that, his particular vice, these only are steadily checked, while the others are not checked but seem to flourish. So have we in our own experience seen a man *utterly licentious*, in whom the feeling of justice in money matters was so great that he prided himself upon it to an extraordinary degree. We have seen one most dishonest, whose sense and feeling of Compassion was so great, that to his sick and distressed neighbours, that same man, who when they were in health would act in the most rapacious way to them, would be the most kind-hearted and the most sympathizing of attendants upon the sick-bed. And again, those who to the world have been cruel and harsh, by the force of the natural feeling have overflowed with natural affection towards their own family.

Nay, from experience and history, we conclude that the *heart of no man*, while upon this earth, is so utterly hardened, so that the fountain of all his Emotions shall be entirely closed; but in all men, there remains still some feeling of the Heart which shall flow forth to their fellow-men, *so that some shall love them still.* The monster Nero had still some fellow-being, who had loved him, to scatter flowers upon his grave; and the hideous Marat, and the cold-hearted and merciless Robespierre, had surviving friends that could weep for them.

In the mere emotion, then, the moral value of the virtue does not rest; or rather the highest possible amount of emotion may exist, and yet there be no moral value in it at all. Or to speak more precisely, such an amount of emotion as ought to lead naturally to any one virtue, may exist along with the most utter viciousness of life and action, even in respect to that virtue. In Emotion, therefore, whether considered in reference to intensity, or continuance, the virtue does not consist,—not even in the very emotion that is kindred to the virtue and leads naturally to it.

Again; with regard to Action, it is perfectly manifest that momentary or irregular actions, *in consequence* of the Emotion, may be done without any true merit or true value belonging to them.

For instance, the above persons specified,—the dishonest man did acts of true compassion from the emotion of Pity,—the licentious man acts of true honesty from the emotion of Honesty,—and he who was utterly cruel to the world, acts of true Affection; and yet none would call them moral men, even in those acts.

Nay further, it is manifest that acts, which in themselves upon principle had been good, may be done upon grounds entirely unbenevolent, and motives entirely selfish, and so be evil. So the man who acts in a strict compliance with the laws of Honesty, or the dictates of Affection, for a course of many years, in order that thereby he may attain to such a character as will put him in a position in which he may be enabled to defraud largely. From these instances, it is manifest that Action, and especially momentary Action, is not necessarily virtuous.

And in addition to this, we would practically remark, that in accordance with the principle that evil is a deficiency, *goodness consists of many elements*, all of which, especially as far as concerns the Affections, must go to making it up; and the deficiency of *one* element shall be evil. And *one* evil ingredient shall be enough to destroy a whole character.

But to resume, with regard to the Affections, we have shown that the "Emotion" has not necessarily a moral character, that the Action upon the Emotion in itself, is not of necessity virtuous. But the *Habit* shall be so, according to the principle laid down here by Bishop Butler,—that is, the *Habit* of *acting* steadily upon the *emotion* as a **fixed principle* and *law of life.*

He, therefore, who feels in himself generous and lofty emotions of the Heart, or tenderness and kindness of feeling, if he would improve the natural advantages that he has, *let him not dwell in the emotion*, as something in itself satisfactory; still less let him content himself with the applause of those he benefits, or even the approval of his own Heart upon *straggling and desultory actions*, done at hap hazard, upon the spur of the mere emotion.

Let him act upon it, *steadily and habitually*, until *it form itself as a principle*† of his conduct, and so shall that be easy to him that required effort, and that habitual that was done with a

* Herein are the Affections connected with the Reason. See in the Second Book, the Chapter wherein Moral Principle is examined.

† See again the rules of Moral Principle, in the Second Book.

struggle. For "Emotion" is not in itself virtuous, or the means of "moral progress," nor is action considered by itself, but *virtue is in "Habit,"* and *virtue* is a "*Habit.*" And to act steadily and systematically upon one affection of the Heart, until this become a principle, habitual, and even unnoticed in its impression, but *constant* and *ever-present*, this is the way of moral progress by means of the Affections.

And as it is in reference to the Spiritual Reason, that he who acts in view of one of the "qualities of God," steadily and calmly so that "moral perception" becomes "moral principle," to him shall another open; so is it with regard to these emotions of the Heart that bind us to our fellow-men. That the Emotions should lead to the Action, and both be interwoven into the chain of Habit, which finally becomes of our nature,—this opens new fountains and leads the way to a greener verdure, a more luxuriant growth.

Have no emotions, then, towards your fellows, of benevolence, pity, or compassion, that, under the Supremacy of the Conscience and the Law of Reason, you do not act upon; none that you do not form into a principle and a habit of life.

For, as in a future world, we must conceive the same bodies to arise and the same features to be possessed by them, and yet shall they be perfect in beauty and radiant with the light of heaven; and therefore each form and each face here upon earth, must contain the elements of a celestial beauty peculiar to itself, and yet of the highest and most exceeding glory; so even in this world, all characters, even those that have been the most utterly vile, *have had*, in their Heart, the elements of an exceeding and peculiar loveliness of the Affections, which might have shown forth from them as a celestial halo.

Men know not the power of the Affections, acted upon as habits, to renew the whole character. They are so besotted with mere mental influences and the belief that everything can be done by arguing, and information, and talking, that they do not see the power of the Heart. Here, I will suppose, is a man of the hardest heart, and the most avaricious and grasping habits, or a man of the harshest temper, or of the greatest selfishness. Let that man, seeing his own faults, let him go forth with only the one word, "*I will*,"* and translate that word into action of, and upon the Affec-

* Here Intention or Purpose comes in manifestly, and therefore here is seen the connexion of the Will with the Affections.

tions, even although the feeling be almost frozen and dead in him, that action shall awaken the Feeling a little. And this, attended by the "Will," shall move again towards another action. And the Action again shall increase the Feeling, and so until the whole force of the Heart is awakened. And then, under Habit, it shall become a Principle, and way be made for another, and again another, until the man to his neighbour's view is entirely changed. And by a reverse process, the most lovely Nature is capable of being hardened until it be utterly deformed.

Let no one then despair because of deficiencies of natural temper; for the coldest heart may glow, the most selfish heart be generous, the most irritable be calm and meek, the most stern and rude become gentle and courteous, but *it is no mental effort that does all this*, none but a *moral one;* the effect of the "Will" and the "Affections" and the Reason acting upon the character by the laws of their nature.

This is no mysterious or baffling discipline, it is a thing that each man can do; a practical rule that all can act upon. Let them try it, and they will see it to be a true one. For as the ancient Grecian Sculptor saw in the block of unhewn marble, the statue that in his mind he had pictured forth as to be made from it, and said, "This marble contains that statue, and I shall uncover it;" and did not say, "I shall make it," but "I shall uncover it," as if all his work were merely the removing of portions of marble that covered and hid the image; so it is with the mass of men—they are, as far as the high Ideal image of moral beauty is concerned, shapeless, and yet there lies in each and every one of them an image and a translucent glory of moral loveliness that even in this life can be "uncovered."

But *Educating as the notion goes* will not do it; *Information* will not do it; Knowledge or mere Mental Culture will not do it. The *only thing that will produce these results upon the moral character is direct cultivation of the moral powers of the Affections.* And this that we call loveliness of temper is to be reached only in this way, by "the Will" and "the Affections," *directly and consciously acting.*

Again, we would notice the fact laid down by Butler, that "Passive Habits" as he calls them somewhat infelicitously, or as they might be called "habits of impression," grow weaker from repeated action, while habits of "action upon Principle" grow stronger.

Two most important conclusions are to be made from this maxim, especially by the young.

The first is, that he who shall *desire to do* a moral act, especially one belonging to the affections, an act of compassion or pity: he shall often *find himself carried on towards it by a rush and glow of emotion, which shall at the same time be the highest inducement to the action, and in some measure its highest reward.* Upon forming the principle, and going upon it steadily, this *glow shall diminish,* he shall no longer *feel the emotion* as he felt it at first; but instead of it shall come a calm, settled, tranquil conviction of doing as he should do according to his nature—a mingled feeling of kindliness, and wisdom, and patience, and assurance, and joy, permanent and unexcitable, which shall take the place of the first and more vehement emotion.

Now I would caution the young not to think of that first emotion otherwise than as *a temporary aid to carry them onward over the gulf of old habit,* so as to do that they were unaccustomed to do; otherwise than as a stimulus *to carry out the feeling to action,* until *it is delivered over to Habit and Principle;* and to think that that feeling *must pass away,* and that *if we would live in it* we could not. And the *attempt to keep it up* in the mind, instead of carrying it out into "Action" and "Principle," and thereby confirming the Habit, and so changing Emotion into *virtue,* this, shall end as the use of bodily stimulants does upon the body, in ruin and destruction of the tone and health of the moral power.

But to carry the *Emotion* into *Action,* and both by *Habit* into *Principle,* this makes and forms a *virtue,* and from that comes the deep and calm self-assurance that we have spoken of.

And to those who understand not this, but imagine the "emotion" to be a thing especially desirable to keep up, it is a very customary thing to seek after means whereby they may so stimulate the feeling as to retain it in its original strength. The readiest means to this is, first, our own mental powers internally, and secondly, language, or the speaking much about the matter. These are the usual means employed.

Now, with regard to these, let any one consider Butler's principle, "*that going over the theory of virtue in one's thoughts, talking well and drawing fine pictures of it, this is so far from necessarily or certainly conducing to form a habit of it in him who thus employs himself, that it may harden the mind in a contrary course, and gradually render it more insensible; that is, form a habit of insensibility to all moral considerations.*" Let a man consider this principle, and he shall plainly see that it is perfectly possible that a man may be led to believe that he is improving his Affections, while at the same time, by trying to stimulate, he is destroying them. For emotion carries us to act, *it exists without words* and *without reasoning*, being independent of both, and *in a higher sphere;* to bring it, then, into words, is so far to destroy its power, seeing that it naturally terminates in actions, and the process that Butler speaks of is to stop it short of that its end.

But to bring forth another principle. "*Resolutions in the mind to do well are properly acts.*" So that over and above the mental actions specified in the extract, which harden the feelings, there are others that are real actions of the mind, that do not do so, but quite the contrary.

From these two principles, then, we draw the second conclusion, "that all mental action upon ourselves or others that tends *merely to stimulate* and *keep up emotion* is directly injurious, and tends to destroy the Affections and the moral powers generally."

The observations made upon "Sentimentalism," in the last chapter, are more fully confirmed by those upon Habit in this. We, therefore, shall proceed to other diseases of the same kind; they may be enumerated as "Affectation," "Unreality, or Romance," and "Day-dreaming."

Now, with regard to Affectation, it is only a slighter form of Sentimentalism,—a mental state in which an individual of naturally noble feelings, instead of carrying the feeling out into action, *merely speaks of it, and praises it;* at first, from a real and overflowing apprehension of its moral beauty, and finally, from custom, vanity, or any sort of notion of being "eloquent," or "in-interesting," or "agreeable," or "entertaining"—until the tongue comes to run over and parrot a set of phrases that did originally signify and convey feeling, but now have no such meaning or power. A very slight fault this, and very usual in youth. The sorrows and the strifes of life, however, usually amend it, and the man or the woman who has been forced by them *really to feel*, often looks back with a kind of wonder and astonishment at the mock pathos and affected fervor of his youth.

Unreality is another thing of the same kind, a feeling towards high, and noble, and generous actions, of admiration and self-esteem, which thinks that these are easy to ourselves, and therefore is ready to undertake everything of this kind, but *has not counted the cost.* An uncalculating generosity it is, arising in the very contrary direction from Sentimentalism—for the "Sentimentalist" substitutes his own flights of emotion, and his glowing words for true action; but the man who is "Unreal," he has looked at things as they are presented to him ordinarily in literature, surrounded by a glow of Romance, a halo of rainbow colors; he takes them to be such as they are represented, and hence no appreciation has he of the truth and the fact. Garlands of flowers for him festoon all circumstances. Odors, not of Araby, but of "Lubin et Cié, à Paris," breathe a soft fragrance; the whole world is a Boudoir to him:—and he does not understand *what it is to struggle and to endure, to bear and to forbear.*

The Literature of the day has done this,—it has created this Unreality,—it presents stimulating fiction and sweetly poisonous untruth to the young, who spend upon these dreams the nobleness of feeling, and fervor of heart, that truly cherished and truly expended, would lead to the loftiest action. And then, at the first real contact with life, they find the falsehood and untruth of these Romantic views,—they fling them aside, and with them, too often, alas! the nobleness of feeling that had been thus mislaid upon an imaginary world, and sink into calculating Selfishness,—the fixed determination of mind, that all nobleness, all tenderness of thought, all generosity of heart is folly and imagination, and that self is all and in all.

And hence it is, that they who might have been the noblest, sink into self-enjoying Epicureans, whose business and thought is that of the old pagan: "Eat, drink, enjoy thyself, the rest is not worth a fillip."* Or else the still lower and viler sentiment engraved upon the tomb of the English Poet:

> "Life's a jest, and all things show it;
> I thought so once, and now I know it."†

And this Epicureanism is destroying the Educated Classes: they are perishing and decaying by it. And they who have been led

* Inscription upon the tomb of Sardanapalus.

† How wretched *in* life must the man have been, if these sentiments were really and truly the opinion of his heart. Although perhaps we may charitably

by their strife with poverty and labor from childhood, to feel the world as it is as a reality, and life as a reality, they fight their way to the wealth the others waste,—that their children may go through the same process of self-indulgence and consequent mental and bodily decay.

We have spoken of this at length; we say to the rich: "Train your children in religion, *a disciplinary religion*, a religion, not of *emotion*, but of *duty*. Let them feel and know a power superior to Wealth; let the Home, *a holy Home*, open their minds to the sense of the Unseen God and His realities,—to the Affections of the Heart, to an obedience to the Conscience, and to a sense of the power and glory of the Will. Let the Father train the child to Obedience, and the Mother to Love, and the Clergyman to a Religion verifying itself in Faith and Works. And so shall he

suppose that they were rather the offspring of that good-natured foolhardiness by which, in the last century, men of Genius were seduced into trifling with subjects, upon which they actually believed with trembling, in order to show their wit.

That such might have been the case with poor good-natured Gay, we may believe. But it was carrying the joke too far, to inscribe such blasphemous flippancy upon a tomb!

How much loftier and truer are the lines of our great American poet, Longfellow:

"Tell me not in mournful numbers,
Life is but an empty dream,
For the soul is dead that slumbers,
And things are not what they seem.

Life is real! life is earnest!
And the Grave is not its goal;
Dust thou art, to dust returnest,
Was not spoken to the soul.

Not enjoyment, and not sorrow,
Is our destined end or way,
But to act, that each to-morrow
Find us further than to-day.

* * * * * * * *

Let us then be up and doing,
With a heart for any fate,
Still achieving, still pursuing:
Learn to labor and to wait."

grow up as a Man, not as an animal whose one idea is that enjoyment of the senses is all, and that riches is all-mighty to procure this enjoyment, and that the whole world has for this reason only its existence. And so he shall not, because he has merely grown up as an animal (for it is not Education), be prepared to give up to a stimulating and unreal literature, whatsoever natural earnestness and natural nobility there was in his Heart."

"Let not this be so, but let the child have, and obtain a truly religious training, and then this sense of Unreality, this hankering after stimulants for the mind, this inward Selfishness of Heart shall be abated."

And for those who feel that Romance and Unreality makes a part of their moral character, and who would themselves get rid of it, I should think that an abstinence from such literature, a direct contact, self-sought, with the misery and sorrow of existence in the way of *relief* and *sympathy*, as well as a direct and steady employment and object in life, would be of great service.

And above all things, I would recommend as a remedy for Unreality and Romance, a duty enjoined in the Scriptures as a Spiritual discipline,—the duty of fasting. I mean not merely the change of one kind of food for another, but *an actual abstinence, for a set time, from all food*, say once in the week, of course under the advice of a physician,—so that it shall not be an injury to the constitution,—but with this limitation, fasting sharp and severe, so as to acquaint the man with *the suffering of hunger*. It is astonishing how much Unreality this will do away with, how much Romance it will destroy; how much sympathy with poverty and misery it will produce. It is a Spiritual Discipline, prescribed in the New Testament, and we here advise it as a remedy, much to be used.

We now go on to speak of "Day Dreaming," or "Building Castles in the air."

Now to bring this forward in a book upon morals, may seem, to some, superfluous. And yet, we believe, to notice it, is absolutely necessary, for it is a disease of the two noblest powers of man, the Imagination* and the Affections. And one which, we are convinced, from our experience as an educator, wastes more energy

* What is called Imagination, distinguished rigidly from Fancy, is a great deal more nearly akin to the Spiritual Reason, than men imagine.

and destroys more naturally high and lofty minds, than perhaps any other.

The Day-dreamer feels himself limited in power by the situation wherein he is placed; ordinary life is not enough for him, but he would do wonders of Benevolence, requiring mines of wealth and inexhaustible power. Therefore, he turns away with disgust from active life, and revels in dreams of overflowing wealth, of which he is the possessor and the dispenser, and of lofty and splendid deeds, of which he is the hero; and inwardly, upon the theatre of a prolific fancy, he enacts many scenes which would, in themselves, be perfectly ridiculous, but for their sad effects upon the mind of the man.

For life and its duties pass by him unheeded, while he is occupied with these inward visions; mental energy is dissipated by the morbid effect of the Imagination; decision of action and of aim is utterly lost; and too often, alas! it is directly true that, according to the principle of Bishop Butler, "the going over the theory of virtue, and drawing fine pictures of it, is so far from necessarily or certainly conducing to form a habit of virtue in him, who thus employs employs himself, that it may harden the mind in a contrary direction." I consider that this "day-dreaming," upon these grounds, is directly injurious to the Moral powers, directly Evil.

Hitherto we have supposed it innocent, as far as the thoughts are concerned, but often, especially in those not baptized with the baptism of Christ, it is the introducer to direct sin. It leads in wandering thoughts and these become gradually vicious and evil, thoughts of rioting, lasciviousness, violence, avarice, revenge, indulged in, cherished by the Heart, and swarming in it, ready to burst forth into evil words and evil actions, before the man is himself aware of it.

For "*thought*," as Butler remarks, "is action," "*words are actions*," and "*deeds are action*." That is, thoughts *voluntarily cherished, assented to, agreed with*,—words *freely and intentionally* spoken—acts *willingly done*—all these are action for which we are responsible.

And so does it often happen, owing to the seductive influence of this vice of the moral habits, that in the family, unknown to the parents, the youth shall have been laying up for years the materials for a moral explosion that shall bring upon him sudden ruin and destruction. Well was it that our Saviour placed in the Heart the "issues of life and death," truly according to the facts and the reality of our nature, did he insist upon watching over the "Heart;" for there is the source of almost all evil.

Now in reference to this disease so expounded, I give this advice; first:

Let the person who has fallen into the habit of "Day Dreaming," let him set before himself, in view, a fixed and determinate end to fulfil, an object and employment in life that he judges worthy of an effort, and let him steadily struggle and labour towards it with all his energies and all his powers. Again, let him avoid solitude, as this especially gives room for these reveries of the Imagination, and keep in society, except so much as may be absolutely necessary for the business of life. If alone, let him be employed; for an idle solitude, an unbusy loneliness, is in itself a temptation to reverie. And lastly, let him avoid long sleep in the morning as enervating to the body and the mind; for in fact, the state of morning sleep, half dreaming, half awake, is injurious to men's energies, mainly because it leads to this habit of dreaming reverie.

And as the last and most efficient remedy, especially if those scattered and wandering thoughts have become evil and have led to evil; I advise the person, especially if a youth under the care of a religious and thoughtful Father and Mother, to lay open to them *under strict confidence*, the state of his mind, and to be of them guided as to his conduct. For evil thoughts *hidden* shall rankle and become as ulcers to the moral being; whereas *laid open* to the eye of a Father or a Mother, they shall by their care be healed.

And here I would add a remark for the Parent and for the Child. The fact is, that between a "Lawyer" and his "Client" there exists a "Legal confidence," to which the lawyer is sworn that he will maintain it, in consequence of which the client consulting with him, may inform him of many matters, that discovered, would bring detriment, but all which the lawyer is bound to conceal. Between the "Physician" and his "Patient" there is a confidence also by which the "Physician" is bound to keep secret and entirely unknown, all matters so revealed, if not in law, at least in the common law of honour that exists in the Profession. And this exists in consequence of the natural position of "Lawyer" and "Client," "Physician" and "Patient;" and is recognized in the law of the land to a degree that but few have any perception or apprehension of.

And so do I imagine that it is or ought to be by nature between Parent and Child. I do believe that such is the trustful nature of the relation between Parent and Child, that if the Child understood clearly that his Father held the principle of "Parental Confidence" as a fixed rule, and considered himself thereby bound to a deep and unbroken silence under all circumstances whatsoever, as to that which his children had so confided to his knowledge,—if this were so, I believe that the child in nine cases out of ten would lay open to the Parent's eye evils that now are left to rankle and ulcerate, because they are concealed; and half the injuries that come upon families unawares, would be avoided, and the parent become the repository of the most inward thoughts of the child, his guardian against secret temptation.* So would he be enabled to check those first movements towards evil, whether arising from individuals without, or from evil thoughts, half the power of which depends upon their hiddenness.

But to do this, manifestly requires a father who is in himself a religious and a truly good man; for such I leave the suggestion to be considered, and I hope by many to be acted upon.

In reference to this matter I shall bring forward another thought, which though it may properly appear to belong to another part of this book, yet finds its practical place here. We have seen under the head of the Reason, that we are surrounded by the Unseen World; nay, that we have a peculiar sense, if I may use the word, by which we feel its reality and are brought in contact with it. We know further that it has *good* and *evil agents*, that can and do act upon us. Now I would take notice that there are *powers of suggestion* by which thoughts that are in truth *not our own*, are pushed forward as it were upon and into our minds, so that they become supposititious, *appearing to be our own*, and yet *not being so*. Secret adits there are in the channel of our life, whereby these flow in upon us, and by a sort of immediate unconscious action, may be adopted as ours, or rather *unwittingly considered* to be the offspring of our own Hearts. Now these *suggestions* are especially dangerous, being acquiesced in by many, even at once; and to

* The same advice has been before given in regard to scruples of conscience. I give it now again in reference to a subject more important.

others giving the most distressing feelings of self-accusation, and even of despair.

I would advise the Person upon whom the name of Christ has been named to bring them forward into full consciousness—to interrogate them, to say to each "does this agree with my principles, my life, my actions?" and then finding they do not, to condemn them as suggestions and temptations of the Enemy of Man, and be not disturbed.

But for those who have not had the seal of the Christian Covenant impressed upon their foreheads, for them no doubt these thoughts suggested from without have great advantage in the Habit of Day-dreaming that we have referred to; and the whole matter, even apart from the principle of Butler that we have cited, may be looked upon as the readiest school that the Evil Unseen World has of training and educating man to Evil.

There are other mental vices connected with Habit, which we might discuss and examine. But the principles are the same that we have cited from Bishop Butler, and the student can, as an exercise, apply them for himself. We therefore leave to him all further application of them as an exercise of moral study, begging him again to put upon these Principles the high value and estimation which they so truly deserve.

CHAPTER IV.

From the Heart proceeds the greatest Evil.—Cause of this, Original Sin — Effects: 1st, Uncontrolledness, or Self-will; 2d, Selfishness; 3d, Sensuality.—Uncontrolledness discussed.—The Passions.—Selfishness.—Paley's Theory discussed and refuted.—Unselfishness.—Annihilation of self.—Sensuality.—There is a threefold instinct to guide Man: of the Spirit; the Mind; the Body: 1st, the Spiritual Powers; 2d, the Desire of Having.—The nature and origin of Property, and the immorality of its assailants.—3d, Pleasure and Pain; uses of these last.—"Good and Evil" is not determined by "Pleasure and Pain."—Systematic Sensuality.—The Christian Home alone cures these three faults.

Our readers have seen, we trust, in the last chapter, the truth that the highest moral development possible to man's nature is through and by the Affections; that therein there lies the germ of all that man may become to man, a vessel full to overflowing of all kindly affections and humane and unselfish feelings, blessing his fellow, and therein himself twice blessed. So that because of the capabilities of moral and spiritual transformation, possessed by this governing power, he that is embruted and debased so far that his fellows shall find no epithet to express his nature save metaphors from the lowest animals, shall be able to arise from this abyss, and deserve and earn all love and affection : the beast transformed into a man. And he that is hated, despised, detested, scorned, shall be loved and reverenced almost with worship and adoration. Such is the wonderful power of this faculty of the Spiritual Nature.

And yet true it is, that this same power is the main adit and entrance to evil. The Heart, in its state of nature, affected by Original Sin, unaided by gracious influences, is the source by which and from which almost all evil flows in upon man. Of almost all moral depravation and moral guilt, these feelings and affections of our nature, which collectively we call the Heart, are the cause;—*uncontrolled, that is*, and *ungoverned*, by *their own law*, the *law of man's nature*, and *the law of God*, all which are, in their power and their results, the same. So guided perfectly, or even so governed in some degree, these powers are the source of the highest moral perfection and the highest happiness in the relation of man tom an—uncontrolled, of the greatest debasement, the worst immorality.

We have stated the one possibility and capability fearlessly; and now do we state the other with as little fear. From the "Heart of Man" those feelings, namely, and emotions, *which naturally should rest upon his fellow for his fellow's good*, come the greatest evils and the greatest abasement. And this is the assertion of our incarnate LORD, who assumed our nature: "Out of the Heart proceed evil thoughts, murders, adulteries, fornications, thefts, false witnesses, blasphemies, these are the things which defile a man." And again, in the Old Testament it is said, "Keep the Heart, for out of it are the issues of life." And everywhere, if we shall take a practical view of human life, we shall find it true, that there is a body of natural feelings which should carry us on to do our duty to our neighbor, which we call the Heart, and that the perversion of these and the corruption of them produces "evil thoughts, murders, adulteries, thefts, fornications, blasphemies," (or as it should properly be rendered,) "slanders."

And each and every one of these crimes and vices is the perversion of some feeling or affection which was in itself good, and which under guidance and control, instead of producing evil might have produced good, unmixed and unalloyed. Murder, for instance, is the offspring of Revenge,—and Revenge is, as Bacon says, "wild justice"—so that the strong sense and feeling of being injured, and the natural desire for justice, this which in itself is perfectly right, provided it be in a legal and just way, becomes, *being perverted*, the root of murder. And with regard to Adultery—this also is the same; the adulterer lavishes upon his paramour the same feelings and affections which, placed under the law and rule of God and man, would have been innocent conjugal affection towards his lawful wife; one of the loveliest of all the natural feelings thereby being corrupted into one of the most evil and degrading of all vices. And so the "desire of Property" in the same way becomes changed into theft; and the desire of purity in society, and of seeing our brother's life pure, this becomes slanderousness. So that in the Heart and Affections of man there is hardly one emotion that is not capable of being the cause of the utmost vileness and degradation. This is the experience of all men in all ages; and howsoever men may declaim of "the dignity of Human Nature and its purity," howsoever we may boast of our nature,—yet standing by ourselves, alone and apart from the influences that are brought to bear upon us by the institutions of Society, and the unseen and unfelt hand of an ever-present God, none there are that can adequately feel how easily betrayed into evil is this part of our nature.

We have already, in the commencement of this our treatise, explained the nature of Original Sin as an inherent insubordination in our nature, whereby "it is not subject unto the law of God," nor can adequately fulfil it;* which law of God is also in a measure the law of man's nature, his Conscience and his Reason, and also his Affections.

And in our examination of each faculty of the spiritual or governing powers, we have shown how far that particular power

* "For the carnal mind is enmity against God, for it is not subject unto the law of God, neither indeed can be."—Rom. viii. 7.

"Animal Mind," as well as a Spiritual Being, can become, as it were, an "Animal." His "Affections," as they can be alloyed, or rather supplanted by "Desires," and so become selfish, so can they be alloyed or supplanted by "*mere animal appetites*," or lusts. The man may make of himself so far a mere animal. This substitution of the appetites for the "Affections," we call "Sensuality."

These, then, we count to be by nature the deficiencies of the Heart of man considered in itself, apart from all subduing influences, "Uncontrolledness," or "disobedience to law," Selfishness, and Sensuality.

And considered apart from all exterior influences that are brought to bear upon man,—that is, *if man were as he hardly can be*, shut out from all Gracious influences of his natural position in a world of Probation, and also from the Evangelical influences of the Gospel; we believe that the situation of the man would be as one having limbs, and muscles, and bones, and nerves to walk with, the very harmony and proportion of which suggested his walking,—and yet these all under the influence of palsy. Or, as it may better express the effect of "Original Sin" upon this part of his nature, we believe that he would rather be as the man to whom all his organization naturally, as well as his position in Society, suggests rationality and decorousness of conduct; and yet insanity having taken possession of his frame, overcomes, by the nervous influence, the "mental powers." And thus in him the body may be said to be warring with the mental power in equal strife; so equal, that to each he may apply the term "I," and say, "*I* wish to rule *myself*"—that is, the "I" which is sane, wishes to overcome, and control the "I" which is insane. So it seems would be the situation of man's Heart by nature; that is, apart from all gracious exterior influences. There would be in it the feeling and strong desire of control according to the harmony of God's law; but this only a feeling and persuasion, lying unable, insufficient, palsied, dead. And close by it would be the three evils that we have mentioned, uncontrolled and carrying the man hither and thither in defiance of all law of God and man; now swelling and blazing up into exuberant and overpowering Passions, and now sinking into cold and dead callousness and apathy. And the Affections, all of them, would also be perverted from their due ends, and Self-will, and "Selfishness," and "Sensuality" take their place, and reign, and rule, having the *power*, and overbearing the Feeling of *right* and of *control.* And thus would the most intense misery be produced between the strife of the Spiritual Sense and the Desire of the Heart, thus left to itself ungoverned.

But this can *never completely* take place, because, as we have urged again and again, "Society" and the "Course of God's providence" give some aid, nay, in many cases very great aid, against such a state of matters. And secondly, to counteract this, the influence of the Holy Spirit, properly called "Grace," acts so as much to prevent it, even in many that know it not. But apart from the influences of God's Moral Government, and apart from God's Grace, such would be the position of every man—a position of the most wretched misery and self-torment.

How far God may permit the Natural Heart in any individual to overpower the influences of Society and of the Spirit, we do not know, and the question is one of the most awful mystery; but it seems, from the history of our race, as if there had been plain instances in which men had been left to themselves, and that in such men Selfishness, and Sensuality, and ungoverned Passions, that might have been noble-hearted Affections, had reigned, and the acutest misery and bitterness, self-contempt and self-accusation, had been the result. And such would seem to be the destiny of each man by his nature, apart from all external divine influence, operating upon his Heart.

We proceed now to notice these three natural faults of the Heart.

The first we have mentioned is "Uncontrolledness," the natural tendency that there is, because of Original Sin, in each and every affection severally, and in them all as a body, to fall from out their Natural Harmony, imposed upon them by the Law through the Reason. This might be expressed by the word "Rebelliousness;" for every one that has had experience of Human Nature, has seen that it is not enough that a course should be rational, and even for the actual and immediate interest of the individual, and that he be clearly convinced that it is so, in order that he should pursue it. Nay, he who shall look at children in the Family, and men in Society, shall see, that because of this very thing, they shall sometimes, out of mere "Self-will," as it is called, reject proposed actions that are such. It might be called "Perverseness," or

"Frowardness," or "Self-will,"—all these express more or less the same thing; but more fully do I think that this word "Uncontrolledness," expresses that quality in the "Heart," which is the cause of "rebelliousness," and "self-will," and "frowardness," and "perverseness."

Now I suspect there are very few, indeed, that comprehend to what an extent this quality of "Uncontrolledness" exists by nature in the Heart of man, and what an immensity of Discipline in God's providence is to him administered, consciously or unconsciously, by the direct action of Society upon him, the immediate effect of which is to conquer and subdue it. This alone shows how great naturally it is. In fact, to look at it aright, the Scripture is *absolutely* and *scientifically* correct, that states frowardness to be bound up in the heart of a child,—for this quality is the first manifested by children, and to give "Self-control" is the direct effect of our providential training in the Family for so long a time as children; and in the State as men. But the amount of this in us by nature, may perhaps be best seen by considering the following extract from Bp. Butler's Analogy.

"But if we consider a person brought into the world with both these (bodily strength and understanding) in maturity, as far as this is conceivable, he would plainly at first be as unqualified for the human life of mature age as an idiot.

"He would in a manner be distracted with astonishment and apprehension, and curiosity, and suspense, nor can any one guess how long it would be before he would be familiarized to himself, and the objects about him, enough even to set himself to anything.

"It may be questioned, too, whether the natural information of his sight and hearing would be of any use at all to him in acting before experience.

"And it seems *that men would be strangely headstrong*, and *self-willed*, and *disposed to exert themselves with an impetuosity which would render society insupportable, and the living in it impracticable*, were it not for some *acquired moderation and self-government*, *some aptitude* and *readiness in restraining themselves and concealing* their sense of things."

Here, then, is the idea we have been urging plainly set forth,—it is here shown, that by nature, the long training from childhood unto manhood,—this whether the parent is conscious of it or not, is, of effect, to repress the natural "Self-will," to give "Controlledness" to that which is "Uncontrolled." And he that has seen "Savages," or even the "Semi-civilized," he shall see that the main difference that exists between them and the civilized, is the want of this "Self-control." The Savage's eye is caught by any trifle. He cannot check that desire, govern it, or in any way control it. He will, for the whim of the moment, subject himself to any amount of future misery. The civilized man, on the contrary, by all the training he has got in Civilized Society, is taught to check, rule, govern himself, and this makes all the difference between them. A great difference, indeed,—the difference of Law, and of Knowledge, of which, as we have said, Society is the channel to all who are in it, in a degree more or less to all, but highest to those who are in a Christianized Society.

Again, if any one look at a child from its birth, he will see that this very thing of "Uncontrolledness" is one born with it,—a fault of deficiency, which is supplied more or less in all who live under the guidance of Parents in the Family; but most of all in those who, being brought into Covenant with God, have all the influences attached to that state, the influences of the Spirit promised them, the teachings of God's Providence, the guardianship of the Holy Angels, the Communion of Saints, and the influence of an holy home, of a Father and Mother pledged unto God, and training up their children in Faith and Love.

This is *the complete and entire remedy*, as we have said, this and this alone. The *influences of the Gospel seen and unseen brought to bear upon the Heart from childhood*. And he that is without this may indeed, in latter years, become a Christian, but he shall be a very imperfect one, with many faults, and all of them arising from this one great natural fault of "Uncontrolledness," left in his youth unremedied. For the great cure of this fault is the Grace of God, awaking *in the Child* the Spiritual Mind *in its youth*; the *living sense*, we say, not the *verbal knowledge* of Truth, Purity, Justice, Holiness, Gentleness, Goodness; all these that we have pointed out as truths of the Spiritual Reason. These so held are the proper and only perfect checks of this "Uncontrolledness" natural to man. And we say plainly that this teaching is the only security against this fault, the only complete and entire security. And he who denies it to his child, he does with reference to his moral being as much incapacitate him as the parents of that German child Caspar Hauser did as regards his body. For he was found in the state which Butler describes, grown to maturity and yet a child, unknowing any language and untrained in any art.

We have seen ourselves youth who certainly had seen at home no viciousness, who had lived at home without vice, and then the first time that the external check of a mechanically virtuous Home was cast aside, they rushed off into all sin; and men wondered, without any cause,—for if the Spiritual Reason, that which is the image of God, is unawakened and inactive, and the Desires uncontrolled, the man so far is an animal, and will live and act as an animal. There is no wonder at all in such cases.

So far with regard to general "Uncontrolledness," as it exists as a quality of the Heart itself; as it is more generally manifested, it comes in connexion with what are called "Passions."

"This term is applied to Desires and Affections *when uncontrolled by Reason*, as if men in such cases were merely *passive* and acted upon. Thus we speak of a man *being in a Passion*, meaning an uncontrolled fit of anger, and having *a passion for an object*, meaning an uncontrolled desire.

"Still it is to be recollected that man under the influence of such Passions is not really passive—when he acts under such influence he adopts the suggestion of Desire or Affection; and rejects the control of Reason. * * * Passion does not prevent a man knowing that there is a rule and that he is acting in violation of it. To say that Passion is irresistible is to annihilate Reason and to exclude the most essential condition of Human Action."*

Upon this matter of the Passions, and their escape from control, we shall at present remark no more than that the Spiritual Reason is the Great Governor of them, and that Habit, Sympathy, Time, these are the conditions of its operation. For the very nature of a Passion is that it is momentary, and therefore it can be overcome in its vehement assaults by *preparing against it long before*, through the awakening of the Spiritual Reason, the chain of Habit, and the shield of a just and equitable Sympathy with those that passion otherwise would have injured; or else, if this have not beforehand been prepared and habitually established, at the time it can be arrested by delay, occupation, surprise, or any

* Whewell's Elements of Morality, vol. 1, p. 58.

one of those things that takes its violence from the immediate moment, and spreads it out over a space of time. For what gives a Passion force, is that it is concentrated in a moment,—resisted for that space, and its violence by any means expanded over time, it shall be conquered.

Hence the mechanical means of conquering anger by saying the Creed, counting one thousand, putting in a mouthful of water and keeping it there for some time, turning aside for ten minutes, all of these very good because they take advantage of that principle in the very nature of passion, *its momentariness.*

But a thousand-fold better is it to prepare beforehand, to think and guard ourselves against it, and thus *to conquer it before it arises.*

Another remark we would here make in reference to Passions. "An Affection, it seems, uncontrolled by Reason is a Passion;"—again in the case of the Heart, it would seem that this governing faculty belongs in some measure to the body as well as to the soul; and that we might say, that *when the Body rules then the Affection becomes a Passion, when the Spiritual power then it is an Affection.* This we say not in a precise scientific way, but in a popular one, in order to explain our meaning more perspicuously.

Now this being so, it would seem that if the Divine Reason is unawakened, and systematic and habitual controlledness is not established, that the Lusts, Desires, Appetites, bodily Passions and emotions have the power of rising up and taking the sway, but that to awaken the Spiritual powers will be to keep off and keep down the others. Love will render the individual proof against Lust, true Benevolence against Prodigality, the sense and habitual practice of Justice against brute Anger, true Joyfulness against riotous and revelling Emotion, steady Hopefulness against that variation of the same natural feeling that leads men to gambling; and so each and every emotion of the Heart under the Spiritual Reason, habitually awakened, keeps down a passion or a lust that has hurried multitudes to destruction. But nought else will effect this than that youthful training under the influence of God's Grace which I have above mentioned.

But from the nature of Passion, from the nature of the Affections, as spreading to Body and Soul, from the nature of the Reason also, to seek for *momentary remedies* instead of *permanent ones*, is merely to delude ourselves.

It is the Habit only, formed by the Reason and the Will guiding, governing, controlling *systematically* the Affections, and these Affections themselves ruling according to their nature, this is the only thing that can raise the rampart broad and high to resist the momentary rush and thunder-gust of the passions.

But that a man shall live through his existence, making it his only object to eat, and drink, and enjoy himself; and his only rule of life to be honest enough, and just enough, and fair enough, to go through life, and all this barely external honesty, and justice, and fairness: and then internally to make Self his only rule, and to laugh at the restraints of the Conscience, and overleap them, to set aside the Spiritual Reason, and in his heart despise its laws, and turn Affection into Animal desire and Lust,—for a man to do all this, *is to make himself ready to be overthrown and destroyed by the assaults of the passions.*

And for ourselves, when we look out upon life and see how many are in the situation we have just described, as to their Inward Heart,—satisfying themselves, if they satisfy Society, with an outward show, and inwardly destitute of all principle, except a systematic Selfishness,—the wonder is not to us that so many awful falls into ruin have taken place of late years, but that so many have stood. So far with regard to the Passions, as far as their governance is concerned; and with these observations, we close our remarks upon "Uncontrolledness."

With regard to the next fault of the Heart,—Selfishness, we have already spoken of it in Chapter Second of this book,—we have shown that it is the "turning *after things* of those Affections that ought to rest upon *persons* exclusively," and have sufficiently enlarged upon it.

Another matter in reference to it we would remark, that the most destructive of all modern "theories of Morals," is the doctrine of Paley, that "Selfishness, moderated and guided by Reason, is the leading principle of morality." This in fact is only the theory of Hobbes, "that the state of man naturally is a state of war; that as birds of prey are supplied with talons and beaks, and beasts of prey with teeth and claws, and both with rapacity to set at work and cunning to employ these natural arms,—so is it with man, that he is an animal *naturally at war* with his fellows, and with all other animals, rapacious by nature, and cunning, with reasoning powers given him to supply and frame the arms that he has not by nature." This is the theory of Hobbes, fully and plainly laid out; the theory of Paley, it will be seen, is much the same. It says that all that man seeks, he seeks *for himself*, and only for *self*, that this *is* the centre of all actions *and must be so*. Hence that all he can do is to moderate and guide his natural selfishness.

Hence there can be no Conscience, no natural feeling or knowledge of Justice, Truth, or Honesty,—for these are put aside, if the gratification of self, by nature, *is* and *must be* the main object of the Man. Hence there is no natural Heart or Affections for these, say "not for Self, but for *Persons who are not your Self, should you act;* and to bring in Self therein, is to pervert and destroy." This notion destroys the Conscience, the Reason, the Heart, it reduces man to the level of a beast without governing powers, led by appetites alone. Nay, it brutalizes him wholly, it says "there is no highness, no loftiness, no nobleness of moral being, for all is Appetite, all is Self;" only regulated a little by the consequences to others, and to yourself,—so that your "Self" shall last out to the end of your natural life, and not end upon the scaffold or in the prison.

This is the notion of Paley, a notion which, we will say, every man that thinks a moment, will see to be false; for the man who acts in obedience to Conscience, acts so not for any motive but that *immediate* one; just as in case of "Simple Pleasure," or Pain, with respect to his body; he that brings his hand in contact with fire takes it away, not from any reasoning upon thoughts of Self, but without any thought of it, from the Pain. And so with regard to simple emotions of Pleasure. Thus also it is with regard to him who obeys Conscience; "Good" is sought as "Good," "Evil" avoided as "Evil." "Conscience" is the natural sense of these in reference to Eternity, as the physical sensibility is of "Pleasure" and "Pain:" and as the consequence of action, attended by the one, is to the body "preservation" or "destruction," it being certain that such to the physical frame is the use of "Pleasure" and "Pain;" so to the Moral Being is the *consequence* of "Good" and "Evil." Each faculty is *an instinctive warning*, a *natural sense*, existing *in all men* without reference to knowledge or experience. And each one who acts upon Conscience, knows as much that he is acting upon it without reference to Self, as he that acts upon

"Pleasure" and "Pain," physically knows His action to be immediate *upon the instinct.*

Again, in reference to the Spiritual Reason, the man who acts upon moral principle of any kind, upon motives of Justice, Honesty, Veracity, Benevolence, he knows that it is *upon the principle* he acts, without reference to the consequence; and the *very perfection of the principle is, that upon it he would so act in despite of all consequences to self,*—strong, and upheld by the principle,

> "Unhurt amid the war of Elements,
> The wreck of matter and the crash of worlds."

So in respect of the Affections; the man who loves his family knows that he loves them for *no selfish* motives, but *for themselves* —his wife is loved for herself—his children for themselves—his friends for themselves. As we have before said, the introduction of Self here is the very destruction of the Affection.

Not according to this *moral* doctrine of Paley is the doctrine of the Holy Scriptures, but quite otherwise. "Except a man deny *himself* and take up his cross and follow me, he cannot become my disciple." In fact, herein does the spiritual doctrine unite with and crown the moral one; herein is the scion of heaven engrafted upon the progeny of earth; the scriptural doctrine of Self-denial, this is the crown of the moral doctrine of the Affections; and in the Home, in the Nation, in the Church, this is in a measure the completion of all practical philosophy, for those whom man is bound to love, to *renounce all self* and selfishness. If the Husband, the Wife, the Father, the Mother, the Daughter, the Son, the Brother, the Sister,—if these love, and for this their love, *renounce and deny and give up Self*, and cause their desires to be towards the happiness of one another;—then is the Home a pure fount and crystal spring of happiness and sweet calm joy. If those Affections that should be disinterested are set upon the *advantages that affection brings*, then Selfishness ultimately brings its own punishment, and that which ought to be happy shall be miserable.

So it is with the Nation;—to labour for the Nation's good, this brings happiness, being disinterested; but Selfishness spoils and destroys Patriotism: and so it is with the Church.

To *deny* oneself,—to love whom we ought to love with an affection *pure from all motives of self*,—this is the height and completion of all wisdom of life, in the Home, the Nation, and the Church.

And as it is the most difficult of all moral tasks, so it is the best rewarded. For if the most selfish soul only knew the calm and certain joy of him who has trained himself to Unselfishness,—if he only knew how soon Selfishness is found out and hated when even buried under the deepest disguise;—and how soon Unselfishness is found out and loved and respected, and given of men *power* and *influence* and *authority*, these things which the selfish man most desires to get, and the being baffled in the attainment of which, is his most frequent torment and truest punishment:—if he only could find out and experience this, even his *selfishness* would drive him to cast away *selfishness.*

But again, I would impress upon my readers that "Selfishness" is the substitution of Desires for Affections; and that merely to fling away the Desire or the object of the Desire, this is of no avail except the Affection take its place: and herein lies the difference between Abstinence and Fasting, Benevolence and mere Prodigality, money-careless Goodnature and Compassion. To renounce things is not hard; to *have Affections rightly directed*, in consequence of which "Desires" are kept away, and "things" renounced, this is the completeness of "Unselfishness."

One thing more in reference to this and I have done with the subject; "*Selfishness*" is not "*Self*" verbally or actually. A man's "*Self*" is his *Being*, his *Identity*, that which makes him what he is. Now there is a religious philosophy that now and then springs up, an error that the noblest often fall into, that confound these two, that says "*let us annihilate self;*" and then prescribes a denial of all emotions whatsoever, an attempt to be without emotion and almost without being, and calls this Perfection.

This is the philosophy of the Mystics or Quietists, and plainly takes Self as if it meant "Selfishness." It is a verbal error, one nevertheless that many have fallen into. We mention it here merely for the sake of caution. Selfishness you can annihilate completely by the Grace of God, given in his Covenant—"*Self*," that is your individual emotions and feelings, you cannot annihilate—if you could your situation then would be that of an idiot—the Perfect Man of the Mystics only and merely exists as an idiot.

But man as God made him, and as God intended him to be, was to enjoy all the emotions of an Heart overflowing with love to God and man, under the guidance of God's law and the ruling power of his own inward being, and not to dream of annihilating them, for these all are *good* in themselves and *not evil.* That they should be guided, governed, controlled, repressed, moderated under God's Law, and by God's Grace, with and by means of the internal governing nature of man, this as a right and true desire ;—but the "annihilation" of them is a Quietist dream that has led many astray.

We come now to the last natural fault of the Affections, that is, Sensuality. Upon this we have already remarked, that it consists in the substituting habitually the mere "Animal Desires" for the Affections.

This, in the Scriptures, is called "Lust," or the "Carnal Mind," these words meaning one and the same thing, the man's acting merely as an Animal, and *putting aside altogether his moral and spiritual being.* This we have termed "*Sensuality.*"

Now, it is worth while to examine the ground and foundation of this. We have seen that man is made up of three elements—the Body, the Animal Mind, the Spirit. We have looked at the Spirit, and seen whereunto its desires tend, in our examination of its various powers. Again: we have seen of the Animal Mind that its desire is towards visible things—things of the Senses, which, by virtue of his organization, man desires *to have.* Again: we look at the Body, we find that it has Sensibility, the power of being affected by external things, that is, of feeling from them the sense of Pleasure and of Pain; that this is strictly and scientifically *the sense that preserves the body from disorganization.* Hence has man, as such, a threefold natural instinctive guide, born with him and awakened in him to act, by the action upon him of Society and Nature—first, the four spiritual senses, that we have so often enumerated, which bind him to God and to things eternal, immortal, invisible.

Secondly: he has with reference to things seen, the sense "of *having,*" the natural feeling of the Possession of Property, of Life, and of Rights—this, we take it, belongs to the Mind, as one and the first of its faculties.

And he that considers the origin of Property, he shall see that there is a natural instinct and ineradicable feeling in Man, by his being, the Desire of Having, which urges him to labor of mind and body, and thereby to obtain as *his own* that which he desires. It is an indestructible and fundamental faculty and feeling of his nature—to be ruled, of course, by law and equity, but not originating in them, but in the man's nature, concurring with the external means of gratifying it.

The Desire to Have—Labor—Property—these are as the eye —its power of sight—things visible. They belong to the Individual Man, as the power of making honey,—the desire to make it,—and the honey, to the Bee. Inherent in Man, they are connatural, always existing; belonging to the very nature of the being, and to that of the world wherein that being is. *They can be regulated, never destroyed.** This is the second natural tie, and it connects man in a very strong way with the world of things palpable to the senses and perceptible by them.

Thirdly: the "Body" is manifestly a material organization—a living organization, too, in the midst of forces, some of which are destructive, some tend to its support. It needs, evidently, a protective sense, by which it shall be instinctively guarded against those that are destructive, and turned to those that are for its

* I have stated thus briefly the foundation of Property to be,—First, in an *inherent faculty* of our being, that cannot be eradicated from it. Secondly, in an action of the man, *labor*, that is always necessary to man's being, always has its Rights, and always must exist. Thirdly, in the provision in the external world of rewards for Labor, and incentives to the Desire of Having. If, then, from the system of the world you would destroy Property, you must be able to eradicate from the nature of man in each individual and in the whole race, an inherent and essential faculty of the mind. You must destroy Labor, and the value of its rewards. Better rule this desire by wise laws, and true and rational principles of Morality and Policy, than waste strength in doing that which cannot be done.

Another thing I would just say to those who may read this book. As in beasts, a certain shape of hoof always implies horns, and horns always imply that peculiar shape of hoof, and yet we cannot trace the logical reason, or even the natural one,—only as a fact of Natural Science it is so;—so with regard to the doctrine of "Community of Property," always through history *as a fact*, we see it has implied another " Community—*that of Wives*. These two always have been connected, one always has inferred the other. The "hoof" has always implied the "horns"—the "horns" the "hoof." Let those, therefore, who may have been pleased with these notions, *be slow—look carefully—examine cautiously*—and perhaps they may see the "hoof" and the "horns,"—and escape from both.

good—this is manifestly in what we call Sensibility* "the power of Sensation in the various tissues of the body, by which it has perceptions and emotions of Pleasure and Pain." This is branched out into the five Senses, which, besides their giving us knowledge of many qualities in bodies of which without them we should be otherwise ignorant, are of themselves organs of Pleasure and Pain.

Now, with reference to this subject, let us consider a little. Here, we will say, is a Child—its eyes are delighted naturally with anything bright, clear, sparkling—it has never had experience—a lamp is brought close at hand to it—it puts its hand directly into the flame. And *instantly* the *emotion* of *pain* is caused in a very great degree, and the *hand is withdrawn.*

Now observe, had there been no Pain, the hand would have remained there, and have been destroyed; and secondly, the pain occurs before any material injury takes place, or rather cotemporaneous with the smallest, so as to be an immediate warning. This emotion, therefore, is in its simplest form, purely defensive and protective.

Again, look at Physical Pleasure, this in its simplest form tends manifestly to the preservation of the body, guiding us towards those physical things external, that most conduce to that end. To the uncorrupted appetite, the most pleasant food is always the most healthy. The things that to the senses *uncorrupted* give a natural feeling of pleasure are to them the best—and those things that are not pleasant but painful, are destructive.

Now, when we look at the power of Habit and Experience, we find that these experiences of Pleasure and Pain, by man and by the animals having bodily organization, are enrolled in the memory, so that the experience of the past is a guide to the present and the future, and thus, that the period of infancy in the animals as well as in man is by this means a period of Education with respect to outward things.

Here then are three guides. The Spiritual Sense in reference to man's Spiritual being. The Sense of Having in reference to the mind. The Sense of Pleasure and Pain in reference to the integrity and preservation of the bodily organization.

Pleasure and Pain then are strictly bodily, *for the preservation*

* Sensibility is here used in the Physiological sense.

of the Body, and when we apply them to the mind it is in a purely *figurative* sense. The delight for instance that a conscientious man has in obeying his conscience, is not only not bodily pleasure, but is of a kind so wholly and entirely different, that it may exist along with the highest degree of bodily pain, caused by that very action.

Good and Evil then are not determined by Pleasure and Pain; for the Good is not always pleasant, nor the Evil always painful. The Good may bring exceeding Pain and the Evil exceeding Pleasure; and yet we shall be bound to do the Good and not to do the Evil; nay, to do the Good when the Pain is so great that it ends in the utter destruction of the body, as martyrs that have suffered death in fire, because they felt themselves bound to maintain the truth; as patriots that have died in torments for their country's sake; and as women that have borne all affliction for their children, have found, and received the applause of all ages for it.

Pleasure and Pain then are for the Good and Evil of the Body. They meddle not with the Good of the Spirit. *It is not to be measured by them, but itself is to be superior to them.*

I have already, in the early part of this treatise, shown that each man has in his estimation some one object that he considers to be his *Highest Good*:—now let us take these ordinary objects we see men pursue, and we shall plainly see that they admit of a threefold division. If the man places his Highest Good in obeying his Conscience, or living with justice, holiness or truth—then shall his Highest Good be in and within the regions of the Spirit or Moral Being. If he places it in "Having," no matter what form of it,—having power, or having wealth, or having fame, or having property; then it is within the animal mind. The man is Selfish. Again, if his main object be bodily Pleasure, no matter how or in what way it is, the man is Sensual.

This is the true definition of Sensuality. The Sensual man makes the *pleasure of the body* his Highest Good—*he lives for the sake of feeling bodily pleasure and avoiding bodily pain.*

When we consider the glutton, the drunkard, the epicure, the licentious man, in them all we shall see that they are all Sensual, they make the pleasure of the physical frame the end for which they live, and that by which they measure their Good and their Evil.

And we see plainly that these are the Good and the Evil of the beasts that perish;* they have no other Good and Evil than physical Pleasure and Pain.

We have already shown how what is ordinarily called viciousness of life is Sensuality in a great degree, properly so called. Another form of Sensuality we would now notice.

There are persons who look upon vice and its pleasures, and pains; and who by mere reason argue in this way: "Vice is injurious and destructive even to its own object,—the desire of high-wrought Physical happiness and its ecstacies of pleasure are attended by revulsions of the deepest physical distress—it shatters, destroys, ruins life and fortune and character,—*and therefore man ought not to be vicious*. But he may take the same desire that urges on the vicious man, the same Sensuality; he may guide and govern it by reason and so his enjoyment shall be permanent, steady and equable. He may *live for it* and *it only*, and suffer no evil."

There are multitudes that do so; that look to the Home, only as a place of temperate sensual pleasure; that steadily and system-

* Now let my reader look at the Sensualist philosophy of John Locke, and make his choice between it and that in this Treatise.

"*Good and Evil what*—Things then are Good and Evil only in reference to Pleasure and Pain. That we call Good which is apt to cause or increase Pleasure or diminish Pain in us; or else to procure or preserve us the possession of any other good, or absence of any evil. And on the other hand, we name that evil which is apt to produce or increase any pain or diminish any pleasure in us; or else to procure any evil or deprive us of any good. By Pleasure or Pain I must be understood to mean of body or mind, as they are commonly distinguished; though in truth they be only different constitutions of the mind, sometimes occasioned by disorder in the body, sometimes by thoughts in the mind."—Locke's Essay on Human Understanding, Book II. Chap. 20, Section 2.

To follow this out we shall show what that philosophy ended in. Listen to the estimate of its result and its tendency, made by Louis Blanc, a bold and daring Socialist, but unquestionably a man of genius.

"It was in England that Voltaire had drunk in that Epicurean Wisdom, which he carried among the French, * * * he read the works of the wise Locke, 'the only one who has taught the human mind to understand itself,' and he had yielded without effort to the doctrine received from Aristotle, that *our ideas are derived from our senses*. * * * Thus Voltaire, on returning to France, carried with him the education England had given him, his religion was *Deism*, his philosophy *Sensation*, his system of morality *Tolerance*. *The overthrow of Christianity was his aim.*"—History of French Revolution, Philadelphia, 1848, 1 vol. p. 214.

Can this Philosophy end in anything else?

atically pervert all the Affections to means of Epicurean enjoyment, and quietly make, as far as they can, all things terminate in their own "pleasure," or bodily appetites. This is just as much Sensuality as is that of the openly and lawlessly gluttonous or licentious man.

Well, is it not lawful to enjoy oneself? Certainly it is; *but not to make it the main end of life; not to make it the Supreme Good.* It is lawful to keep the home comfortable, but not to make comfort the sole end and object of life. For as I have said about Selfishness, so Sensuality, however tempered and modified, is still Sensuality, and both are immoral in any shape.

According to Paley, Selfishness so tempered and guided is the right and only spring of action. According to the principles of Locke, in reference to Pleasure and Pain, Sensuality is so too. But not according to what I conceive both natural and Christian morality to be; the Sensual and the Selfish are as plainly condemned by Nature and in the Scriptures as may be; and therefore I must conclude that *no modification of either quality* can be moral.

What then is the true course of action here and the true remedy? —the same that we spoke of in the case of Selfishness do we give in the case "Sensuality." Make not your home a mere place for the pleasures of Sense, that you there receive, *or soon will you cease to love it at all,* you will soon *become* and be *Sensual:* but love your home and your family *for themselves,* and permit not Selfishness or Sensuality to come in and to spoil the holiest of all Affections, that of the Family. Let the Home be in your mind *for them, for their* comforts, *for their* pleasure, and not for your own; and so will you find in them and in their love a degree of actual pleasure that you never could have found in Self or Sense.

But the completion and perfection of this is to be attained only in the Christian Home,—this alone can completely and entirely put an end in the Family to these two evils. The Family is the natural School to *unteach** man these two faults of the Affections; and only as sanctified and perfected by Christianity, is its function to this effect complete.

Having thus discussed the faults of the Affections that come upon man's heart naturally because of his fallen state, we shall in the next chapter consider the "Body."

* Dedocet uti.—Horace.

CHAPTER V.

The Body—it is not evil—but it is affected, first, by Self-will, Selfishness and Sensuality. Second, by death and disease entering the frame, and by the loss of the Sacrament of Life. Third, by weakness of those mental powers that remain, and by total loss of others.—False imaginations about a future state recounted and reproved, and true ideas in their stead.—Our "body" is not that of brutes, and thereby contemptible, but is to be reverenced; and of this the reason is, that the Word assumed Flesh, was born, lived and died as man—And is now as Man upon the throne of heaven.

IT will have been seen in the last chapter that two of the main faults of the Affections arise directly from the "Animal Mind" the one, and from the "body" the other, these feelings taking the place of the Affections, and being substituted for them; and hence Selfishness and Sensuality both come from the animal part of our nature.

The question, then, may arise, "Is not this material organization, therefore, that we call the Body the cause in itself of our Evil?" We answer, that to make the Body rule and be the main object of our Good, this is to be Carnal or Sensual, and is, as we have shown, the source of multitudinous evil; but the Body in itself, no more than the Spiritual part, is evil. The Body, *ruled and governed*, is in its proper place, and the Spirit, *as ruling and governing*, but one is no more evil by its nature than the other.

The inordinacy that comes from Original Sin, and inability to be obedient to the Law of God, run through *all parts* of man's nature,—"the whole head is sick and the whole heart is faint"—and the Body is wounded as the Spiritual part is. But the one is not in its nature wholly or essentially evil any more than the other. The *Body* with its powers is in nature *good*, but *fallen*, just as the whole man is; nay, there is not a function, or a desire, or appetite, or instinct of the Body that is not in itself good, when it is *guided and governed* by the Law of God. This is the decision of the Ancient Church against the Manichæans, a decision worthy to be brought up again and again, and impressed and urged upon all men as one of the primal truths of a real Christian Science.

And this being laid down, the question then will arise, "What, then, is the Body in quality, and what is its condition and nature?" The answer to this is, good still, but fallen,—this its condition. How it is good we shall afterwards determine—but how it is fallen is answered in two ways; first, as concerning its desires, which are "Uncontrolled," "Selfish," "Sensual,"—which may be seen also to be the resolution of that true Ethical Philosopher, St. James, when he declares that "this wisdom,"* that of the Flesh, is "earthly," "sensual," "devilish"—three epithets that most distinctly are identical with Uncontrolled (devilish,—rebellious, that is against the Law of God,) Selfish, that is, "Earthly" and Sensual. Hereby, then, do we count that the mere "Animal Nature" is perverted itself, and perverts and destroys the Heart, and through it the whole man.

This we count to be upon the Animal Nature of man one great injury wrought by "Original Sin," and the three elements of that one† injury are called in the Scriptures by the name of the *Will*, or *Lust* of the *Flesh;* and are, in the estimate of the Scriptures and of the Ancient Church, the chief bringer in and leader into sin. And indeed, this embracing these three, shall be what St. Augustine calls the "fuel of Sin."‡

This, as we have said, is the first way in which the body is injured by "Original Sin."

Again: manifestly man was originally an immortal being. God made him not imperfect, but perfect in all his parts. And existing as he did in Time and Space, and the particles of his frame being in a perpetual flow, it must necessarily be that this immortality of his should be *an immortality of supply*, a power in his frame of supply commensurate with decay, of restorative power, both internally and externally, equal to repair all possible deterioration of particles.

And accordingly we find that even now, in the very nature and being of man, there are what the physicians call the "Forces Medicatrices de la Nature," the "Medicinal powers of Nature

* I take it that this "wisdom" or "philosophy" is an Epicurean worldly wisdom, that makes interest and self-gratification its Highest Good.

† "Self-love," "Selfishness," "Sensuality," together, are the constituent parts of what St. Augustine calls "Concupiscence," or "Evil Desire."

‡ "Concupiscentia est fomes peccati." "Concupiscence is the fuel of Sin." —St. Augustine.

Herself;" by which self-restorative power, in fact, all diseases are cured, the effect of what we call "medicine" being only to remove obstacles in their way, while *these cure.* So that the human frame is a self-repairing machine, a self-healing animal organization. And this consideration led one of the greatest minds* of this century at once to pronounce the fact of the original immortality of man; for a self-repairing machine, if its repairs *are* or *can be* equal to its decays, *is* or *can be* an always lasting machine.

And again; by the Holy Scriptures we find that there was to man externally the means of a perpetual supply in the "Tree of Life" in the centre of the garden, the fruit of which seems to have been, as it were, the Sacrament of Life, a perpetual means whereby from without him a constant and adequate supply was given to the lamp of immortality that burned in his undying Body, the *food of life*, and appropriate nutriment to the immortal organization. So that as to the Spiritual part there was that Supernatural Gift that we have specified; in like manner, also, unto the immortal frame there was the corresponding external supernatural supply of immortality. And† the true difference between man as he was originally in reference to life, and the post-Resurrection man is this—that the first man was *able not to die*, and man as raised shall be *not able to die.*

Upon the "Body," then, another effect of Original Sin is this: "Sin entered into the world, and Death by Sin," and "Death has passed upon all, inasmuch as all have sinned."

But over and above this, or perhaps in consequence of this, it seems that the "Animal Mind," or, as others call it, the "Understanding,"—the "Mental Power," that is, which deals with the things of Sense, the objects of the Visible World—has been injured.

And this, we can see, has taken place in a two-fold way: the first by a superinduced imperfection in the action of its faculties; and the second, by an actual diminution of them in number. These two mental injuries we shall now proceed to examine.

When we look at the possession of mental powers, we feel in ourselves the sense of imperfection, both in the comparison of some men's powers, with others naturally, and also as to the effect of cultivation. There seems, as regards *mental power*, to be about

* Napoleon Bonaparte. † This distinction is St. Augustine's.

as much difference between a rude European peasant and an American citizen, with an ordinary education, almost as between a beast and a man.

The effect manifestly this is of Education entirely and completely. For the whole of the Institutions of Society in this country, and the whole of its influences, are Educational; so that in fact to him who truly contemplates the Republic in this point of view, it is fully manifest that that saying of the ancient Greek philosopher* is, in effect, entirely correct; " that a True Republic is truly a School." And the more perfect the Republic becomes in spirit and action, the more perfectly all its institutions must have an Educational effect.

Again; over and above this difference between one man and another, as to mental culture, each one who lives has the internal feeling of weakness and effort in all his mental exertions. It seems as if there was a feeling that inability, weakness, deficiency, were inherent in the mental powers of every man.

There is no one that I have ever met that has not, in a measure, acknowledged this; has not had before his mind constantly an ideal, or mental image, or model of his own powers of mind, to which, if he could reach, his mind would be perfect; and after or towards which it is his constant struggle to labor.

And this internal feeling is met and nourished externally by two facts: the first, the fact of Instinct, that animals do, without effort, almost unconsciously, and with unerring precision, things that we do laboriously, strugglingly, and feebly. This seems to cherish in us the feeling that, *if perfect*, then without labor, or struggle, perfect, complete, and almost unconscious, though still voluntary, would be the action of our mental powers.

The second fact that responds to and cherishes that sensation of mental imperfection and weakness in all men is, that now and then some powers reach, in individual men, almost, if not altogether, to that degree of effortless and perfect action that we attribute to them naturally. Mozart had the sense and power of music so strong, that, as an infant, he beat time to the carillons or chimes from a neighboring church. Zisca, the chieftain of the Hussites, had such a perfect sense of locality, that the whole country of Bohemia was so mapped out in his brain, that when he

* Plato.

had lost both his eyes, he fought pitched battles and conducted the whole operations of the war as if he were able to see. Barret and Magliabechi forgot nothing they had ever read. Colburn performed the most difficult arithmetical problems almost without an effort. And Geometers have not been wanting that had in Geometry the same power. These facts responding to the internal sense of effort and labor that ordinary men must employ in mental efforts, seem to say that mental imperfection is in weakness and inability. And that strength is that which is required, so that if strength could be given to the mental powers generally, and to each faculty individually, then would they be perfect; and that perfection would consist in action, unimpaired and complete, as regards the individual faculty, and without effort or labor. This part of our nature, then, shows manifestly the traces of the effect upon Nature that we have attributed to "Original Sin,"—that is, *inability* to fulfil the law of its being.

But it is now time to consider the second effect of Original Sin upon the "Mental Powers." The first we had stated to be "imperfection of those powers that we have;" the second, is "an actual diminution of our Mental Powers in number." I think, from the relation that we can see the Human Nature of man once bore to the external world, and the position of perfect obedience, in which all created beings in it stood towards him, and the dominion which we are told he had over the powers of nature by his very being: from this, as also from the disjointed way in which, at present, he stands towards the external world, I think that it is a very natural and easy conclusion, that originally there were in man's nature, *powers and faculties of body and mind which now he does not possess.*

And that these powers having been fully developed, and in full operation in the Primal Man in his state of Original Righteousness, have, by means of the changed relation of man to all things, in consequence of his sin, *shrunk back, as it were, into his being,* and been withered up, until hardly the vestiges and indications of them remain.

So that with regard to man, we may say, in reference to these powers and capabilities, that they *lie folded up in his being*, never coming to maturity of action or ripeness, as the germ of the fruit in buds that never come to flowers, or as the wings and plumage of the butterfly in the chrysalis, or as the ramifications of trunk and branch, twig and foliage in the acorn of the oak.

This, I would say, seems to be the case with man's being, in reference to a multitude of powers, whose existence and nature we can hardly guess at, save in the one way of analogical conjecture, that they must have been of those that bound the external world in obedience to his commands. The being, nature, and extent of these powers, what they are, or how, in what condition they would place man if *now* called forth, seems to be wrapped up in utter darkness; but that such have an actual existence *as possibilities*, it seems to me all things around us, by their analogies, lead us immediately to conclude.

The subject is an extensive one, and capable of a great many curious and interesting inferences and conclusions being drawn from it; but it is enough, for our present purpose, merely to indicate it as a thing very probable, and agreeing strictly with man's position as he is at present.

We shall consider, then, that upon the Body of Man, the effects of Original Sin are: first,—Concupiscence, embracing "Self-will, or Uncontrolledness," "Selfishness," and "Sensuality."

Secondly,—the loss of natural immortality, and the Sacrament of it; and the varied consequences of disease and decay.

Thirdly,—the utter loss and ruin of some mental powers, by their becoming shrunken and decayed in his nature, so that now they exist as germs and possibilities only, not as actual powers.

And lastly,—the weakening and decay of all the remaining mental faculties.

This, I conceive, embraces all the effects of Original Sin upon the Body, so far as we are able, according to the analogy of faith, to draw them from the meditations of the Church for many ages upon Holy Scripture and her practical contemplations upon the nature and being of man.

And the conclusion practically that we may come to, is this: "it doth not yet appear what we shall be, but we know that when He shall appear, we shall be like him."*

But one thing I think of sufficient importance to be noted is, that we should look *more to changes in ourselves*, and *less to changes in external things*, in reference to our resurrection and its

* 1 John, ii. 3.

consequences. For I do think, one of the most predominant faults of this age is, that in reference to the Future Life, men, in a way almost unknown to themselves, a sort of unconscious and unwilling self-deceit, take it for granted that all the weaknesses, feeblenesses, imperfections of their present state of being, shall still remain in them, and be transferred with them to Heaven. And then by the aid of a lively and constructive imagination, they go on to build themselves up a material Paradise, that shall contain *in itself externally* the supply of all these weaknesses and imperfections. And thereby fall into a Mohammedan dream of a sensual Heaven; a paradise in which the full supply of bodily wants shall be the happiness; as if the body were *now* perfect and Sin Original were not its imperfection, to be removed then with all its consequences.

To them, we say, if "Uncontrolledness" remain, then the power of doing absolutely whatever we will, under certain limits, shall be a part of the happiness of Heaven. But if this "Self-will" be a consequence of "Original Sin," and with it is to be taken away, then most likely *an absolute and entire* obedience to God's Law,—so that, like a planet around the sun, we shall eternally move round the central light of God in one undeviating course, suspended from his Being by a law ever one,—this, if "Uncontrolledness" be taken away, may be our completest happiness.

We say again, if "Selfishness" still remain, then most likely, in having all possible power, riches, knowledge, everything which in this world we can have, may be a part of our happiness, and it is but a fair and decent employment of the intellect, to build up such an imagined paradise of Having. But if this be not so, and Selfishness is not a part of our nature, but a consequence of the Fall, to be taken away at the resurrection, it may be that having and self-appropriation may not exist in the future life. But our supremest joy may be in perpetually receiving, that we may perpetually pour forth upon others in a less perfect state the favors of God's mercy. Our happiness may not be *in possession at all*, but in being the channels of benefits to others,—vessels of mercy—urns wherein, from the crystal sea, the waters are eternally lifted, and wherefrom they are eternally poured forth.

And if Sensuality still be, in heaven, a defect and tendency of our nature, then in earthly Desires and revellings, in the enjoy-me nts of the Animal Desires and Appetite we may naturally place one blessedness of a future life. As the old Chiliasts did, who, under decent shapes, as Dionysius, the Bishop of Alexandria, says, "made of heaven a place of sensuality," saying, in decent terms, that "it was a place" in which "they were to offer sacrifices and feast upon them continually, and to be perpetually celebrating marriages." Or else men may, as Mahomet, imagine his heavenly tree of paradise, the Tooba, of which so many different dishes were the fruits, and from which sprung the Houries, damsels of Paradise, to wait upon the blest;—a sensual and licentious heaven. These follies are fair reasoning if Sensuality yet remain. But if it be as the dross mingled with the gold, an imperfection that is to vanish with this life, then these dreams are evil and absurd, and we are not to attribute to the glorified body the *Concupiscence of that which is fallen, but to content ourselves with the certainty, that "as He is so shall we be also," "when I wake up after thy image I shall be satisfied with it."

For there is no idea that contains a wider range of mystery and of possible glory than this of a "Spiritual Body," "a body which being material, shall yet come as nearly to the nature of Spirit as being still body it can come."† Nay, even the heathen philosopher Pliny had a glimmering idea of this, when he stated that man was naturally a being, "all eye, all ear, all sense, in each and every part."

* The Concupiscence of St. Augustine, which he counts to be "the fuel of Sin," (fomes peccati) embraces then these affections, Self-will, Selfishness, Sensuality. It is properly an affection of the Body and of its representative, the Animal Mind. And through these it rises up against and into that part of the Moral Nature that we call the Heart, and debases and adulterates it, so that for obedience there is rebellion and lawlessness; for nobleness and Christian beneficence there is meanness and selfishness; for love and affection there is lust and exorbitant passion. In Scripture, this Concupiscence (evil desire) is called "lust," the "carnal mind," the "Will of the Flesh." It is that by which and in which Sin Original issues forth in actual sin. While we remain on earth it abides in our bodily constitution, and therein existing, it is the occasion to temptation,—and this it is that makes our life a constant struggle. But when we rise again we shall arise without Concupiscence. Selfishness, therefore, Sensuality, Self-Will shall have no place in heaven. And Paradises, Selfish, Self-willed, or Sensual are but the dreams of men ignorant of the nature of man on earth, and man in heaven, and untaught in the Spirit of Christ our Lord.

† See Bishop Nicholson on the Catechism.

Nor would men dream of a Paradise of learning and knowledge and physical science, if they could feel how truly in this world "Knowledge" and "Science" are only helps to imperfection, and how if the man were restored to his Original State, through his Gift of the Holy Spirit, working upon his perfect being, "knowledge" would be swallowed up in Intuition and faith in Sight, and from the Spirit of God the omniscience as it were of the Almighty would so dwell in the man as the water in a vessel plunged in the ocean, which being in itself limited, is yet filled unto its fullness, and communicates with the unlimited:—and so through this omniscience poured into his soul, according to his measure and his necessity, man with entire and immediate certainty, would then see and know all things necessary to him.* And thus even that which we call "Knowledge," its means, instruments, struggles shall vanish in the fuller and completer sight of the Spiritual being.

If men could at all see this, would they make a Heaven of knowledge? Would they not rather see that "holiness," and "peace," and "joy," and the calmness of eternal bliss,—and the seeing of Him face to face, to whom all things are present, and all things known, would make their *happiness?* And this while it confers knowledge, yet makes it of but little avail;—as to the Blind the knowledge that he can gather, from the descriptions of others, of the visible world is most precious while he yet does not see, but when his eyes are opened,—then, this otherwise a help becomes useless, and having sight, he thinks of it no more; so must it be with regard to what we call knowledge, nay more with regard to Faith, when we are brought face to face with the Almighty and enabled to look into the mirror of his omniscience, wherein all things are portrayed.

Away! with these dreamings, this wish to frame externally, imaginary modes of supplying imperfections, arising from "Original Sin," and idly supposed to be carried into our heavenly abode. "Original Sin" shall pass from us and with it its defects; and "Self-will" and "Selfishness" and "Sensuality" and "restless intellect,"—these shall perish and die, and have no heavens built for them. But "*we shall be as he is;*" and the entire removal of these faults and deficiencies, which in itself would make of this

* This is the effect of the "Vision of God"—that seeing Him as He is, we shall see all things in Him.

earth a heaven, if their root* were cut up and eradicated from man's nature, this shall fit him for the New Heaven and the New Earth wherein dwelleth righteousness.

But to return from this digression, we have shown wherein the body and the mental powers that belong to man are injured by the taint of Original Sin, and wherein and how it is possible that this may be improved by the casting away, at the gate of the Resurrection, of those deficiencies.

And this should sufficiently show that this "Body," made by God as part of the whole nature, "which is in his image," is not of man to be despised, is not to be looked at with Cynic scorn or Stoic contempt, not as a "mere envelope of the soul," a "garment coarse and filthy, that we wear only of necessity;" nor yet in the Platonic style of thought, as "our tomb, the sepulchre of the soul;" still less with the brute indifference that looks upon it as it would look upon the carcase of a beast, dead and cast out. But that it is the "*corporeal*" which, the dross being refined away, shall *become and be* the *Spiritual, remaining yet the same, but purified;* it is the mortal which, raised up by the Life of God, shall be the immortal; the Body now crude and imperfect, full of flaws and weaknesses, that shall then be holy and upright and pure and perfect—a plant now buried and hidden darkly in the earth of this present life, that shall shoot up yet into the realms of upper day.

This is a point of Morality which we would have men see, and learn, and feel, and act upon; for we have seen and know that to despise the Body, to look upon it merely with indifference and contempt, as brutal, or our "brute part," as men have said who thought themselves wise—this easily leads to evil: but reverence and respect to our bodily frame, and that of our fellows, this is of itself moral.

Let the man be supposed to look upon the body of man because of its similarity of function, *to be no more than that of a Brute,*—show me such a man, and if he be a non-professor, I will show you one who has low, and mean, and filthy thoughts and words,—and

* The doctrine of the Church unquestionably is, that even in the regenerate Original Sin remains, although its Stain is blotted out, its Guilt removed. This the Church holds in opposition to the Romanist doctrine, that by regeneration, all men are put again in the same position as Adam was in Paradise. Query – if so, why then do the baptized die?

by this very thing, if he is young, is likely to be seduced into vice —if he be a religious man, he is one who has a tendency to sensuality, and is coarse, and hard-minded, and unaffectionate. But he who takes the other view, and reverences the body as, even though fallen, still part of a nature "made in the image of God," his tendencies shall be entirely the other way. And as the conclusion of these remarks, I say it is a great moral principle and precept, "Reverence the Body," a dictate which nature herself utters with no faint voice, and which revelation explains and elucidates.

But this principle that the "body of man, although fallen from its original state, and so infected with the weaknesses that we have specified, is still not a body the same as those of the beasts, but something altogether different;" as the Apostle says, "there is one flesh of man and another flesh of beasts:"*—this principle we say, that the Body is thus to be reverenced, we shall not leave to these proofs only, but we shall seek a higher and loftier reason, one that concerns all humanity, and that gilds it with exceeding and abundant glory.

And this is, that as a fact and truth, the Eternal Word, the Son of the Father, he who from eternity was "the manifestation of his glory, the express image of his person," "dwelling in light unapproachable," the Word who "was in the beginning," and "was with God, and was God," "by whom all things were made," "in whom was life and that life the light of men"—"HE *was made flesh*, and dwelt among us."

This is the grand and glorious truth that makes the Body of man, even as it is fallen and imperfect, a glory, not a shame; a thing to be reverenced and respected, to be thought of with honour and tenderness of feeling.

This, the fact that the "Everliving Word" of God assumed to himself *really and truly*, a *body*, the *same* as that each of us possesses; this is the great mystery of godliness, "*God manifest in the flesh.*"

And see! how wonderful it is. Here is a babe—new-born, upon its mother's knee—and that babe, with its undeveloped mind, its speechless tongue, its soft and tender body, with no knowledge, no experience; this is "God of the whole earth!" its Maker and King! "God of God! light of light! very God of very God!"

* 1 Cor. xv. 39.

and all the natural feeblenesses, and weaknesses, and miseries, and distresses of childhood—these are his! God, born a child! and the Natural Body,—this he has assumed and bears!

The Body of the child, the Animal Mind, the Spirit—all these God the Word has assumed! and unto them inseparably and eternally he is united! This is a great wonder.

And surely that Body, that Soul, those Mental Powers, made originally in God's image, and which God assumed, these cannot be in themselves essentially evil; they must be good—"good, though fallen." The Body which the Eternal Word assumed, this is not to be scorned, or despised, or looked upon as brutish, but held in all reverence.

But more than this: the Word assumed it *not as perfect;* all its weaknesses, and deficiencies, and liabilities to temptation were still in the Redeemer's Body,—in the Body of "God, who shed for us his blood," were all these by which sin has access to us. "So that he was tempted in all things as we, *only without sin;*"* and until he had passed through the resurrection gate of the grave, it to him was a "Natural body," or a "Terrestrial" body. And thus remaining in substance the same, the dross being cleansed away, the weakness having vanished, it became the Spiritual and Celestial body.

So that unto a body having in nature but not in effects the same feebleness, deficiency, weaknesses that our body has, was the Word of God united. Our Bodies, then, we should not despise, or think brutally of for this natural weakness, but rather tenderly, since Christ passed through this life in a body that had the same weaknesses.

Again: that body that he assumed of the Virgin Mary, his mother, this same flesh that was born of her was weak and mortal; suffered, and died and was buried; this body of the same humanity as mine, of the same blood, the same flesh, the same bones; this rose with the Word from the grave, a Glorified, Heavenly, Spiritual Body, never dying and perfect, *and yet the same that was born of the Virgin.* And this Human Nature is thenceforth one with God the Word, two natures,† God and Man

* He had neither at birth Original Sin, nor during life Actual Sin.

† This is called the Hypostatical or Substantial Union of the two Natures in one Christ forever.

forever joined and forming one Christ, seated upon the right hand of the glory of God, upon the eternal throne of heaven.

Thou that wouldst despise the body, look to this;—the "body," the "mind," the Spirit of Man,—Human Nature,—a true man, and at the same time God the Word, is seated upon the throne of Omnipotence! *Man* is almighty, omniscient, eternal, immortal! The Body of *Man*, the same as this my body, the same Flesh and the same Blood is exalted into heaven, there to sit for evermore upon the right hand of God.

Should I not, therefore, reverence this my body, seeing that there, in the council chamber of Omnipotence, in the most inmost shrine of the Presence, upon the most shining throne of glory, in the central light and unapproachable depths of God's splendor, there is united to the Word for ever, the Body born in Bethlehem, laid in the manger, the Human Body, that suffered and died, was buried and rose again?

Great, truly, is the glory to me and to my Body that this is so. And, therefore, with all reverence and respect shall I look upon the "Body of man" even as it is, beset with the effects of Original Sin. To others I shall leave the pagan dreams of scorn and contempt for this our earthly frame. And the bodies of the dead, these I shall look at as no carcases,* no cadavres,† but as holy and sacred; shrines from which the spirit has departed again to return; dwellings, that by their frame-work and fashioning, were made after His own image, fitted in their nature to receive and be forever the dwelling of the sanctified spirit.

This is the Christian feeling of reverence to the body. And because of this thought of a human frame made perfect and seated upon the throne of God,—because of this thought is it that the aspect of the grave has changed from dreary and blank despair to the calmness of a living hope. Because of this it is that instead of casting out our dead to the birds and the beasts, instead of giving them up to the devouring flame, or of exposing them to the wasting elements as the carcases (caro casa) of dead beasts; with all reverence and tenderness we wash them free from all pollutions; we dress them in the pure raiment of death; we weep over them; we shield them even from the too rude contact of the earth, and we commit them to her bosom in peace and in hope.

* Carcase—caro casa—flesh fallen, or cast away.

† Cadavre (French) Caro, data, vermibus,—flesh, food for worms.

These are, as respects the Body, the effects upon our morals of the fact of the Incarnation,—the fact that the Word of God was made flesh and dwelt among us, and is now, together with that Human Nature which he took of his mother, seated on the right hand of God. And therefore should man reverence his Body, and neither scorn nor despise it, but even in its weakness count it not evil, but good, although injured by Original Sin.

CHAPTER VI.

The nature of man has, 1st, a capacity of life through the Word Incarnate; 2d, of receiving His Body and Blood; 3d, of the Indwelling of the Spirit. Love is the highest Christian state.—The Eucharist is hence a school of Works and Love.

The great fact with which we closed our last chapter, while it fully manifests the truth, that the body of man is not of the same kind as the body of the beasts, but an organization wholly different in its nature, inasmuch as it could be united with the Word of God; and these two natures, the Human and Divine, *become* and *be* eternally one Christ; while it shows this as a fact, it enables us, upon the strength of that fact, to proceed still further.

Can the Word, eternally begotten of the Father, assume the flesh of man? It can be so. Then as made of God, that Human Nature had, by its constitution, as of God created, *this capacity of union with the Word*,—a capacity no other created being has. This is a quality of man's nature which is not manifested by mere organization, and yet which evidently exists and distinguishes clearly between his body and that of the beasts.

Human Nature, then, has the capacity in it of eternally being in Christ upon the throne of God as God. It must, then, have a capability of Life everlasting through him. There must be in our nature secretly, and it may be unconsciously to us, a capability and a power of having His Life dwelling in us. There must be in nature as it is, the power whereby the same Holy Ghost that in Christ united the Word with Human Nature, so that both should be one eternally, can implant in our human nature, that is, in our body, our soul, and our spirit, the Life of the Eternal Word. For if the Human Nature, as created in His Image, had the capacity of being united with the Word, so as to be one Christ, then has it of the same constitution the capability of receiving the Life that comes from the Word only. And so of being of Him new born through the same Spirit, so that the man shall become a "member of Christ, a child of God, and an inheritor of the kingdom of Heaven." Hence also, it has the capacity that it should receive of the "Body and Blood" of Christ our Lord. For that Humanity which he assumed here upon earth,—which was born, "suffered," "died," and was "buried," and all this being "corporeal," "earthly," "natural," "fleshly," "rose again," *being then* "spiritual," heavenly, perfect. For it is most distinctly the doctrine of holy writ that the body, after the resurrection, remains the *same* and *identical as to its actual being;* but all imperfection and incompleteness is then done away. For the Natural body is changed into the Spiritual body, the corruptible into the incorruptible, the earthly into the celestial,—not losing its identity, but casting off its imperfections. And the body of our Lord having been, until his burial, a Natural body, as ours, (save only in sin,) at his Resurrection was changed, even as ours shall be through Him. It became a Spiritual and glorious body from having been a Natural body,—its qualities being changed, yet did it still remain the same in being that he bore on earth,—nay, even the same that was born in the manger at Bethlehem. God-man on Earth, even while yet a speechless and feeble babe on his mother's knee! God-man in Heaven, seated upon the throne of power! Great, truly, is the mystery of godliness, that God should be born of a woman and shed his blood and die for us here on earth! Greater still its crowning glory, that Man should take his seat upon the throne of the universe! forever to be worshipped! forever to reign as God! And thus the Word and the Human Nature, united in one Person, are at the head and on the throne of all being.

And the Human Nature of the Word, as far at least as his Body and Blood are concerned, this by the Spirit of God, can we, *having faith,* receive as the food and supply of the Life of Christ in us. For the very fact that Human Nature in Christ is capable of being united with the Word, and being invested with all the attributes of God, this proves that Nature to be capable of bending down from its eternal throne and giving itself as the food and supply of the Life to its kindred nature in us here upon the earth.

Only grant the great central fact that "Man is God," and no Time, no Space, shall prevent "omnipotence," omniscience united with Humanity forever, from conferring upon us, really and truly, the gift of his Body and his Blood, not in figure, not in metaphor, but *actually*, *really*, and *truly*, and by means which, while *they are not themselves* the "Body" and the "Blood," *are means* of its being most certainly conferred. Think upon the great fact that Human Nature could be joined unto the Word,—and Human Nature can, by virtue of this capacity, receive that gift of the perfect and glory-crowned "Body and Blood," that now sits upon the throne of eternity, and be fed and cherished by it in body, soul, and spirit. No figure this is of an absent body, no metaphor, save the Incarnation of the Word be a metaphor, and his conception of the Holy Ghost a metaphor.

But if the Human Nature is eternally united with the Word, so that a *real man*, one who has, as I have, a body, a soul, and a spirit, is seated on God's throne, and is God,—then this capacity exists in him to give to me in whom, by spiritual regeneration, is His Life, his glorified, spiritual, heavenly "Body and Blood," as food and nutriment of that His Life in me. Then in me exists, by my "creation in his image," and the suitableness of my very nature, the capacity of receiving that true gift of his *real* Body and Blood.

But if "God" and Man are not truly united, the two Natures in one Christ eternally,—then this union is but a figure, a metaphor; and the reception of the Body and Blood is only a figure and a metaphor; and the frame and nature of man is as the frame and nature of the beasts, flesh made to live and then to perish; but having in it no capacity of the divine nature,* no capacity of a Spiritual Life, or of spiritual support to it.

But it is not so. We can, by our nature, receive this heavenly food. The capacity is in us; because our very "flesh and blood," the Humanity of Man united with the Eternal Word, is God eternally; and because of this that we are created "in His image." For these reasons we can receive actually, really, and truly His Body and His Blood.

* "Wherefore unto us are given exceeding great and precious promises, that by them ye might be partakers of the divine nature." 2 Peter, i. 4.

This is the doctrine of the *real presence, which may thus be seen, not only to be plainly declared in the Scripture, universally upheld by the Ancient Church, the manifest and evident opinion of the Churches of England and of America in their standards, but also to be the highest reach and pinnacle of the philosophy of Christianity, the doctrine which unites earth with heaven; and frail and feeble, weak and afflicted as my human Nature may be in body, in soul, and in spirit, yet binds me to the Humanity that now is seated upon the throne of eternity, and tells me, "as he is, so shall I be also."

We see, moreover, from this also the capacity existing in us, our "Body," our "Soul," and our Spirit, that the Holy Spirit of God, should, as in a temple, dwell in us actually and really, as much as "Jehovah" of old by the Shekinah dwelt in the material temple of human building, in the glory that rested between the Golden Cherubims over the Mercy Seat. So it is possible that the Holy Spirit should dwell in this material temple of our Body, made in God's image originally, as he does also in the Humanity of our Lord, which is by him united with the Word forever. So that as our Soul, a limited Spirit, can dwell in our body, so can the Infinite Spirit indwell in the same Humanity to them born of Christ, through his regenerating power,—and by an immediate influence, uphold the body, the soul, and the spirit, through his Grace. So it is that through "Christ in him and strengthening him," the

* I would have my readers notice, that while we believe in a real presence it is, first,—spiritual, as not *local* nor *corporeal*, but of the Spiritual Body, which is free from the bonds of Time and Space. Secondly,—It is spiritual as it is conferred upon us by the gift and operation of the Holy Spirit, the same God who is the Giver of Life,—he gives us this Grace to maintain that Life. Thus the Sacrament is a real means of Grace. Thirdly,—It is spiritual as received in us by Faith, one of the highest operations of the spiritual being in man. This, with what I have said in the text, distinguishes the Church doctrine from the Romish figment of Transubstantiation.

One word more. This doctrine is one easily misrepresented, easily misunderstood. We have in our Services, our Catechism, our Articles, a most complete and perfect system upon it. To those, then, who think they see inconsistencies, I would give this advice, *let them wait a little before they speak*—let them in silence use *the Prayer-book practically*, and the *Holy Eucharist practically*, and they may grow up to the measure of this doctrine,—they may see that the inconsistency is in their own fragmentary notions, not in the Prayer-book.

Christian man can do all things, and yet of *himself*, of *his own power*, of *his own ability*, nothing,—but all things *through Grace.*

These are then facts, first, that Human Nature, a man as we are, with a real body, a real soul, and a real spirit, as mine is, is now and for ever God.

Secondly, That from this fact comes the truth of our nature's capacity for a new Life and birth derived from him our risen Lord, a spiritual birth of the whole nature, the body, soul and spirit. And that this birth takes place in us through the Word, and by the agency of the Eternal Spirit, the Holy Ghost.

Thirdly, That this Eternal Spirit and the Eternal Word Incarnate, the one can and does feed the flame of life in us, with the peculiar gift of his Body and his Blood; and the other "dwells in us richly," in our bodies, our souls, and our spirits, with Grace and strength.

These, then, are plain facts of the Gospel, for those that have been redeemed by Christ's blood, and having true faith in that atoning blood, and true repentance, have been "baptized in His name for the remission of sins," and have so been "born anew of water and the Spirit."

How high, then, can the Affections of the Human Race ascend? So high by nature and natural capacity that Humanity joined with Deity as one Christ is God; so high as this,—our Lord, ever blessed, yet still a real and true man in all things that appertain to Human Nature,—he is God, with all the feelings, all the emotions, all the affections of the heart that belong to our common Humanity. Love, joy, sympathy, pity, hope, all the emotions whereby man in Society is by his Heart carried on towards the good of his fellow-man, and made to rejoice in it—all these belong for ever to God the Word Incarnate. So that Compassion is almighty and all-seeing, and "Pity" ever-present, and "Sympathy" omniscient, and "Love" is crowned with the diadem of Eternity, clothed with the royal robe of infinite power, gifted with the sceptre of omnipotence. And the same Heart that upon earth overflowed with all emotions of gentleness, and compassion, and kindly feeling towards man, that same Heart has become of the same emotions an infinite fountain towards man, gushing forth from the central throne of God.

Well might men feel that the highest summit of Humanity is the Affections; that this, if it cannot reach to Heaven, at least can rise towards it, and catch the beams of its light, while all beneath is sleeping in darkness. Well might all men put so great a value upon the Heart above the loftiest powers of Reason, when the Human Heart reaches its full glory in the one Incarnate God, risen from the grave and ascended into heaven.

Think not, my reader, and I hope my disciple, of station in this world; of poverty, or of wealth, of mental ability or mental power; for deficient in all these, thou hast a loftier and a nobler gift and endowment in the Heart. One internal struggle, to cleanse thy mind from Selfishness—one inward strife, to cast away Self-will, and bow to the Will of God—one effort, to purify the Heart from Sensuality—one emotion of pity towards thy fellow-man,—this, through Christ's power and in Christ's name, is worth all these other matters and possessions of visible attainment, and shall outlast them all, and in the balance of Eternity and the judgment of heaven's King outweigh them all.

This thought of the man Christ with the heart of a man reigning for us in almighty and eternal power, this is that which inspired the holy apostle, Paul, with that divine Hymn of his upon "Love," which more than any passage in the Scriptures seems a melody from the tongue of Heaven, translated into the language of earth.

"Though I speak with the tongue of men and angels, and have not 'love,'* I am become as sounding brass or a tinkling cymbal; and though I have the gift of prophesy, and understand all mysteries, and all knowledge; and though I have all faith, so that I could remove mountains, and have not love, I am nothing; and and though I bestow all my goods to feed the poor, and though I give my body to be burned, and have not love, it profiteth me nothing. Love suffereth long, and is kind; love envieth not; love vaunteth not itself; is not puffed up; doth not behave itself unseemly; seeketh not her own, is not easily provoked, thinketh no evil, rejoiceth not in iniquity, but rejoiceth in the truth; beareth all things, believeth all things, hopeth all things, endureth all things. Love never faileth: but whether there be prophesies, they shall fail; whether there be tongues, they shall cease; whether

* 'αγαπη, in the original, means "love," literally, and cannot mean "charity," in any sense that the word now bears in the English language. So translated, in fact, it is perfectly meaningless.

there be knowledge, it shall vanish away: for we know in part, and we prophesy in part, but when that which is perfect is come, then that which is in part shall be done away."

"When I was a child, I spake as a child, I understood as a child, I thought as a child; but when I became a man, I put away childish things. For now we see through a glass darkly, but then face to face, now I know in part, but then shall I know even as also I am known; and now abideth faith, hope, love, these three, but the greatest of these is love.

The same feeling is manifested also in St. John the Divine. In him manifestly the highest and loftiest feeling is of the affection of Love made perfect in Christ upon the throne, and love made perfect in us in this world through Christ. In him that feeling constantly exists that is seen in St. Paul. "My little children," he says, "Let us not love in word, neither in tongue, but in deed and truth."

And history tells us that this the Apostle, "beloved of Christ," when in the infirmity of many years, he was, in Ephesus, carried into his church, and could, from feebleness of mind and feebleness of body say no more, he said this, "let us love one another," and when they asked him to say more, he said, "in Christ this is all."

This, then, is our practical conclusion. The "Heart or the Affections," is the highest of all the Spiritual powers. In and through Christ only can it attain that perfection of which in us it is capable, and this is a state higher than Faith, higher than Hope; so that he may have faith who has not "Love;" he may have faith and moreover hope, and yet not reach to this;—and that this state, the state of Love, wherein the heart is changed, so that its affections are sanctified and made perfect, this is the highest Christian state that man can reach upon earth,—the state in Christianity that answers to the whole spiritual power of nature and brings it all to perfection.

And when, in some further advance of the Church in Holiness and Sanctification of Heart, it comes to be asked by men of faith and zeal, "how and by what discipline of the Church shall we so cultivate our Hearts, that towards our fellow-men they shall be actuated by complete and perfect Love, according to the capabilities of the nature of each?"—then may it come to pass, that men shall be enabled to see that in the glorified Humanity of Christ our Lord, there is the perfection of Love, and the Human affections complete and perfect. Thus may they see, that of that Humanity, that Body and Blood, the Holy Spirit can make the faithful participate. They may then discern, that in our body, our soul, and our spirit, which are his, that His Spirit may eternally abide, as in his temple, as a supply of all deficiencies,—a help against all weaknesses—an indwelling strength and power not *of us* but *in us.* And while by no means they neglect exhortations, prayers, and sermons, yet seeing these things with the eye of faith, they may act practically upon their convictions, and go back to the old universal Christian custom, that the *communion should be a stated and systematic part of the worship of every Lord's day.*

When this comes to pass, then shall be seen that which was seen of old, that the sanctifying and humanizing effect of Christianity exerts itself mainly upon the individual man, through the secret influence of the Spirit, and very directly and manifestly through the sacrament of his Body and Blood.

And, then, the Communion, instead of being a meeting for incidental and uncustomary purposes, shall be a Society, organized not of man, but of God, having each week its regular and stated meetings, a Society of "Faith" and "Works," of "Mercy and Love."

The effect of which, upon the individual's heart, shall be, that it will train him gradually and unconsciously, yet most surely, so that his Faith shall mature into Hope, and Hope be succeeded by the full ripeness of Christian Love. And holiness and sanctification of Heart, shall be once more a general attribute belonging to all Christians in the Church, and by its tenderness of feeling and freedom from all ordinary faults of the Heart, distinguishing them from common professors of Christianity.

This would manifestly, from the principles above discussed, in relation to us, be the natural result of such a discipline, habitual, and used not as a thing extraordinary, which there was some peculiar merit and effect in adopting, but, as a *matter of course,* in the *ordinary quiet routine of things.*

For we cannot disguise it from ourselves, that in these our days, even the best motives and the best measures are often adopted and advocated by presumptuous and overweening self-will, and the holiest polluted by party, and the noblest and the loftiest lowered by presumption. So that that which carried out *quietly, in faith, by the individual,* would have been of great use, being made "*his great idea*" of which "he is the *great advocate,*" comes to be offensive to all well judging men.

For this reason was it that we said that the Holy Eucharist, used *weekly*, would have such an effect upon the Christian holiness of the individual man, when it comes to be used *as a matter of habitual discipline*, and not *as a thing extraordinary, which there is some peculiar merit and effect in adopting, but as a matter of course in the ordinary routine of things.*

With the exception implied in these words, we believe the effect would be from the principles we have laid down, the training of *all Christians* onward towards that higher state the apostle calls "Love," instead of its being the attainment of only one or two here and there, as it is at present; and the rest being left as they are in the first and initial state merely of Christianity, the imperfection of a crude and unripened faith.

So should this be for each man baptized into Christ a school, in which Faith would be transformed to Hope, and Hope to Love; and thus his Heart be filled with the fullness of Christ, and his affections have to all men that sweet and saintly character which they only possess who are made "perfect in Love."

Again: I look upon this practice to be a school of Works of Mercy, so great and so efficient, that upon the general practice of the Holy Communion Weekly, I place my hopes for the decision practically of a question which theoretically has been the cause of many disputes, the union of Faith with Works, in the great work of our salvation.

I believe that no sooner would the Church have returned to that practice of "Weekly Communion," as an *usual and customary thing*, than the feeling in the hearts of those who enjoyed that privilege, would arise to the practical fruits of mercy—the clothing of the poor, the feeding of the hungry, the Christian education of youth, the support of Missions. All these things would be effected by as natural a process as is the produce of the fruit from the flower; not under stimulus, not under excitement by means of eloquent addresses, or as something greatly and meritoriously done, but as the unboasted and usual duty of all Christians.

Let the Weekly Communion come in every Church, then by the very nature of its effects upon the Heart, when it is so established as to be customary and of the usual routine,—by the nature of man's Heart naturally,—by the nature of that Heart as sanctified,—by the nature of Christ our Lord, the God-man, with a Heart human as ours is,—by the nature of his Church as giving to those who have faith, his "Body and his Blood,"—by all these it shall be, that when this takes place, that as of old, the members of his Church come each Lord's day to the Communion of His Body and His Blood, then shall feelings of Faith be poured out in works of Mercy, Almsgiving and Love, and no appeal, no vehement exhortation shall be needful, but the stream of Christian benevolence shall flow from motives purely Christian, fed instrumentally by that ordinance from week to week, which the most raises in our heart the feelings that are Christ-like towards God our Father in heaven, and our brethren here upon earth.

And both these effects the Ancient Church experienced through her Weekly Communion and her Weekly Offertory, which went along with it. For during four hundred years the Communion *was weekly in all Churches*, and *there never was a Communion without an Offertory, nor an Offertory without a Communion;* and this with Oblations given according to each one's pleasure, was her sole revenue.

And with these free-will offerings of the people, and the oblations at the altars, so abundant was that spring of systematic and principled liberality, Ancient Christianity supported all her Clergy, all her poor, and all her schools; and never was there a state in which Holiness, and Sanctification, and the perfection of Love was more prevalent. Such, until the fifth century, when Christianity was endowed by the State, and therefore more or less corrupted by it, was the influence of the "Weekly Eucharist" upon Christian Faith and Christian Works.

And again: the same cause can produce the same effects,—ripeness of Christian character and fullness of Christian benevolence in us, the first Apostolic Church that is free altogether from the fetters of the State.

I make no apologies for introducing the subject I have examined in the last few pages. Treating as I am upon the Affections, it was necessary to see in what living man the affections reached unto their highest perfection, and this I found in Christ our Lord, and in the fact of his Humanity still possessed by him in heaven.

Hence the humanizing influence of His Religion upon the Heart. Hence, too, that highest state of the Christian, the state of Love.

Hence, too, the influence of the Eucharist upon the Heart, as nutriment of the Christ-like Affections. Hence the effect of the habitual use of this Holy Sacrament in producing to their perfection Faith and Works, hand in hand.

These are questions and resolutions of Morality and Ethics of the highest importance. And these I have thought myself bound to enter upon and examine at length,—for surely the questions, "What is that which most humanizes the Heart of man?" "What discipline in the Church is thereunto most efficient and most useful?" and "How shall Faith be perfected into Love, and true works of Love and Mercy be done spontaneously?" These *are* high and lofty questions of Christian Science.

And all spring from the one great fact of "God in our flesh and our blood," God, our brother, in this flesh *forever*,—and thus as Man, eternally seated upon the throne of power.

And although in this age, plunged in selfish ambition and the pursuit of pleasure, these things may be thought strange deductions, yet the time shall come when universally it shall be a practice in the Church that all shall come weekly* to the Communion. And then it shall be visible and manifest, as it was of old, that the sacraments, especially the Eucharist, are, by their relation to the nature of man, peculiarly suited and adapted to work upon that portion of our spiritual being that we call the "Heart," and to ripen Faith into Love, and cause true Works of Mercy and Benevolence to be done in Faith, through Love.

With this we end this Book, and in the next books we shall discuss the affections of the Home or Family, of the Nation and of the Church. The ensuing Book shall be occupied with those of the Family.

* While I am so much in favor of the practice, I must say that the adoption of it, on the part of the Clergy as well as of the laity, *needs peculiar caution*, lest we sin by haste or by presumption. I would, therefore, recommend the careful perusal of "the Tracts upon the Weekly Eucharist," by Dr. Muhlenburg, of the Church of the Holy Communion, New York.

BOOK V.

THE HOME AND ITS AFFECTIONS.

CHAPTER I.

Society.—Of Divine institution.—Coeval with Man.—Man's nature answering to it, and it answering to Man's nature.—The fiction of a Social Contract examined and refuted.

We have in the foregoing book examined the Affections as existing in the heart of the individual man. We have defined them as finding their ends in Persons, and these persons existing in Society. We have again and again expressed our opinion that Society is of a threefold organization, the Home, the Nation, the Church: that it is a divine institution, and coeval with man, an organization for fixed and determined purposes, and in set and determinate forms. These opinions of ours are familiar, *as opinions*, to our readers.

We have also, at different parts of this book, as it came up according to the subject, shown the uses of Society; that Society in itself is one grand school of teaching, divided into three, which teaches in the Family, Love; in the Nation, Justice and Equity; in the Church, Holiness. These uses we have, at various periods of our work, illustrated. The uses, however, manifestly are facts; they could exist as uses of Society, whatsoever its origin: the question now is of its origin. Our opinion that we have expressed is, that it is of Divine Institution, coeval and congenital with man; the organization, just as much as the individual, an existence made of God for set purposes, and in fixed, unchangeable forms.

This it must be, or else made of and by man; not of divine origin, but made by a multitude of men consenting thereunto, as men, after an unanimous plan, frame and build a house.

There is no alternative—either Society is by God intended for the purposes that we see it fulfil, and *is of his building;* or *else it is made by man after his own will:* one thing or the other must be true.

Now of this latter opinion there have been in modern times many advocates; their theory is called the "theory of the Social Contract." It is, we conceive, in its main features fairly represented thus:—

"There was a time when there was no Society, but men were in a State of Nature. Then they came voluntarily together, and by contract they constituted Society. Hence that agreement is called the Social Contract: and so doing they each renounced a portion of their individual rights, as the price to Society for the securing of the others." These three clauses will embrace, we believe, all the elements of this theory.

We shall examine these asseverations one by one.

Now with regard to the fact of contract, what evidence is there that this which we call Society was constituted by contract among individuals, who formerly *not being in society contracted* to make it, and *after it was made* were thenceforth in it? What evidence is there of the contract which the theory takes to be a fact?

Of such a fact there is in existence *neither record, witnesses, registry, evidence of time,* or *place,* or any one of those circumstances which are requisite to the proof of the fact of contract.

Let us go back, and we shall see there is no evidence to the effect that the theory requires. We go back to our American Constitution, established at the Revolution. We do not see that this answers at all to the "Social Contract," for the theory says that *by that* contract, Society was constituted; *that previously there was no Society,* but men were in a State of Nature. Now before the American Revolution *there was Society,* there were families, churches, magistrates: the change then was *from one form of Government to another,* not from *no-government to government;* not from *no-society to society.* Men were not in a State of Nature before the Revolution, and after it stepped at once into the Social State. Whatsoever the Social Contract may be, and whensoever it may be imagined to have been made, it certainly was not made at the time of the establishment of our Government, and our Constitution does not answer to the description given of it.

We go back, then, to our English ancestors. We have the history of the nation for a thousand years at least. If a fact so remarkable as this, of a Social Contract, by which a whole nation stepped from a State of Nature in which *no Society existed,* into the *Social state;* if a fact so remarkable ever occurred in that people, we should have, in all reason and common sense, some record of its happening. But there is no record of time or place, nor of any thing that can prove this alleged fact of a Contract, in the history of the English nation.

But we may have evidence of it, perhaps, in the times anterior to the national existence of England: and lo! in the historical records of the whole world there is not the slightest evidence of such a transaction, such a Contract! The matter is a supposition, a theory, a fiction, so far as evidence or record of it is required or searched for—not a matter of fact.

Wherever, even in the fewest numbers, the Man is seen, there is he seen in Society; he enters into Society as member of a Family; where there are only two or three families, there is Government in the Tribe, which is the Nation in little; and there is Worship. Where there is, either from newness or from desolation by famine, pestilence, war, or emigration, only one family in the land, the three elements are seen coexisting in the one social organization, which is at once a Family, a Nation in little, and a Church; and the head at once is Father, and King or Chief Magistrate, and Priest. These relations are not made by any supposed compact, but are coeval with man, for as far back as we go we see them to exist, and we see no evidence of Contract constituting them.

But again, this theory supposes that there was in existence antecedent to the Social State, a State of Nature! This is a fact asserted, a thing of which we ought to have evidence. It is supposed to be a state opposite to that of Society, a state in which there was no society, but *only individuals;* in which, of course, there were no Families, no Nations, no Worships; in which therefore there were no husbands and no wives, no property, no magistrates, nothing, in short, but the individual man eating and drinking, and freely doing whatever his heart moved him to! Was there ever such a state as this?

As a matter of fact, there never was: because, as we have said, the very first sight we get of man in the records of our race, sacred or profane, shows him in Society; shows all its three forms to exist; and shows his nature too, so framed and adapted for Society, that it is manifest that he *was made and organized for it*, and it *was made and organized for him*. So far with regard to the fancied State of Nature as supposed to exist before and in opposition to the Social State.

But again, the "Man," in acceding to the "Social Contract," and entering into the Social State, is supposed to have surrendered a portion of his "Original Rights." I confess I do not see that in Society *any rights* belonging to the individual *are surrendered.* Life and Liberty and Property are certainly secured against outrage, which, if the Nation did not exist, they would endure. Except, perhaps, that which society makes a *crime*, is a "*right original;*" except "rapine," and "theft," and "brutality," and contempt of the marriage bond, except these, which Society calls "Crimes," are "Original Rights."*

I cannot see how Man in Society "surrenders a portion of his rights." To secure life at the expense of contributing perhaps three days' labour in a whole year, instead of being perpetually in peril and constantly in arms; to secure property by a like expenditure of time, instead of being able only to possess that which with armed hand we can take and hold; this, so far from a "Surrender of Rights," seems to me an enlargement of them.

And looking steadfastly at the civilized man and at the man

* Here is the immoral element in this theory, the concealed premise, always held back yet always implied and *insinuated in various forms*, by Rousseau and his followers, the doctrine that the Law of Society only made those actions vicious, which, before that law, were not only *not vicious*, but *rights of the individual man*, at that period, the golden age of Rousseau, when

"Wild in woods the noble savage ran,
Ere arts and manners first corrupted man."

And so, it seems, murder, theft, rapine, promiscuous concubinage, all these are "original rights" of the individual man, which he surrenders to society by being under the Social Contract,—not wrong in themselves by any means! The evils of this theory are thus manifest to any mind; they were in fact and reality manifested in the corruption of manners that preceded the French Revolution. This vile theory had taken possession of the whole mind of the nation of France, and such was its result.

Such is the power unto evil of one base, "bad-hearted" man of Genius. In this has Rousseau a bad pre-eminence. He is the one, the only thoroughly bad-hearted man of true Genius the experience of the past reveals to us.

who approaches nearest to that fancied "State of Nature," so far from a "surrender of rights," the consequence of Society is an *enlarging, developing, securing of rights*,—and the man in a Social State has a thousand rights the savage cannot possess.

Never, in fact, did this fancied State of Nature exist; never did a "Social Contract" take place either between men to make Society, or between any Individual to enter into Society; never were any rights original to man surrendered. And the facts which they twist into proofs of a contract are proofs *of this only*, "*that the 'Individual Man' is made for Society*—suited and adapted by his nature to dwell therein always and for ever; and *that Society is made for him*, so that his nature responds to the organization and the organization to his nature:" and this, in accordance with the principle so often laid down in this book, and urged as a primary one in Morals, that all things are double, one against another, and God hath made nothing imperfect. In fact, the whole theory existed only in the brain of that man whom before we noticed as the most base and bad-hearted of all writers:

"The self-torturing sophist, vain Rousseau."

It was a fiction and a theory, *for the time* and *for the place*. When the tyranny of the king and aristocracy of France had become so oppressive as to shake the very grounds of all confidence; when faith had become a mockery to intellect; and the conduct of men of rank a base and filthy scandal; so that all things were preparing for downfall and ruin, then came forth this theory of the "Social Contract," as a banner to men who seemed to themselves to see no hope of justice or equity save in the destruction of all things.

And these men took this theory for granted, because thus they were enabled to say, "You are bound to us as we to you, by *contract;* do that duty, or we shall break *our contract;* we are entitled to do it, and if you compel us, why then we recur to our original rights, and one of them is *the holy right of insurrection*," a phrase ten thousand times employed in the French Revolution.

It was a theory for the times; it may be as well put aside now: we may as well found our duties and rights upon truth, and holiness, and equity, and the nature of Man, of God, and of Society, as upon *Contract*.

The theory of the "Social Contract" having thus been examined and rejected, upon, we conceive, good grounds, we take it that "Society" is an Institution of God, coeval with man, adapted to his nature as his nature to it, and so fitted to it that it is not only merely the best, but the only condition for him to exist in.

CHAPTER II.

The Family always existent.—The Home its realization in Space and Time.—Heathen notions of its institution.—The feeling that the Law makes it.—Man's nature.—Nature of Society, and the express Law of God.—These, not mere legislation cause it.—Pretty fables about marriage.—Natural feeling of unity.—Doctrine of the Roman Law.—Common-Law Doctrine.—Doctrine of the Scriptures.—Conclusions: 1st, Law does not make marriage; 2d, Marriage is no Sacrament, but a Mystery; 3d, All bound to marriage, except, first, it is wrong for them to marry—secondly, for a religious motive.

WHEREVER, as we have shown, Man appears, there Society appears, simultaneously as it were, and coeval with his existence. Man *as made* was one, it is true, at first, but afterwards, when "the LORD God said, It is not good that the man should be alone," from his flesh and bones was made a partner for him. And since then, man *as born* has always come into Society—he has been born into it. And this society made up of a pair, a Man and a woman living together—a Husband* and a wife.† This pair, with their offspring, constitute the Family. Their dwelling is called the Home.

Hence result a multitude of relations of Persons—of Husband to Wife—of Wife to Husband—of Parents to Children—of Children to Parents—of Brothers to Sisters—of Sisters to Brothers. All these manifestly are relations between Persons in Society, and that Society composed of these Persons is the Family.

And again, owing to the Nature of man, which is a nature in Space and Time, this Society, the Family, has a *place of inhabitation*, a dwelling to itself exclusive, in which only the one

* "House-band"—the union of the house.

† Wife from "weiben," to weave or unite.

Family dwells, or ought naturally to dwell, the Home: and the Society therein is, as it were, set apart from the rest of the world by visible and tangible limits; defined by them to be, although composed of many members and many relations naturally, still *One only.* One by exclusion of others from without; one by union of interests and feelings and mutual aid within; one by authority and by love. A oneness of organization with manifoldness of members and relations and affections. There is authority there, in the authority of the Father. And there also naturally exists the unity of love, represented in all its possible relations, and flowing, as it were, from one fountain, the Mother.

We come now to examine into the nature of this Society, and the Affections that are in the heart towards it. "The Home," we have entitled this book, "and its Affections."

And first, the question is, Whence comes it? How was it organized? Whence its Laws? This I conceive a question worth noting, but not worth examining. I see the man that was made by the hand of God, by him brought into Society—but all men that *are born*, born into a family. The Family, I see, by the most ancient of histories—the Bible—to have been instituted of God. I then, as a plain matter of fact, take it for granted that it was so: that for *one man* and *one woman* to live together as Husband and Wife all their days, that this was the original institution. That those who lived otherwise were not they who *lived as at first*, but they who *broke off and diverged from the original institution.* Heathens* may say,

"First men crawled out from the earth, a brute and dumb class of animals, fighting with fists and nails for acorns and wild fruits, then with cudgels, and then with arms which necessity invented. Then their rude cries they gradually formed into

* Quum prorepserunt primis animalia terris,
Mutum ac turpe pecus, glandem atque cubilia propter,
Unguibus, et pugnis, dein fustibus, atque ita porro
Pugnabant armis, quæ post fabricaverat usus:
Donec verba, quibus voces sensusque notarent,
Nominaque invenêre: dehinc absistere bello,
Oppida cœperunt munire, et ponere leges,
Ne quis fur esset, neu latro, neu quis adulter.
Hor. Sat. lib. i. 3.

articulate language; and lawgivers came, who taught them marriage and instructed them in law."

This is the heathen view entirely. The Christian is, that marriage was the Original State, and Language a Divine gift,* and Law† a thing natural to man from his own Reason and from the nature of Society and of God; and that if men were found in a state such as above described, it was because they had sunk voluntarily into it.

But to resume: Men, asked any questions with regard to the Family when they are possessed with this Heathen notion, will answer, the Law makes it so; taking it for granted unwittingly that the Law could make it otherwise.

But with regard to Marriage, does not the Law enact it? Does it not inflict penalties upon those who shall transgress this enactment? and thereby first cast the Family into a precise and definite shape, and then by its action so retain it?

Granting that it does all this—all this will not be *to constitute it*, but only to *protect*, *guarantee*, and *define* it, by the consent and legislative power of the nation. If the thing be "*right*,"‡ then legislation sanctioning it is good; but if it be not "right," then no legislation can make it so.

The foundation, then, of the Family, and its Law, I seek in the Nature of Man and of Society, and in the express Law of God. These are they that make and constitute the Law of Marriage and the Law of the Family; and human legislation is good so far as it expresses and reflects these.

But when human legislation upon any point opposes these, and says that it shall not be so, but otherwise, then human legislation fails. Mohammed permitted and enacted polygamy—and Nature starts up and says, "Nay, it shall not be: polygamy, the allotment of many wives to one man, cannot be the Law of a Nation, for only one woman throughout a nation shall be born for one man." And thence throughout the nation that *human law* is wholly inoperative as a law, that is, as an universal rule

* See an essay on the Divine Origin of Language, in Magee on the Atonement.

† See Hooker, first book of the Ecclesiastical Polity.

‡ Right—rectum, *ruled*—that is, by the inner law of man's moral being; and by the external law of God corresponding to it, wherever and however revealed.

of life; and the only effect is tolerated licentiousness among the rich and great, and a decay of principle among the poor, and a decrease of happiness and prosperity in the nation.*

If Law be according to the nature and being of Man and according to the Law of God, then it is Right, and sanctions that which is Right; but if it be not "right," "ruled," that is, according to the Eternal measure of immutable and unchangeable morality, then it is not so good. The will of God externally—the Nature of Man internally,—as interpreted by the Universal Reason in Society,—these are the measure of all human legislation. And these always and for ever agree.

Having so digressed, we shall, for a while, leave the legal consideration of "Marriage," the "Family," and the "Home," and go to the Ethical consideration, that which examines not its Laws under Legislation, but its foundations in the nature of man, and in the Law of God.

Now with regard to nature, we find the feelings of the oneness and exclusiveness of the marriage so prevalent among men from the beginning, that it gave rise to many pretty and interesting fables. "The soul of man and woman," says one ancient Greek fable, "was originally one; it was then divided by Jove into two portions, half to one body, and half to the other; and hence the one soul, with instinctive patience, seeks its lost half, and will wander over the world for it, and, if united with it, shall be happy, if not, miserable."

Behold a theory which at one blow accounts for all travelling and emigration, as well as all happiness and unhappiness of the marriage tie, and yet expressing sufficiently the sense the author of it had of the Spiritual Harmony of Marriage.

"Behold," say the Cabalists—those Jewish retailers of absurd philosophy and foolish wisdom—"man was originally one, both soul and body, the 'Ish Kadmon,' or primitive created being, and then God separated them, and man fell!" a most absurd and ridiculous notion, and yet showing the sense these strange philosophers had of the intimate relation of unity which the Masculine character bears to the Feminine.

* It is, I believe, a well ascertained Statistical fact, that the population of Turkey—the exclusively Turkish population—has not increased during the last two or three centuries; and that this is owing exclusively to the legal toleration of Polygamy.

Strange fables, these, and yet bearing witness to the natural fact of unity brought about and realized by the marriage tie.

In fact, through all time antecedent to Christ, the fables of all nations, extravagant as they may be, still bear witness to the feeling and persuasions of an union the most intimate between the parties, an union of Body, Soul, and Spirit as effectual as if they had actually become *one body*, *one soul*, *one spirit*. And this persuasion and universal sentiment assumes manifold forms, some amusing and ridiculous, and some interesting and even sublime, according to the nature and temper of the narrators.

And in philosophic earnestness and truth, when we examine the nature of Man and of Woman, we shall find that one is, as it were, the complement and counterpart of the other, that which renders it perfect; so that in the natural quest to feel and determine what would be the perfection of humanity, we should have to combine and unite the various attributes and qualities of both minds, the Masculine and the Feminine, and would find that all qualities of the one nature would, as it were, combine with and perfect those of the other.

For instance, the intellect of man, being intellect, is still a very different thing in nature from the intellect of woman, but so different as to correspond to and complete it. And when we come to imagine the height and perfection of intellect, not barely great intellect, but the utmost degree and topmost summit of all greatness of mental power, then we naturally fall into a combination of both. We unite the tenderness, the grace, the delicacy of the Female Intellect, with the boldness, and strength, and robustness of the Masculine Mind; and we find this combination actually to exist in Shakspeare, Dante, Homer, in the men of the highest reach always, but not in men of second-rate powers.

And when we look at these faces of the loftiest genius, then shall we see the tenderness of the female countenance uniting itself with the strength of the masculine; as may easily be seen in the portrait of Dante, of Shakspeare, or even of Milton.

In the same way, if we take the whole nature—the Conscience, the Reason, the Affections, the Will, the Understanding—in the case of all these, they are the same in both sexes; but in one there is a certain quality we call "Masculine," and in the other, a quality we call "Feminine," and one is supplementary, as it were, to the other, completes and perfects it. No wonder then that this constitutional adaptedness, this natural agreement of two different natures towards unity of end, should be explained by such extravagant philosophies, existent as that harmony is in all faculties of the whole being.*

But the sense of harmony in two towards one purpose, or rather towards oneness of life, is manifested exceedingly in the ordinations and definitions of legislators. "Nuptiæ sive matrimonium," says the Roman law, "est viri et mulieris conjunctio individuam vitæ consuetudinem constituens." "Marriage is the union of a man and woman, constituting an united habitual course of life, *never to be separated;*" and again the same Roman law defines it to be "Consortium omnis vitæ, divini et humani juris communicatio:"—a "*Partnership of the whole life,—a mutual sharing in all rights, human and divine.*"

But much as the Roman law acknowledges this natural unity; or rather tendency and adaptedness for unity of life, much further the English Common Law goes, for it actually considers, for all legal purposes, man and wife to be "*one person.*"

To quote a modern writer, "The English Law goes further, and considers the Husband and Wife as one Person. As the lawyers state it, The very being or legal existence of the woman is suspended during the marriage, or at least is incorporated and consolidated in that of her husband, under whose wing, protection, and cover, she performs every thing, and is, therefore, in our law-French, called *feme coverte,* and her condition during her marriage is called her *coverture.*

"Hence a man cannot grant any thing to his wife by a legal act, or enter into covenant with her, for this would be to covenant with himself. The husband is bound by law to provide his wife with the necessaries of life; if she incur debts for such things, he is obliged to pay them. Even if the debts of the wife have been incurred before marriage, the husband is bound to discharge them, for he has espoused her and her circumstances together. If she suffers an injury, she applies for redress in her husband's name, as well as her own. If any one has a claim upon her, the suit must be directed against her husband also. In criminal

* I have seen, somewhere, notice of an absurdly ingenious book called "Sex in Souls." To this the reply is easy; "in Christ there is neither male nor female." Souls are of no sex, although different in quality.

prosecutions, indeed, the wife may be indicted and prosecuted separately, for the union is only a civil union. But even in such cases, husband and wife are not allowed to be evidence for or against each other, 'justly,' say the lawyers, 'because it is impossible their testimony should be impartial;' but principally because of the union of Person. For being thus one person, if they were admitted witnesses *for* each other, they would contradict one maxim of law, 'Nemo in propriâ causâ testis esse debet;' 'no one can be a witness in his own cause:' and if against each other, they would contradict another maxim, 'Nemo tenetur se ipsum accusare;' 'no one is bound to accuse himself.' "*

This is the doctrine of that English Common Law, which its ablest advocates have pronounced the "Perfection of Reason," and which, undoubtedly, from the oldest Saxon times, has been the Free Element in the constitution of England. This dogma, therefore, that civilly the effect of marriage is the union of the two into one Person, is the decision of the Common Law; a decision, we fear not to say, that nearer expresses the truth than any other. For, as we have shown, the natural feeling of the human heart, expressed in many fables, many philosophies, and many legal enactments, is such that it confesses an union of the closest and most intimate kind between the Husband and the Wife—an union so closely drawn and intimate, that by no other words can we clearly express the fulness of it, than by these of the Anglo-Saxon law—"these two individuals make one Person."

So, when we come to the Scriptures, we find the same doctrine most plainly held forth. The doctrine that these, being two individuals, "are one flesh," one humanity; that is, one, not only in union of interests, will, sympathies, and affections, for this is a figurative oneness, but one as no other oneness is: so one, that by Christ's law nothing but death can disunite them; one, so that the unbelieving husband or wife is sanctified by the believer; one, as Christ and his church are one; one "in a mystery," that is to say, the fact is *to us* impossible and incomprehensible *as a fact*, yet, as being revealed to us by the word of God, is true; while the means whereby it is so, the grounds, the consequences of it, these lie far beyond us, deep hidden in the limitless power and the inscrutable wisdom of the eternal God. This, as may be seen from the words of St. Paul and of our Lord Jesus,

* Blackstone's Commentaries.

is the true doctrine of the Scripture and the Church concerning the marriage union.

"Wives, submit yourselves unto your own husbands, as *unto the Lord.* For the husband is the head of the wife, even as Christ is the head of the church: and he is the Saviour of the body. Therefore as the church is subject unto Christ, so let the wives be subject to their own husbands in every thing. Husbands, love your wives, even as Christ also loved the church, and gave himself for it; that he might sanctify and cleanse it with the washing of water by the word, that he might present it to himself a glorious church, not having spot, or wrinkle, or any such thing; but that it should be holy and without blemish. *So ought men to love their wives as their own body. For he that loveth his wife loveth himself. For no man ever yet hated his own flesh; but nourisheth and cherisheth it, even as the Lord the church:* for we are members of his body, his flesh, and his bones. *For this cause shall a man leave his father and his mother, and shall be joined unto his wife, and they two shall become one flesh. This is a great mystery;* and this I apply to Christ and the church."*

* Eph. v. 22. It will be seen, in the above citation from St. Paul, that I translate two phrases somewhat differently from what they are in our English version. The first, in our version, is, "*they shall be* one flesh." The Greek expresses it differently; it is, "they *shall be unto* one flesh;" that is, "shall become." There is in the original a Greek word corresponding to our English word "unto," which seems to be wholly neglected in our version, and yet upon it the stress of the argument lies. The same phrase, "shall be unto," I shall translate in this way in citing our blessed Lord's words: I shall not therefore notice it at that place.

Again, there is another peculiar phrase, which in the Greek original is, τοῦτο δὲ λέγω περὶ." I translate it, "and this I apply to." Let my reader examine the passage, and he shall find that the first translation makes a jar in the sequency of the argument; the second brings it clearly out. The argument is from the idea of the mysterious nature of the marriage union, with which idea every Jew was well acquainted, to the doctrine, entirely new to them, of the *vital union* of Christ *with His Church.* The argument and illustration is from the one to the other; a logical connexion that is dislocated completely by one version, but expressed by the other in the text.

But are not the words, "but this I say concerning," the translation, even a literal translation, of the Greek? Yes. And so of the French, "Il fait froid," the English, "It makes cold," is a translation, and yet it is nonsense; and of the English, "So wo-begone," "Ainsi douleur va-t-en," is a translation. The fact is, as keen old Selden, from whom I take the illustration,

This is the plain doctrine of Scripture: a doctrine that says that, in the very being and constitution of man by his creation, there is a mystery in reference to marriage.

A mystery, in the Scripture language, is "a thing declared to us as a fact, and therefore to be received upon the evidence of Almighty God, and yet the reasons and causes of which are hidden from us." So is "the Incarnation," the fact that God was born of a woman and assumed flesh,—this is a "mystery," a fact declared and shown, and for which, on natural grounds, the grounds of mere reason, we cannot account.

Thus marriage is a "Mystery," and the Mystery is, that as "Christ and the Church" are actually one, so should the husband and wife be one,—that as we, having mortal bodies here upon earth, are united with his Spiritual and Immortal Humanity upon the throne, and are thus one with him, so should these two, the Man and the Woman, being two, *become* and *be one flesh.*

And hence *that*, as the church obeys Christ, so should the wife obey the husband: not through compulsion, force, or fear, but through love, because *obedience in love* is the natural consequence of her position; and so should the husband love the wife, as Christ loved the church, because this is the natural consequence of his position, and because "she is his flesh, and no one hateth his own flesh."

Here is the mystery. The apostle takes it for granted that they are *actually and really one*, and argues therefrom *as it is so;* but the ground and the reason of the union that makes it so he does not declare—only that *it is.*

From this fact, then, we shall deduce several consequences.

1st. Marriage is not an institution of the Law, so that the Law institutes it as it institutes a Savings Bank, a Senate, a

has remarked, "there are two kinds of translation, *literal* and *idiomatic;*" and to translate an idiom literally is *no translation*, but is nonsense.

This Greek idiom, then, "this I speak of," or "concerning," is used idiomatically for "I apply unto," or in "illustration of." Of this, any scholar that may think it worth while, as I have done, to search through Stephens's Greek Thesaurus upon the point, may easily satisfy himself.

The translation, then, that gives the full sense of the idiom is, "And this" (that is, the mystery of the union of man and woman in marriage assumed as a fact) "I apply to" (illustrate that vital and equally real union of) "Christ and the church."

School, or an Observatory, and then can unmake it and reach the same end by another institution of a different kind. This it is not, but an *institution of man's being*, a *law of his nature as created*, a fact *antecedent to all Human Law.* So is marriage in Society, a *law before all laws;* and therefore the work of human law and man's legislation is *to enforce upon the citizen* these two laws, the innate law of nature, the outward law of God's revelation; but not to dream that they shall be able to make and unmake, form anew and remould that which is superior to them all, and to them all antecedent.

Another conclusion we would draw from this: As marriage is a Mystery of our nature antecedent to all law, and Law has, as we have said, the power only to enforce, to regulate, and to protect; hence all marriages wherein the individuals legally declare their desire and intention, before authorities constituted and established by law, to live together in the state of matrimony, are *legal* and *valid** marriages; the individual thereby enabling the State to maintain and enforce that contract and agreement then made.

But marriage contracted with prayer and religious rites, and the blessing of God's church, and solemn and appropriate services—this marriage is *legal also and valid, and more than this, is blessed*, being in accordance with the precept, "Whether ye eat or drink, or whatever ye do, do all to the honour and glory of God."

And this in accordance with the doctrine of the Church, which holds marriage *not to be a Sacrament of the church and instituted by Christ*, but to be a *mystery of man's being*, an adaptedness of his nature as originally created.

And this in opposition to the Romanists, who declare marriage to be a Sacrament; and therefore, seeing that among themselves they think the only valid sacraments are, do in effect declare all marriages except those among themselves invalid, and bastardize all offspring save their own. Because, instead of being content with the Scripture doctrine, "that *marriage* is *a mystery*," they

* Provided always the law of the State do not contradict the law of God. A Turkish marriage to a second or third living wife may be very legal according to the Mohammedan law: in the law of God it is adultery, or concubinage.

would add to it still greater sanctity and greater effect, and make of it a "Sacrament."

Another inference I would draw is this: Except a person be incapacitated for marriage by reason that he cannot support a family, or by any other reason that renders it *positively wrong* for him to enter upon the marriage state, he is *wrong in not being married.*

Marriage is, by its very nature, and by the very nature and being of man, a better state than singleness, a more moral state, a more natural and useful state; and except, as I have above said, there is some impediment that makes it *positively wrong* to marry, ALL are *bound to marry, and are better mentally, morally, and physically, because of it.*

And thereby, to remain unmarried merely for expediency-sake, or for mere Self-Will, or capricious motives, this is wrong and evil, from the nature of man and of society. So that, save one actually is disqualified for marriage so that it *shall be wrong* for him to marry, he is naturally in a better situation marrying than not so.

But there is one exception made by our Saviour; that is, "for Religion's sake." "Some are eunuchs made of men, and some have made themselves eunuchs for the Kingdom of Heaven's sake." "He that is able to receive it, let him receive it."

"For the Kingdom of Heaven's sake"—for a *religious motive,* our Lord permits men to remain unmarried; and not only permits, but requests and desires them so to do.

For a religious motive:—Say that thou art a son with a widowed and helpless mother and her feeble little children, left with only thyself to look to; thou canst marry, have a family of thine own, enjoy comfort and satisfaction. *Surrender all these;* give thyself up to be the support of the feeble mother and her helpless children, and to be a father to them; *and this, done in faith and trust in God and his Christ*—this shall be for thee a blessedness, *permitted* and *sanctified,* to remain unmarried for Christ and his kingdom's sake.

Daughter! the last child of a widowed mother, who thinkest whether it would not be better to comfort her declining years than to be at the head of thine own family: this the first to do, is to remain unmarried for the Kingdom of Heaven's sake. And so of a multitude of other cases of the same kind, among which come possibly cases of missionary labour,* in which particular men may feel that to preach among the heathen is a duty so bound upon them, that for it, through Christ, they are to remain unmarried. Such was St. Paul.

But in all such cases, it is a duty of which, first, the individual is to judge himself: "He that is able to receive it, *let him* receive it." For that Self-denial that is compelled by Law is not Self-denial at all, but compulsion.

And, secondly, the person must be able to receive it, that is, be a person such by nature and by Grace that he can remain as moral unmarried as married.

With these two qualifications, Self-denial for religion's sake is an exception made by Christ himself, and blessed of him. But this case and that exception above stated are the only ones that at all exempt men from the principle that says, "Marriage is honourable *in all*, and the bed undefiled."

* There is a great deal of good sense in the following passage from the works of Dr. Miller, of Princeton, an eminent Presbyterian. Although I must say that I think "Itinerancy" has done almost all the good it can do, and the sooner it is replaced by a settled parochial clergy, (who, according to the deliberate opinion and primitive usage of the Greek Church, ought *always* to be *a married clergy*,) the better. I must say, also, that of all institutions, I believe an *unmarried Itinerancy* to be the worst. Still, however, on a delicate subject, the following extract contains a great deal of good sense. The small capitals are his: the italics inserted by me.

"I. In reference to this subject, my first leading suggestion is, THAT THERE ARE SOME CLERGYMEN THAT OUGHT NEVER TO MARRY. While I firmly believe that the doctrine which *enjoins celibacy* on the clergy generally is, as the apostle styles it, 'a doctrine of devils,' and that it *has led* and *must always lead* to the most enormous evils, I have at the same time no doubt that the minister who deliberately resolves to spend his days as *an evangelical itinerant*, ought, if he can be happy in a single state, to continue in that state. * * * There ought to be a few such ministers in every church of large extent. Yet no one ought to be *constrained* or even *persuaded* to choose this plan of life. Nor should any one adopt it unless it be the object of his *deliberate* and *devout* preference. And even after having adopted it, he ought to feel himself at liberty to retract and assume the conjugal bond whenever he is persuaded that he can serve the Church better by doing so." Miller's *Clerical Manners*, let. xii. sect. 1.

CHAPTER III.

Laws of Marriage:—I. Permanence.—The Scripture Doctrine of Divorce discussed.—The Uses of Permanence.—Causes of frequency of Divorce. St. Paul's Advice in regard to Marriage.—Adultery *a Crime:* Nature and the Divine Law forbid it.—Its evil Consequences.—The Causes of Marriage unhappiness.—II. Law of Mutualness.—Marriage a Moral Good in itself.—Highest motive for Marriage is affection.—Children should not marry without consent of Parents.—Third Law: The Supremacy in Marriage belongs to the Husband.—This doctrine is made tolerable by Christianity.

WE come now to the laws of Marriage—those principles, namely, of the ordinance, which arise, first, from its nature, as an institution of God in our very being and the being of society; and, secondly, from the Laws of God concerning it.

And of these principles the first is its permanence—"that it shall be an union for life, capable of being dissolved only for one cause, that of Adultery."

This is plainly asserted in the words of our Lord: "The Pharisees also came unto him, tempting him, and saying unto him, Is it lawful for a man to put away his wife for every cause? And he said unto them, Have ye not read, that he which made them at the beginning, made them male and female, and said, For this cause shall a man leave father and mother, and shall cleave to his wife: and they twain shall *become* one flesh? Wherefore they are no more twain, but one flesh. What therefore God hath joined together, let not man put asunder. They say unto him, Why did Moses then command to give her a writing of divorcement, and to put her away? He saith unto them, Moses because of the hardness of your hearts suffered you to put away your wives: but from the beginning it was not so. And I say unto you, Whosoever shall put away his wife, except it be for fornication, and shall marry another, committeth adultery: and whoso marrieth her which is put away doth commit adultery."*

* Matt. xix. 3—9.

Here is the word of the Scripture plainly: "He that made them in the beginning, made them Male and Female."

God made man—He was the author of man's constitution and being: and in that being and constitution they were made by him, first, *male and female*—adapted by their very nature as man and woman to union in marriage;—and, secondly, they were *only two*.

"And because of this"—arising from this harmony of nature originally established by God, so that in every way the one should be the aid and counterpart to the other, the male to the female and the female to the male, by natural being and constitution,—upon this is founded the law of God, "*for this reason*, a man shall leave his father and mother, and shall be united to his wife, and they two shall *become* one flesh."

"He shall leave father and mother,"—the dearest ties shall be left of him; those that by nature are the closest being superseded by one still dearer and closer. And this in consequence of the mystery of his own being, as so made in the beginning.

"And shall be closely joined unto his wife,"* united in such a way as to void even the closest natural ties, and to take their place in priority of obligation: so close the bond.

"And they two shall become one flesh,"—not "they shall *be*," but "they shall *be unto*," "they shall *become*."

"Wherefore they are no more twain, but one flesh." The effect of their marriage union shall be an inseparable union into one humanity. So that as in a Son all the elements of his being come from the Father and the Mother, and the Father and Mother *in him* are inseparable and indiscernible, *so* mysteriously are the husband and the wife united into "one flesh," or "one humanity."

"What God therefore has joined together, let not man put asunder." God has united them "in one flesh" by the original constitution of their nature as made by him, and by his express and positive law in accordance with that nature. *Therefore*, let *no human legislation* separate them.

And then He shows that only in reference to the hardness and brutality of the national heart was the liberty of divorce *politically* permitted; but that originally it was not so.

* "Cleave unto," in our version. The word is in the passive in the original. It signifies the closest permanent union.

And the conclusion from these premises is, "Whosoever putteth away his wife, except for fornication, and marries another, commits adultery."

Although human legislation may permit divorce, or even decree and enjoin it, for *many causes*, still the man who is *divorced for any other cause than the adultery of his wife; or the woman who is divorced for any other cause than the adultery of her husband*, and then marries again, *that man or that woman*, notwithstanding man's legislation and human law, is, by the law of his own being as man, by the law under which Society is of the Almighty constituted, by the law of God from the beginning, and by that law as again declared and promulgated by Christ, the Word Incarnate—AN ADULTERER OR ADULTERESS. And he that marries a wife *so divorced*, divorced by the law of man, but still married by the law of God, is an ADULTERER. THIS IS THE LAW OF CHRIST, WHATSOEVER BE THE LAW OF MAN, AND, AS SUCH, IT IS TO BE OBEYED BY ALL CHRISTIANS.

And, by a parity of reasoning, since the clause "save for fornication," excludes him or her who, because of this sin *in his or her partner*, is divorced and marries again, from the sentence of adultery; it is manifest that he who, because of the adultery of his wife, is divorced from her, is legally separated so as to be entirely free from all fault, *even if he do marry again.*

Upon this ground we place the Christian law of marriage,—upon nature first, as originally made of God,—and secondly, upon the express law of God as cited and re-enacted by Christ. And we believe that as in all cases of the express law of God, so in this, obedience to the express command of the Almighty, even although human law and human wisdom sanction disobedience, shall be found ultimately to confer the greatest amount of lasting and permanent happiness. And more than this, *the sincerest wisdom of man shall be ultimately driven to re-enact and re-establish the Law of God.*

But still, although upon the Law of God and upon the Nature of man, we found *the obligation* of permanence, and not upon expediency, yet still it may be advantageous to show the uses of this permanence. We quote, therefore, from a writer* whose principles of morality we dislike, but whose logical acuteness was very great, who, in tracing out the advantages of permanence, says:

* Paley.

"A lawgiver whose counsels are directed by views of general utility, and obstructed by no local impediment, would make the marriage contract indissoluble, during the joint lives of the parties, for the sake of the following advantages:—

"1. Because this tends to preserve peace and concord between married persons, by perpetuating their common interest, and by inducing a necessity of mutual compliance.

"There is great weight and substance in both these considerations. An earlier termination of the union would produce a separate interest, the wife would naturally look forward to the dissolution of the partnership, and endeavour to draw to herself a fund against the time when she was no longer to have access to the same resources. This would beget peculation on the one side, and mistrust upon the other, evils which at present very little disturb the confidence of the married life.

"The second effect of making the union determinable only by death, is not less beneficial; it necessarily happens that adverse tempers, habits, and tastes, oftentimes meet in marriage, in which case each party must take pains to give up what offends, and practise what may gratify the other. A man and woman in love with each other do this insensibly, but love is neither general nor durable, and when that is wanting, no lessons of duty, no delicacy of sentiment will go half so far with the generality of mankind and womankind, as this one intelligible reflection, that they *must* each make the best of their bargain; and that, seeing they must either both be miserable or both share in the same happiness, neither can find their own comfort but in promoting the pleasure of the other. These compliances, though at first extorted by necessity, become in time easy and mutual, and although less endearing than assiduities which take their rise from affection, generally procure to the married pair a repose and satisfaction sufficient for their happiness."

There is a great deal of good sense in these remarks, although we see in them the low and mean views Paley had of all things. He argues upon men and women "united in holy matrimony," as a man would upon a pair of oxen united by a yoke, or of dogs in a double collar! "They won't kick or bite, but will learn to run quietly together, when they find they can't be separated!"

But, to proceed, he goes on to assign other reasons for the permanence of the marriage tie:—

"Because new objects of desire would be continually sought after, if men could, at will, be released from their subsisting engagements. Suppose the husband once to have preferred his wife to all other women, the duration of this preference cannot be trusted to. There is no other security against the invitations of novelty than the known impossibility of obtaining the object. And, constituted as mankind are, and injured as the repudiated wife generally must be, it is necessary to add a stability to the condition of married women, more secure than the continuance of their husbands' affection. Upon the whole, the power of divorce is evidently and greatly to the disadvantage of the woman, and the only question appears to be, whether the real and permanent happiness of one-half the species should be surrendered to the caprice and voluptuousness of the other?

"We have considered divorces as depending upon the will of the husband, because that is the way in which they have actually obtained in many parts of the world; but the same objections apply in a great degree to divorces by mutual consent, especially when we consider the indelicate situation and small prospect of happiness which remains to the party who has opposed his or her dissent to the liberty and desire of the other.

"Milton's story is well known. Upon a quarrel with his wife, he paid his addresses to another woman, and set forth a public vindication of his conduct, by attempting to prove that confirmed dislike was as just a foundation for dissolving the marriage contract as adultery; to which position, and to all the arguments by which it can be supported, the above considerations afford a sufficient answer."*

And we proceed, ourselves, to add a few considerations, of a different spirit, we hope. We have shown that man is of three parts, the "body," the "animal soul," and the "spirit;" of these three is the entire oneness of his nature framed. We have shown that, according to the Scriptures, these two human beings become "one flesh;" there is an actual union of the nature of the one unto that of the other; so that they are no more twain, but one flesh. Now, as a preparation for this, there ought to be a meetness and suitableness of the one for the other. I ask, then, is it not a fact that there are masses of men and women in whom the Spiritual part is wholly uncultivated, who use not the Conscience,

* Paley's Moral Philosophy.

who have no Spiritual Reason or sense of the Unseen World, but live only for the things of time and sense, whose Affections, at least so far as the Heart is concerned, are become Sensual and Selfish?

Every one knows that there are multitudes of such men, multitudes of men whose moral faculties are utterly uncultivated and undeveloped, and whose main principle therefore, in life, is either the Sensual one, "to live for pleasure," or the Selfish one, "to live for acquisition."

If a man be in such a state, then that man's heart is in the state naturally that the hearts of the Hebrews were, *his heart is hard;* hard through Sensuality, and hard through Selfishness.

Say that such a one marries; he marries, not for higher objects than his nature reaches to, or for higher ends than his Greatest Good will measure. The man that marries for beauty, when the beauty is gone, having had no higher object, and no loftier feeling than that mere sensual admiration* of beauty which the ancient heathen and Paley call "love," and the Scriptures call "desire," or "lust,"—why, if this be the object of his marriage, why should he be confined to one wife? why not more than one? why not the utmost latitude? Surely, if this be the highest end and the highest aim, the *real affections* will be neglected, and the utmost latitude of divorce sought for and desired.

And again, if objects merely Selfish be sought for, if the husband want a housekeeper only, and the wife only a man who can give "a comfortable home," this very thing—this attaching a Selfish end exclusively to marriage, this too infers, in reasoning upon

* An old poet beautifully contrasts this with true affection:

He that loves a rosie cheeke,
  Or a coral lip admires,
Or from star-like eyes doth seek
  Fuel to maintain his fires,
As Old Time maketh these decay,
So his flames must waste away.

But a smoothe and steadfast minde,
  Gentle thoughts and calme desires,
Hearts with equal love combined,
  Kindle never-dying fires;
When these are not, I do despise
Lovely cheekes, or lips, or eyes.

it, the utmost latitude of divorce. For if the man's highest end is to obtain a good housekeeper only, and this is the view he takes of marriage, and he is disappointed, naturally he will think he ought to have the liberty again to try and suit himself.

Suppose the end of marriage to be either Selfish or Sensual, and that rightly and properly a man can, for these motives, and *no higher ones*, engage in it. And then, naturally, there is a craving for unlimited divorce; then, naturally, the Scripture doctrine is changed, and husband and wife are, and should be *on these grounds*, allowed to be separated *for every cause.*

Now there are, unquestionably, a vast number of divorces at the present day. I trace them to these reasons,—in the first place, to *the philosophy of the day*, which is the Sensual philosophy of John Locke, who asserts that Pleasure and Pain are to be the rules of action, and that Good and Evil are to be measured by them:* and therefore, so far as in him lay, he has made man utterly Sensual and Unspiritual. In the second place, to the "Selfish" philosophy of Paley, which makes "selfishness regulated by reason" the rule of action, and is very commonly held among us. And in the third place, to the absence of a regular and systematic cultivation of the Spiritual powers in the mass of our people.

Because of this, multitudes are even, as were the old Jews, hard-hearted—Selfish that is, and Sensual, with no sense or feeling of the sacredness and the mysteriousness of marriage; looking upon it as upon any other contract made by the consent of two, which by the consent of two can be dissolved.

This is the case with multitudes of men at the present day; and therefore I say to Christian men and Christian women, "Keep *ye* by the law of God and Christ, and it shall bring to you a content and satisfaction that these men cannot comprehend. And as by religion, *your moral* and *spiritual being* is educated and developed, so take care that *with regard to those with whom you may be united*, it be so also, as marriage is an union mysteriously of the whole nature. For otherwise, much suffering, much sorrow, much affliction you will have, if to the Unspiritual, to the Selfish, or to the Sensual, you are united. For in Ethics it is, by the very nature of the scientific principles of it, a true advice, 'be not unequally yoked with unbelievers.' "†

* See note on Book IV. chapter 4. † 2 Cor. vi. 14.

The proper preparation for marriage that shall come up to the Christian idea of it, is an adaptedness of the whole nature; first, a Religious and Moral development of the Spiritual nature, so as to enable the man to appreciate the sacred mysteriousness of marriage, and to exclude Selfishness and Sensuality from being leading motives; secondly, a development of the mental and intelligent part, so as to manage well the affairs of life; and thirdly, full age and maturity of person.

When these three are united, there exist then all the qualifications for a Christian love, and then for marriage: but when only the last two, then there always will be a want of the Christian feeling in the most of persons, and a desire that divorce should be easy and unrestrained.

And the first qualification, the full development of the Moral being, this can exist only in those who are *trained up in the religion of our God;* and for this reason I do conceive, as I said above, that Christian science supports the advice of St. Paul, "Be not unequally yoked with unbelievers."

The same reasons in nature and in the law of God that prohibit divorce, also may be seen to prohibit Polygamy, or the marriage of one man to several women, or one woman to several men, during the life of the parties, whether this be simultaneous or successive: for from the mystery in our nature it is prohibited; "they *two* shall become one flesh," and not they three, or they four. The natural adaptedness is that "two shall become one," and any more than two will violate the law of the nature.

But in addition to this, and to the other arguments against it, it will be seen by any one who chooses to look at the ordinary tables of statistics, that the number of males and of females born in the world is so very nearly the same, that it never could have been intended that one man should have more wives than one; for if it were so, then for the one that had four, three must remain unmarried. In fact, again to quote Paley,

"Polygamy not only violates the constitution of nature and the apparent design of the Deity, but produces to the parties themselves and to the public the following bad effects;—contests and jealousies amongst the wives of the same husband,—distracted affections or the loss of all affection in the husband himself,—a voluptuousness in the rich which dissolves the vigour of their intellectual as well as active faculties, producing that indolence and imbecility both of mind and body which have long characterized the nations of the East,—the abasement of one half of the human species, who, in countries where polygamy obtains, are degraded into instruments of mere sensual pleasure to the other half,—neglect of children, and the manifold mischiefs that arise from a scarcity of women."

Such are the evils of Polygamy—evils that manifestly arise from the fact that it is a violation of the natural law and constitution of man and of the express revealed law of God.

Now, the same principles of nature and of God's law, besides that they enjoin an union for life and with only one, not with more than one,—these same principles of the junction of two in one, manifestly forbid "Adultery," as an act which severs and disunites the conjugal tie, so that in consequence of this act the Law of God and of Man shall *pronounce judicially* the marriage at an end.

In reference to this crime, we shall remark at the very first, that the husband gives himself to the wife and the wife to the husband, so that, in the words of the Roman law, there is "omnis vitæ consortium," a "partnership of the whole life,"—"divini et humani juris communicatio," "a community in all rights, human and divine;" according to the English law, "a oneness of Person" as to all rights of life and property; according to the Scriptures, a "oneness of flesh or humanity," so "that they twain are no longer two, but one flesh." All this manifestly confines to the one man and the one woman all the peculiar privileges of Marriage.

This also establishes the Home as the habitation and realization of the Family, which, as it were, draws the line expressly, and says, "Within this house there shall be *one* master and *one* mistress, one husband and one wife: they have given themselves mutually up to one another, so that the husband's interests are no longer his, but the wife's—his pleasures no longer his, but his wife's—his profits no longer his, but his wife's; and her interests, profits, and pleasures no longer her own, but her husband's." There is, then, a mutual surrender of Affections and Interests by each to the other in the Home.

Hence, the most grievous of all injuries of one to the other is Adultery, since it terminates and destroys, by the law of God, *pronounced judicially by the State*, that union *so entire, so inti-*

mate, and *so exclusive*. It is therefore, apart from the evils that flow from it, apart from its consequences, a crime of a most aggravated and atrocious nature, as breaking up and destroying an union that is for life in all pleasures and interests and pursuits.

And here I must say, that by the very nature of the Union, as existing in the constitution of man, and by the very nature of Society, as being an organization as real as that of the individual, marriage is no mere "Civil Contract," the breach of which can be repaired by damages; but "Adultery," the violation of the Marriage *vow* on the part of *man* or *woman*, is a *crime* that deserves the *infliction of punishment*—a crime in its own nature against the Nation, of the most grievous and ruinous kind, and therefore *to be punished*. And by-and-by all men will come to the same opinion.

It is not, as foolish arguers imagine, wholly from the Contract that one is bound not to commit Adultery, as they might contract to do or not to do any thing that before that contract was lawful; nor from the law, so that anterior to the law it was part of man's "Original Rights." Nor is it only because of the consequences. But, anterior to all law of man, the law of Nature said so: anterior to all notion of contract or utility, anterior to all sense of consequences, the law of God said, "Thou shalt not commit adultery." And the whole Spiritual part, the Affections, the Conscience, the Reason, the Will, all say the same. The nature of man everywhere accedes to and ratifies the law.

And even among the most brute and barbarous races, the sense and feeling of the savage heart will receive it; and although, in respect to his neighbours, the "Uncontrolledness" and "Selfishness" and "Sensuality" that come from want of cultivation of the moral being impel him, acknowledging the law, yet to break it, still, *in reference to himself*, he shall feel its breach most acutely, and confess the obligation to be divine. Until finally the evils of such a state, slaughters and savage feuds and fierce revenge, compel Society, for the sake of its own interest, to enforce the law according to the dictates of nature and the express will of God.

But this commandment, adopted as it was by our Lord with the rest of the decalogue, was not simply left in this way in reference to external law: inwardly it was traced to its foundation in the "Sensuality of the Heart;" and therein it was branded with the reprobation of the Almighty Judge—' He that looketh upon a woman to lust after her hath already committed adultery with her in his heart;"* "for *from within*, out of the heart proceed murders, adulteries, fornications, lasciviousness,"† &c. And again, "Marriage is honourable in all, and the bed undefiled: but whoremongers and adulterers, God will judge."‡

And accordingly the spiritual law excludes, as well as Unchastity, all things that lead to it, all sensuality, lasciviousness, wantonness; and all that may feed the tendency to this sin or be a provocation to it, as luxuriousness of diet, idleness of life, indulgence in inward voluptuous thought, corrupt company, lascivious and wanton books, obscene and filthy words, and gestures wanton and loose;—all these, as unchaste in themselves, leading directly to adulterousness, and every thing that in the sphere of human action, in thought, in word, or in deed, is adulterous, is by the spiritual law of Christ forbidden, as of the same nature with actual adultery. And this shall all men's hearts and consciences tell them to be true. And happy are they that act upon it, and avoid the very beginnings of evil: they only are secure.

And the consequences that follow from this sin and crime to individuals, to families, to nations, these consequences will ever engage, or, I may say, force all men to uphold the law of Nature and of God. The consequences are of the worst kind: the breaking up of the family, and rending the heart of the innocent with the most agonizing of all afflictions; the making of orphans by a worse bereavement than that of death, a bereavement that renders the name of parent, that ought to be a glory and a joy, a disgrace and shame—that separates the children from affection and love, and connects disgrace and sorrow and a suspicious shadow with that household for ever. And then to the guilty party, if it be a woman, strips her of all modesty, all self-respect, all character—sends her forth as a branded outcast from Society, and delivers her over almost certainly to the foulest of all lives and the most abandoned of all deaths;—and, if a man, lays the foundation for all abasement of character, and is an easy stepping-stone to all evil—the first step in man's progress to the most desperate villanies, and to that

* Matt. v. 28. † Mark vii. 21. ‡ Heb. xiii. 4.

depraved state of profligacy that scorns all public and private obligation.

What wonder then that, in view of all these consequences,—in view too of the "Law" that "*gave damages*" for "*loss of services*" and "*breach of contract,*" instead of "punishing for crime," and that with the uniformity and the certainty that alone gives to punishment its restraining power,—men, outraged in their dearest rights, should take upon themselves revenge? And then, that other men,—who felt, that although the law made it not so, yet adultery IS a "crime,"—should, under the same influences of feeling, with that of sympathy and of pity also, bring in *verdicts of insanity* to excuse *murders of revenge for adultery and seduction?* Let Crimes be crimes upon our statute-book,—let them be visited with punishment adequate, certain, and inevitable, and then we shall have no more such "Wild Justice,"* and no more such verdicts.

But to continue the subject. As "they two are no more twain, but one flesh," it is manifest that the tie of Marriage involves the most complete mutualness, if we may use the expression. And besides this, marriage is a systematic and fixed mode of life, under an external habitude and law; wherefore the Roman Law rightly calls Marriage "omnis vitæ consuetudo," "of all the life a custom or habitude."

Let us look at these two facts:—Herein is the natural cure for Selfishness; for under the Law of marriage, by the very constitution of nature, be a man or a woman as selfish as they may be originally, another "Self" is substituted which the coldest-hearted are compelled to love, to feel for, to sympathize with. Nay, such is the nature of this mystery of our constitution, that even such persons will feel a high and pure pleasure in loving that other unselfishly and rendering her happy. Even *of itself,* by its own nature, that is, apart from considerations of duty, mutual love and mutual affection is the law of marriage; and he that can, in reference to his wife, remain "Selfish," and escape from the mutualness of affection that is natural to this society, must be hardened indeed. In all ordinary cases, it is a natural cure and remedy of "Selfishness," to a certain and indeed a very great degree.

* "Revenge is a sort of wild justice."—*Lord Bacon.*

But with regard to "Sensuality," also, the tendency that is to make mere pleasure the object of life, here too exists a natural and efficient preservation against this, in Marriage. It takes an individual apart from the world—it opens up to him a new life and new enjoyments. It shows him, as it were, a sphere of uncloying pleasures in the domestic society of his home and his fireside. A whole new world, as it were, in the present and in the future, is unsealed to him; and this world is his, fenced in and shut from external intrusion by the Home.

And at once to him it says—"To these calm joys and uncloying delights will you prefer the lascivious gaudiness of theatres, the revelling of the drunkard and debauchee, the insane frenzy of the gambler, the filthy and abominable conversation of the harlot and the prostitute?" From these, and from their consequences—loss of character, destruction, and ruin—does the Home and its chaste pleasures and secure happiness preserve multitudes. For because of the mutualness of marriage in all happiness and in all joys, as well as in all sorrows, it is the most complete cure there is naturally for that defect of the Heart that consists in our tendency to make mere pleasure the object of our life; which tendency we have called "Sensuality," or the inclination to pursue, as the main object, the pleasures of "Sense."

And, as we have before remarked, the living after a certain habitude and way of life, dependent not wholly upon our own Will, but upon a multitude of other circumstances and laws which all spring from the words "Marriage," "Family," and "Home;" this, in most men, is a very strong corrective of "Self-will," or "Uncontrolledness."

So that by the constitution of the relation, the marriage state, in consequence of its mutualness, or identification, is, if we may so say, a sort of "Natural Grace," or help that God has given us if we will improve it, against the three effects of "Original sin" upon the Affections or the Heart. I do not say a perfect or a complete remedy, but still one that is an aid more or less.

And from this, if we were asked what are those things that will the most destroy the happiness of married life, and turn the most its felicity into sorrow, we say these three—"Selfishness," "Sensuality," "Self-will." They are incongruous to its very nature, unsuitable in every way, elements, which, however evil they are elsewhere, here become tenfold more poisonous, tenfold more destructive,—being, to those united in marriage, the very elements and fountains of misery and wretchedness, as being in their very nature antagonist to that Mutualness or complete reciprocal identification of all pleasures, interests, affections, between persons united in marriage, which results from its very nature, and may well be counted the second law of marriage.

And they that would be happy, let them keep these evils away; let them ever avoid them, and instead of thinking of "Self" in any way, of will, of pleasure, or possession, let them think of that other "Self" whom God has given them. And of all possessions, all pleasures, all the objects of life, let them make that other Self the end. So, by these simple precautions, shall much sorrow be avoided, and much happiness secured.

I do not deny but that many are able to hide pure Selfishness under an appearance of carefulness for their families, and even at the time that they appear the best to the world, are most entirely Selfish. I will admit also, that some men are so entirely Sensual as to look upon their Home as a mere means of systematic Epicurean comfort. Nay, such men will secretly calculate to hide this, and to escape. But of the Un-house-like affections, for such are these, then the Family is the true avenger. Children detect these secret feelings of the Heart. They see, with a subtlety of discernment few imagine them to possess, whether a father or mother is Selfish, or Self-willed, or Sensual. They pierce through the veils and wrappings whereby these faults are hidden from the outer world. They discern the pretence of that which is claimed, but does not exist, the unreality of that which appears. And thus they are *driven to believe* that these are real principles of action, *and they act upon them.* Thus, Selfishness in the parent, especially when disguised, begets Selfishness in the child; so with Sensuality, and so with Self-will. The natural punishment of these offences in parents against the law of the Family, is the same in their children against themselves. Their vengeance is from evil and rebellious children. We do say not that this is always so, for there are many cases in which the good are afflicted in this way. But we will say, that of these things in the family, this is the natural result. And this we say, that one of the wisest men we have known, remarked to us that in this way he had seen the Selfish oftenest punished,—in their families.

The basis, it has been seen, and foundation of marriage is laid upon the mystery, *in us, of our nature*,—and externally to us, upon the law of God corresponding unto that mysterious constitution of our being.

The qualifications for it are the adequate and equal perfection, by training and education, of all the parts of the nature, the Spiritual, the Mental, the Physical. The completion and perfection of marriage, as to adequacy of these conditions, is that both should have been baptized in the "Name* of Christ," trained in the Law of Christ, and obedient unto the Faith of Christ. A completeness this is of the Spiritual Nature that will compensate for many deficiencies, and ensure much happiness.

The laws then of marriage are the laws of Permanence and of Mutualness,† from which spring all its duties.

And, according to these laws, the one cause of divorce is Adultery.

And the causes of misery in marriage life are "Selfishness," "Sensuality," and "Self-Will;" and the absence of them a great cause of happiness.

This synopsis we have here given of the preceding contents of this chapter, that our reader may see the whole matter summed up clearly and distinctly before we enter upon other parts of the subject, of which we are to speak less certainly.

The first of these questions is this: "Upon what motive, and upon what inducement, is a man or woman to marry?" Upon this we say, that the completeness and mutualness of the union will enable us to decide. The very basis of marriage is "that they two are henceforth no more twain, but one flesh." Should there not then be such an agreement of affections, such a mutual love, that the one would give up for the other all things, as it were, and make the happiness of the other the main object and end in life?

Certainly it seems by the very fact that they two are henceforth *to be one*, that no other motive or inducement should be sufficient but that of affection and love.

And this furthermore will be confirmed by the conclusion before educed, that "Selfishness," and "Sensuality," and "Self-

* The "Name" here is something more than the mere verbal appellation.

† The third law, that of the Supremacy of the Husband, I do not here touch upon, for plain reasons.

will," all of these are the most destructive of marriage happiness, and, therefore, naturally before marriage are as motives to be excluded; this, therefore, I say, *is*, or *ought to be*, the measure of the affection upon which, as the highest and purest motive, one may found his desire for marriage and his best prospect of happiness in it; *affection that shall be entirely unselfish,—that shall be unsensual, seeking mainly the happiness of the other instead of its own,—and steady and determinate, free from caprice and self-will.*

If a man or a woman feel in themselves such an affection, and measure it thus, they may be assured that this is "Love," such love as is the highest and best qualification for happiness, and the highest and best motive for engaging in marriage.

At the same time, I do not deny that there may be a multitude of other subordinate inducements upon which it is morally right to found our motives for marriage; but in all cases, whatsoever else there be, *there must be Affection as the great and leading motive*,* and, if not, there will afterwards be much unhappiness.

External circumstances, therefore, such as the natural taste for female society, the desire of companionship, the inability to manage the cares of a household, or in fact any external circumstances not "selfish" and not "sensual," may induce man or woman to wish for marriage, and to move towards it. And these may be, and are undoubtedly lawful and permissible motives, *provided there be real and sincere Affection.*

The other question is, "How far should parents interfere in the marriage of their offspring?" This question is, within certain limits, decided by the law, which, until a certain age, renders their consent necessary. An extended discussion of the subject we do not wish to enter into, as it is rather a difficult point, and one which would take more ground than we can appropriate to it. But we shall give the result of a good deal of thought upon the subject,—the conclusion, that is, that we have come to, without the arguments that have led us to it. We think that for *Christian children*, who are not only *baptized, but also communicants*, it will be a very safe and useful rule if they impose it upon themselves "never to marry without the full consent of their parents; always, that is, to allow them a full veto upon

* See, in the first book, the doctrine of the Supreme Good, or the Highest Motive.

their marriage." This, I think, they will find to be a principle according to the analogy of Christian faith and Christian practice.

Another, and a most important part of the marriage relation, is the relative position of Husband and Wife as regards control.

Now, manifestly, if marriage be merely a "Civil Contract," this shall be regulated in the way that the same question is managed in other "civil contracts" or "copartnerships,"—the one that is able to lead shall lead, and the one that is not able to lead shall obey, in all things that by the contract are common; and in all other things, each one shall manage in his own way. This must be the case under the Roman notion of "two persons;" "Person" being not merely an individual, but one who has all legal rights of holding property, suing and being sued, &c. Now between two "persons" in this sense entering upon "a Civil Contract," the idea, it seems to me, of Obedience is very foolish —these notions exclude it altogether. The proper idea herein, that is, the idea appropriate to these notions of Roman Law or Heathen Wisdom, is this: "I enter into a contract with you; I fulfil my part—do you fulfil yours; we are two persons still —and compliance with the terms of contract, this is all: fulfilment of the contract is all that is requisite, and Obedience is quite a different matter."

But the Common Law and the Scriptures, that teach that husband and wife are "One Person," and to be "no more twain, but one flesh," resting as they both do upon the doctrine of a mysterious union,—they imply by these very doctrines *that one must govern* and *one obey*. They send them not to a civil contract, to examine and decide upon their mutual rights—they set them not up as different "persons," to have a diversity of interest: they say, "You are one person and one interest, and one must lead and govern by your very position, and one be governed."

Hence the Scriptures are very plain and manifest in their directions to both husbands and wives in this respect: "Wives, be obedient unto your husbands,"* "The husband is the head of the wife, even as Christ is the head of the church,"† and so forth.

And this decision, inferior as it may seem in wisdom to the other, yet shall be seen and felt to be ultimately the wisest; for

* Tit. ii. 5. † Eph. v. 23.

differences of opinion are very likely to exist, and either they must be decided *judicially*, by *one out of the society*, or else *one must yield.* The first is the Roman notion; the second, the Christian doctrine. And every one knows how much a separation of interests, a debating upon them, a bringing in of a person extraneous as a judge and arbiter, tends to render irreconcilable the disputes and dissensions of marriage. Every one also knows how easily husbands and wives, *under the influence of love** and mutual respect, can yield the one to the other. And they who look at the different spheres of action which Husband and Wife fill in unity of life, and consider that the connection is not betweeen two men or two women, but between two of different sexes, upon the whole nature of which the difference is imprinted, and this difference in nature manifestly tending unto unity of action, shall see that to two natures so adapted unto unity, occasions of disagreement shall be infinitely few, compared to what they would be in those of the same sex. The occasions then of complete and entire unity of action shall be with them innumerable—the occasions of dispute very few indeed; and, in fact, with those that love sincerely and entirely, if they, as we have said, in the spirit of Christ, avoid Selfishness and Sensuality and Self-will, none at all. And the husband shall maintain his natural position of love towards his wife, and the wife her natural respect towards her husband, and in these be, through mutual and sincere love, entirely and completely happy. But to the fulfilment of this conception of marriage, *Christian love is a necessary ingredient* of the marriage; and having it, the husband shall not act unjustly, oppressively, or tyrannically towards his wife because he has a right to her obedience, nor shall she feel herself to be wronged in that she has promised to obey.

And, in truth, he that shall look through life shall see that there are multitudes of facts that will strengthen the belief that this last doctrine is the true one; of which I shall mention only two. The first is, that the wife shall be the last to see her husband's faults, even when she is the most keen-sighted as to those of others. There does seem to be, as it were, a veil cast by nature between her and those things the sight of which would

* Here I would be understood to mean the natural affection Christianized, under the influence of the Spirit of God.

weaken her obedience. Again, I have noticed that the wife shall feel and see the husband's love to wane when he is as unconscious of it himself, and he in reference to her love shall just be as hard and dull of sight as she of his faults. These things I have myself seen in many cases.

I have remarked that *love on both sides*, true and sincere, renders natural and rational the *Christian doctrine of the Supremacy of the husband* and the obedience of the wife; and I believe it will be seen that it is the doctrine upheld by reason and confirmed by experience.

But Christian faith and Christian holiness, this completes and perfects it—this alone is that which completely and entirely brings forth the marriage vow in its beauty, and enables the Husband and the Wife to estimate the marriage state as "Holy," "Sanctified," "Honourable in all." This alone says, "Husbands, *love* your wives *as Christ loved the Church and gave himself for it*:" this compares the marriage union to that of Christ and the church; this, instead of "Civil Contract," makes it a vow before God, and that a vow of that which no "Civil Contract" can prescribe or enforce—of mutual love, honour, obedience, affection, respect—in fact, love unselfish and unsensual. And a true and sincere faith in our Lord Jesus Christ, a living faith in the heart and in the life, these, when they exist, display and manifest unto the married the suitableness unto our nature and the adaptedness to our happiness of the doctrine of the Gospel in reference to the position of husband and wife.

But a deficiency in these will naturally lead in the way of the other notion.

And for this reason I should not at all be astonished to view the gradual growth and prevalence of the Roman-Law view of marriage, and the decay of the other, until, finally, only in the Church of Christ may we see those views and that law of marriage prevail that are peculiarly Christian.*

* I would not be understood wholly to condemn the proceedings of the Roman Law. No. I say, only Christianity can render the Common-Law doctrine possible. While the mass of the people, then, are unchristianized in profession and in heart, there must be recourse more or less to the principles of the Civil or Roman Law. Let women, therefore, in their property be protected. But let us the clergy, and others who feel its value, spread the true doctrine of marriage until it again become the sentiment of the whole people.

CHAPTER IV.

Law of Parents and Children.—Not merely an Animal Relation.—Evils arising from this notion.—Parents are bound to Children: 1st, Corporeally; for Maintenance.—Limits of this Obligation.—The State can enforce it.—2d, Mentally; for Education.—Limits of this Right.—The State has no Power of Religious Teaching: of Moral Teaching only up to a certain point.—3d, Spiritually; for Religious Education.—The State has no right in this whatever.

THE relation of the parent to the child and of the child to the parent is very simple indeed, if we look upon man as an individual animally existing, and consider Society as having no existence and no rights. "The animals pair by the force of one instinct, implanted in their nature for that purpose, and so does man." Here is the Animal or Physical account of marriage. "And by another instinct, the animals provide for their young until able to provide for themselves, and so does man. And that's the end of it."

Now, I do not say that men precisely and distinctly hold these views; but this I do say, that there are thousands and hundreds of thousands of parents in our land who *act* upon these views, and discharge themselves, *as far as they can*, from all duties of Education, of Religious Training, of Moral influence and superintendence, and, at the bottom, hold the mere physical view that the Home is *not* sacred, but is the mere dwelling-place of a pair of Animals having reasoning powers, whose mutual relation is merely to minister to one-another's comfort, and who have positively no moral duty, no religious, no educational one to fulfil to their offspring—nothing but a mere physical one: that of giving them food and clothing until they are able to give it to themselves.

I say, too, that of so-called religious men, there are multitudes who take precisely the same views, who, upon any and every pretext, are ready to devolve upon others the duties they themselves should perform towards their children.

And then have I seen these parents unhonoured by their children in old age, unreverenced, unobeyed. I have seen the children despising the age and infirmity of the parents, ashamed of their poverty, speaking openly and contemptuously of their errors, vices and infirmities, froward, rebellious, and disorderly, until, finally, the tie was severed—without love and trust upon the one side, without gratitude or filial affection upon the other. And then such parents complain. Wrongly and unjustly; for this result they themselves did all they could to bring about.

Man is a threefold being: "Spiritual," "Rational," "Corporeal, or Animal." If you act in the Home, towards children, as a mere animal, then shall the reward you obtain be nothing but this. I do not conceive that nestlings, when grown to maturity, make any difference between their parents and other full-grown birds—that dogs or horses, or any other animals, have any feeling towards the parent for a longer time than they are attached to them by physical wants and physical instinct. And so of all other animals wherein that which in man is done by the Affections is done in them by animal instinct. There is no gratitude, no love, no reverence, no respect, after the time of growth is past. Full growth and maturity of age puts the parent upon precisely the same ground as all other animals of the kind.

But man is a Spiritual being as well. His marriage is not a bare Animal Union, but one moral and spiritual in the highest degree. His Home is Spiritual and Moral too, and parents have Spiritual and Moral duties to do. If they do them not, but evade them, neglect them, free themselves from all obligation of them, so that really only the mere physical duty of supplying food and clothing is done, then the Animal result is the consequence—thanklessness, disobedience, neglect, want of respect, and want of affection, upon the part of children. I excuse them not for this: children of such temper and conduct sin before God, and are guilty because of it; but this I do say: the sin of the father is *the cause*, bringing most certainly, *as effect*, the sin of the children.

But let us be clearly understood, and not misapprehended. We said not that these merely animal duties and rights do not exist. We only say that they are *not the only duties*, so that all should be void except these. The father, in virtue of his threefold existence, has duties merely and entirely physical towards the child as an animal; *but these are not all.* There are, besides these duties, duties Intellectual and duties Moral. Let us look at these three in order.

"Maintenance" is the first. "The duty of parents to provide for the maintenance of their children," says Blackstone, "is a principle of natural law, 'an obligation laid on them,' says Puffendorff, 'not only by Nature herself, but by their own proper act in bringing them into the world. For they would be in the highest degree injurious to their issue, if they only gave children life that they might afterwards see them perish.' By becoming their parents, therefore, they have entered into a voluntary obligation to endeavour, as far as in them lies, that the life they have bestowed shall be supported. And thus the children will have a perfect right to receive maintenance from their parents. * * * The Municipal laws of all well-regulated states have taken care to enforce this duty. Though Providence has done it more effectually than any laws, by implanting in the breast of every parent that natural "Στοργὴ," or insuperable degree of affection, which not even the deformity of person or mind, not even the wickedness, ingratitude, and rebellion of children, can totally suppress or extinguish." * * *

"The Civil* law obliges the parent to provide maintenance for his child, and, if he refuses, 'Judex de ea cognoscet,' ('let the judge take cognisance of the matter.')"

Blackstone then goes on to show how the Common law enacts the same duty, and by what measures it can be enforced. But this belonging to Law and not to Ethics we shall merely say that the principle is maintained by the Laws of all countries, and dismiss it: only remarking that the duty and the right are purely physical and animal, arising from the fact that the child has a body and bodily life, that requires daily support,—that this life and body he has derived as part of his whole nature from his parents, and *from no other individual or individuals*,—and that, of himself, he is unable, in every or any way to support that life. These are the whole foundations of that right and that duty, both of them, it is manifest, purely animal, and both done by the animals under the influence of instinct.

The duration of this maintenance, or rather of the right, manifestly being until the offspring are perfectly able to support them-

* That is, Roman.

selves, is a period depending upon many elements, and usually settled by law. The expensiveness of it depending mainly upon the ordinary manner of life of the parents, is by this to be determined. And because, although it is in and within the Family, still, however, questions of Life and Property are involved; herein the State comes in, and enforces by its outward Law that which the inward and natural law, or, as it was called by the ancients στοργὴ (storghe,) or natural, parental, and filial instinct prescribes.

The parents, then, are bound to give to their children this maintenance, by the law of their own nature. The State, as an external institution, divinely appointed, and having the power of protecting by law, rights of Life, and rights of Property, has the right to enforce and regulate this question of maintenance, and to compel it from parents that are unwilling to obey the law of their own bosoms.

These, then, are the first duties of parents, the first rights of children;—the physical and animal rights arising from the body, the rights of helplessness and inability to support.

And here we shall remark that there is a very great difference, morally, between the ways that these things are done in; of themselves they are merely Animal, and may be done merely as such, —still are they done. And the same duties may be done in a spirit of love, affection, tenderness of feeling, sympathy; this last ensures love and gratitude;—the first, ingratitude and thanklessness.

The same remark may be made with regard to all aid to the hungry and the miserable. Bread, with pity and sympathy, is that which ensures gratitude and thankfulness; bread, unblessing and unsympathizing, is bread that receives no thanks.

But we come to a matter higher than the Animal duties. When the bird or the beast arrives at maturity, then it has, by its nature full grown, the capacities to continue its life, to acquire its food by the faculties its organization gives it, and in the way that organization requires. Now this is partly by an unerring instinct, and partly by the Understanding, as instructed by experience. And so we find the parents give the young the benefit of their own experience, as any one may see who will watch a parent bird with her fledgelings, or a cat with her kittens. But mostly are they left to Instinct, and to the effect of that allotment, which, for the most part, causes animals to be born in the peculiar region and place suited to provide them with the support of life. The work of Education is very small in them indeed.

But in man, on the contrary, the Instinct is very small, and the Understanding, or mental faculty, very great. And hence do we see the time during which men are placed under the direct influence and guidance of their parents, to be very long indeed, and to bear a large proportion to the whole of life, compared with the same period in other animals. Man's growth to maturity is exceedingly slow, the period of subordination and parental control exceedingly long. That which other animals learn by instinct, with only brief hints from the experience of parents, man learns slowly and gradually by the process of mental growth and mental development, through experience, imitation, instruction, example, emulation, sympathy.

Now, taking the Understanding, or the Animal Reason, as that whereby we reason and think upon things visible and perceptible by the senses, it will be manifest this is the faculty that does in man what instinct, with a few hints from experience, does for the animal nature, when separated from its parents—enables it to continue life, and support itself after this separation.

There is then, manifestly, a duty bounden upon the parents, an express obligation so to educate and train the Mental Powers of children, that they shall be enabled, after separation from their parents, to support themselves honestly and reputably; although the measures and limits of this are manifestly very indefinite.

And the child has a right to that Education, and that training of its mental powers, and may claim it by law, and the law may enforce it. And it does do so, so far that if parents rear their children as vagabonds, or in occupations evil and immoral, the Law will then step in, take away the children from the parents, and place them under persons who shall give them that training.

The parents, therefore, are under the obligation to give such an Education. The Children have a legal right to it. The State can enforce that right. But still the Laws of most nations, while they acknowledge the right, seem very little to enforce it, save in such cases as those we have mentioned, or save in the case wherein a parent teaches his children doctrines, that, *practically*, interfere with Life and Property, and those Rights which the State enforces, and the Wrongs that she forbids. If the parent taught the child systematically and practically, thieving, murder or adultery, so that the children were instructed in these crimes as a part of education, it seems that the Law can step in and put a stop to such Education. But with regard to anything else, it seems the State can hardly interfere.

In fact, as to the interference of the State in Education, it seems, as it has the office of establishing Rights and forbidding Wrongs, as far as concerns Life and Property, so to have the negative power of forbidding all education that shall train men to Crime. *Education in crime* it can forbid; a negative and prohibitory power it has to prevent Criminal teaching, so that it can interfere to prevent men being trained to break the Law, this seems to be *the limit of the moral teaching of the State*, in regard to parents and children.

But the State cannot interfere with Conscience, or with Religion, or with the Morality taught by the parents on any other grounds than these. The State has no control over the consciences of men. It can neither, under the pretence of Union with the Church, usurp to itself her offices of religious teaching, and thereby make heresies crimes, and opinions penal, and doctrines laws, and dogmas statutes, and compel all to religion by statutory enactments, and by the sanctions of law, fines and imprisonment. Nor can it reach the same end by a different route, pretending that the State is a Moral Teacher, a Religious Institution, for the purpose of instructing in religion, as the old theory of Pagan Rome, the new theory of Dr. Arnold, has it. The Church has to deal with Religion, Doctrine, and Spiritual Government and Instruction: these are HER sphere. Her punishments touch neither Life nor Property, but are spiritual. Sin, not Crime, is the transgression of *her* law; and although a Sin may be a Crime, and a Crime a Sin, it is *only as Sinful* that she deals with it, not *as Criminal.*

In fact, the Church is wholly and entirely separate from the State by nature and by the Law of this land. Hence, the State cannot interfere with education given by parents to children, so as to teach any doctrine, or *to forbid any doctrine to be taught*, except that the doctrine, over and above its character as doctrine, be also *criminal.* I conceive, then, the right of the State in interference with the education of children to be such that, first, it can require an education that will enable the child in after-life to get its bread honestly and reputably; and, secondly, that the edu cation given shall not be criminal. Without these limits, the State cannot touch the Parent in his education of his children.

Such an education the child can legally claim of the Parent as a right: the parent is bound to give and the Law bound to enforce it.

This is the second class of rights of Parents and Children; what may be called their Mental Rights.

But at the same time, although the State cannot interfere to enforce any above these "rights of maintenance," which are corporeal or animal, and "rights of education," which are mental, and cannot interfere as regards religion, still the father and the mother have a Spiritual Nature, and this puts *them* under the obligation to give a religious education, and to instruct Spiritually in every thing that shall exercise and bring to maturity the Conscience, the Spiritual Reason, the Affections, the Will. The training of these powers in the children, this is Religious and Moral Education; and the parents are bound to this by the Law of God and the Moral Law of their position. For the Family is a Moral and Religious institution by its very constitution; and the parents who are deficient in this culture are deficient in the duties of their position. And the children, too, by the Law of God and by their position, have the right to this Spiritual Education,—are by their position fitted to receive it, and have by their nature capabilities for it that they never have at any other period of their lives.

So that the whole obligation of parents, human and divine, shall correspond to the three parts of nature, and be three in number: Maintenance—Mental Cultivation—Religious or Spiritual Cultivation. These three must go on simultaneously; and without fulfilling these three, the duty of the parent to the child shall not be completely and entirely done; nor, without this, shall the fulness of the relation be felt and acted upon by either parent or child.

We purpose to follow out these remarks by some observations upon the spiritual and moral education of children by their parents, which will be most conveniently discussed in another chapter.

CHAPTER V.

The Right of the Child to a Spiritual Training, from its being always a Moral Being, and from the Needs of its Nature.—That Right extends to, 1st, Direct Instruction as to its own Nature and Position, *i. e.* Ethical Teaching—2d, As to the Nature of God, *i. e.* Religious Teaching—3d, Personal Sanctity in the Father and Mother—4th, Practical Guidance and Governance—5th, Baptism, or Covenant with God.—The Perfection of the Home is Love.

We have shown, in the last chapter, the claims of the child upon the parent in reference to the Body and the Mental Powers. In this, we shall examine his rights in relation to his Spiritual being.

Now, the claim for bodily Maintenance, the claim for education of the mental powers, these come from the needs of the child—his having faculties which require them; the situation of the parent producing at once the responsibility and the capability of fulfilling that responsibility. These four,—on the part of the child, the *faculties* and their *needs*—on the part of the parent, the *duty* and the *capability*,—manifestly are the foundation of the natural right of the child and the obligation of the parent in reference to the supply of bodily food and of mental training.

Let us take the child, then;—and long before the mental powers awake, there is in it, alive and vigorous in its being, the sense of Right and Wrong. This sense the Conscience awakens as an instinct, at the slightest hint. The Will is seen in the mere child; the Spiritual Reason, too; and, chiefly, the Affections. The whole experience of the Human Race manifests that at that precise period when the mental powers, owing to the rapid growth of the frame and the corresponding feebleness of the brain, are weakest and most unsuitable to exertion or to training, then are these most susceptible of impression, most capable of emotion.* So much so, indeed, that men shall often

* All physicians of knowledge or eminence are now well agreed upon the doctrine that mental education begun before the seventh year is of itself

look back with feelings of wonder, and almost of awe, to the high and radiant glory that they feel to have shed its beams upon their infant soul,—the glow, undoubtedly, of the moral powers in their first awaking. Of this emotion in the child, Wordsworth the poet speaks in his celebrated ode:—

"There was a time when meadow, grove, and stream,
The earth, and every common sight,
To me did seem
Apparell'd in celestial light,
The glory and the freshness of a dream.
It is not now as it hath been of yore,—
Turn wheresoe'er I may,
By night or day,
The things which I have seen I now can see no more:
The rainbow comes and goes,
And lovely is the rose,
The moon doth with delight
Look round her when the heavens are bare;
Waters on a starry night
Are beautiful and fair;
But yet I know, where'er I go,
That there hath pass'd away a glory from the earth."

This glory, which the great poet so justly and beautifully attributes to infancy and childhood, we recognise as the first awaking glow of the moral affections of the child, demanding that spiritual food and support to them which the parent is authorized to give; that training which they are then best qualified to receive.

highly destructive, as prematurely exciting the nervous system, and laying the foundation for many diseases. The physiological considerations upon which this is founded, I omit. I shall only remark that this hot-bed forcing of the childish mind into premature action, produces mental feebleness in advancing years; and in many cases it causes mental oddity and distortion; just as the forcing a young tree to bear fruit before its maturity, stunts and dwarfs it. *No child should learn a letter of the alphabet before seven years of age.*

People, then, will say, What shall we do with them? Shall we give them no education till then?

I say, there is *an education* that dwarfs not the infant mind, but invigorates its powers and enlarges its calibre—*the training, that is, of the moral faculties.* At that time of life, parents *are teachers of God appointed,* to *that end;* and *viva-voce moral teaching* is worth ten times all the reading done before that age by children even of the most cultivated mental powers. This, I conceive, is answer enough to the objection. The parent will find the subject further carried out in the text.

Nor need the "glory pass away," if the parent walk himself in the faith of things Unseen and Eternal; if the child be trained by him to walk in the "light of heaven," and "under the shadow of the Almighty;" if the Home be a sanctified temple and dwelling-place of God's presence and his teachings. Then, indeed, the eye of the child would in all things continue to see the "Glory of the Unseen God," and not the external world alone be "apparelled in celestial light;" but from youth to age the human being so trained would walk through life, canopied by the light from that unspeakable glory; crowned with a halo and a radiance of moral beauty that we see in few at the present day.

In few,—because, though some appreciate the value of giving Education to their children, and almost all feel the necessity of supplying bodily Maintenance, yet very few seem to know that there is a Spiritual faculty in man, that that faculty needs education, and that the Parent is the Teacher of that faculty appointed by God, with peculiar privileges, peculiar powers and abilities, unto that purpose adapted, which *he* can exercise, and *no one else.*

Now, the child has a Conscience even from its birth,—just as it has mental and bodily powers that will enable it, where they are duly trained, to obtain a livelihood in mature years. The parent is counted cruel that does not so train these powers as to fulfil their end. What shall we say of him who trains *them*, but trains not the sense of Right and Wrong, or so perverts it by his own negligence that it is by the child neglected or despised? What but this, that, whether he intended it or no, he has sent out his child,—*without an internal principle—to do evil;* and sooner or later to fall upon that external law of God and man that forbids evil by penalty and suffering? The man who permits his child to pass into life with a conscience not *educated* to the utmost of his power, that man prepares for his children countless miseries, —and the man who trains it, happiness to an untold extent.

And he who trains them in the high and lofty truths that come from God's being, and teaches them in childhood to appropriate these to themselves, to walk in and by them as moral principles, how much is he to be praised, compared with the man who either positively, by actual precept, or by example in his house, instructs his children that there is no moral principle or moral truth, but that all a man has to do is to make the most of the world in a moderately selfish and sensual way? Does not the one teach moral truth, the other moral falsehood? And has a parent any right thus to corrupt the Spiritual Reason of his child more than he has a right to destroy his Body or his Mind?

Again, in reference to the Heart—half the miseries of life come from Selfishness, Sensuality, Self-will: have the Parents of a feeble babe any more right to leave the child unprotected from these, untaught and untrained in reference to these, than they have to permit the body to be devoured by wild beasts?

Let such persons look at a miserable Byron,—look how Selfishness, Sensuality, and Self-will tortured him through his whole life; look, then, at the character and temper of his mother, and I think that it will be very manifest, that her teaching and example was such as to cherish all these, and that a different mother would have produced different results. And then, looking at the natural nobleness of temper that he seems to have had *originally*, it would appear that the infant, and the boy, and youth *had a right* to a direct training of the Affections which would have prevented these things; and that *because* he went forth with these untrained and untaught, *therefore* he spent his life in a fiery agony and storm of Self-will, and Sensuality, and Selfishness.

So might I go on and show that each child has upon its parents the *right* and *claim* to a proper development and education of its moral powers; and that no parent ever sends forth a child in this respect uneducated, without being the cause of great misery to it.

But I think there is no further need or necessity of illustrating it any more. My first two propositions I consider all men will acknowledge—1st, that "children have, from the earliest years, Moral Faculties which require education;" and 2dly, "that physical maintenance, and physical training, and mental education, are not that Spiritual Education, *but entirely distinct from it*, so that one may *be mentally educated* to the very highest degree of cultivation, and *have no spiritual education at all.*"

This Moral Education, then, the child has the faculty for, because he has a Moral Nature that requires and needs, yea, and yearns for it, and searches after it. And the man is not perfect as a man without it; going forth into life without it, he goes forth halt, and maimed, and imperfect, as he would if he went forth with a limb of his body incapable, or a sense destroyed, or a mental faculty decayed. The child from earliest years has a Moral Nature capable of a peculiar moral education, which is distinct from mental education; and the needs and nature of Man's life and of Society demand that training to the future man from his parents.

Now, admitting these two primary assertions to be true,—that the child has moral faculties, and that they require and need a peculiar training,—what shall be the Spiritual or Moral education the child has a right from the parents to claim?

Manifestly, the answer shall be, first, a proper training and development of *the faculties themselves;* such an education of the Moral Powers as shall strengthen, invigorate, establish them in due operation, correct their faults, and supply their deficiencies; this in reference to the faculties themselves. Secondly, in reference to their action, the supplying them *externally* with the proper objects.

We may compare these two ends of Spiritual education in this way:—With the body,—the stomach, for instance, is the organ of digestion; you can strengthen it, *considered as an organ*, as to its health, its tone, its action:—this will correspond to the one kind of education of the Moral faculties. And then you can supply it with healthy and digestible food, in certain measures and after certain laws:—this supply of nutriment will correspond to the other. A Parent, then, we consider, is bound, first, to strengthen and develope the Moral Powers of his child; and, secondly, to supply those powers with suitable and appropriate nutriment.

With regard to the first obligation, is there a true doctrine of Man's Nature and Position, or is there not? As there are certain internal principles of physical being that belong to the nature of the dog, the horse, the elephant, which when you know, you know their nature and the way in which that nature works upon external things; is it so with man? Has he an internal constitution, with internal faculties of Body and Soul and Spirit, which are the same Internal Nature, corporeal, mental, and spiritual, in all men—in all to work in the same way upon the external world?

Surely, if this be so, the first duty of the parent is to *appeal* to that Internal Nature,—to *manifest it*,—to teach the solution of its various problems to the child,—and to trust for the proof to the nature itself. By the very fact that man has an Internal Nature, and that Nature is the same in all, there must be one, and only one true doctrine of Nature and Position; and the highest and chiefest of all duties of the parent is to convey that doctrine to the child, and its solution of the various problems which to every one each part of that Nature suggests.

For, as I have remarked, most of the moral errors at present in vogue in the world arise from misinterpretation of facts and problems of our nature: and, indeed, when we look at the two-foldness of all Moral facts, we find it, we may say, perfectly impossible for a person *wholly untaught* to give a right solution of them.

For instance, here is the "Conscience," as shown in the second book of this volume. There are two clear and equally distinct impressions naturally of it: the first, that it is fallible; the second, that it is infallible; the one as strong as the other. It would seem that here is a very difficult problem. And, indeed, if you look at what it has resulted in, you find that to men untaught in youth, the solution is generally *by rejecting one or the other as untrue.* And the practical result has been, in one class of persons, the making of the faculty a God, without any reference to Jehovah or his Law; or, secondly, the rejecting altogether the Conscience, and the denying its existence. The true solution being that deduced from revelation, as in the second book: "It is *fallible* so far as it is a faculty of the man, an eye seeing the light, an ear transmitting the voice; but *infallible* so far as it is the Light of God's Word, so far as it is the voice of God's Spirit. *Fallible* and *infallible!* When governed by the Law of God, habitually obeyed under the influence of the Holy Ghost, morally infallible;—but outside these influences, fallible, and the more so from its very loftiness." Is not this problem one which is of our nature,—comes up to every man sooner or later,—is impossible *almost* to be solved without teaching,—and yet is absolutely needful to know? Surely, the fact that man has a Moral Nature that is one, implies *one solution, one teaching*, and the need of *that one teaching.*

Again, look at the Heart. The Scriptures tell us that the Heart is *the source of all evil.* We feel this to be true: we feel it also to be the *source of the highest moral good.* Two contradictories, seemingly, again; and, as in the other case, the source, in a practical way, of much evil; and yet both meeting in one, and both true, and reconciled only by a true and high scriptural philosophy of our nature.

But I may refer back to the antecedent pages of this treatise, to manifest the truth I am now illustrating,—to show that our Nature is full of the hardest problems, the most contradictory, rising up of themselves in all men, and solved only by a high Christian philosophy—the philosophy of Faith and Hope and Love—a philosophy that is one, because the Church is one, and Human Nature is one, and the Father, Son, and Holy Ghost are one—and therefore is to be seen, more or less, in the Church, in all ages, as Her solution of the problems of our nature and situation. In Augustinus, the African, of the fourth century, in Gregory, the Roman, of the seventh, in the church of Egypt, of Constantinople, of Greece, of the whole world, in all ages and times, this *one* Ethics is everywhere visible. This the Christian view of Human Nature, I conceive, should be taught by every parent to every child. What is man's Nature? what Conscience? what Reason? how binding? how guiding? All the proper ethical knowledge that is necessary, could be taught within a small compass, and very easily, even to the young, and would make up a branch of education hitherto very little touched upon,—the "Doctrine of man's Nature and Position."

I conceive, then, that, as a part of the Spiritual Education for which all parents are responsible to their children, one of the first requisites is this, to instruct them in the "*doctrine of their own nature and position.*"

And corresponding to this system of truths of man's nature, is the system of "truths of the nature of God," or the truths of revealed religion, which explain and illustrate the others, and upon which all truly scientific elucidation of those others depends. So that would it seem that there is not a *subjective* truth of the nature of man, that has not corresponding unto it some *objective* truth of revelation that illustrates, confirms, teaches it, and, being in this relation, sheds a flood of light over it. Hence, in reference to man's Spiritual Being, the parent is bound to teach the truths of religion and Christianity in their fulness and completeness, as corresponding to and harmonizing with the Spiritual nature of the child.

And so, for his moral nature, shall he supply him with high

and holy precepts and laws, which the child will feel and know to be in accordance with his Nature, its necessities and uses.

But there is more than this: Mental or verbal teaching is not always moral teaching. To act upon a moral truth is to learn it —to *cause to act* is to teach;—hence, the relation of the child to the parent in the Home, demands of the parent, first, *that his own life be holy and true.* Moral teaching that is merely verbal will not do; as for a parent in the Home to *act* is to *teach.* Children are taught by actions: if holy, just, sober, true, honest, holiness, justice, sobriety, truth, honesty, are taught; and so of the contrary.

Thus children may be educated spiritually, by their parents first acting themselves, then causing them to act, upon principles of true morality;—causing them to *act first*, and then trusting that expanding mental powers and increasing experience will manifest the truth of the principles.

From this it follows that the Child has a claim upon the Parent for *sanctity in his own life* and *sanctity in the Home;* and not only for instruction, but also for *guidance and governance* in the ways of true morality.

And then, if Baptism be not merely a sign of profession, but also a seal of the Covenant of Faith—a "means of grace," as the Church holds it, so that "by baptism we are members of Christ, children of God, inheritors of the kingdom of heaven,"— if this be so, and the faith of parents can place the children *in covenant* with the Incarnate Word, through the Life-giving Spirit, then is the parent bound, by the Spiritual nature and wants of the child, to secure to it that blessing of being consecrated unto God in the "name of the Father, and of the Son, and of the Holy Ghost;" and thereby unto them, as the Elect of God, assuring the teaching of God's providence, "so that all things shall work together for good to them;" assuring to them the Redeeming influences of the Son; and the instruction and influence of the Holy and Infinite Spirit upon the spirit of the child; the Spiritual teachings, too, of the Church of God, with all its ministries, from Angel and Archangel, Cherubim and Seraphim, in heaven, downward unto the ministration of God's Church and ministers on earth. All these benefits is the parent bound to procure for his children. And all these are consummated and completed through the parent's faith and vows, and by the dedication solemnly by Baptism of the child unto God,—the bringing of it thus within the Church, the fold of God's Elect.

But upon this point of Christian morality, having already, in a separate treatise more than once referred to, discussed this subject, I shall direct my reader's attention to it, merely remarking that therein the right of the infant to baptism, and the effects of it in sanctifying the Home, are fully examined.

Here, then, is the last right of children upon parents—the right of being dedicated to God by the formal act of their parents. And from it, how many consequences flow!—the right that they should be trained up in His name and His word,—that his Law should be made the rule of their lives,—that the Written Word should be their study,—that the Home should be a Sanctified temple of God's presence and graces, and not a mere abiding-place to eat and drink in, but a temple, wherein father and mother shall be, as it were, "priests and kings," sanctified teachers and sanctified governors of their household in Christ perpetually!

This is the last claim the Child has upon the Parent; and this claim is verified and established by all parts of the human nature of the child, which cry aloud for such a consecration; and are then, and then only, placed in their proper position towards man and God, when so dedicated, so united in covenant to the Eternal Son through the Eternal Spirit. This is the highest teaching to the Spiritual Nature, and the most complete and perfect education that its faculties and its necessities require and demand.

And for them who have placed their children in this position, and then themselves have, through the sense of their responsibility and the grace of God aiding them, lived up to the requirements of their position,—for them we have seen the highest grace of the Christian Home to ensue,—the "living in Love." We have seen them, not by constraint nor compulsion, not by the interposition of any Human Law, but by disinterested Love and unselfish devotion, fulfilling all duties, gladly and rejoicingly.

And from this spirit of Love in parents, we have seen the spirit of affection and love arise on the part of the children. And we have seen that all *legal* thoughts of right on the one part and obligation on the other have ceased to have any influence—the affection of parents to children, and of children to parents, joyously and overflowingly fulfilling all duty, almost without feeling it. So that here we have seen the truth that "Love is the fulfilling of the law;" and all its duties are done through no external compulsion, but by that internal principle that makes them all, pleasures and springs of happy feeling.

This, then, we count the perfection of the relation of parents to children and of children to parents, of wives to husbands and of husbands to wives—the perfection of the Christian Home:—that all within it be sanctified and duly dedicated unto God, and live up to the sum and completion of their profession—that is, live in Christian Love: the completion, not only of all happiness, but of all Christianity.

And this being done in the spirit of Christian Faith, we fear not that love, and honour, and reverence, and gratitude, and respect will flow forth naturally from the child unto the parent,—that children so educated will feel the truth and incumbency of the precept, "Honour thy father and thy mother, that thy days may be long in the land which the Lord thy God hath given thee."

Our readers may then say, "But cannot parents and children, apart from religion, live in a state of love?"

In respect of this we say, that the feeling is natural to the heart of man, a natural affection, and so comes forth naturally from parent to child, and from child to parent: and so we do not deny but that natural affection may exist in a *very great degree;* but *not to that degree* we have spoken of; *never to that perfection.*

And that for this simple reason that our Nature, made in God's image, only obtains its completion and perfection when in direct covenant with the Almighty Father, through his Son, the Mediator,—and therefore directly taught and trained and formed by the Grace of his Holy Spirit.

With this remark we shall end this book, having brought the duties of the Home upward, until we have seen in it, as in all else that concerns Man's Nature, that duty is perfected by religion, and Nature is crowned by Grace.

BOOK VI.

THE HUMAN WILL.

CHAPTER I.

Arguments upon the Will generally mere thorny quibbles.—The opinion of Milton to this effect.—Censure upon its harshness.—The opinion of Bishop Beveridge.—The sentiments of Hooker as to the Will of God and the nature of His Decrees.—St. Augustine, his character and temper.—Two ideas held by him to be connected, Grace and Predestination.—These are not so connected naturally.—Evil consequences on both sides of taking it to be so.—The Theological Controversy waived.—The Will discussed as a faculty of our nature.

IN the works of Thomas Aquinas, there occurs an argument to prove that God has a body,—is, in other words, material, which the great Schoolman states gravely, and then as gravely refutes. It is from a passage in the book of Job, which reads thus: "Canst thou by searching find out God? Canst thou find out the Almighty to perfection? He is as *high* as heaven, what canst thou do? *Deeper* than hell; what canst thou know? The measure thereof is *longer* than the earth, and *broader* than the sea."*

Therefore, says the ingenious fool whom Thomas refutes, "God has *length*, *breadth*, and *thickness*, (depth or height,)—these are expressly attributed to him in the passage of Job,—but these are the three dimensions of body; God then has the dimensions of body!—therefore, God is body!"

Whatever one may say about the argument above given, we must admit that it is a most ingenious absurdity; so absurd, indeed, that its very folly makes it startling: and yet no one would give any weight to it; it is merely verbal, a knot of words that expresses nothing.

* The quotation is from the Vulgate.

Such, we humbly conceive, and we have bought our knowledge by dear experience, is the staple of almost all books upon the Will that we have read—ingenious absurdities, startling paradoxes, knotted words that bind not nor define the realities, definitions gravely laid down, that, like conjurors' magic boxes, hold secretly all consequences afterwards drawn from them,—fruitless ears that seem full, and yield no fruit, and are yet always seeming-ready for threshing. Such are the disputes upon the Will as we have seen them managed, and we believe that the man who has had the most of such discussions, that man will the most see the fruitlessness of them on the one side and on the other. With all due respect to the illustrious dead, in this quality of a fruitless and thorny verbal logic, the argumentations for "Free-will,"* and those for "Slave-will,"† are upon a par,—the one about as unsatisfactory as the other.

Such has been the effect of them upon many of the greatest, and soberest, and most judicious of men. Such, too, was the effect upon one, who, although certainly great, was as certainly neither sober nor judicious, but fiercely fanatical, and injudicious in the highest degree: we mean John Milton. He places his demons in hell, arguing upon these themes:

> "Others apart sat on a hill retired,
> In thought more elevate, and reason'd high
> Of Providence, Foreknowledge, Will, and Fate,
> Fixed Fate, Free-will, Foreknowledge absolute,
> And found no end, in wandering mazes lost."

This, then, is the opinion upon this matter of the great poet who, in his younger days, had been most conversant with these argumentations; that they are lost in such labyrinths that no clue is to be found; that they are so difficult, so unsuitable to the calmness of Christian faith, that only in the evil angels

> "Late fallen, and weltering on their bed of fire,"

could be found intellect enough, and fierce restlessness enough, to discuss these subjects. In the opinion of John Milton, fallen angels in Pandemonium are the only fit and proper disputants upon the Calvinistic and Arminian controversy! We excuse not Milton for this strange poetic license. We only point it out as

* "Liberum Arbitrium."—*Erasmus.*

† "Servum Arbitrium."—*Luther and Calvin.*

the expression, in a very strong way, of a very fixed opinion, by a man of great genius, as to the peculiar nature and tendency of this class of disputes.

And if the reader please, we shall put it into plain, unimaginative prose, that Milton had come deliberately to the opinion,—that to contemplate the Almighty Father solely as a Being of Infinite Power, is to involve and entangle our minds in the most complicated questions, to produce in us, as regards ourselves, the temper of despair,—as regards our neighbours, that of unyielding and unsympathizing harshness. Such might be the meaning drawn from this Miltonic parable, when we soften down the hatred and scorn for this Controversy that manifestly was the motive for such an extraordinary procedure. For surely, whatever Calvin, and Luther, and Erasmus, and the Dort divines, and the Arminians had done, they had not deserved this, that the angry theological poet should give a synopsis and summary of their opinions on both sides, and then set them forth as subjects of debate for the devils in Hell! However, while we protest most fervently against the spirit of this passage of Milton, we cite it here as strong evidence of the matured opinion of that great mind, as to the fruitlessness of this harsh controversy.

The same impression is made upon Bishop Beveridge of the incompetency of the human mind to deal with such subjects. In his Commentary upon the Articles of the English Church, he expresses himself thus:

"A cockle-fish may as well crowd the ocean into its narrow shell, as vain man ever comprehend the Decrees of God. And hence it is that, both in public and private, I have still endeavoured to shun discourses upon this subject; and now that I am unavoidably fallen upon it, I shall speak as little as I possibly can unto it."*

But that Intellect, the greatest perhaps in the English church, who, by the judgment of all modest and sober men, has earned the title of the "judicious Hooker,"—he has expressed himself, perhaps, more fully than any upon the inutility of bringing into logical and mental examination, the subject of the Will of the Infinite and Eternal God:—

"All things, therefore, do work after a sort according to Law,

* Beveridge on the Seventeenth Article.

whereof some superior, unto whom they are subject, is author, only the works and operations of God have *Him* for their worker, *and for the law whereby they are wrought. The Being of God is a kind of Law to his working.* * * * [Our purpose] is only to touch upon such operations [of God] as have their beginning and being by a voluntary purpose wherewith God hath eternally decreed when and how they shall be, *which eternal decree* is that we term an *eternal law.*"

"Dangerous it were for the feeble brain of man to wade far into the doings of the Most High, whom although to know be life, and joy to make mention of his name, yet our soundest knowledge is to know that we *know him not indeed as he is*, neither can know him; and our safest eloquence concerning him is our silence, when we confess without confession that his glory is inexplicable, his greatness above our capacity and reach. He is above, and we upon earth, therefore it behooveth our words to be wary and few."*

Such are the resolutions of Hooker: 1. God's decrees are the eternal laws of His Nature—Justice, Holiness, Wisdom, Truth. Aught, then, unjust, unholy, untrue, cannot be attributed to God.

2. The finite mind of man cannot comprehend the *Infinite by reasoning;* and therefore we should not systematize, argue, or reason, but trust in Him, with faith, and fixedly distrust ourselves and our reasoning concerning His action, knowing that of his Secret Decrees we can neither by argument nor system attain any knowledge, save only that they are not against the eternal laws of his being, holiness, justice, truth, and mercy.

This seems the doctrine of Hooker, as it is manifestly that of the English church.

That God has Secret Decrees, the determinations of His Will which were made in the bosom of his Infinity, when no external creation existed, and only the Infinite Father dwelt alone with the Eternal Word and the Eternal Wisdom,—this we must acknowledge. And our business, then, is to bow before Him in adoration—to know that of these we can know nothing, save that they are not contrary to those laws of his being that he has revealed to us; and, secondly, to be assured, that by no logical

* Hooker, vol. i. p. 156–7.

systematizing can we reach to a comprehension or a knowledge of them.

We must not argue and reason and systematize, and frame out schemes and plans of this ineffable action of the Eternal, that took place before matter and time had any existence,—as Edwards, or Hopkins, or Beza, or Calvin; although, indeed, this controversy, dated, as it usually is, from Calvin, goes far higher up the stream of time. Higher far than Calvin are we to seek the origin of this controversy, in the works of St. Augustine, a Christian father of the fifth century, and unquestionably one of the greatest and holiest men of the church, as well as a man of immense genius and ability. He was the first to introduce into the Church the peculiar views at present called Calvinistic.

And much as we revere the memory of Augustine, we must say, that we think that in bringing into Christianity the Stoic doctrine of Fate, and the logical and verbal debatings by which it has been sustained, he inflicted a grievous wound upon the simplicity of the Gospel. Far better would it have been fully to confess God's almighty power and man's feebleness of mind—to think that there are mysteries above our reach,—and to refrain from the vain attempt, by logical and verbal arguing, to shape out a system of action for the Inscrutable and Ineffable Jehovah.

In fact, there are in the works of St. Augustine, to be found united together in close connection, two ideas: the idea of Original Sin and Grace, a true and real Christian idea; and another idea, the pagan one of Doom, or Fate. These two are so joined in *his* mind, by his natural fervour, that one seems to him the logical consequence of the other. And even to this day, such is the influence, at the end of fourteen centuries, of that great mind, that to many, these two ideas seem absolutely connected, so that one must infer the other,—when they are, in reality, wholly separate. Men cannot conceive how the doctrine of Original Sin and Grace can be held without holding Predestination, or how Predestination can be held without holding Grace; whereas, as I have said, the ideas are not in any way naturally united: as may be seen from two examples. Mohammed, the Pharisees, the Stoics, Diderot the French infidel, all these held most distinctly the doctrine of Absolute Fate; and yet no one will say that any of them approach at all to the doctrines of the Grace of God and the Inability of man. And, on the other hand, before the time of

St. Augustine, the Ancient Church universally proclaimed the doctrines of man's fall and the all-sufficing power of Grace; and yet there is no trace of the doctrine of fate among them. And the Church in America, at the present day, says distinctly that without Grace no man can do any thing pleasing in the sight of God, and yet distinctly reprobates the fatalistic doctrine.

But in the mind of St. Augustine, the two ideas dwelt together. Penetrated to his inmost soul with the idea of man's fallen state, his inability of himself to do any good, or in thought, word, or deed to satisfy the just demands of the law of God, we see the stern will that could have swayed the sceptre of the Roman empire—the lofty mind that soars to the most empyrean heights of mental science—the great heart so overflowing with love,—all this nature bowed before the throne of God, confessing its own unworthiness, its inability to do aught of good, its guiltiness, its deservingness of condemnation before the pure and holy bar of Infinite Justice. And then, as the counterpart of this, is seen his conviction of the mercy of God in Christ—his feeling of the all-sufficient and almighty influences of the Grace of God through Jesus Christ.

No greater, no more glorious sight has Christianity ever seen, than the great Augustine,* bowing before the throne of God, and under these convictions crying out, "Not myself, but thee, O my God—not my power, but thine, O Infinite and Eternal Father—not my merit, but thy death and thy love by me undeserved, O Eternal Son, the Word Incarnate—not my ability, or my purity, or my merit, but thy Grace, Almighty Spirit; proceeding from the Father, endued then with his omnipotence; sent by the Son, conveying then his love and his pardon—not myself, then, the creature of clay and the dust, but thee, O Father, Son, and Holy Ghost—Creator, Saviour, and sole Sanctifier of Man!" Such are the feelings wherewith, throughout the works of this great saint, the doctrines of Grace and Original Sin, practically held by him, abide upon his mind and find vent from his heart.

Such are and such ought to be the feelings of every true Christian who holds these doctrines, without any reference to Absolute

* See throughout the Confessions of St. Augustine: a book that perhaps has been never equalled for true Christian feeling, and which every one that desires to know the true spirit of the Gospel should read. There are several English translations of it.

Predestination at all. The two doctrines, in fact, are entirely and completely distinct. Only in the ardent mind of Augustine were they united, by the fact that he held them both.

For, alas! the Stoic doctrine of Necessity, or Doom, or Fate,—the doctrine that sees power as the sole attribute of God, and considers his sole act to be the issuing of infinite and uncontrolled decrees,—this idea, familiarized to the mind of Augustine from his previous philosophic studies, offered apparently an easy solution for the mysteries of Grace, seemed to honour the Almighty sovereign of the universe, and to be a ready answer to all gainsayers, a ready means of accounting for all mysteries of external nature, and of providence, as well as for all the dark problems of man's nature and position; and so it was too readily adopted. The fervent genius and glowing heart of Augustine thus united two ideas wholly incongruous—the Christian idea of Almighty and All-sufficing Grace, and the Stoic idea of Fate uncontrolled and irresistible, predestinating all things by an absolute doom.

From that time, in the apprehension of the ordinary mass of Christians, such is the far-descended power of one great soul even in its mistakes, it has been found almost impossible to separate these two ideas. Most probably it may take place even with this very book, that many who read it and see that it upholds so strongly the doctrine of the guiltiness of man before God, and the All-sufficiency of Grace, may wonder that the other idea they think to belong to it, that of Fatalistic Predestination, is so strongly rejected. Nay, perhaps, they may be inclined to accuse me of inconsistency in accepting the one doctrine, and rejecting the other.

Let them know then, that for the facts of Creation, of Providence, of Grace, I seek not the solution in the Pagan doctrine of Doom, but in the Christian doctrine of the Trinity. God governs not the world by Doom, executes not his decrees by the rigid machinery of an iron Fate, but by the Word, a personal, ever-present being, proceeding from the bosom of the Father; God *from* God, Light *from* Light, very God from very God; consubstantial, coeternal, coequal with the Father. He is the governing power in this world, HE, and not an impersonal, unintelligent, mechanical Doom; a present God He is, and a present King. If I believe in Stoic Doom, I more or less deny the government of the Word, the personal and present agent of the purposes and decrees of the Almighty. If, on the other hand, I fully conceive and apprehend the Christian doctrine of the Word, I must cast aside the idea that a predestination system is to this world the executor of God's will. One idea destroys the other. I cannot hold them both. I therefore hold to the peculiarly Christian doctrine, and reject that taken by St. Augustine from the Stoics.

Again, if the way wherein our thoughts are subdued unto Christ, be conceived to be by the infinite power of the Almighty crushing them into conformity with his will by an overwhelming force, this is one idea,—a solution for the problem which cuts the knot instead of untying it. And manifestly by this there is no agent can interfere between our thoughts and the power of *the Infinite Decree.* It is the agent that subdues the soul. Here then again, the idea of Doom is substituted for the Christian idea. The Christian idea is, that a *personal being*, the *Holy Spirit*, the Lord, (that is Jehovah,) proceeding from the bosom of the Father, as God *from* God, and receiving from the Son Life and Light for men, that he, the Love of the Father, the Free Gift of the Son, the Spirit of grace undeserved, and all-embracing, is the agent that works upon our thoughts and turns them to God. HE and not Doom. If I hold, then, in its fulness, the doctrine of the Holy Spirit and His office with regard to men, I cannot hold that other predestination doctrine. If I should hold that doctrine of Doom, I make the Spirit of God,—if I admit His existence,—a subordinate agent working *in consequence of the decree*, and only its instrument, and therefore, I am, by my very doctrine, tempted to deny that he is God *of* God. In the mystery of the Trinity, as I have said, not in any pagan philosophy of fatalism, is to be sought the solution of the problems of Grace. Happy had the church been if Augustine had never united these two ideas together, so discordant as they are, in their sources, in their effects upon the mind and temper of man, and in their consequences.

Happy, too, for modern Christianity, had men been content with the humble and calm views of Hooker, as given a few pages back, but, in both cases, so far from taking this moderate view, they attempted to systematize the admitted facts of God's omnipotence and of man's subjection, into a rigorous logical theory, and thereby, as the natural consequence of the system, they changed the Almighty and Omnipresent "Father of Mercies," into a Lord of rigorous and unbending destiny, predestinating to heaven and reprobating to hell independently of all the laws of his own being, save that of almighty power. The external world, the great school of Probation, whereby, in its various forms, man is taught by a living and present God, they made a machine driven by an eternal Fate, and man so crushed within its wheels, as to be externally bound by infrangible chains, and internally driven by an irresistible Will, not his own. This is the issue of the argument for "Slave-will."

And then the opponents of this fatalistic system, in attacking it, argued just as unfairly upon the other side. Instead of abstaining from the attempt to measure the Infinite by the Finite, to systematize by man's puny reasoning, the power and the acts of the Eternal God; they, too, had their *system by which* God made the world; their *reasons why* he did every thing; they, too, could penetrate into the *motives upon which*, before time was, he decreed; and "being His counsellors, they had instructed Him." And so the end of the one system, as well as the other, came to be false philosophy with reference to the Being and Attributes of God, the uses of the external world, and the nature of man; and presumptuous dogmatism flying away from all living faith into absurd and unpractical speculation.*

* The author will, perhaps, be asked, what there is in your own doctrine, seeing you count one scheme to be harsh and unsuitable to the doctrines of the Gospel, and the other, that of Predestination upon foresight of good works, to be presumptuous and evil in its tendencies,—what then is your scheme?

I answer, that which I think to be the doctrine of the standard of the Protestant Episcopal Church in the United States, to which I belong. That is the doctrine of Original Sin and Grace, upon which, as I have dwelt upon them so plainly I need not enlarge. In reference to the Decrees of God, the doctrine of Hooker, that we cannot know any thing of them, only that they *are*, and that they are not against the revelations of His nature that he has given us. And with regard to the Election, that every man in this world who is within the church of God, in the visible covenant, he is Elect, predestinated *to those privileges*, to an opportunity that is, of all the means of grace, and therefore bound "to make his calling and Election sure." Upon this last point I would refer my readers to Faber on the doctrine of Election.

I think that the Church is not Calvinist, much less is it Arminian:—upon Grace and Original Sin, Her doctrine is that of St. Augustine; upon the decrees of God and the nature of Election, that of the Greek church; and upon the whole subject, her desire is due reverence and freedom from the bondage of systematizing dogmatists.

How much better than Calvinistic or Arminian controversialism it is to say, with Hooker and Beveridge, that "His Decrees are secret and infinite, and therefore by no exercise of mental power in us to be ascertained or expounded—and that they are according to the unchangeable laws of his being, mercy, goodness, truth, and therefore only by living faith to be contemplated and believed in!"—How much better to impute no evil to God, no good to ourselves, but to bow before him in silent adoration and acquiescence in his Will!

The reader, then, may consider that we purpose not to take either the one side or the other of these thorny questions. The above resolution of Hooker's is all we shall give upon the point—a resolution which excludes the one side as well as the other. Calvinistic and Arminian controversies we meddle not with, as, upon the grounds taken, being profitless and idle. The practical truths of God's Power and of Man's Freedom* we shall not be slow to argue and expound in a practical way; but these other thorny verbal argumentations we shall, we hope, ever eschew.

But although a subject may have been abused, still this is no argument against its rational discussion. Although Calvinists or their opponents have talked nonsense about the Human Will, that is no reason why the subject should be neglected—no reason why it cannot be treated rationally. And, indeed, that persons have falsely and foolishly discussed any subject, especially if it be of the importance of this one, is a very strong reason why it should be set in a true and sober light before men. This subject, therefore, of the Will of man, we shall take the liberty of rescuing from the position it hitherto has had as a part of Theology, and vindicating unto it its own proper place in Philosophy—an element, and a most important one, in the Philosophy of Human Nature, which is Ethics. We shall, therefore, as I have said, omit all consideration of the *will of God* and *his decrees*, as belonging to Theology, contenting ourselves with the resolution of Hooker that we have given upon this point, and hoping that it will content our readers. But, in the ensuing chapter, we shall

* A very important distinction must be noted here. The Will is the faculty of freedom, whose function it is to act freely—in that sense the *will is free*. The question of fact, "How far it is actually capable of acting, in the race or in any individual," is a different one. The eye is the organ of sight—and yet I may be blind. But of this more further on.

examine the Will of man, as a faculty of his being, and a most important one,—in fact, one of the highest of his moral nature. This shall be the subject of our next chapter.

CHAPTER II.

Definitions of the Will: Three given.—Objections answered.—Logical and Real Examination of the sophism, "The Will is determined by Motives, and therefore is not free."—Motives are of two kinds: Spiritual and Temporal.—The first frees the Will; the last-mentioned enslaves it.—Two Powers that combine in every Human Action: the Will of the Man, and the Effect of Circumstance.—From this fact, a new ground taken upon the subject of the Will.

Our readers will remember that in the last chapter we announced our intention, as far as possible, to keep clear of the Theological questions upon the Will of God, and confine ourselves to the examination of the Human Will as a faculty of man's nature. In conformity with this intention, we ask, What is the Will? "It is the internal power of self-guidance in reference to action." This is one definition.—Another, and a very good one, is that of the Greek church universally—that "the Will is the faculty of Autexousia, or Self-Power."—A third is, that "the Will is the faculty of voluntary choice in man."

One may say, "If these definitions be true, there is no further need of dispute, for they all take for granted and imply the Freedom of the Will." "And so," we say, "they do." The question is not to be decided verbally, at all, but actually—by the experience of Human Nature. And we say to each of our readers to decide it so. Let a man read the definitions of the Will, and see whether there be in him—in his nature, that is—a power answering to them. If he finds in himself existing "an internal power of self-guidance in reference to action"—"a faculty of self-power"—or "a faculty of voluntary choice, whereby he can choose to do or not to do,"—if he experience this in his own nature;—and if this be the universal experience of man in general,—all logic and all systems to the contrary notwithstanding, the definitions above given are true.

Let us see what these imply. First, that the power is internal, proceeding from the inward nature of the man—therein originating, in the inward faculty, and not from external circumstances: in other words, a part and faculty of the Spiritual Nature of the man.

Secondly, "self-guiding"—the power, that is, of guiding the "Self"—the person—the man. This implies three things: first, the possibility of choice between one act and another; secondly, the power of determining, or making permanent in the Will, that choice; and thirdly, the ability, *more or less*, to carry out into action that choice and that determination.

If a man tell us that he has felt no internal power of choice, of decision, of action,—we say, "Very well; it is possible in extraordinary cases of malformation of mind,"—and we do not intermeddle with him, any more than, in writing a treatise upon light and colours, we should with a man born blind. But the mass of men, in all ages, have, in language and in fact, acknowledged a power internal, that is not Conscience or Affection or Reason, to which these qualities belong, and which they have called the Will. All, therefore, we can do, is *to describe it*—to ask our readers to look within, and if they see it there, as they shall do, to go on with us to examine it practically, and practically to apply the doctrine to their own moral culture. The full proof of the facts of this science, as we have before said, is the self-knowledge of the reader; and the writer who truly describes the facts of nature so that his readers can recognise and confess their truth, and who then applies them to practical purposes,—he is right, and not the best arguer and debater. It is too late in the day to fill books with such babillations as have been perpetrated in reference to this subject of the Will. If a man have felt no such internal power, we pity him: if, more than this, he prove, or try to prove that no one else has, we leave him to the enjoyment of his ingenuity—and say no more about it.

Of like character are such other asseverations as this: "I acknowledge a Will to exist, but the Will is not free." That is, the man acknowledges a Will that is not a Will—for the very notion of Will implies freedom, in faculty, at least, and function.

The very idea of a Will, the very meaning of the word, is, that it is the faculty whose function is freedom.

"He doubts whether the idea of a Will implies freedom; nay, he proves the *Will not free*, but Slave."

And this is his argument: "The Will is determined by motives"—"it does not then determine itself, but is determined"—"therefore it is not free."

This is the famous argument for Slave-Will, a mere verbal catch, and nothing more. However, in order that our readers may see it to be so, we shall put it in the shape of a regular syllogism:—

Major premise: "The Will is determined by motives."

Minor premise: Whatever is determined, does not determine itself.

Conclusion: Therefore—The Will does not determine itself.

As the logicians say, "Nego minorem," I deny the minor premise to be true. What proof is there that whatever is determined does not determine itself?

Another syllogism:—

Major: "That which is determined is passive."

Minor: "That which is passive does not determine itself."

Conclusion: Therefore—That which is determined, does not determine itself.

A syllogism false through a double Middle Term. That which is passive is the *verb* "is determined," in the first premise; and in the second it is real, a thing;—the middle term in the major is *verbal*—in the minor, *real:* the conclusion, then, is inconsequent—it does not follow. So it seems this great argument is merely verbal; a sophism, which proves the Will, the faculty of our being, to be *passive*, because a verb in a sentence put together by the writer is a *passive verb!* The same may be seen by multitudes of other arguments constructed upon the same model: *e. g.* from the premise, "John is loved," you can prove "that he does not love himself;" from the sentence, "This man is slain," that "he has not slain himself;" and so on, through as many false argumentations upon the false model as are required.

In reality, that "the Will is determined by motive," does not exclude it from being "self-determined:" being so, it still comes under the assertion, "it is determined."

All Motives are divided into two classes: the External and

the Internal. All that come from the outward, physical world, and work upon us through our senses, are External. Those that come from our internal and Spiritual nature—from the Conscience, the Spiritual Reason, the Affections,—these are Internal. The first enslave the man; they bind his Will in an obedience to the things of Time and Sense; they make outward, material and corporeal objects to have the dominion over him. His Will, determined by this class of motives, then, is *so far* enslaved, not free. Again: Internal motives—those that come from our Spiritual nature and from the Spiritual world—these are internal; they do not enslave the Will;—they free it. He, for instance, that is determined by his Conscience to go in the right path, against the temptation to go in the wrong,—he feels that, in the one case, *determined by one motive,* he is free; in the other, determined by it, he would be a slave. So in matters of Reason: walking by the rule and law of Moral Principle, determined by it as a motive, he is free; led against it by any motive, he is a slave. And so with respect to the Affections: to be led by them is to be free; to be led by Sensuality, or Self-will, or Selfishness, is to be enslaved.* This is the truth upon the subject of Determination of the Will by Motive. One class of motives enslaves the Will; the other frees it. How accordant it is, both in nature and in philosophy, to the truth of our Saviour's words, "If the Son make you free, ye shall be free indeed,"† every one can see; as also how distinctly it agrees with the nature of Motive and of the Will.

What, then, is the use of entangling verbally the mind of uneducated men in such sophisms as that which I have above examined, and of really supposing all Motives to be external, and the Will not to be a faculty, but a mere machine for motives,—a water-wheel, whereupon these are poured from without, and which thereby goes?

But, although men may not be able to answer these sophisms or logicians enough to put their finger on the unsound part of the argument, they *always act* and *always have acted* as beings that have in their nature a faculty whose function is Freedom. Nay,

* The Sensual and the Dark rebel in vain,
Slaves by their own compulsion.
Coleridge.

† John viii. 26.

the very upholders of these arguments—even they act as if their own reasoning were false. No Necessitarian ever yet acted consistently with his scheme. Their actions show that the scheme is verbal merely, and not real. We shall, therefore, pass by and neglect as frivolous such argumentations, and go on according to our own consciousness of Human Nature, and our knowledge or penetration into that of the race, describing the moral powers, and leaving the proofs to our reader's knowledge of himself; and then urging moral action and moral culture upon these truths, instead of fruitless speculation and dry verbal paradox.

We ask, then, any individual,—we suppose the one who now has this page open before him,—to consider this illustration we are about to give.

My reader, then, has arrived at a certain point and period of life, that he calls NOW, in reference to Time and events past, and HERE, in reference to place. In reference to Time, a certain definite series of events has happened, through which he has passed; and his present point in the series he calls "NOW," or the "present time." In reference to Space, his course, from beginning to end, might be traced exactly upon the globe; and the present point he calls HERE. The result, then, of his course in Space and in Time, is that "NOW the man is HERE." What, then, has produced this result? What forces have brought him so far that NOW he is HERE?

Let him consider, and he shall find that his course hitherto is naturally and aptly described as a voyage—the man, as a vessel that started upon the voyage of life, and has got so far. What, then, has brought the vessel so far on its course? Two forces only—the internal power that is within the vessel—the external force without: the combination, or rather the resultant* of these two, is that which brings all vessels thus far. So it is with the man: two forces he shall recognise to have brought him so far as he has come on his voyage—the force of *external circumstances* and the force of *internal power*. And never has there been a life in the course of which up to any given point the two forces do not unite. External circumstances, in their result, are modified by

* The "Resultant," in Statics, is that force which "results," in direction and amount, from the combined action of two others upon the same body at the same time.

the internal power: and it is modified by external circumstances. The course of the vessel is shaped by the two powers combined.

Now, by looking at the matter in this way, the individual shall see that, in each act of life, these two powers—the internal and the external—both exist: the Will is never so weak in any man that it does not modify the effect of the external influences; nor is it, again, so strong in any, that by its force, exclusively and entirely, the man's course is guided. The external force and the inward power exist together in bringing to an issue all actions. The sternest and strongest Human Will never was so potent as to annihilate the influence of circumstances, so that this last force should become nothing: and the most crushing force of circumstances never did nor could reduce to nothing the effect on action of the internal power; but both, in degrees that vary much in relative power, exist in each act of man's life.

As a practical matter of the consciousness of all men, they know and feel the internal force to exist: the external force also to show itself in each action, in all actions; and that neither in the course of the whole life, nor yet in any one single action, does this twofoldness cease to exist, or one of the forces become all and the other become nothing.

Now, before we go further, it is worth while to see how paradox upon this matter arises. The Fatalist supposes Circumstance to bind man in with an irresistible chain, so that all actions are predoomed by an eternal fate. Is not this to exaggerate the one force, to suppose it irresistible, and to suppose the other to come to nothing,—a mere theory that each one's own experience can assure him to be false? For each one in each circumstance feels the two powers, and knows that the one, as well as the other, ever exists. Because things are to be touched, have I no sense of touch? Because things visible are to be seen, have I no sight? Because there is a power without me, which can and does act upon me in a degree which I cannot measure, have I no power within?

And, on the other hand, there are some men who eke out an Atheistic philosophy by an argument for what they call "Free-will," but which, in all senses and meanings of the word, is not "Free-will," but "Self-omnipotence." They first take it for granted that mere physical laws embrace all action; and then that by his internal power man can modify, as he likes, all these laws.

And so man is wholly and entirely free, no external power upon him, his inward power is lord of all. That is, that internally he has *an intelligent power* which meets nothing from without but *unintelligent physical laws*, and so is entirely without control.

So might the dove, that by chance had fallen into the grosser element of water, and found it to obstruct its flight upon rising into the thinner fluid of air, imagine that all resistance was gone; or that the more it was diminished the more progress it would make.* Whereas, for all external resistance to vanish entirely, would be for all its inner power to be rendered wholly unable. Just so it is with these men, they imagine away the outward Intelligent Power that bears upon man through what we call "circumstance," and think in this of freedom! If this dream were realized, their "Will," would be as the doves' wings, idly fluttering in vacuum, unable and useless.

And their dream of an internal Will, with no external Will modifying it, this is just as vain a paradox as that of the Fatalists; just as vain, for the same consciousness that tells me and all men of an inward power, the Will, that can modify all external circumstances, that same knowledge of myself and of the world shall tell me of an external power working through what I call circumstances that shall modify the result of my action.

The so-called arguments or verbal riddles, that deny, the one the internal power, the other the external power,—occupy, in some books a great space, with us they shall take up none. The evidence that I have for the internal power, the Will, that same evidence, I have in my own experience, and in that of all men, for the external power that acts upon me through the "Circumstance."

And my course of life, both in itself as a whole, and in each act of it singly, is a resultant of these two powers, varied in force, it may be, but still existent each of them in each event, and in the whole result, or entire sum total of my life. I think the experience of each considerate man, apart from prejudice or system, will show him that this is true; and that it is not only in

* This illustration is taken from a well-known, but not well-understood German writer. I use it because as an illustration it suits my purpose admirably. And I mention it lest some censorious person should bring a charge of plagiarism.

accordance with his own experience, but with the nature of power and of action.

And so the two powers being established, the matter of discussion is changed from the old ground—which was, whether the Will was *self-omnipotent* entirely, or entirely a *slave to circumstances*—to a new ground, which, instead of denying one force or the other to exist, and arguing for the irresistibility of that which it supposes, admits both to exist, and then *discusses their relative powers and effect.* This new ground having taken, and thus fairly opened the subject, we shall leave our readers to meditate upon it, and go on to another chapter, wherein we shall discuss the meaning and purport of this that we call "circumstance."

CHAPTER III.

The meaning of "Circumstance."—It does not imply Doom or Physical Necessity, but an ever-present God acting upon us, according to the Laws of his nature and the laws established for us by Him, and therefore good -The question of Freedom different from that of Power.

In the last chapter, we have shown that in each and every human action, two forces conspire—the internal power and the external "circumstance." It is manifestly necessary to discuss the meaning of this thing "circumstance."

Now the origin of the word, I believe, is not classical, but of the Lower Ages, and it implies "things standing around" us, not simply "*things*" that exist, but things that *are around and act upon us.*

And I conceive that the word, whosoever invented it, is a good and an useful one, for, from birth to death, we find that the "I," the being to which we apply "Personality," is ever brought in contact with external forces that act upon it, modifying circumstances itself, and being modified by them. And howsoever men may exaggerate the one force or the other, this is true,—in our being, the internal force exists, nay, is at the centre of the sphere; and the external force of "circumstances,"—"circum stat," "stands around," is everywhere in contact with us. So much for the meaning of the word.

For the meaning of the thing, how are we to interpret it? Circumstances are manifold, various, innumerable. Are we to take it, that by chance and accident they roll upon us, as the sea-weed and marine rubbish from the storm rolls upon the rock, and along with the fortuitous sand surrounds it? Are circumstances the product of chance?

Certainly not. The same marks of design, of purpose, of will, which we discern in the acts that spring from ourselves, and which manifest them to be those of a *person*—those same evidences we see in the circumstances that operate upon us.

If our own acts are those of a Person, the influences that act upon us show "Will" and "Personality" as much. In fact, by the unanimous agreement and sense of all men, by all the indications that we have from the thing itself, external Circumstance *is taken to manifest an external personal* agent. The internal power by which we act upon outward things,—this is so far analogous to that external power, that we feel personality as ours is, to be its natural explanation.

And corresponding unto this interpretation is the Revelation primevally given, and thence passing downward through the channel of the knowledge of all nations, of a Being that wields that external power that we find to bear upon us; against whom we can raise no ramparts or circling fortress strong enough to keep Him out: for, from the Heavens above, He shall rush down upon us; from the earth beneath, He shall rise up against us: nay, the very armour with which we gird and enclose ourselves against that Power, becomes means and ways of access against us to that Power.

Yes,—let man as he will cut himself away from Christianity, and from Revelation, and still, in the sphere of Circumstance by which he is enclosed and environed, he has evidence of another power than his own, that works upon and modifies his action. And even he who in fact has left God, he shall be forced to say,

"Who can feel and dare to say, I believe him not?
The All-Embracing, the All-Sustaining,
Does he not embrace and sustain us himself?
Does not the heaven arch itself above, and earth lie firm below?"

Even such a man as the writer* of this, from the bare consideration of the relation of an external power to the internal force, had to confess an "All-embracer," an "All-sustainer."

But to the Christian, and, in fact, to all men, save those that have of set design placed themselves apart from knowledge, this fact and feeling receives its true interpretation, in the belief of a Personal, Omnipotent, Omnipresent, Omniscient God, surrounding each man, embracing each man within the sphere of Circumstance.

Such, of the two facts of the internal force and of "Circumstance," is the interpretation given by the primeval revelation, and henceforth, in the Tradition of the Nations, taught by one generation perpetually to another.

But, more than this, the World, as I have shown, is a school of probation, and teaches us this eternally, by the one great idea of Law perpetually suggested—the Law of the Affections, that is, of Love in the Family; of Justice and Equity in the Nation; of Holiness in the Church: and so are "Circumstances" arranged under these three natural organizations, that not as a God of Power only He appears, but a Being of Love, of Justice, of Holiness; for all these moral qualities we, by the fact that the world is a "School of Probation," must attribute to the Almighty, in addition to that of Personality. God is Good, both in name and in reality; and each idea of Him that Society or Nature awakens in our Reason,—each manifestation of his glory that He makes unto man,—at the same time enables us to see in Him a higher degree of goodness, to feel it, and to reach after it. The interpretation, then, that we give to the action of Circumstance upon us, is this:—

First, that "God is not absent,"—that he has not made the world to go by the machinery of an all-embracing Fate, or of an universal physical law or system of laws embracing all possible contingencies, and then has departed, having by his own machinery filled up the world he had made so that he no longer works personally therein, or is therein present, save by the Decree or by the Law. But, on the contrary, that he is *here, present, acting*, and *that all power comes from him.*† This is the

* Goethe.

† The reader will remember that it is with regard to the *physical system* of the universe that I speak here, and not in reference to the acts of intelli-

doctrine of the Scriptures as to God and his acting, plainly and manifestly laid down.

And he that shall take it and the objections against it, and then take the mechanical theory,—whether the fatalistic one of Doom, or the other of a machinery of Physical Laws,—and the objections against them,—he shall find more objections against the Unchristian* than the Christian doctrine.

The objections which may be brought against the Christian doctrine of an ever-present God, are such as this: "I see the phenomena to be regular, and therefore I argue that they are effected *by a law*, and not by the direct action of a personal being."

To this the answer is easy: Such arguments will exclude a *finite personal being*, not an *Infinite*. The action of an Infinite Being is and must be regular, according to the laws of Infinite Perfection. Man's action is and must be irregular; but the action of God upon the physical world is, and must be by his nature, regular, according to the law of his perfection. To see, then, the world so regular that we can express *some* sequences of its events in regular geometrical formulas, which we call "Laws," this shows the presence of an "Infinite Cause," whose acts are regular. And to be incapable of expressing *all*, but day by day to be attaining new perceptions of regularity, this expresses the same idea of *one cause* working in manifold ways. The sense of regularity excludes a *finite personal agent*, but not an Infinite one.

Again, it will be said, "When a personal being acts, we see Will, but not here."

Will, we answer, in all finite beings, is more or less Self-will, more or less capricious, unsteady, faulty; but the more perfect it is, the more it approaches to a Law. And God's Will is and must be a Law, not capricious, not Self-willed as is man's Will, but uniform. Hence, the actions of God's Will are not

gent beings. All personal agents have the capability of exerting self-derived power by their own being. The evil, then, that they do, they do themselves: God does not do it. Spiritual beings, of their own nature and constitution, as formed by the Almighty, have the capability of originating power, separate and apart from material and physical causation.

* I say "Unchristian," because Fatalism, in its perfection, has been held only in Mohammedan or in pagan countries.

arbitrary decrees, but *uniform laws*. That no "Self-will," or "arbitrariness," or capriciousness, is seen, this is so far from arguing against an Infinite Agent, that it argues for it. He whose eternal decrees are determined by the eternal laws of his nature,—justice, holiness, and truth,—his Will must act regularly, and without variableness, caprice, or shadow of turning.

But in reference to all theories that suppose a machinery of Doom or of Physical Law, the grand reply is, that this supposes *mere power*, but that our own constant feeling is not of *mere power*, but of gentleness, kindness, mercy, benevolence, wisdom, forethought,—in short, not of Power only, but of all and every one of the *moral powers; to beings possessed of which alone we attribute personality*. In each "circumstance" that is brought to bear upon the life of man, we see *moral influence* in manifold ways, not *power only*, and therefore we naturally conclude the presence of an Infinite Moral Being—that is, God.

This, then, is our estimate of "Circumstance:"—In reference to its agent, it is the external force of the Will of an Infinite Moral Being, Personal and Ever-Present, applied unto Man. And this not according to arbitrary decrees, or the caprice of self-will, having no other motive but its own consciousness of power, but according to the eternal laws of a Being infinitely good, just, gracious, holy, merciful—a Father, a moral Governor, a God to be worshipped,—and not merely a being conceived as possessing only the one attribute of Infinite Power and Will omnipotent and unchecked.

This, then, is the interpretation:—That not the machinery of an Infinite Doom, or of an all-embracing physical law, but an ever-present God, Father, and Moral Governor, with a Will so determined, creates all Circumstances surrounding me, and by them exerts, in all things, upon each action of mine, an influence whose extent I cannot comprehend nor measure; which yet I know is not an influence contradictory to his nature, and, although I see not its end or extent, still must consider it to be good and to tend to good.

And while with regard to the material world I may form systems, and say that events are bound together by Physical Laws, but with regard to my own voluntary action I must suppose it above Physical Law, and to be expressed by no formula; so with regard to the Circumstances that bear upon me, no formula will express them, no physical law embrace them: they show the personal action of a moral agent who is ever present, acting voluntarily upon me. Such is the moral interpretation of "Circumstance," an interpretation which men put naturally and easily, which agrees with the express words of Scripture, and only by a false philosophy can be put aside from the persuasion of any human being.

If this explanation be true, then it may be said, "Man is not free,—for of the two forces that determine any act, and from which it results, one is the finite Will of man,—the other, the infinite Will of God;—the Finite must ever be overpowered by the Infinite."

In answer to this, we say that *the force put forth by a being of Infinite Power is not necessarily infinite.* God has infinite power, but in his dealings with man, of his own will *he modifies his power.* When my finite will comes in contact with an obstacle and overcomes it, such an amount of hindrance has been put in my way as I can overcome; and I can easily conceive, that for wise purposes the infinite God might have put only such an amount,—and yet it certainly is not the less an exertion of His power.

Again, he may put such an amount as will be insuperable; according then to *His measure*, which is *His wisdom*, He may direct his influences upon us, so that in various ways our actions shall be modified. But in each circumstance the influence of the finite Will is seen, and the influence of the Infinite.

This then is the result:—Central amid a sphere of Circumstances, man feels that external things and actions he can modify by an internal power. He feels, too, that they can and do modify his action. These two forces he is conscious of in each action of life, and the sum total of life is made up of the results of these two. He, therefore, by his constitution feels these both to exist; he feels that one does not annihilate the other, but that both coexist, the Free-will of Man, the Power of God.

This he knows by his own knowledge, and his own feeling of his actions both singly and in the mass, and it is in vain to argue the non-existence of the one or the other. Such arguments to all men are mere verbal knots that touch not the reality of things. The question is a simple one: "Do I, by action springing from an internal, self-guiding power, modify external circumstance?" If a man knows this to be so, according to his own experience, then argument against it is mere babbling, mere talk. For the thing must be decided by man's consciousness of the fact, and not by metaphysics. If a man be conscious that it is so, and the race generally have the same consciousness, millions of treatises are unavailing against the fact of such self-knowledge.

The question of the existence of Free-will is sometimes confused with another, as to the extent of its results. "Have I the power, according to internal choice, to modify external circumstances *more or less?*"—this is the question of Free-will. "What is the extent of that modification?" is a different question. "Can I do what I will, uncontrolled by any outward power?" This does not ask "Am I free?" but "Am I omnipotent?"

The question as to the extent of the power of a Free agent is quite a different one from the question of his Freedom. God may grant me such a power of Will, that all external circumstances that come in contact with me shall be ruled, swayed, and governed by it. He may grant me no such power of Will, and yet make the outward Circumstances to yield to my weakness. And so in manifold ways may modify, guide, govern, direct, teach, rule; but all this action is *according to the laws of his infinite being.* And if evil is brought about, it is not of *God's action* upon man, but *by his permission* that it exists.

The rules of his action are the laws of his eternal being. Thus "God cannot lie," the Scripture tells us: this we shall take for a law of his being,—no power of God, then, can make man lie. "God cannot sin;"—God's Almighty power, then, cannot pre-doom man to sin, and so forth.

And again, God is of himself infinitely free; he has made man free; it is a part of his constitution established by God; God, then, cannot make man un-free, save by annihilating the constitution he has made. In like manner, he cannot make two bodies at once to occupy the same space, because it is a fact of the constitution of body, that it cannot be so. So it is a part of the constitution of man that he shall be free, that of each action, *one force* should be the power of man's Will, and the other a *portion of external power*, brought to operate upon him by the Will of God, for his most holy and most secret purposes.

This, then, I conceive to be the interpretation of "Circumstance;" that it shows neither Chance, nor yet Fate, but a

Personal and Ever-present Being, Almighty, All-just, and All-holy, directing, according to his wisdom, a *portion* of his *power* upon us.

And from that external power and our internal power, both existing in each act, all our acts do come.

And the relative proportions of these two forces we know not, only that they both exist, and that the power of God works upon us, not according to caprice, but according to the Laws of His Being, and according to the Constitution wherewith he has framed us.

These are practical decisions, which the experience and knowledge of our race has a thousand times affirmed, and which only false philosophy as to the nature of God, the being of this world, and the constitution of man could deny.

We have placed them here because, so placed, they will enable us, in their light, more fully to examine the internal power which thus acts along with the external power of God. We shall go on, then, in the next chapter, to examine the nature of the internal power which we call the Will, as to the modes of its action, which we before have enumerated.

CHAPTER IV.

The Will has a Power of Resistance to Motive.—Motives upon the Will do not act necessarily.—The evil Results of Fatalism.—Analogy to the Will and its Motives of the Concurrence of Forces, Mechanical, Chemical, and Vital.—Brute Animals are really and truly what the Fatalist thinks Man to be.—Man has a Will: Brutes have properly no Will.—The question of Free-will is a practical one.—As a matter of fact, there are Men whose Will is not free.—The Two Wills: The "Will of the Flesh," and the Spiritual Will.—Society trains the Will.—The Spiritual Law sets the Will *de facto* free.—Examples from Conscience, the Reason, the Heart.

HAVING thus examined the nature of Circumstance, and shown that herein the power of man meets with and is united with the power of God, we go forward to examine the nature of the Will in itself.

The Will is "inward and spiritual:" this is the first part of our definition. By this we mean that the faculty, as far as it is a faculty of our nature, is one that belongs to man as a Spiritual being.

The answer is not hard to this question:—"Admit that your Will is capable of being influenced by external motives—has it yet such a power that all these, by its own internal force, it can reject, and go contrary to the course they indicate?" If this be so, it is internal, and, at the same time, Spiritual.

Is there an inward power by which, giving riches their full value, and on certain occasions pursuing them,—upon certain other occasions I shall permit the desire of them to have no power over my actions? Is there an inward force by which, desiring food, I shall, at certain times and upon certain occasions,—abstain from it? desiring pleasure,—I shall resist it? being tempted to evil,—I shall oppose the temptation? being excited unto anger,—I shall yet quell it? Certainly: every child feels within himself this *power of resistance.* He may not feel it to a perfect degree; but a power he does feel whose faculty this is, and which may be brought to greater perfection by exercise. It is a testimony of all men, that there exists in all *this internal power of resistance to external inducements to action.*

We shall put the question again, in this way:—"Cause and Effect," we shall say, "in Physical Science, is a law absolute and certain. In consequence of this, it is in Physics a true axiom, 'Like causes produce like effects,' and therefore, *without exception*, when you find the *identity of cause*, from it invariably follows the *identity of effect* in physical science." This we believe to be invariably true. Now, "Motive" we shall define to be an "external cause of action." Is the law of "cause and effect" true in reference to human actions? If it be, the same amount of external cause shall always produce the same effect—the *Will shall always be determined by motives*, and shall not be free in any way.

But each man's reason can tell him that it is not so—that although Motives to action are upon the will as "causes" in Physical Philosophy, still there is an internal power of resistance, by which the "effect" of motives is limited in a very exceeding degree, so that no amount of "motive" shall *compel* or *force* or *determine*, *physically*, the Will of any, if it freely from within resist.

And so the law of "cause and effect," however well it may do in Physics, has no power in Ethics. No external motives compel or necessarily determine the "Will of man." Apart from religion, we shall say, even the weakest and the most vicious knows that his acts are uncompelled—that the external temptation may have been *very strong*, but yet *never so strong* as *to necessitate* his action upon it.

So would it seem that man has an inward force, which, even while he is in the world, sets him free, by a faculty dwelling in him, from the general laws of Physics, and puts his action upon a loftier ground,—an inward power of resistance to the causation of outward motives. This is a fact of our knowledge; we see it with regard to ourselves, and we see it in our intercourse with our fellow men. And they who deny it, either do so out of vicious motives, that they may be enabled to cast the blame of their vices upon external circumstances, as the woman and the man, our first parents, in paradise, did, or else they do so under a false notion that by applying the doctrine of "Cause and Effect" to the Spiritual part of man, in the shape of "motive" and "determination," they thereby do honour to God's power, by making man's acts, *all* of them, to be determined and doomed of God. A false philosophy this, and one that would be immoral, but for the fact that the very men that preach it do not act upon it, but in their every act of life proclaim that they believe it untrue.

And yet, as Mohammed and Gengis and Bonaparte bear witness, not without its danger is this dogma. For never in the course of history has military and religious frenzy been united, that it has not for its fulcrum had this doctrine, that human action is predoomed by an irresistible chain of external motive. This is that force that urged the swarthy Saracen over half the world, until the larger frames and sterner souls of the Frankish war-king and his Germans flung back from France and Europe the tide of Mohammedan invasion, and the light limbs and slender sabre of the Arab were crushed by the iron mace of Charles Martel.* This that doctrine that drove the count-

* Charles the Hammerman, so called from his weapon and his exploits in the great battle at Poitiers, against the host of the Arab general Abderrhame. But for this victory, Europe, historians say, had been Mohammedan. But men are made for their times; and if a Mohammed is sent to wreak God's vengeance against a corrupt church and a degenerate nation, again a Charles Martel is raised up to turn back the scourge.

less hordes of Tartar horsemen over the world, and made China and Russia, Persia and the shores of the Baltic Sea, and the wild regions of Siberia, alike to groan and tremble at the barbarous names of Baatou and Houlagou, the vicegerents of the "Universal Sovereign," "Lord Predestined of the Universe!"* This also the doctrine that urged incessantly for two centuries the military fanaticism of Turkey against European civilization.

And this the doctrine of each vain man who, living like an animal, has not cultivated his moral or spiritual powers, but has permitted his Conscience to cry in vain, has lived without the control of Reason, has given up his heart inwardly to Selfishness, Sensuality, and Self-will, merely keeping up decent appearance, and complying with the outward requirements of society. And such a man, with his moral faculty wholly uncultivated—the fortress it was given to protect wholly unguarded—this man, having neglected all inward moral preparation, yields to outward temptation, and then cries out, "It was too strong for my Will, and determined it!" and "I was predoomed!" or "Overpowered by the influence of circumstances!"

I do not say that they who hold this doctrine are always vicious; for, as I have said before, nature often corrects the effect of doctrine that is untrue to it, and truly pious men have held it. But this I do say, that history represents it as an element that gives an immense strength to military fanaticism; and the experience of life and nature tell me, that whatsoever may be its effects upon the good, when *believed in by the weak or the bad*, or *taught to them*, it is a ready excuse for all vice, a ready means of shifting blame from themselves, and justifying a continuance in sin. And this the author has seen, both in case of the Fatalism of Absolute Predestination, and the Fatalism that supposes our affections and moral state to be the consequence of mere physical organization.†

* "The nation held a convention on the banks of the Sellinga. A Khodsha, or Sage, revered for his age and virtues, rose up in the assembly, and said, Brethren, I have seen a vision. *The Great God of Heaven, on his flaming throne*, surrounded by the spirits on high, *sat in judgment on the nations of the earth: sentence was pronounced*, and *he gave the dominion of the world* to our chief, Temudsin, *whom he appointed Gengis Khan, or Universal Sovereign.*"—Universal History, by John von Müller.

† The author here alludes to the principles that ensue from the doctrines of Combe on the Constitution of Man.

The author then will be asked, does he suppose this internal power of resistance in the Will to external motive to be, in its immediate action, entirely free from the law of "cause and effect," so that if the man will, he can resist the highest and weightiest motives that can be brought to bear upon him, or admit the very feeblest and weakest.

I consider that it is so; that so far the Will of man, when under its law, is independent of the law of Causation. And this as a part of the constitution of man, in virtue of his being a spiritual being, made in the image of God. I consider that of the Almighty, all His acts are from within, *none caused from without*, so that He is purely, perfectly, absolutely free. And so he has made man that he has the inward *power* of Will, capable, under its law,* of resisting all external motive, how weighty so ever it be; that he has this power as a spiritual being, endued with the faculty by God.

Men may say this is speculation,—"man is body, and under the laws of body."

And we say, "No more than it is speculation to say Man has eyes." The fact every one knows and acknowledges to himself and to others a hundred times every day of his life. We admit, then, that man is body,—and we say more, we say man is matter, and subject to the law of matter; man is living or animal body, and subject to its law; and man is spirit, and subject to its law; *the laws coexist, and the higher outrules the lower.* The man is matter,—the mechanical forces then act upon each particle of his frame; the chemical forces, too, act upon him as matter, and their result would be decay; but he is also an animal body, and the *vital forces* neutralize the chemical and mechanical forces, and cause their effects not to ensue. And so say we: the mere physical motives would have overcome man, if he were only an animal; but since he is a spiritual being as well, he has the power of resistance by an inward Will that is not animal, but spiritual. The truth of this to nature and to our constitution may be seen from the above analogy.

And this leads us to the remark that the brute animals do really and entirely fulfil the notion of beings led altogether by circumstance; for in them we see that external motives, appealing

* See the next chapter.

to animal desires, invariably bring about the same result, act as *cause and effect* in determining action,—sufficient cause producing the proportionate action invariably. Nor is there, in the brute, any power of internal resistance, that cannot be overcome by an additional force of external motive. Instincts *are* irresistible in the animal nature, and appetites in their nature addressed by external motives in sufficient degree, *can become* irresistible; such motives are incapable of being resisted; in fact, there is no internal power to resist them.

The man of the Fatalist is no real man, made in the image of God with a Spiritual Nature, and having thence free-will as a faculty; only in those vertebrated mammalia that are the likest in physical organization unto man, the pongo or the ourang-outang, is it realized.

It may, perhaps, add a good deal of clearness to these illustrations, if we ask, since the animals act, and have therefore some guidance unto their action, what is there in them that corresponds to the "Will"? We answer, that the *immediate desire, which is the strongest* towards any thing external, *that is to them* for a "Will." The Desires, as it were, reign by turns in them, and, answering to the variety of external motive, each Desire, in its turn, is in some measure a sort of Will. The external allurement addresses the animal appetite, so as to arouse it into action, and this rushes onward toward the outward object, with a force that leads the whole animal: thus, in them *animal desire* is produced by "external motive," under the law of cause and effect; the motive producing the emotion of the appetite, and that again the action of the animal according to that law. And we must say that, in most cases, it is not a single motive, but a complication of motives external, and that these tend generally to the preservation of the animal, and to its uses in the system of Nature, as of course we should expect from the creation of a Being infinitely wise.

But the general distinction that man has by his nature a "Will capable of resisting all motives from without, how weighty and forcible soever," and that the animals, on the contrary, are wholly and entirely governed by Desire, external circumstances acting upon their appetites, according to the law of cause and effect, this I count so generally true, that every one at once will see the distinction in Will between man and animals. Man *has* a Will *inward*, and *spiritual*, and *free;* animals an appetite, *wholly animal*, and *under the dominion of outward motive.* Animals properly *have no will.*

And this brings us to the examination of a most important question with regard to the action of man. We have shown that there is no action of man's life wherein will not come in man's power; and then that man is not a puppet or a machine, driven by irresistible power, and dreaming that he moves when he only *seems to move*, but that in all circumstances he *has power* coming *from himself:* we have shown, too, that he has an internal faculty whereby he *can* resist *all motives* coming from without, and accordingly admit or not admit their influence. And from this last train of argument and illustration that we have employed, our readers may see that this *power of free-will* is a *natural faculty* of his constitution, not *animal*, but *spiritual and internal.* And now comes the question of fact, "as to Free Action upon Free-will,—*how far* is man free?"

This I conceive to be a plain matter-of-fact question, as to each individual of our race,—a practical and scientific question also, which, in this last point of view, may be put in this way: "Seeing that I have the faculty, by my constitution, of freedom, how shall I train it so that the power in itself and in its action shall attain the highest degree of perfection? And, on the contrary, what is that course of action by which, if I pursue it, the faculty may be so injured as to lose its natural powers, and not to have its natural effects?" This to answer, I conceive, would be to examine the subject practically and scientifically, with a view to life. We shall proceed, then, to this examination.

Now, taking it for granted that man's power manifests itself, and is not wholly extinguished in any, and that each one has this faculty of resisting outward motive according to an inward power; as a matter of fact, are there men that *do not* exert this power, but are led as the animals, by external circumstances, and therefore are *not, in fact and in effect, free?*

We answer, and each one who has looked upon the world can answer, that *in fact* and *in effect* there are men *so led*, and *not free.* And secondly, that the men themselves, every man and all men that are under such bondage, know that it is not by an external irresistible power they have been so enslaved, nor by the want of an internal faculty of resistance, but because *of* *themselves that they have not used that faculty they had*, habitually,* and under the guidance and governance of the Conscience, the Reason, and the Affections.

And the situation of persons under such bondage, we shall see to be truly and really the situation of brute animals, roused to action, and stimulated by the animal appetite, and the outward circumstance that awakens and excites that appetite, so that the peculiar desire, whatsoever it be, takes the place of the Will in the man, and is to him *for a Will.*

This is the state of the man that is enslaved. We have seen gluttons, and drunkards, and licentious men, and liars, and misers, and vain men, and ambitious men; and while we saw the faculty or power in them of Free-will to exist, we saw that in effect they were "slaves," *as much perhaps* as if the faculty had no action and no existence. And we saw, moreover, that in each step of their progress towards this state, their own power and their own Will had been exerted *suicidally*, until both *power* and *Will, as against* the ruling appetite, ceased almost to have any being.

As a matter of fact, I have seen a drunkard, who, against all motives of religion, against all of reason and conscience, against all of happiness and self-interest, knowing that he was ruining and destroying his own life, and rendering miserable all those that he loved and was bounden to,—and against all this, the man indulged the one appetite, and would indulge it. Now, as a matter of fact, that man's Will *was in bondage*, he *was not free.* And as a matter of fact, there are thousands and tens of thousands that are so.

Is it not, then, just as well, while we admit that in all Man's acts, his own power comes in, and that he ever has the faculty of Free-will, to consider these cases that are before our eyes, and, instead of *arguing* that they are free, and closing our eyes *to the fact* that they *are not*, to examine how the faculty may become diseased and lose its strength and its power, and the man *become a slave.* Abstract proofs that "all men have the faculty and power of sight," avail not much to him whose eyes are diseased so that he cannot see; nor will the fullest demonstration of the laws of Optics be of much use to him: the practical

* See particularly the chapter upon Habit, and generally, the second, third, and fourth books of this treatise.

science of the surgeon is much better in such a case than the abstract theory of the philosopher.

We are treating of the "Will" *ethically*, with a view to practice, and not *metaphysically;* and we remark that, having established as a fact of the constitution and being of man, a faculty of freedom—and as a fact of man's position, that he is not actuated by an irresistible power not his own,—these two things being established, then,—as a *matter of fact* and of daily experience, men are *in action* oftentimes *as completely enslaved* as any of the animals *that have no will.*

We shall go on to examine this state of disease, the causes and the cure of it. And we shall ask our readers to go along with us and to realize our principles, and if they think them true, to employ them upon their own life, and upon the life of others dependent upon them. This, then, brings us onward towards another part of the examination that is very important, and is, in fact, a further step in our progress. The fact that there are *two wills** in man, if we may use the phrase : he is an animal, he is also a spiritual being; as an animal, he has the Animal Mind, which corresponds to external things and external motives, which, were he an animal only, would place him as all the animals that have no spiritual faculties are, *completely under the power of external circumstances;* that is, completely in bondage and in slavery. And this appetite perpetually exists in him, being an animal; external appeals to it perpetually arise; and the tendency of them is to have their full force to produce action in him necessarily, and therefore to *enslave him,* in one point of view *to circumstance,* and in another to his own *appetites.*

Now, this *animal will* that is in man, this perpetual tendency to follow Desire, and to be under the control of outward circumstance, this is called in Scripture the Will of the Flesh; and the man that considers it shall see that it is indeed a power in man which is the insubordinacy, the ingovernance of the lower part of his nature, which, were he without the spiritual faculty of the Will, in despite of Reason, and Conscience, and the Affections, would make him even as the other animals, but most wretched, inasmuch as then he would feel the Good and love it, and yet be enslaved to the Evil.

* We use the word not scientifically, but in ordinary language, and not strictly.

And then, if a man look at the true Will, he shall find that it, by the power we have specified, can resist these mere external motives, this is its faculty,—and thus free the man from the outward dominion of circumstance and motive, so that he shall not be governed by them.

Now, were man's nature perfect, "that is, free entirely from the deficiency and inability of the spiritual powers that is the consequence of Original Sin," his Will would be perfect also, and his nature *in entire subordination;* and then this that we call "the Will of the Flesh," would exist only as desire *completely controlled by the Will;* and the man, as far as internal desire and external temptation is concerned, would rule himself according to the measure of a Will perfectly free from disease and deficiency.

This, to use cases often cited, was the case with Adam and the case with Christ our Lord. Adam had the most perfect control of his Will over his animal part, yet he could sin; and this possibility of sinning shows the essay of outward circumstance upon him. And our Lord and Saviour, he too "was tempted in all points, like as we are," he had all parts of human nature as we have, the Animal part as well as the Spiritual, and we find that external circumstances acted as temptations upon Him. And yet the "Will" was perfect in him through the Godhead supporting the Humanity, so that he sinned not. So I suppose it must be with the perfect nature,—the Will is perfect in its functions, and consequently the Will of the flesh does not exist, save as desire *governed*, and *directed*, and *perfectly subordinate* to the superior spiritual power.

But has not man the faculty yet? Certainly he has. His own feeling shows him that he has, but the same feeling tells him also, that it is impaired in its *powers*, that it is injured in its *functions* and in its *effects*. This is the universal feeling of man, and his universal experience. And this also is the experience of each individual of us. Now, this of the Will, that it is impaired in its functions and in its effects,—this is the consequence of Original Sin.

Thus, through this faculty also of the Spiritual Nature is carried on the great problem of contradictions. "I can rule and govern myself, and I will do it," says one, feeling truly;—and the interpretation of it is this: "I have by nature a faculty whose function and effect is self-governance, and I fully wish and desire to employ that faculty." And then the other side *as truly* says, "I cannot rule and govern myself, nor am I able,"—a truth also, the interpretation of which is, that this natural and spiritual faculty of the Will is decayed and weakened in function and effect, so that only very imperfectly does it fulfil its uses. The two truths of nature that are contradictory, both being true in the solution given of *the existence* of the faculty as an endowment of our Spiritual Being, and of *its injury* by Original Sin.

If this be so, one would say, "Shall not life then be an internal struggle between the faculty whereby man is free, the Will, and that other inclination called the 'Will of the flesh,' or the animal desire?"

Certainly it shall be so. If man were a beast as the beasts are, without any Spiritual Nature, and therefore without the Will, and completely under the dominion of external things,—he would feel no misery because of this, being a brute: if he had the faculty of Will perfect in itself and in its action, then would he have under his dominion completely that external desire, and he would be happy. But now he *has the faculty*, weakened and unable; and therefore, sometimes overcoming, sometimes being overcome:—there is then by nature in him a *strife in his nature*, which is in his very being, and exists in its existence, and cannot be stopped or put an end to by any thing *save that which will restore the Will unto its whole power.*

That strife is in all men by nature;—all have felt it, and all must feel it, for it is in their being. Xenophon, before the coming of Christ, testifies to the existence of that strife. Seneca, too, a Heathen, in his fifty-second Epistle, testifies the same thing: "What is this, Lucilius, which, while we are going one way, drags us another, and impels us thither from whence we are struggling to recede? What is this that struggles with our soul, and never permits us to will any thing? We vacillate between two opinions: we will nothing freely, nothing perfectly, nothing always."

Again, the trite lines,

Video meliora proboque
Deteriora sequor,

bear witness to the same feeling and the same experience. And Lactantius, in his treatise upon true wisdom, has put into the mouth of a Heathen these words: "I wish, indeed, not to sin; but I am overcome, for I am clothed in weak and frail flesh. This it is which lusts, which grows angry, which grieves, which fears to die. And so I am led away *against my will*, and I sin, not because I wish to do so, but because I am compelled. I feel that I am sinning, but *my frailty*, which I cannot withstand, urges me on."

These testimonies to the actual existence of that internal strife, as a fact of man's nature, are sufficient; but, indeed, they might be multiplied a hundredfold; for that this exists in man by nature, as fallen and *apart from grace*, is the universal experience of all, both of Heathen, who, by their position, knew not the cause of it, and of Christians, who, by revelation, are acquainted with the fact of the Fall.

But perhaps the most vivid description that is given of man in respect to this internal strife of Will, is given by St. Paul, in his description of the *natural* man:

"For we know that the law is Spiritual: but I am carnal, sold under sin. For that which I do, I allow not: for what I would, that I do not; but what I hate, that do I. If then I do that which I would not, I consent unto the law that it is good. Now then it is no more I that do it, but sin that dwelleth in me. For I know that in me, (that is, in my flesh,) dwelleth no good thing: for to will is present with me; but how to perform that which is good I find not. For the good that I would, I do not: but the evil which I would not, that I do. Now if I do that I would not, it is no more I that do it, but sin that dwelleth in me. I find then a law, that, when I would do good, evil is present with me. For I delight in the law of God after the inward man: but I see another law in my members, warring against the law of my mind, and bringing me into captivity to the law of sin which is in my members."*

Here is the experience of all men's nature, of this inward strife, most vividly portrayed; a strife that has no end until, of set purpose and constantly, the man has *sought after the law of God's Grace*, and *found it*, and *given himself* up to be ruled by it, through the *set purpose of his will*—or until he, *with his eyes open*, *voluntarily*, and of *set purpose*, *has given himself* up to be

* Romans vii. 14–23.

ruled by this other law, *the will that is of the flesh*, and *its law, the law of sin and death.**

We can see then the deficiency of the Will, that, being in us an internal and spiritual faculty, the faculty of freedom, it participates, through Original Sin, of the deficiency and inability of the rest of our nature; and *of itself* it is *unable, weak, deficient*, both in its *power* and in its *results.*

Hence, when it is *utterly apart* from all Divine influences—a situation in which we cannot believe the ever-blessed God has left any of our race—the man would be the most miserable of all beings,—knowing, willing, desiring, feeling the duty of resistance to temptation, and yet being the *absolute* and *utter slave of circumstance and appetite.* This would man be *of his nature, apart from all Divine influences,* in consequence of the infirmity of his Will, its inability to resist external impressions, and the influence of external motives on it.

But, as we have shown that Society is a school for the other spiritual parts of man, so is it a very strong discipline for this. And, indeed, if a man will look at the course of events through which he has passed in this life,—that is to say, the effects of God's providence upon him,—each one, in his own course, shall hardly miss to say, that the schooling of the Almighty, which is so strong an exercise and trial to the rest of our Moral Nature, in no small degree tends to develope the powers of the Will, in all men that are teachable by circumstance and the course of events. So far are none apart from influences that come from God, and directly tend to strengthen the Will and give it control over the mere power of Desire and Appetite.

Taking into account, then, and allowing it as a fact, that there is this external education of the Will in various degrees conferred upon men by God,—setting, I say, this case aside, as mainly beyond our examination and our powers of explanation, let us come to the consideration of the Freedom *de facto* of the Will, or of that which enables it to control the Will of the Flesh.

And here I think that we shall find that the motives which *free the Will* are, *of its own nature, inward and Spiritual,* not Animal; and that that man whose Will is so guided, he shall

* I would refer my reader to the fourth book, for the description of Concupiscence, or Evil Desire, which is the origin of that strife here described, that comes up to man's self-knowledge in his Will.

have the power of resistance to enslaving circumstance, in a degree greater or less, just in proportion as his Will is so actuated.

The Will is like the other Spiritual faculties: *it is not a law to itself;* it seeks not its perfection *in itself*, but by an influence *from without* is it perfected.

And if a man, the most having the control over himself,—if he looks at it clearly, he shall find that to be steadily under the Law of Conscience, this gives freedom,—this sets a man apart from the enslaving influence of external things. It tells the man—"Thou art no slave to gold; for, under the law of Conscience, the Will so actuated can resist all amount of treasure rather than do evil, rather than break through the checks of the conscience, rather than incur the Stain and the Guilt written down by it, or bear its Fear and Shame." Conscience, in its action upon the Will, sets a man free from a multitude of evils, from the strength of a multitude of appetites and lusts.

It avails not that men, with vain babble and idle logic, say, "Then you are not free, for you are governed." Certainly, governed; but, as certainly, by an inward power, which *is my own* highest and loftiest faculty. And, as certainly, by this freed from the heavy dominion of external circumstance and the hard and unhealthy rule of the lower parts of nature.

Certainly free,—for when, under the sway of Conscience, the Will is determined by it, then is it determined by the highest and most perfect faculty of my nature. And, according to a similar harmony, the rule, that is, of His Infinite Perfections, is God's Will determined. And therefore, as He, being Infinite, is free, so am I, in like proportion, free, according to my finite nature. So that in vain shall men, with verbal quibbling, argue, "that since the Will is determined by the Conscience, then it is not free;"—seeing that men whose will is determined by appetite, *know* and *feel* that then the *Will is certainly not free.* And most certainly do we and all men know by experience, and feel, *that determined and ruled by the conscience*, it is *then free*, and enables the man to resist all enslaving circumstances.

In like manner, if we look at the Spiritual Reason, and see the man under its guidance, each fact and attribute of the nature of the Most Holy God that by it he receives and applies, in the shape of Moral Principle and Moral Habit,—each one of these frees the Will,—each one of these sets and places man apart from the possibility of a heavy burthen and grievous yoke, which many have borne and groaned beneath. He in whose life the feeling and sentiment of Justice reigns as a Principle, or of Benevolence, or of Purity, or of Holiness, that man, by the Spiritual Principle so upheld, is freed from a multitude of heavy burthens and grievous sorrows that are laid upon the unjust, the cruel, the impure, the unholy, *besides that greatest burthen of all, the internal strife, the inward agony of self-reproach, the despair of a nature feeling the sinfulness of sin, and repugnant to it, and wrestling against it, and yet, by the chain of appetite and outward temptation, tied down and bound beneath the burthen!**

Tell me not "that for the Will to be determined by Moral Principle is a proof that it is not free! just as much as when it is determined by appetite!" when I see that one is Spiritual, according to the height and perfect harmony of the whole nature, and the other, Animal, and against its perfection,—when I see that the one is a state such as is that of God, Willing according to the perfection of his attributes, and the other makes a man a beast, and ruled, as the beasts are, by Circumstance and Appetite!

And, lastly, that the "Will" should be determined by the Af-

* Perhaps the great Stoic poet, Persius, expresses more distinctly than any Heathen the despair and agony of being conquered in that Life-struggle, the strife which each man has to undergo, between the "Will of the Flesh" and the Spiritual Will, when he makes it for the highest criminals the greatest punishment:

> Magne Pater Divom, saevos punire tyrannos
> Haud alia ratione velis, cum dira libido
> Moverit ingenium, ferventi tincta veneno;
> *Virtutem videant intabescantque relicta.*
> Anne magis Siculi gemuerunt æra juvenci,
> Aut magis auratis pendens laquearibus ensis
> Purpureas subter cervices terruit, *imus*
> *Imus præcipites,* quam si sibi dicat?

His prayer for them is, "When the poison of evil desires fires the soul,—then let them in despair look back with longing to the virtue they have deserted—then let them, in their certainty of utter and unavoidable ruin, cry, '*We fall, we fall, and there is no help for us.*'" This, in the opinion of the Stoic, is the most agonizing torture of life. And truly, I must think that he is right. I have been told so, in so many words, by those in whom the will was habitually enslaved by appetite.

fections, this frees from Slavery, that instead of being determined by Selfishness, it be by Unselfish Motives,—instead of being ruled by Froward desires, it be obedient unto law,—instead of being Sensual, it be Pure. Manifestly, when we look upon the evils brought upon man by Concupiscence, or Evil Desire, ('Επιθυμία it is called by the apostle,) embracing these three, "Sensuality, Selfishness, and Self-will," and see how opposite the Affections are to these, it is the highest degree of freedom that the Will should be by the Affections determined, instead of by Concupiscence.

This, then, is that which enables the faculty of Freedom to be in action and effect most free, that its action be determined by internal Motive,—that motive, namely, that is Spiritual, arises from the Spiritual part of man's being.

Let a man draw the line between the good of the animal being, body as well as mind,—let him suppose the highest object and aim of a man to be without and below the line of Spiritual Good,—then, how lofty soever it may seem in the eyes of the World, it confers no Freedom. But let the motive be Spiritual, from the Spiritual nature,—then at once Freedom is manifested, and we see it and feel it to be so. The power of resistance is given by this, of emancipation from appetite and external circumstance. Whatsoever men may talk in *their logical* and *verbal way*, the man of Conscience, of Moral Principle, of pure Heart, knows and feels in this his freedom to exist; and freedom *just so far* as he has perfection in and of his Spiritual Nature. He, and he alone, has that inward power that enables the man to resist the external action of that law of Cause and Effect under which the animals are bound, and to be, *according to his limited nature*, as God is—free! And it is manifest that this shall take place only when the measure according to which these inner faculties determine the Will, shall be the Will and Law of God. "Not my will, but thine be done," was the prayer of our Lord and Saviour Jesus Christ unto the Father. And, secondly, the means of bringing this result about, the agency that shall subdue our Will unto the will of the Father, this is only Grace,—Grace given through all the means of Grace, and Grace given without means, according to the Will of God. But if we despise the first, we may be certain that in the last we shall have no share.

CHAPTER V.

The Second Power of the Will that of Purpose; illustrated by a comparison of cases:—1. Sets its object in the Future.—2. Prescribes a law to the Will.—A rebuke of the Heathen Morality that tells us not to look to the Future: *we must, by our being,* look towards it.—This fact interpreted.—True Christian Hope, 1st, looking steadily to Christ, and, 2dly, imposing voluntarily the Law of God upon the action, is that only which perfects Purpose of Will.

In the last chapter we have examined the first part of the power of the Will—the liberty, that is, of choice; and we have shown its relation to human life and action. In this chapter, we enter upon the consideration of the second power of the Will, the power of Purpose, as we have defined it, "the power of fixing and determining choice."

This we consider a separate and distinct power altogether from that of liberty of choice; the one consisting in the ability of resistance to motive, however strong, and, consequently, of the admitting voluntarily of it, however weak—and the other, the motive being received, of a determination of the will, or a fixation of purpose, subsequent in time to the admittance of the motive, and distinct from it. In fact, the word, "I will," embraces, when you examine it closely, the two ideas—the first, of choice, in which "I will" is equivalent to "I wish," "I desire," or "I choose," —the second, that of determination or purpose, "I am fixed and set in that choice which I have made." "Will you go to the city?" is equivalent to, "Is it your wish," or "desire," or "choice, so to do?" "I will," the answer, expresses determination or purpose.

This would, perhaps, make the idea plain enough, and sufficiently show that the power of Choice in the Will is different from the power of Purpose; but perhaps we may be able to illustrate it still more, and to make it still clearer. When we look at men in life, we see some men whose Wills are at the moment vehemently impressible by motives both internal and external, and their action thereupon correspondingly energetic, who, in a little time, are just as vehemently excited in an opposite direction. The Will is impressed now by one motive, then it is again impressed by another; and no impression seems to have the power of lasting, or of enduring for any time. Others there are, who, when they come under the influence of motive, seem to have the power of *fixing that motive in their Will as a future guide, of stamping, as it were, the immediate volition* in the Will, and sealing it therein, as a set decree and law of future action.* This power of determinate Purpose, this capacity of ordaining a present decree, upon present motives, that shall be an inward law and rule for future action, is manifestly quite a different thing from that other of admitting or not admitting motive. We can distinguish them in the action of our own minds; we can see them as distinctly in other men's actions; and we mark them by a variety of words, implying the difference: the words "freedom," "choice," "liberty," express the one action of the will; "purpose," "determination," "fixedness," "decision," the other.

Nay, this fact of Purpose you shall see manifest itself in every department of life. Enter into a school, and you shall find one class sent there by their parents, and *there for that reason;* rising in the morning at the appointed hour, because of another *external circumstance*, studying because there are lessons set, and there are tutors that teach,—obeying for the reason that obedience is the law of the place,—and so making *circumstance their law*, and never once looking forward beyond the day, never troubling themselves for any thing beyond the circumstance immediate to them in time and place. What is their Purpose? they have no Purpose;—they mean to get through. What their determination?—they have no determination: they let Chance and Circumstance, Position, and the Will of any that think it worth while to rule them, decide for them. Such persons I have seen in all states and conditions of life, in schools, in colleges, in professions, in trades, in society, in whom the faculty and power of Purpose and predetermination either had never been trained to action, or else had perished; floating weeds upon the waves of circumstance; ships, with sails and helm, but unprovided with chart and compass, or hand to hold the helm,—such are men without the power of Purpose.

* *Volition* means an act of the Will.

Others I have seen quite different from these:—*who look around them*, that they may see their relation to existing circumstance, and *what they can do* in modifying it for their good;—*who look inwardly* upon themselves, their hopes and fears, and power and desires, and *see what they wish*, what is their Will, and their Desire;—and who then form steady purposes, which, inwardly framed and inwardly settled, are laws of life and of action, binding, self-imposed upon the Will, ruling it as the helmsman's hand and eye rules the helm of a vessel,—and who henceforth guide it, according to that inner law of Purpose, *across* the waves, and *through* them, against the wind or with it, but still according to the inward law *self-imposed*, of set *Purpose*, and fixed *determination.**

So, while the power of resistance to external motive is in the will by nature, and in it is freedom, the power of Purpose is that by which the will sets and establishes to itself a Law of action; appoints to itself an end in the future, after which to struggle, lifts its eye up from the present, its objects and its delights, or its miseries and sorrows, and setting to itself a distant point, perhaps in tracts of time so distant that it only may reach them, perhaps upon the extremest bounds of possibility, fixes its aim upon that remote and distant point.

Ask whether there are such men, and who they are? And the same experience that shows us the one class, the men of infirm and uncultivated Purpose, wandering through the wastes of life as animals that now rest upon a sunny bank, now move a few steps towards a greener patch of herbage, now flee from the heat to the shelter of a grove,—the same experience that shows to us these men without purpose, will show us that other class, that have an aim to which they are pressing, that know what they want to obtain, and are struggling towards it, *that have an object and an end in view*, and are not mere animals, chance loiterers in the paths of life.† And wherever they are, in whatever situa-

* I would, of course, have my readers note here that there may be a power of purpose, which, being determined and set to evil, may, *because of this*, be evil. Still the same might have been set to good as strongly. This faculty, then, of fixedness and decision, *is, in itself* good; only by being set towards evil is it bad.

† The lofty Stoic poet, whom I before quoted, illustrates this well. The Stoics placed all virtue in a self-governing Will exerting itself by a fixed and

tion of life they may be, of whatever sex or age, *they have respect from others*, and *they respect themselves.* The man without a Purpose is a mere animal, the man with a Purpose is so far a man.

Let us look at this faculty of Purpose, and upon analysis we shall find in it indications of many things Spiritual. Every one sees that to have Purpose, this is man-like; to be purposeless, this is to be like the animals: and, therefore, that to have an aim to the future, according to an inward law of the Will superior to external motive, this is most in accordance with man's true being. Three things are there in this: 1st, an object; 2d, in the future; 3d, a law of the Will self-imposed, which has the power of rejecting other motives. Look at all men of Purpose, and these three things are clearly and distinctly seen in them. Men place the object in the future. There is no man would say, I would be content with the Present and all its circumstances, and see it established as one eternal NOW. All men desire the Present to pass away, and the Future to arrive. . And, although they may, as travellers do, set limits to themselves, and establish in their imagination a period and a station further on, wherein they shall desire no Future, and pursue no object after they have arrived at them;—still, when they reach the destined point on their journey, greener vales and shadier hills expand to their view, another object further on is marked out for their final resting-place, the terminal station, which reached, they shall no further purpose, but dwell and abide there satisfied and no more desiring;—is not this the nature of Man, and this his doom?

Philosophers have talked of this as a "fault of Human Nature," a "delusion," and have said to men that they should repress it, that they should rest in the Present and enjoy it, and think not of the Future, and so forth. In short, they have talked an im·

stable Purpose,—and I must say, not without a considerable degree of truth, although *not all*, for assuredly half the miseries of life come from weakness and instability. In conformity with this, he addresses such a charactei as those whom we have spoken of in the text as "chance loiterers in the paths of life,"

> "Est aliquid quo tendis, et in quod dirigis arcum?
> *An passim sequeris corvos testâque lutoque,*
> Securus quo pes ferat, et ex tempore vivis?

mense amount of that vain babble of Heathenism, those "morals of Seneca," that might have done well enough in a pagan, to whom the Present is absolutely certain, the Future and any existence in it, a shadowy possibility, and a vague uncertainty; and feeble, narrow-minded Moralists have vented a great deal of this heathenish philosophy, and thought it Christianity, and have wondered how absurd and perverse men are, that they cannot be prevailed on to live in the Present, and to set for themselves no object in the Future.

We give no such advice. We say, "Here is a power of mind and a peculiar action, by which you, by your nature, are compelled to travel onward in aims and desires towards the Future;—this is no vain desire to be repressed by moralizing or self-restraining effort, but a power and an instinct having its proof and its perfection in Revelation and in God,—a living proof that there is an end in view onward still and onward, where *there is* rest and contentment: a sure inward proof that man is no animal, to dwell in the Present and its delights, but a traveller onward through a road which he wishes perpetually to end,—and which *will end*. And in despite of Heathen Morality upon the duty of dwelling in the Present, in despite of Heathenism of belief, this* "feeling of the Traveller," as the middle age Christians call it, ever shall make man know that his dwelling is not here, but out of Time, out of Space, in Eternity!

We then tell not men to dwell in the Present, to fix no object in the Future. We tell them to look through that flitting and changeable future of things temporal that hitherto has been so unsatisfactory, to look through this painted veil, this gorgeous bank of sun-tinted clouds that we call Time, upon Eternity, and there they shall find their true and satisfactory object of Purpose. The power of purpose in us that exists in Time, leads us of its own nature towards Eternity, thereunto it points, therein its proper and peculiar end and object is.

Again, in this power of Purpose in the Will, besides this looking to the Future, we see the fact of a self-imposed law. The Will is not in man simple in action, but it acts according to Law; in the case of Purpose, to a law self-imposed and self-applied. A motive, for instance, engrosses the mind of a man; this motive he

* Animus Viatoris.

has the power of making to be a law of his Will that shall henceforth work upon its action, and make it within him capable of resisting, habitually and constantly, even stronger powers than the original one has been. This is essentially one of the elements of Purpose, the bringing of the will under the rule of a voluntary Law, for such it may be seen is the act of Purpose. The man who says "I will," in reference to future action, he evidently prescribes a law of action for that amount of time, to his Will.

Hence we see the relation of the Will, the faculty of Action, to the Reason, the faculty of Law; hence, too, we see the permanent freedom of the Will reconciled to the fact of its being under fixed law, that so far as it freely makes the principles of Eternal Morality its Law of Purpose, so far it is permanently free: but this subject has been so fully discussed in other parts of the book, that we need not now more than indicate it.

But one may say, do not we see this second law of Purpose to exist in the animals, this of a law self-imposed, that shall control immediate desires?

And we say, No;—you may see long and continuous action upon a *present motive*, giving an appearance of Purpose, but when you examine it closely, it is no Purpose, no law of action self-imposed, but the permanence of an animal motive, inducing permanence of action. The lion lies for days by the one lonely spring in the African desert; the wolves follow the track of a deer for days together: there is *continuance of action*, from permanence of the animal motive of hunger,—that gone, the action comes to an end: there is permanent action continuing under a motive as long as that motive exists,—but no Purpose. The animal *not hungry* would not hunt,—the man *without hunger* chases after animals with the same perseverance, from a set purpose for the future, under a determination self-imposed, and not necessarily under the movement of an immediate appetite.

And when it is necessary that something should be done for the Future by the mere animals, we find it done in them by an irresistible instinct, framed and formed in entire accordance with the circumstances of their natural habitation: and to confirm this view of ours, that the animals have not, in such cases, any real Purpose, but an instinct that in its stead prepares for the Future; when they are transferred to climates wherein circumstances are different, we see them still acting upon the instinct, although it be idle;* for purpose, properly so called, there is none in the animals. Indeed, it is very hard to think that they have any proper idea of the Future; purpose and thought for the Future belong to man as modes of Will,—and Will is his as a part of his Spiritual Nature.

Now, again and again, in the course of this book, we have insisted upon the truth that there is a Spiritual Education—an education peculiarly belonging to the Moral Powers, and to be conducted under its own rules and modes of training, and after its own methods. And this is distinct entirely from Mental Education, so distinct that the highest degree of Mental Cultivation may exist with the lowest of moral development and of Spiritual Education: and, then, we have laid it down again, that Physical Education is distinct from the other two, each of the three needing and requiring its peculiar knowledge in the teacher and in the pupil, and its peculiar education, whether given by another or self-imposed.

As an instance, we point out this Law of Purpose to parents and instructors as a power of the Will peculiarly to be cultivated, and the cultivation of which is a peculiar benefit. We mean, not *verbally* but practically cultivated,—not by a teacher who should set a verbal lesson to memory, to be learned by rote, but by one who had felt and known himself the facts we have noted and their power.

Let such an one take a youth who is growing up, and is ordinarily intelligent; let him bring him, as Socrates brought his pupils, to think upon his Spiritual Nature practically, to recognise its powers and their relations, so that he shall have a general view.

Then let him take this of the Will and its Purpose, and, by easy illustrations, make him feel the *power* of Purpose, the

* Birds that migrate from one climate to another, about the particular time show a great and overpowering uneasiness, the working of instinct preparing them for their flight. Hibernating animals, on being transferred to temperate climates, do not sleep through the winter; nevertheless, although the need of it be gone, they often make all preparation for their winter's repose. But perhaps the most ridiculous instance given in Natural History, is that of a beaver, who, being kept as a pet in a gentleman's house in London, at the set time built himself a dam out of the best materials he could find, across the floor of a bed-chamber!

capability of governance of the Will by a fixed Law, and the duty of looking to the future with a fixed object; and he shall have done more for that youth than by giving him the knowledge of twenty books of science or art.* And, then, if having his confidence, and thence knowing his deficiencies, mentally or morally, he shall teach him how to apply this knowledge—he shall realize his instruction, and make the youth feel it as true and precious.

For, as regards talents or mental power, when we look at the history of men celebrated for this, in nine cases out of ten we shall find that it was some circumstance apparently fortuitous that called into vehement action and vehemently developed some one of those that we have called the Governing Powers,—the Conscience, the Heart, the Spiritual Reason, or the Will. And that this, *then*, has awakened to action and developed the Mental Powers;—especially manifest is this with regard to the Will. Let any teacher, then, who is in doubt about the general principle, let him take the most stupid, seemingly, of all his scholars, get his confidence, instruct him practically with regard to the power of the law of Purpose,—teach him to apply it, and he soon shall see, under its influence, mental power developing and acting that perhaps he had not dreamed to exist. This I have seen myself, in reference to many pupils who have come under my care, and I believe others that try it will find it true, and thence perhaps may be encouraged to test the assertion, and, finding it true, to act upon it systematically.

* There has been, in this country, a great deal of good done, and a great deal of harm, by "Foster's Essay upon Decision of Character." A great deal of good, because in that essay he manifested, to many who had not before known it, the power of a fixed and determined Will, and showed practically, by very interesting narratives, what such a Will can effect.

A great deal of harm, because he taught the bare power of Will apart from any law, and making itself its own law; and, therefore, by the third general principle of the governing powers, being in that evil. For the Will that is ruled by itself, when it should be governed by Conscience, the Reason, the Affections, is a curse. And to be taught merely the power of Will, apart from its connection with these, is no advantage, but harm.

However, making this exception, I would advise all students of Ethical Science, to read and think upon that essay. They will find it a most important contribution to the Science of Morality. But, without this exception, I recommend the book to no one; and, to a certain character of mind, I conceive it is capable of doing great and permanent injury.

I have shown how the law of Purpose fixes for a man an object in the Future, and how its leading and tendency is only satisfied by an object in Eternity. I have shown, also, how naturally and easily, through the same power, the man imposes upon his Will a law and rule of action, internal and spiritual, which is a Law. And yet, in it is freedom,—in that very Law, —and in being ruled by it.

Now, the Christian who steadily looks at this power and instinct of the inner man, he in it shall see how the faculties of nature answer to the gospel privileges. The Unseen World, with its joys and its crown of Life Eternal, held out for us to look towards with the eyes of Faith;—this is that object upon which the Purpose that is truly perfect must be fixed. And, so directed, so guided, the action of the natural faculty is changed into the Christian grace of Hope, fixing its sight upon the throne and mount of God, and upon our Lord and Saviour Christ, there sitting and making intercession for us.

Perfected then is Purpose of Will, when, illumined by the light of heaven, it pierces through all the temporal things of this visible world, glories alike and clouds, and sees through them all the effulgence of Eternity. Then is the path of the vessel directed across the waters, then it is guided aright by the chart, steadied by the helmsman's hand, when Purpose is transmuted into Christian Hope, by means of faith, which, as the Apostle tells us, is "the substance of things hoped for."

And then the Law of faith,—the royal law of liberty,—the inward grace of the Holy Spirit, reigning and ruling in the heart,—this becomes the law of action that the Will imposes upon itself. And, so governing itself by an inward Law, in accordance with the inward faith, the Will is entirely under subjection to the Law of Christ, and, by this, rules and guides itself. By this, the natural faculty of Purpose, through the inward law of a living faith, becomes the "assurance of (Christian) Hope,"— the "anchor of the soul, sure and steadfast, and which entereth into that within the veil."*

This is that alone which can render our Purpose perfect, both in the object upon which it is fixed and in the Law self-imposed. This only can make the Will perfect in this part of its faculties.

* Heb. vi. 19.

And this will do it. This is that sure hope which "looks to Jesus, the author and finisher of our faith," and thus finds in Him alone its object in Eternity, and its rule and inward law for the Will. So the inward faculty of Purpose of Will, this is converted into a living Hope, looking immovably unto Christ the Saviour, and as immovably ruling the man by the "law of the liberty of the Gospel."

Purpose of Will becomes not Christian Hope of itself, by any effort or struggle of its own; but it is so crowned and perfected by the influence of the Holy Spirit. Earthly faculties are changed into heavenly powers and gifts, not of themselves, but only by the "engrafted Word" and the "grace of the Spirit."

To him, therefore, who is regenerated, to him we would say, to cease not to improve the grace of faith already possessed, by ruling the Will inwardly, according to the "Law of Love,"—the "perfect law of liberty,"—the "royal law" of our King, making this, with the most inward earnestness of the Heart, the rule of all purposes, and by all means of meditation and prayer and inward thought, fixing the eye of faith steadily upon Christ our Lord.

Thus shall the faculty and power of Purpose of Will be completed and perfected, and this world, which to the unstable is a delusive and unsteady wilderness of changing objects, bewildering and confusing,—this shall be seen with the "Mind of the traveller." And, neither desirous to hasten our course nor yet to loiter by the wayside, we shall travel onward with clear views and distinct hopes until we reach our home; for there is nothing that so directs our course and so clears our views as "true Christian Hope:"—this alone is that which perfects the faculty of Purpose, and enables it to be complete, both in its action and in its objects.

CHAPTER VI.

The question of Power.—Man's Will originates Power, and is not merely an agent of it.—The evils of Fatalism, exemplified in a quotation from Diderot.—Man's Will is free in act and fact, when it coincides completely with the Will of God, in Choice, in Purpose, in Power.

WE come now to the third prerogative of the Will, that of Power; a very difficult question, we admit, but still, one that may be made, we believe, sufficiently plain, if first we clear away the thorns and brambles of pertinacious and self-centred controversy; the arguments of men who uphold various modifications of the fatalistic system, under the idea that such a scheme is *absolutely necessary for religion*, and the counter arguments of others, who cared *nothing for truth*, *but only wished to be free from restraint.* Such, we think, are, on either side, the arguments that have perplexed, not decided, this question.

Strange arguments! of which the one side proves, that man has no power, can do absolutely nothing! and the other, that he can do any thing he pleases! is absolutely omnipotent!—and both unite in relying upon abstract and verbal argument, and agree in considering human nature and man's experience as generally delusive! We put these argumentations aside, and go straight to the question, "Is there Power in the Will of Man?"

Now, we have shown the vainness of the argument, with reference to "Cause and Effect," upon Choice and Liberty; manifesting, in reference to that power of the Will, that while the Physical World of the mere animals is bound up in a Causal system, which, *from without*, predetermines their choice,—man, *because he is a spiritual being*, is free. And that this freedom consists in this, that, as a spiritual being, man has the power of resisting or admitting the motives which, so far as he is merely an animal, would absolutely determine his Will. Again, the Power of Purpose, which we have treated of in the last chapter, may be seen to belong to man peculiarly as a spiritual being, inasmuch as no animal has Purpose. This, too, will set man apart from "the great external system of Physical Causation.

In the same manner, by self-experience, we know, that we, under certain conditions, exert Power, which originates from ourselves, and is not under a physical law of causation in its origin, or an absolute law of doom in its operation; both of which theories leave to man only an appearance of doing, and a self-delusion by which he vainly imagines he does that which he only seems to do. And both theories employ as their argument the Law of Causation, the assertion that the system of the world is driven by it, and that man is a mere part of that system or machine. A mechanical system of the universe, in other words, that asserts, that in His world, God *does* nothing, and is *absent himself*, and that the only thing present is *Power* exerted *according to fixed law.*

These three theories, viz.: first, of a Mechanical System of the universe; secondly, of an Absent God; and, thirdly, of Mere Power; these are the premises that deny the Freedom of the Will, whatever talk men may make about other matters and other motives. Get men to believe in a Present God, a Father, a Governor, a holy God, to be worshipped and loved, "upholding all things by the Word of his power," "in whom we live and move and have our being," and the fatalistic arguments soon vanish. And then there is no difficulty in admitting of Free-will or free Power in man.

But take these three vile and abominable notions, and the man who takes them as true, consciously or unconsciously, must be a physical and mechanical atheist, (so far as atheism is possible to man,) or else an absolute Fatalist.*

* We speak advisedly, for such they are, being contradictory to the express declaration of the Scriptures, to the truths of God's nature and being, and to man's experience of his own inward constitution, and of the outward face of the world, and the course of events. We say, then, that they are vile and abominable, and their vileness consists in this, that the man who holds them has no escape from a Pantheistic Atheism, save in a system of Fatalistic Doom. For, *if God be absent,* I have no proof in the outward world, and in my experience of a God. If *I meet only power,* I cannot argue for a father most gracious, or for a moral governor, but only for *one maker,* working on one plan, or *twenty makers working on the same plan.* And not for *an Almighty maker,* but only for one sufficient in power to the work of this material world. If *it be only a mechanical system,* this, with the other

And but small choice there is between any kinds of fatalism, if only they be consistent to their own principles. Although we must always remark, that Human Nature in practice, to a greater or less degree, renders men inconsistent in evil principle; yet the evil may be seen by the ensuing passage: it is a citation from Denys Diderot, a physical and organical atheist; we take it from "Upham on the Will:*"—

"Examine it as you will," says M. Diderot, "and you will see that the word liberty is a word devoid of meaning. That there are not, and there cannot be, free beings; that we are only what accords with the general order, with our organization, our education, and the chain of events. These dispose of us invincibly. We can no more conceive of a being acting without a motive, than we can of one of the arms of a balance acting without a weight. The motive is always exterior and foreign, fastened upon us by some cause distinct from ourselves. What deceives us is the prodigious variety of our actions, joined to the habit, which we catch at our birth, of confounding the *voluntary and the free*. We have been so often praised and blamed, and have so often praised and blamed others, that we contract an inveterate prejudice of believing that we and they *will* and act freely. But, if there is no liberty, there is no action that merits either praise or blame, neither vice nor virtue, nothing that ought to be either rewarded or punished," &c.

Here is physical Fatalism boldly and without subterfuge professed; founded and distinctly placed upon that "Cause and Effect" doctrine from which we have shown man's Spiritual Nature is free; urged upon that logical quibble of motive, external and irresistible, that we have exposed; and boldly then driven out to its natural consequences, *that there is neither "vice nor virtue,"* nothing that "*ought to be rewarded or punished, praised or blamed.*"

And that these are the natural consequences of a physical fatalistic philosophy, every one can see who shall take the premises of Diderot, and go onward to his conclusions. The pre-

two, cuts off personality,—makes all power and action mechanical,—makes all individuality vanish,—all persons become parts of the great All,—and all things to be parts of the one machine. So that, to escape Atheistic Pantheism, the reader must believe in a God of rigorous Destiny.

* Page 271.

mises once established, the conclusions follow as a matter of course. Only teach man that "motive externally and irresistibly determines the action and Will of man," and the morality of M. Diderot follows as a matter of course,—his theoretic morality we will say, and his practical morality, both which were on a par;—M. Diderot at least was consistent.

What then was his doctrine? This that we have rejected, that "motive acts upon man necessarily and invincibly;" so that his Will is in every thing externally determined, and consequently that all power in him existing, and by him exerted, is not *in him really*, or *by him actually* exerted, but only apparently, in consequence of this "causal machinery of sufficient motive."

The axe splits wood, and were it intelligent, would say, "I split;" but yet it is only the agent of power, not itself originating, not itself exerting power: such is the man of the fatalist, a mere tool through whom power flows, and by means of whom it is exerted, but nothing more. And therefore, naturally the man that holds this doctrine comes to the doctrinal and practical morality of the celebrated Encyclopædist, M. Denys Diderot.

Now, in opposition to this, we shall say that man has these two qualities: first, that he originates power, and secondly, that he voluntarily exerts it and applies it. I say not, that all the power that he exerts and applies is originated in himself, for this would not be true; but some power unquestionably he does originate, and other power he applies, and both independently of the law of Causation.

Let one look at it, and seeing man "is made in the image of God," he shall find it no more difficult to believe that God has made man capable, voluntarily and freely, of originating power by his being and nature, than that he should have made plants capable of producing particular fruit. And everywhere this is the natural feeling and the natural persuasion of the race: they feel that it is a faculty belonging to their being, they feel it to be theirs, in their constitution, truly and really belonging to them. And why men should allow "this is *your* faculty of sight, this is *your* faculty of muscular action, this *your* faculty of thought," and then turn round and assert that the sum total of these, which they had allowed in separate items to be man's, was not his! is very hard to say, except that the mind is preoccupied with these three prejudices above mentioned, framed into a system. Why as to other parts of our nature, men should acknowledge that this, because you feel it to be so, is a faculty of nature having such and such products, —you call them yours, and such they are, for you have had a life-long knowledge and consciousness of their possession, and your neighbours see and know the same; "but with regard to *this one only*, you are mistaken,—your Will that you count free is not free;—the Power that you exert, you only seem to exert;—your will is bound; of that power you are only the agent,—you are a puppet, and although you feel no wires, yet they are there,—and you are a puppet, made of wood and leather, completely and entirely!" Why men should talk in this way, it is very hard to see.

And by what means they have got it into their head that such notions, which make of man a mere machine, tend to exalt the character of God! is stranger still.

But the persuasion and knowledge of man that he can act by a power originating in his Will, is a sufficient refutation of all these specious paradoxes. The fact that to hold them does, *if we are consistent*, lead at once, as in the case of Diderot, to the denial of any responsibility and to the destruction of all moral distinctions,* this I think is sufficient to exclude them from being held by any who desire to think of man as a moral being.

We hold then that man is no mere agent and instrument of Power through whom it flows, as the lever is, physically; that he is no puppet made of wood and pulled by a wire or string, at the same time that he thinks he acts; that he is not a part of a piece of machinery, driven by the same force as the rest, and imagining that he is an individual being, when he is only a wheel or pinion of *one machine;* we believe not that he is the agent of an infinite doom, or a resistless physical law that actuates him unconquerably. This, man is not.

* I ask honestly and calmly of any thinking man, to take the premises of Diderot, and go over them, and he shall see that they absolutely infer Diderot's conclusion, that is, the denial of all morality, and the freedom unto all vice and wickedness. Fatalism, *held consistently* and *acted upon*, implies viciousness of life. I would also ask the same person to go over the ethical doctrines of Christianity, and to ask himself, Do not these doctrines encourage morality? Will not every husband and wife, every father and mother, every son and daughter, who attempts to go earnestly and consistently upon these principles, be more virtuous, more pure, more lovely in the eyes of God and of man? Surely it is and must be so.

But "made in the image of God," as God has of himself *power*, so is man given of himself to have *power*, to originate it, to apply it: it is a faculty of his being, a gift that God has given him; originating in himself freely, apart from the causal necessity of motive, save so far as he will permit himself to be ruled by the Animal Nature, which in him is conjoined with the Spiritual.

The first objection that will be made is,—Shall not this then give too much to man? is not man then made a God, and able to do precisely as he will? The answer to this I have given in the chapter upon Circumstance; and there it will be seen, that while man really and truly, by an inward force, exerts power, yet is there another personal force externally applied, that controls the result in a very remarkable way,—a power, to use the beautiful language of the poet:

> "That shapes our ends,
> Rough-hew them as we may."

Our reader, then, will see that strongly soever as we may act, there is, external to us, a personal Being, gracious, merciful, and holy, as well as omnipotent, who guides all our efforts and controls their results, not according to doom or a fatalistic decree, but with the all-seeing wisdom of a *present* and *personal God.*

So are there two forces that guide the course of man's life, of which two it is the resultant, his power and the power of God,—and this gives, as the practical solution of the question of Freedom, this answer: "When the two powers coincide and are one completely and entirely, then is the man free: when his will, in the direction that he spontaneously gives it, coincides with the Will of God, then these two forces become one, and the man goes onward entirely and completely free as far as regards *effect and power.*" Then his own power from himself arising, and the power and operation of external circumstance so unite, that the waves that ordinarily do oppose, bear him onward, the winds favour, and all things outward coincide with all things inward, in driving the man onward upon his course.

That such is the case often, the experience of all men can tell; that it is not exclusively the case with the good, but that for particular purposes, by the wisdom of the Almighty, such a power, and such a direction of Will, and such success are often given to the evil, is the experience of all ages.* And the meditative wisdom of ancient Greece considered such invariable success in those that were evil, a proof of Divine wrath and jealousy, and prophetic of utter ruin. And, indeed, such it often is.

With regard to the Christian who lives in Faith fixed upon the Unseen, according to the law of grace, he shall find that in him, if he live under the law of God's grace, that his Will coinciding and agreeing with God's Will, he is free perfectly and completely, and he alone; Circumstances may not yield to his power, but may control it; success may be denied to his best efforts, prosperity may not be granted, yet let him bind his *Will* to *that of God*, and therein he shall find Freedom. And more than this, Providence protecting him, with the invisible foresight of omniscience, from perils which himself could not have avoided; sheltering him from accidents no power of his own could ward off, no subtlety escape; upholding him with the mind of a father, staying and guiding the steps of a feeble infant; and correcting and destroying, by the action of circumstance, faults that he himself could never become conscious of:—almighty power, omniscient wisdom, infinite mercy;—these thus wait upon and belong unto that man who, *in covenant with God*, rules and guides his Will according to the Will of the Eternal, the Law of Holiness and Grace!

He is free in thought and act, free in the power of Grace through Jesus Christ! and to him, thus perfect, and to him alone, his nature fulfils its intended purposes. To him the external world is that which to all men it should be. And Society, in reference to him, exerts its complete effect as a school of teaching. All things internal and all things external coincide; inward Nature and outward Circumstance are brought into that harmony of

* Often this stern energy of Will and the invariable success attending it are wondered at, and attributed to the man by all around him, and even by himself, when it is a truth, that the vessel is only in the current of Almighty power, sweeping onward to a certain point, as a vessel of deserved wrath, or laden with mercy. And succeeding ages begin to see, when the results have unfolded themselves in History, that behind the man lay the purpose of God,—behind his Will, the almighty Will of the omniscient God. The thought is gradually unfolding itself, especially in respect to the Emperor Napoleon; men are beginning to see how uses and ends in the policy of the world *that he never intended, have come forth* from his strong will set firmly toward selfish ends, and wholly unconscious of the power that lay behind him, and of the issues that were in the future.

action and reaction that ought to exist between them, and *the man is free.* And this is not, as I have said, of himself or by himself, but the nature of man is harmonized with the sphere of external circumstance only by Grace. And the height and completion of this is, that his Will should be under the Will of God, perfectly and entirely obedient to it, in its three faculties of Choice, of Purpose, and of Action. Upon these three we have treated, and this completes our discussion of the Will.

GENERAL CONCLUDING REMARKS.

We have now brought our work to a conclusion. The Affections we have treated upon in two books. The Affections in the Nation,—this we might have discussed in another book, but it would have made the volume too large. And Law in the Nation is to one part of Ethics what Religion in the Church is to another division of the same science, the completion of it; Law is the objective and external science, which is the completion of the Ethical discussion: the sum, therefore of that which we would have said would have been these two practical precepts: "Obey the Law at all risks, and in every way uphold it and support it, and give it in the State the supremacy over all Self-will." And secondly, "Do your best that it may come as near the Eternal Law of the Almighty, that which is written upon Man's heart internally, and manifested by God externally, as may be,"—these two and their reasons in man's nature and position, would have afforded a wide field. We give the precepts, and omit the Ethical illustrations and development, for the reasons above given.

The Affections in the Church,—this we have also omitted, for a reason very plain indeed; it leads us directly into the discussion of "Spiritual Ethics," or of "Practical Christianity," that is, of the Ethics that ensues from the peculiar position of Human Nature in Covenant with God. The Ethics of a human being endued with this high privilege, placed in this lofty position, while manifestly it is *not opposite* to that of the man who is of Nature only, not of Grace; has only the *capabilities*, instead of the *gifts*, but is the crowning and completion of it,—is still something infinitely higher and infinitely more perfect. As the stately palm in the desert, crowned with its diadem of leaves at once, and flowers and fruit, is to the date borne in the hand of the wandering Arab, so is the true Science of the Christian Life to the loftiest and truest philosophy of Nature apart from Grace. In both cases, it is true, the germ exists the same, but in the latter the influences are wanting that shall develope it.

That germ in the case of the natural man, the Spiritual Nature that is in him existing, which renders him capable of Grace, I have in this book treated of. Spiritual Ethics, the Ethics of Man in Covenant with God, is a distinct and higher part of the same science, and is practical Christianity. At some future time in the ripeness of maturer years, and by the light of fuller knowledge, I may enter upon the examination of this loftier science.

In the mean time I would say, upon these elements, in this book developed, even this depends: just as the highest Astronomy takes for granted the humbler science of elementary Geometry,—so the highest Christian philosophy is founded upon these doctrines of Man's Nature,—these that bring forth and manifest its adaptedness to all external influences, to Society, to the system of God's Providence, and of his Creation, and through all these means to the Infinite and Eternal God himself! And the religion that denies or falsifies these truths may, by adventitious circumstances, remain for a time, but it is about to perish and be taken away. The true doctrines of the Internal Nature of Man and of his Position, are the very elements of all practical religion, even of the loftiest.

I must now, in all justice to my reader, tell him that the system I have here laid before him is not a system of my own, invented by myself, but that it is the Ethical Science of the first Christians, as far as I have been able to distinguish and feel it. This I have, as it were, translated into the thought of our age and time, out of the thought of men of different ages and different times. That is, I have attempted to present, in a scientific form, as *a system*, before the ordinary reader, the Ethics of Christianity, as held by the church unbroken, before the ambition of Rome and the pragmatical spirit of Constantinople had rent the church in two. For much as men may have forgotten the idea, there was a time, and that time lasted for ten centuries, when the church was one. This Ethics of the church undivided, I have then attempted to present to the men of this age and this time.

I have not said all I could say upon each point, only that which I counted enough to convince, and therefore the reader or teacher will often find a multitude of confirmatory arguments and facts capable of being adduced, which I have not adduced. To the teacher, this will be a good exercise of teaching,—to the reader, of thought. But I have been forced to omit a multitude of such things, even thoughts and facts that were to me most delightful, and which I was convinced would be to the reader very interesting. The nature of the science as "Subjective," resting for a good part of its proof upon the self-experience of the man and of the race, will sufficiently account for this.

I would now, as respects my readers, address to them a few words in reference to the book and its results upon them. If the reader who has gone thus far is contented with it, thinks that it gives a sufficient and satisfactory account of Human Nature, its problems, and their solution, in the first place *I* claim from him no praise, personally, in this book. I profess to present the Ethics of the Ancient Church. Augustine, Athanasius, Cyril, Cyprian, Origen, Tertullian, these men whom every puny writer of the present day thinks himself privileged to scorn at,—these are the sources from which I have obtained the principles here presented in a connected form,—men who, often by the meditation of a whole life of holiness and self-denial, thought out and established for ever the Christian solution of a single one of the problems of nature herein discussed! These results the theologian will often discern in these pages, given in a few lines, while, in the original, volumes hardly embrace their discussion. For myself, therefore, I claim no praise of originality or of genius; but that one, of bringing again before the world, in a shape to every one tangible, the Ethical Science of Apostolic Christianity, undivided and at unity with itself.

So far, with regard to myself, I have said to him, who has thus far read the treatise, with satisfaction; now, *with regard to himself,* I say, if he be convinced of the truth of these principles, let him not for a moment abide in a barren philosophy, but *act upon the principles* herein laid down. Let him begin to cultivate his Spiritual Inward Nature at all risks, and under all pain and loss to make it the ruling and supreme governor of his action,—it as perfected and aided by the external influences, through which alone it can be complete in its functions and in its action. This he must do, if he would draw the proper advantage from this book; and the book itself in its several parts, I believe, will be found to contain directions for this mode of action. So far with regard to moral Self-cultivation.

And if, with regard to himself, he has found these principles of the Science of ancient Christianity efficient, I would most vehemently urge upon him to exemplify them in the family, the Home wherein, by God's decree, he has been placed, not to live as an unit, an individual, but as part of a divinely appointed institution. In the Home, then, I would urge the Father, the Mother, the Sister, the Brother, to live up to and distinctly to exemplify the principles herein laid down; for, too much has it been forgotten, that the Home is, for those within it, a sphere peculiar and exclusive, wherein there is for its members a peculiar religious and moral work to do, which *there can be done* and *nowhere else*, by *them* and *by no one else*. There is moral teaching, "with which no man meddleth," as well as sorrow and joy, exclusive of those that are without.

But, moreover, I would urge the person who has read this attempt toward a Christian science, and approves of it for himself and for his family, to put it into the hand of the growing and intelligent youth with whom he is acquainted. The experience of the writer tells him, that for those especially who, in childhood and youth, have been neglected by parents, untrained in the holy teachings of the gospel, there is a period wherein all the problems "of our nature and of our position" rush up and demand a solution; and the youth then is in great doubt; his nature demands a true answer; and, alas! so false is the ordinary Ethics of Christianity, that but seldom that true answer is given. Hence are multitudes in our land Non-professors, for the want of a true Christian philosophy of man's Nature and his Position. This the author has tried to give, not as his own, but as that of the old Christian church. If the reader, then, clerical or lay, finds then, that, *even in a degree*, this book answers that want, *the author would ask of him, whithersoever this book may wander, to bring it into the hands of thoughtful and serious youth, who are in that crisis of life alluded to.*

And, with this remark, the author will bid his reader God speed. He has now come to the end of a laborious work, which he felt to be needed. He has worked upon it sincerely and ardently, for he knew of no book embracing the subjects treated upon herein, so as to be accessible to the mass of readers, and at the same time pleasing to them. How he has succeeded time will tell; but if the reader feels that the author has so far succeeded as to supply, *even in a small degree*, the great want of a book upon these subjects, the author would ask of him, *not to let the book rest upon his shelves, but to bring it before the notice of those to whom it is likely to be of service.*

And, if the author has not succeeded, at least, he has attempted that which *must one day or other be done*,—the answering truly, according to the sentiment of the Ancient Church, the problems that arise in the mind of all men born upon the earth. He has felt that one great want of Christianity, at this day, is the want of a true Christian Ethics, and in his measure, according to his ability, has done his best to supply it. And if he have not succeeded, still to have felt the want, to have known wherefrom it could be supplied, and to have laboured towards that end sincerely, is enough.

But he has better hopes, that this his book will be found to give true answers to these questions, according to the plan proposed, to remove the difficulties that have hitherto kept away multitudes from Christianity, to satisfy objections, and to hold up the clear light of Christian philosophy upon the dark and dubious problems which so perplex, in this day, all men, and especially the young.

And this if he have done in one case,—if he have cleared the path of one from the obstructions that a Heathen Philosophy places in the way of men "who would enter in,"—if he thus, from the way of one individual, has been efficient to remove "an offence," the author has faith to believe, that in the final account he shall not be without his due reward. With this hope he bids his reader God speed.

THE END.

www.ingramcontent.com/pod-product-compliance
Lightning Source LLC
LaVergne TN
LVHW020128110826
845151LV00001B/308

* 9 7 8 1 4 2 5 5 4 0 0 6 7 *